PERSONNEL ADMINISTRATION A

PERSONNEL ADMINISTRATION AND THE LAW

by

RUSSELL L. GREENMAN

*Vice President, Personnel and Labor
Relations, General Cable Corporation (retired);
Adjunct Professor, Industrial Relations,
Union College Institute of Administration and Management*

and

ERIC J. SCHMERTZ

*Arbitrator; Impartial Chairman,
Several Industries;
Professor of Law, Hofstra University Law School*

Second Edition

THE BUREAU OF NATIONAL AFFAIRS, INC. • WASHINGTON, D.C.

Quotations on pages 3, 70, 71, 78, 95, 96, 111-112, 116-117, 122,
127, 231-232, 243-244, 248, 251-252, and 269 are reprinted from
THE NEW YORK TIMES, © 1973/75/76/77/78 by The New York Times
Company. Reprinted by permission.

Library of Congress Cataloging in Publication Data

Greenman, Russell L   1904-
    Personnel administration and the law.

    Includes index.
    1.   Labor laws and legislation — United States.
2.   Personnel management — United States.
I. Schmertz, Eric J., joint author.   II.   Title.
KF3369.G69   1978   344´.73´01   78-62296
ISBN 0-87179-234-6

Printed in the United States of America
Library of Congress Catalog Card Number: 78-62296
International Standard Book Number: 0-87179-234-6

Foreword

> "The more extensive a man's knowledge of what has been done, the greater will be his power of knowing what to do."
> — BENJAMIN DISRAELI
> "A little learning is a dangerous thing."
> — ALEXANDER POPE

Both Disraeli and Pope suggest pitfalls that threaten personnel and labor relations administrators in their continual contacts with the law. To avoid legal pitfalls, administrators must be armed with a broad knowledge of the effects of yesterday's and today's decisions in order to make informed decisions tomorrow. This book attempts to provide the background for tomorrow's informed decision-making.

The scope of the law is enormous. Federal, state, and local governments all have enacted laws regarding personnel and labor relations. Some laws were enacted to protect management and others to protect employees. Punishment may result for failure to comply. Some laws may be taken at face value. Others mean what a governmental board, agency, or administrator says they mean at a given point in time. Some laws have been interpreted similarly by all courts. Others have been interpreted differently by different courts in different jurisdictions.

Obviously, it would be impossible to compress within one book all that personnel and labor relations administrators might need to know to perform their jobs proficiently. They should, however, know enough about the law to be aware of when to ask for legal advice. Therefore, this book's primary function is to suggest guidelines and specific information sources on major statutes and on their interpretation in leading cases.

The authors have acquired a combined total of more than 60 years of experience as industrial relations instructors, personnel administrators, public officials, consultants, professional association staff advisors, mediators, and arbitrators. One also has specialized legal practice in labor relations and labor-management arbitration. From this experience, they have attempted to identify essential issues and to cite landmark decisions that influence or control management options in the employer-employee relationship.

This book is not intended as a handbook for attorneys. It is designed to alert personnel and labor relations administrators to situations in which legal advice may be required to arrive at sound management decisions.

RUSSELL L. GREENMAN
ERIC J. SCHMERTZ

Acknowledgments, First Edition

The authors are indebted to a number of professional associates and friends who have contributed invaluable suggestions regarding case material and its significance. We wish especially to thank Henry Clifton, Jr., Esq.; C. Stanley Lomax, Esq.; Herbert L. Marx, Jr.; Kenneth Nash; Benjamin Naumoff, Esq.; John D. O'Brien, Esq.; Mrs. Theresa Smith; and Roger Vaughan for enabling us to take advantage of their expertise on one or more of the subjects dealt with herein. It is hardly necessary to explain that, important as their advice has been, none of these individuals has assumed any responsibility for the conclusions and opinions expressed in this book. These are the authors' alone.

Our gratitude must also be expressed to Miss Ann Wyant, our research assistant, for her diligent ferreting out of source material and checking of the manuscript throughout seemingly innumerable revisions.

Acknowledgments, Second Edition

For the second edition, additional help in suggesting important legislative, administrative, and judicial developments for inclusion therein was made by Gerald Aksen, Esq., Virgil B. Day, Esq., Edward P. Lynch, Esq., Leo Teplow, Esq., Richard V. Porrett, and H.F. Urban. The authors are also especially appreciative of the assistance of two professional reference librarians with special expertise in labor law. They are Jaia Heymann and Julie von Schrader.

Table of Contents

CHAPTER 1

The Gamut of the Law

Few basic management decisions involving employee relationships can be made without regard for some law. Every industrial and commercial enterprise in the United States is subject to federal and state regulations. Frequently, municipal ordinances also impinge on management's obligations to its employees. Often two or more statutes, sometimes with conflicting provisions, apply to the same situation. The same laws may be construed diversely by courts in different jurisdictions. Management frequently must make vital personnel decisions under conflicting laws which would seem to make a course of action illegal under one statute and equally illegal if the terms of another statute were scrupulously observed.

The complexity of federal, state, and municipal regulations that affect personnel policies need not be an insurmountable barrier for management. Conflicts between administrative agencies and courts of original appeal may be resolved in the appellate courts. Further, the U.S. Supreme Court is often called upon for the final decision on how and whether a given statute controls management's rights and obligations in employee relations. But this is not all. Companies that have entered into union agreements stipulating the arbitration process as the final determination of their contractual obligations to employees may find that the arbitrator can and will construe the terms of their agreements as to what clauses must govern or have to be partially or wholly nullified because of overriding provisions of applicable legislation.

SCOPE OF LEGISLATION APPLICABLE TO MOST PRIVATE ENTERPRISES

The checklist presented below indicates the scope of federal laws with which personnel administrators should be generally familiar. This list is not all-inclusive. The statutes mentioned are some of the most important ones that apply to almost all companies engaged in such fields as manufacturng, distribution, trade, finance, and international commerce.

Federal Laws Relating to Terms and Conditions of Employment

A. Fair Labor Standards Act (Wage-Hour)
1. Minimum wages
2. Maximum hours
3. Child labor

B. Public Contract Act (Walsh-Healey) applicable to firms holding government contracts
1. Minimum wages
2. Maximum hours
3. Child labor
4. Safety and health

C. Civil Rights Act (Anti-Discrimination)
1. Race, religion, national origin
2. Sex
3. Age

D. Immigration and Naturalization Act
1. Hiring of resident aliens
2. Hiring of new or prospective immigrants

E. Labor-Management Relations Act (Taft-Hartley)
1. Employees' rights of self-organization
2. Nondiscrimination for union activity
3. Determination of appropriate bargaining units

F. Labor-Management Reporting and Disclosure Act (Landrum-Griffin)
Protection of members in internal affairs of union organizations

G. Anti-Strike Breaker Act (Byrnes Act)
Restrictions on employment of strike-breakers

H. Anti-Injunction Act (Norris-LaGuardia)
Limitations on resort to judicial processes during labor disputes

I. Social Security Act
1. Provisions for federal employer-employee and self-employment taxes to finance social security system
2. Provisions for old-age insurance benefits, dependents and survivors' benefits

      3. Federal subsidies for "old-age assistance"
J. Employee Retirement Income Security Act
    1. Mandatory federal standards for employees' retirement plans
    2. Regulation of financing and administration of most other types of employee benefit plans
K. Occupational Safety and Health Act
    Formulation and enforcement of federal standards for safe and healthful operation of private-sector establishments.

Before resigning as Secretary of Labor in 1976, John T. Dunlop was reported to have proposed that "the key to improving existing regulatory effort is to give the contending parties a larger role in writing regulations and how they will be enforced. . . . " The number of regulatory programs administered by the Labor Department increased seven and a half times between 1940 and 1975, rising from 18 programs in 1940 to 134 in 1975.[1]

The foregoing list applies to federal government *regulation* of employer-employee relations. There are numerous federal statutes authorizing government agencies, particularly the Departments of Labor and Health, Education and Welfare, to provide financial or other services for employees of private enterprises.[2]

Illustrative of the scope of state legislation for protection of employees' interests is a brochure published by the New York State Department of Labor in 1975. The table of contents lists the following subjects: minimum wages, prevailing wage rates, payment of wages, women, pay and hours of work, employment of minors, industrial homework, employment agencies, health and safety, state employment service, job training, unemployment insurance, workmen's compensation, disability benefits, labor relations, labor and management practices.[3]

Special protective laws for women workers have been common to most state labor law codes. Nearly all of these laws place restrictions on employment in particular occupations and provide special limitations on hours of work, or differentials between terms of employment, for men and women that have been all but nullified by the anti-sex discrimination provisions of the Civil Rights Act of 1964.

---

[1]NEW YORK TIMES, Nov. 9, 1975, p. 70.
[2]Cf., U.S. Department of Labor, Employment Standards Administration, FEDERAL LABOR LAWS AND PROGRAMS (Bulletin 262, rev., 1971).
[3]HOW THE NEW YORK STATE LABOR LAW PROTECTS YOU (Albany, N.Y.: New York State Department of Labor, Office of Public Information, 1975).

PREEMPTION

Fortunately, most federal laws covering employee relations either present no federal-state jurisdictional conflicts or set conditions for preemption if conflicts arise. In broad terms, "preemption" means the overriding authority of Congress to decide whether a given federal statute applicable to industrial and commercial enterprises shall set *minimum* standards and allow states to set higher ones or whether the statute shall do the reverse. The federal Fair Labor Standards Act (FLSA) is an outstanding example. The FLSA sets minimum wages, maximum hours for child labor, and maximum hours that may be worked without overtime payment. State laws may supersede the FLSA by imposing higher minimum wages, lower maximum hours for child labor, and lower maximum hours that may be worked without overtime payment.

The Taft-Hartley Act applies the doctrine of preemption in diametrically opposite ways on different substantive issues. On the one hand, this law expressly sanctions the negotiation and enforcement of union shop agreements, although union shop agreements are not mandatory. On the other hand, Taft-Hartley permits state legislatures to enact so-called right-to-work laws that in part negate the federal statute. Right-to-work laws make it illegal for enterprises operating in the states having such statutes to enter into labor agreements requiring compulsory union membership as a condition of employment.

Unfortunately, from management's standpoint, neither Congress nor the federal judiciary has succeeded in setting clear guidelines as to the powers of state legislatures or courts on all other vital matters of labor relations that come within present or prospective purview of the Taft-Hartley Act. In commenting on preemption problems more than a quarter century ago, the distinguished law professor Charles O. Gregory said:

> In our federal government, Congress is the appropriate body under the Constitution to make our national policies and to crystallize them into law. In each state, the legislature performs a similar function locally. Who is to say what these respective spheres of legislative influences are? The theory is that the federal Constitution makes this clear. The practice is that the Supreme Court sets these boundaries, doing so in the name of the Constitution.[4]

---

[4]Charles O. Gregory, Esq., LABOR AND THE LAW (New York: W.W. Norton & Company, Inc., 1946), p. 335.

Even the U.S. Supreme Court has struggled over weighty matters of preemption for some 50 years without conclusively or consistently interpreting the Constitution's meaning on jurisdictional questions between federal and state governments. Thus the Court said in 1953 in the celebrated *Garner* case: "The National Labor Relations Act [Taft-Hartley], as we have before pointed out, leaves much to the states, though Congress has refrained from telling us how much."[5]

Management has reason for concern over shifting Supreme Court doctrines on preemption issues, both from the standpoint of taking legal action to protect its legitimate rights and from the standpoint of determining what affirmative policies to pursue to assure maintenance of equitable employee relations. Therefore, personnel administrators should have their legal counsel keep them informed of decisions in leading high court cases.

In the landmark *Garmon* case of 1959, the U.S. Supreme Court ruled that in the area of *potential* federal regulation of labor relations through Taft-Hartley, Norris-LaGuardia, and other statutes, the states may intervene only if a labor dispute involves violence or coercion.[6]

Among state labor laws that have been held inapplicable to disputes involving companies subject to federal labor legislation are the following:

1. A Michigan law requiring strike authorization by a majority of the affected employees
2. A New York law requiring bargaining with foremen's unions
3. A Florida law requiring union organizers to obtain licenses
4. A Massachusetts law providing for conciliation of labor disputes (held to be designed to "bring the pressure of public opinion to bear to force a settlement").

As already indicated, the end is by no means in sight. As recently as June 1970, the Supreme Court handed down one of its most far-reaching decisions since it sustained the constitutionality of the original Wagner Act in 1937. This new decision, from which two Justices dissented vigorously, expressly reversed the Court's tremendously significant 1962 decision in the case of *Sinclair Refining Co.* v. *Atkinson.* There the Court had held that the anti-injunction provisions of the Norris-LaGuardia Act of 1932 precluded:

---

[5]Garner v. Teamsters Union, 346 U.S. 485, 33 LRRM 2218 (1953).
[6]Garmon v. San Diego Building Trades Council, 359 U.S. 236, 43 LRRM 2838 (1959).

any federal district court from enjoining a strike in breach of a no-strike obligation under a collective bargaining agreement, even though that agreement contains provisions, enforceable under Section 301 (a) of the Labor-Management Relations Act for binding arbitration of the grievance dispute concerning which the strike was called.[7]

In its about-face, the Supreme Court rejected the argument that, since Congress had chosen not to change by legislation the Court's own conclusions of 1962 holding that the Taft-Hartley Act did not eliminate the Norris-LaGuardia Act's ban on the federal court injunctions in labor disputes, the Court was bound to await congressional action to determine whether Taft-Hartley or Norris-LaGuardia should control federal courts' decisions relating to the issuance of injunctions against strikes prohibited by the specific terms of labor agreements.[8]

The June 1970 Supreme Court decision is of vast consequence to management and unions alike. On its face, it is a setback for labor organizations. Unions can no longer sanction wildcat strikes without risking federal court action to prevent their members from breaching no-strike agreements conditioned on arbitration as the terminal point for resolving labor-management differences.

Preemption in Relation to Arbitration

Arbitrators' decisions on matters involving alleged discrimination for reasons of race, sex, age, etc., are no longer automatically controlling, even in situations where the management and the union had stipulated in a contract that the arbitrator's award in any case would be final and binding on all concerned. In effect, the U.S. Supreme Court so ruled in the tremendously significant *Alexander* v. *Gardner-Denver* decision handed down in 1974.[9]

For some years prior to 1974, many eminent legal scholars and professional arbitrators of unquestioned competence were in accord in the belief that well-qualified arbitrators had the power to make conclusive settlements of disputes involving their interpretation not only of contract clauses but also of applicable laws. But as an American Bar Association Committee adroitly phrased the issue:

> Arbitration as the forum for settling disputes in the equal opportunity field was set back by the United States Supreme Court's decision in Alexander v. Gardner-Denver Co. . . . But private arbi-

---

[7]Sinclair Refining Co. v. Atkinson, 370 U.S. 195, 50 LRRM 2420 (1962).
[8]Boys Markets, Inc. v. Retail Clerks, Local 770, 398 U.S. 235, 74 LRRM 2257 (1970).
[9]Alexander v. Gardner-Denver, 346 F.Supp. 1012 (1971), *aff'd per curiam*, 466 F.2d 1209 (10th Cir. 1972), *rev'd*, 415 U.S. 36, 7 FEP 81 (1974).

tration continues to have a role to play. So an opinion and award of an arbitrator selected to hear a dispute involving the charging party may be received into the record as evidence for trial court consideration.[10]

The crux of the decision considered so important was that a complainant who has lodged a discrimination charge against his employer and who loses his case in arbitration still has the right to go to a federal court to seek redress. If this is done the court may admit the arbitral decision as evidence and accord it appropriate weight. (More detailed comments on the far-reaching significance of this case both as regards civil rights complaints and the scope of labor-management arbitration procedures are to be found in Chapters 3 and 8 below.)

State Statutes Relating to Terms and Conditions of Employment

State laws regulating employment practices of private enterprises do not always parallel federal statutes in the kinds of regulation they establish. This is particularly true of New York State legislation, although the same general pattern appears in many other state laws. For example, on the one hand, the New York Labor Relations Act (Little Wagner Act) applies most of the principles embodied in the federal law to employment relations activities of purely intrastate establishments not subject to federal regulation. On the other hand, the "hours of labor" provisions in New York State Labor Law (Chapter 31 of the Consolidated Laws) include numerous restrictions on working time that are not found in the federal Wage-Hour Act. That Act, as will be explained more fully in Chapter 2, merely requires overtime payments of at least time and one-half the employee's hourly rate for hours worked in excess of 40 in any workweek. (The Walsh-Healey Act, also a federal statute, requires overtime payments for hours worked in excess of *eight per day* to employees of concerns with government contracts of a stated dollar volume.)

To illustrate other types of state ῾regulation, the New York laws, like those in a number of other states, prohibit employment of women, and of boys under 18, in industrial and commercial establishments for more than six days or more than 48 hours in any workweek, except by permit of the state industrial commissioner.

---

[10]American Bar Association, Section of Labor Relations Law, *Report of the Committee on Equal Employment Opportunity Law—Development of the Law, Practice and Procedures as It Affects Labor Relations*, 1975 COMMITTEE REPORTS, Part 1 (Chicago: ABA Press, 1975), p. 38.

Also, New York and other states regulate such matters as rest periods, lunch periods, and night work for female employees.

Regarding minimum wages, nothing in the federal Wage-Hour Act precludes any state from fixing a higher minimum than the $2.30 per hour minimum now imposed by federal law (that is, the minimum in force as this book was being written). New York City has an ordinance setting a minimum of $2.50 for employees of private enterprises providing goods or services to the municipal government. State laws regulating terms of employment usually go beyond federal regulations or may touch areas not covered by federal law.

PENALTIES

If any company official has ever gone to jail for violation of a law regulating employer-employee relations, it has been an extraordinarily well-kept state (or federal) secret. Most federal and state statutes *do* provide criminal penalties as a last resort. It is extremely doubtful, however, that employers are deterred from evasion or overt violation of the law because of penalties. Rather, it would seem that maintaining sound, wholesome employee relationships within the bounds of applicable statutes would itself be adequate reason for full compliance.

Still, ambiguities and uncertainties as to what various regulatory statutes may require of management warrant more than passing mention of consequences of inadvertent or deliberate violation of the law. Labor union officials are painfully aware of such consequences. More than one union official has been imprisoned for violating the Labor-Management Reporting and Disclosure Act (Landrum-Griffin) of 1959.

Most laws that apply to management-employee relationships have teeth of one sort or another. Tens of millions of dollars have been paid by employers held by the Wage-Hour Division of the U.S. Labor Department to have violated the overtime or minimum-wage requirements of the Wage-Hour Act. When Labor Department findings have been challenged by employers in the federal courts, additional millions of dollars have been assessed in what amount to triple penalties for failure to pay requisite overtime allowances. Even though it has not yet happened, employers *can* be imprisoned for willful violation of the Wage-Hour Act.

Penalties for violating the Taft-Hartley Act usually require employers to cease and desist from violations and also "to take such affirmative action, including reinstatement of employees with or without back pay as will effectuate the policies of this Act." The NLRB in the early years of its existence went beyond instituting the penalty of reinstatement with back pay. It concluded that it had the authority, upon finding a company guilty of unfair labor practices, to require it to "instate" — to hire — rejected applicants who had been refused employment because of their union connections. In recent years, the Supreme Court has repeatedly sustained NLRB and appellate court decisions requiring employers to grant back pay to employees found to have been illegally discharged because of their own overt union activities or because of management's deliberate attempts to block or discourage protected union activity. For individual companies, such penalties have cost millions of dollars.

Monetary restitution is by no means the only penalty that may be imposed upon employers who violate such statutes. The Public Contracts Act, for instance, expressly authorizes government contracting agencies to cancel contracts with private enterprises which violate employees' rights to daily overtime, minimum wages, or safety precautions. Agencies may also purchase the products contracted for on the open market and then assess the offending establishment for additional costs incurred. The Civil Rights Act goes even further in sanctioning stringent penalties. If the federal courts find that a company has willfully violated that law's employment discrimination prohibitions, that company could be indefinitely barred from selling goods or services to any federal agency. Or a court might order the company to recast almost completely its hiring and promotion policies, including advancement in management ranks.

A 1976 Supreme Court decision in a civil rights case went so far as to order a company to grant retroactive seniority, with all accompanying rights such as pension benefits, to a group of black workers who the Court found had been illegally denied employment.[11]

The citation of these seemingly extreme illustrations of the impact of the law on the day-by-day functioning of personnel administrators is not intended as a value judgment on the laws reviewed. Many businessmen and union leaders believe that some federal and state regulations, such as those relating to minimum wages and maximum hours as well as to the rights and prohibitions in the Taft-Hartley and Landrum-Griffin Acts, provide benefits by curb-

---

[11]Franks v. Bowman Transp. Co., 495 F.2d 398, 8 FEP 66 (8th Cir. 1974), *rev'd on other grounds*, 424 U.S. 747, 12 FEP 549 (1976).

ing unscrupulous tactics by irresponsible representatives of both management and labor. This book does not attempt to suggest what the structure of government regulation of employer-employee relations should be. Its purpose is to summarize what personnel administrators need to know in order to deal with employees equitably and legally while protecting their companies' interests.

CHAPTER 2

Wages and Hours

Virtually all enterprises of any consequence in the United States are subject to legislative regulation of minimum wages and maximum hours. Such regulation is provided by both federal and state statutes. The meaning of the term "minimum wages" is unambiguous. Minimum-wage laws fix the lowest wage that may be paid by an employer to any employee or to a particular occupational group. Maximum-hour legislation is something different. The basic statutes—both federal and state—do not actually fix the maximum hours that may be worked by employees in any given period. Instead, they establish the top limit of weekly or daily hours that may be worked without payment of overtime. There are, of course, exceptions. Absolute maximum daily or weekly hours of work are prescribed in some laws for women or minors or employees engaged in hazardous or unusually fatiguing operations.

For the first 40 years of the twentieth century there was protracted litigation over the constitutionality of state and federal laws regulating wages and hours for most types of industrial and commercial enterprises. Such litigation brought about the adoption of sometimes overlapping or conflicting laws designed originally, in part, to circumvent U. S. Supreme Court decisions that repeatedly held various statutes invalid. By way of example, when the Supreme Court in 1935 aborted the National Industrial Recovery Act, which authorized enforcement by the Federal Government of industry-adopted standards for maximum hours and minimum wages, Congress enacted the Walsh-Healey Act a year later to impose similar standards on enterprises involved in performing government contracts. There was little or no question about the sovereign right of the Federal Government to determine by statute the terms and conditions under which work could be performed by employees of companies producing goods or providing services for federal agencies.

Attempts by state legislators to devise controls over hours and wages were blocked by Supreme Court decisions for many years.

True, in 1917 the Court sustained the constitutionality of an Oregon law setting minimum wages for women. But the Court in effect reversed itself in 1923 when it struck down the minimum-wage law for women applicable to the District of Columbia. Thus the Court, for all practical purposes, then established the principle that no valid federal or state legislation could be enacted to set minimum wages for women.

In the U. S. Supreme Court, yesterday's minority opinions are often tomorrow's majority opinions. But in the case of minimum-wage legislation, 14 years elapsed before the Court upheld a state law for women, and four years more before the Court sustained the all-embracing federal Fair Labor Standards Act. With respect to maximum hours, however, the Supreme Court in 1917 validated an Oregon law fixing 10 hours per day as the maximum that could be worked by either men or women without overtime payments for up to three additional working hours daily.

The Supreme Court's landmark decision of 1923 striking down the minimum-wage law for the District of Columbia differentiated between the constitutionality of maximum-hour legislation and the unconstitutionality of minimum-wage legislation. First, the majority opinion stated that the right of legislators to limit the hours of work of women had been upheld upon the theory that the differences between the sexes

> may justify a different rule respecting hours of labor in the case of women than in the case of men. It is pointed out that these consist in differences of physical structure, especially in respect of the maternal functions, and also in the fact that historically woman has always been dependent upon man, who has established his control by superior physical strength.[1]

The Court then proceeded to discuss, not the law, but its understanding of the facts. It is highly questionable whether any Supreme Court Justice would subscribe today or in the foreseeable future to the following excerpt from the majority opinion.

> The feature of this statute, which perhaps more than any other, puts upon it the stamp of invalidity, is that it exacts from the employer an arbitrary payment for a purpose and upon a basis having no causal connection with his business, or the contract or the work the employee engages to do. The declared basis . . . is not the value of the service rendered, but the extraneous circumstances that the employee needs to get a prescribed sum of money to insure her subsistence, health, and morals. The ethical right of every worker, man or woman, to a living wage may be conceded. One of the declared and

---

[1]Adkins v. Children's Hospital, 261 U.S. 525 (1923).

important purposes of trade organizations is to secure it. And with that principle and with every legitimate effort to realize it in fact, no one can quarrel; but the fallacy of the proposed method of attaining it is that it assumes that every employer is bound at all events to furnish it. The moral requirement implicit in every contract of employment, viz. that the amount to be paid and the service to be rendered shall bear to each other some relation of just equivalence, is completely ignored. The necessities of the employee are alone considered, and these arise outside of the employment, are the same when there is no employment, and are as great in one occupation as in another. Certainly the employer, by paying a fair equivalent for the service rendered, though not sufficient to support the employee, has neither caused or contributed to her poverty. On the contrary, to the extent of what he pays, he has relieved it. In principle, there can be no difference between the case of selling labor and the case of selling goods. If one goes to the butcher, the baker, or grocer to buy food, he is morally entitled to obtain the worth of his money; but he is not entitled to more. If what he gets is worth what he pays, he is not justified in demanding more, simply because he needs more. And the shopkeeper, having dealt fairly and honestly in that transaction, is not concerned in any peculiar case with the question of his customer's necessities. Should a statute undertake to vest in a commission power to determine the quantity of food necessary for individual support, and require the shopkeeper, if he sell to the individual at all, to furnish that quantity at not more than a fixed maximum, it would undoubtedly fall before the constitutionality test. The fallacy of any argument in support of the validity of such a statute would be quickly exposed. The argument in support of that now being considered is equally fallacious, though the weakness of it may not be so plain. A statute requiring an employer to pay in money, to pay at prescribed and regular intervals, to pay the value of services rendered, even to pay with fair relation to the extent of the benefit obtained from the service would be understandable. But a statute which prescribes payment without respect to any of these things, and solely with relation to circumstances apart from the contract of employment, the business affected by it, and the work done under it, is so clearly the product of a naked, arbitrary exercise of power that it cannot be allowed to stand under the Constitution of the United States.[2]

There was sharp and caustic disagreement by three Supreme Court Justices in two separate minority opinions. The minority opinion of Chief Justice Taft presaged the much later view of the Court when it sustained the validity of both federal and state minimum-wage legislation in 1937 and again in 1941. Chief Justice Taft had this to say:

Legislatures in limiting freedom of contract between employee and employer by a minimum wage proceed on the assumption that employees, in the class receiving the least pay, are not upon a full level

---

[2]*Ibid.*

of equality of choice with their employer and in their necessitous circumstances are prone to accept pretty much anything that is offered. They are peculiarly subject to the overreaching of the harsh and greedy employer. The evils of the sweating system and of the long hours and low wages which are characteristic of it ar well known. Now, I agree that it is a disputable question in the field of political economy how far a statutory requirement of maximum hours or minimum wages may be a useful remedy for such evils, and whether it may not make the case of the oppressed employee worse than it was before. But it is not the function of this court to hold congressional acts invalid simply because they are passed to carry out economic views which the court believes to be unwise or unsound.

Legislatures which adopt a requirement of maximum hours or minimum wages may be presumed to believe that when sweating employers are prevented from paying unduly low wages by positive law they will continue their business, abating that part of their profits, which were wrung from the necessities of their employees, and will concede the better terms required by the law, and that while in individual cases, hardship may result, the restriction will inure to the benefit of the general class of employees in whose interest the law is passed and so to that of the community at large.[3]

THE WAGE-HOUR ACT

The basic federal law regulating hours and wages of industrial and commercial enterprises is the federal Fair Labor Standards Act.[4] This law is commonly referred to as the Wage-Hour Act and will be so designated here.

As originally enacted in 1938, the law applied only to certain classes of employees of establishments engaged in interstate commerce or in the production of goods for interstate commerce. Over the years, however, administrative interpretations, congressional amendments, and court decisions extended the coverage of the law to apply to some employees of almost every type of business establishment except nonchain corner drugstores, undertaking parlors, and so-called Mom and Pop stores — stores operated by members of the same family that have no other employees besides the husband, wife, or children of the proprietor.

The Act's expanded coverage is not primarily the work of over-zealous bureaucrats but of the Congress. Congressional amendments of 1961, 1966, and 1974 added millions of employees of private enterprises to those already covered. Indeed, the 1966 amendments made 29 changes in the coverage of the law, resulting

---

[3]*Ibid.*
[4]The constitutionality of the Fair Labor Standards Act was sustained without formidable opposition in U.S. v. F.W. Darby Lumber Co., 1 WH Cases 17 (1941).

in its application to more than eight million additional employees.

Special Exclusions

The expanded coverage resulting from the 1974 amendments were of relatively little consequence to firms engaged in the principal fields of commerce and industry. Mostly they reduced or eliminated exemptions for basic overtime payment requirements for a limited number of seasonal industries engaged in processing perishable products. By way of example, previous exemption from overtime requirements for employees engaged in on-shore processing of certain seafood products was modified, effective January 1, 1975, to require payment of overtime only after 44 hours; but on May 1, 1976, the partial exemptions were cancelled entirely.

Two unique features of the law make it difficult for personnel administrators to determine easily whether all the employees working for their companies may be currently subject to the terms of the Wage-Hour Act. Unlike most federal regulatory measures, the Act is administered by a single official rather than by a board or commission with multiple membership. Even more unusual, the administrator has no authority to order anyone to do anything. To be sure, he is empowered to issue "interpretative bulletins" explaining, for example, what categories of employees are exempt from the overtime-pay provisions of the law, or from the minimum-wage provisions. Yet he has no power to issue compliance orders when violations seem evident. Instead, he or the aggrieved, underpaid employee must go into federal court to seek redress. And the federal courts do not necessarily see eye to eye with the administrator—or even with each other.

More than 35 years after the passage of the original law, the courts are still busy grinding out decisions as to the coverage of the Act and the application of specific provisions. One reason for the proliferation of litigation over this statute is the multiple basis for determining who is covered by it. Under the law, the status of an employee of a business establishment may be determined (a) by the nature of the enterprise for which he works, (b) by the nature of his own duties, and (c) by the amount of his compensation. No wonder, then, that the courts sometimes disagree, especially since amendments to the act (more than 20 such changes applicable to exemptions were made by the 1966 amendments alone) have prevented the courts over the years from establishing and following consistent precedents that are uniformly applicable to all jurisdictions. Thus personnel administrators in companies having facilities in different areas throughout the nation may at times have to apply one court-determined version of the law for a plant in Massachusetts and a different version for a distributing house in Colorado.

Two actual cases, both decided by federal courts in 1966, point up this problem. The common issue in both cases was the meaning of the phrase "retail or service establishment" within the purview of the law. Both cases ultimately came before the U. S. Supreme Court, and the facts below are as summarized by that court.

The first case involved Idaho Sheet Metal Works, Inc.[5] This company operated a plant employing about 12 workers who made, installed, and maintained sheet metal products used in equipment operated by companies processing potatoes for interstate shipment. When challenged by the Secretary of Labor on behalf of the Wage-Hour Act administrator for noncompliance with the overtime provisions of that law, the company argued that it was a retail or service establishment that was expressly exempt from coverage by the law. It adduced evidence indicating that over 75 percent of its dollar volume of sales enabled it to meet the test for exemption as a retail establishment. A federal district court held the company completely exempt, and it remained so until a federal court of appeals reversed the lower court's decision, and several years later the Supreme Court sustained the appeals court.

The second case, wherein a federal district court took a position almost diametrically opposite to that of the court referred to above, involved the Steepleton General Tire Company, operating in Memphis, Tenn. This company employed nearly 50 workers while doing business as a franchised tire dealer engaged in the sale, recapping, and repair of tires. More than half of the company's income was derived from its sales and services to other concerns operating construction vehicles or truck fleets, some of them operating their equipment in interstate commerce. Upon proceedings instituted by the Secretary of Labor to require Steepleton to comply with both the minimum-wage and the overtime requirements of the Wage-Hour Act, a federal district court held the company to be covered by the law. The federal circuit court of appeals having jurisdiction reversed the district court. So this case, presenting as it did a conflict of rulings between two federal courts of appeals, eventually came before the U. S. Supreme Court.[6]

The Court decided that Steepleton, like Idaho Sheet Metal Works, was engaged in interstate commerce and was not a retail establishment excluded from coverage by the Act. But the point is

[5]Idaho Sheet Metal Works v. Wirtz, 17 WH Cases 240 (1966).
[6]Wirtz v. Steepleton General Tire Co., 17 WH Cases 240 (1966).

that for several years, companies in one area were not considered covered by the Act, and companies doing similar business in another area were covered because of the different judgments of federal circuit courts of appeals. In any event, the extensive amendments to the law in 1966, which became effective January 1, 1967, clarified and greatly restricted the exemptions of retail establishments. Hence, it may be safely assumed that almost every one working in a store with two or more employees (except a purely family establishment) is employed by an enterprise that is subject to some of the terms of the Wage-Hour Act.

The 1977 Minimum Wage Law

On Nov. 1, 1977, President Carter approved an Act of Congress (P.L. 95-21) that substantially amended the original Fair Labor Standards Act of 1938. This statute had been significantly amended several different times, most recently on May 1, 1974, when the basic statutory wage had been set at $2 per hour, to be increased to $2.30 an hour as of Jan. 1, 1976. (The numbers cited below in detailing wage and salary minimum, or exceptions, special maximum hours, etc., are those as prescribed in the 1977 amendments, except where specifically indicated otherwise.)

Basically, the 1977 statute established a new set of minimum rates for nearly all of the gainfully employed persons in the 50 states of the nation. (Separate, lower minimum rates are applicable to persons employed in Puerto Rico and the Virgin Islands). On January 1978, the generally applicable minimum rate became $2.65 an hour. For 1979 the rate will be $2.90 an hour. In 1980 it will become $3 an hour; and on and after Jan. 1, 1980, the minimum will become $3.35 an hour.

The 1977 law also made minor changes in the Wage-Hour Act's general coverage. As amended in 1974, small retail and service establishments were exempted from coverage of any of their employees if their annual receipts were less than $250,000. The test for exemption of such establishments is scheduled to raise to $275,000 as of July 1, 1978; to $325,000 as of July 1, 1980; and to $362,500 as of Dec. 31, 1981. In one other minor amendment, the 1977 law increased from four to six the number of students that may be employed by any retail or service concern at 85 percent of the applicable norm when the Secretary of Labor finds there would be no adverse effects on full-time employment opportunities. Under certain limited conditions children over age 10 can henceforth be employed in the summer as hand-harvest agricultural laborers.

Minimum Wages

The term "minimum wages" is nowhere defined in the law. In the context of the statute, however, this term obviously means the lowest rate of pay fixed directly by law, or by administrative regulation, that may be paid either for a particular type of work or for a particular class of workers or for any individual worker. The present federal standard minimum wage is $2.65 per hour. There are some statutory exceptions. The law permits the administrator, for example, to provide for employment, under special certificates at wages less than the regular minimum, of individuals "whose earning or productive capacity is impaired by age or physical or mental deficiency or injury." Such wages cannot be less than 50 percent of the applicable minimum wage.

One complication in determining the applicable minimum wage arises because of the intricate provisions covering the extent, if any, to which employees engaged in retail activities may or may not be exempt on the basis of the annual sales volume in the establishment for which they work. This situation is reviewed in the operations manual published by The Bureau of National Affairs, Inc.[7] Companies whose operations combine manufacturing and distribution facilities, including direct sales to customers that are directly or indirectly engaged in interstate commerce, may be subject at least temporarily to the differing minimum-wage standards. The BNA manual explains such situations in detail.

Wage Payments Other Than in Cash

Compliance with the minimum-wage requirements of the Act does not mean that the full amount of the applicable minimum rate must be paid in cash. The reasonable cost or fair value of certain "perquisites" may be counted as part of the minimum wage. Official regulations provide in part that the wage paid to any employee includes "the reasonable cost as determined by the Secretary of Labor, to the employer of furnishing such employee with board, lodging, or other facilities, if such board, lodging, or other facilities are customarily furnished by such employer to his employees."[8] There are the usual exceptions to the exceptions in these regulations. One excludes from calculation of minimum wages any pay-

---

[7]THE NEW WAGE AND HOUR LAW (rev. ed.; Washington: The Bureau of National Affairs, Inc., 1967).

[8]These regulations are summarized in the Code of Federal Regulations (C.F.R.), Title 29, *Labor*. See 29 C.F.R. §778.116 (1975).

ment in kind, that is, board, lodging, etc., made pursuant to the terms of a collective bargaining agreement.

Minimum Payable for Each Hour Worked

For those covered by the law, at least the minimum hourly rate must be paid for each hour worked. This was not always so. For example, if a salaried employee's weekly rate was the equivalent of at least 40 times the applicable minimum rate, and he regularly worked only 35 hours per week, no additional payments were due him when he worked more than 35 but fewer than 40 hours in a given week. In other words, assume a clerk's weekly salary was $100 a week, and the statutory minimum rate applicable to his job was the equivalent of $2.30 per hour. So long as he received at least $92 for a workweek of 40 hours or less (40 × $2.30), such payment was understood to be in compliance with the law.

Under the most recent rulings of the administrator, weekly salaries in excess of the equivalent of more than the hours worked (less than 40) times the applicable minimum (i.e., $2.65 per hour) do not count for the purpose of calculating minimum hourly rates payable for every hour worked. Hence, the clerk in the foregoing example who works beyond his regular schedule of 35 hours has to be paid at least an additional $2.65 per hour for the extra time worked up to 40 hours. And, of course, as will be developed in the next subsection, he must be paid at least one and one-half times his regular equivalent hourly rate for all time worked in excess of 40 hours in any one week. In short, unless the employee's own contract with his employer, or a union contract by which he is covered, provides for a higher equivalent hourly rate, an employee subject to the minimum-wage provisions of the act must be paid for each hour worked at the minimum rate specified for his occupational group.[9]

Obviously, employees exempt from the requirements of the law respecting payment of overtime are automatically excluded from any requirement as to payment of a minimum hourly rate, regardless of the number of hours scheduled for them or worked by them in any given workweek.

Maximum Hours

Forty hours is the maximum number that most employees covered by the Wage-Hour Act can be permitted to work in any par-

---

[9]*Ibid.*, §778.322 (1975).

ticular workweek without overtime payments of at least the equivalent of one and one-half times their regular hourly rate.

Determining the regular rate of pay that must be used in calculating the mandatory overtime payments was the subject of a landmark decision by the U. S. Supreme Court in 1948. The decision not only interprets the law but also demonstrates the complexity of the problems management faces in assuring full compliance with the law.

In the case in point, the Court had to decide something that the law itself did not spell out or define. As was succinctly stated in the Court's majority opinion:

> The problem posed is the method of computing the regular rate of pay for longshoremen who work in foreign and interstate commerce varying and irregular hours throughout the workweek under a collective bargaining agreement for handling cargo which provides contract straight time hourly rates for work done within a prescribed 44-hour time schedule and contract overtime rates for all work done outside the straight time hours.[10]

In a footnote to its opinion, the Court then went on to observe that "The use of the word 'overtime' in the contract does not decide this case. The problem for solution is whether rates described as 'overtime' by the contract are such rates as Section 7 (a) [of the Act] provides for statutory excess hours."[11] The Court in another footnote defined the term "overtime premium" as "extra pay for work because of previous work for a specified number of hours in the workweek or workday whether the hours are specified by contract or statute."[12]

In the majority opinion the Court summarized the respective positions of the litigants (the respondents being employees claiming extra pay and the petitioners being their employers) as follows:

> Respondents claim that their regular rate of pay under the contract for any workweek within the meaning of Section 7 (a), is the average hourly rate computed by dividing the total number of hours worked in any workweek for any single employer into the total compensation received from that employer during that week and that in those workweeks in which they worked more than forty hours for any one employer they were entitled by Section 7 (a) to statutory excess compensation for all such excess hours computed on the basis of that rate. The petitioners claim that the straight time rates are the regular rates, and that they have, therefore, with minor exceptions not presented by this review, complied with the requirements of Section 7

---

[10]Aaron v. Bay Ridge Operating Co., 8 WH Cases 20 (1948).
[11]*Ibid.*
[12]*Ibid.*

(a). That is, no rates except straight time rates are to be taken into consideration in computing the regular rate. The petitioners contend that the contract overtime rates were intended to cover any earned statutory excess compensation and did cover it because they were substantially in an amount of one and one-half times the straight time rates.[13]

The majority of the Supreme Court accepted the petitioners' view as correct. Its opinion noted that, since Congress had not defined the "regular rate of pay,"

> we feel sure the purpose was to require judicial determination as to whether in fact an employee receives the full statutory excess compensation, rather than to impose a rule that in the absence of fraud or clear evasion employers and employees might fix a regular rate without regard to hours worked or sums actually received as pay.[14]

The decisive passage in the Court's decision read:

> We think the most reasonable conclusion is that Congress intended the regular rate of pay to be found by dividing the weekly compensation by the hours worked unless the compensation paid to the employee contains some amount that represents an overtime premium. If such overtime premium is included in the weekly pay check that must be deducted before the division. This deduction of overtime premium from the pay for the workweek results from the language of the statute. When the statute says that the employee shall receive for his excess hours one and one-half times the regular rate at which he is employed, it is clear to us that Congress intended to exclude overtime premium payments from computation of the regular rate of pay. To permit overtime premium to enter into the computation of the regular rate would be to allow overtime premium on overtime premium — a pyramiding that Congress could not have intended. In order to avoid a similar double payment, we think that any overtime premium paid, even for work during the first forty hours of the workweek, may be credited against any obligation to pay statutory excess compensation.[15]

Regular Rate for Overtime Computations

The Wage-Hour Act now specifically provides that the

> "regular rate" at which an employee is employed shall be deemed to include [for purposes of calculating statutory overtime] all remuneration for employment paid to, or on behalf of, the employee, but shall not be deemed to include: . . .
>
> extra compensation provided by a premium rate paid for certain hours worked by the employee in any day or workweek because such

---

[13]*Ibid.*
[14]*Ibid.*
[15]*Ibid.*

hours are hours worked in excess of eight in a day or in excess of the maximum workweek applicable to an employee under subsection (a) [the provision of the law establishing a higher maximum workweek for limited groups of employees] or in excess of the employee's normal working hours or regular working hours, as the case may be;

extra compensation provided by a premium rate paid for work by the employee on Saturdays, Sundays, holidays, or regular days of rest, or on the sixth or seventh day of the workweek, where such premium rate is not less than one and one-half times the rate established in good faith for like work performed in non-overtime hours on other days;

extra compensation provided by a premium rate paid for work by an employee, in pursuance of an applicable employment contract or collective bargaining agreement, for work outside of the hours established in good faith by the contract or agreement as the basic, normal, or regular workday (not exceeding eight hours) or workweek (not exceeding the maximum workweek applicable to such employee under subsection (a)), where such premium rate is not less than one and one-half times the rate established in good faith by the contract or agreement for like work performed during such workday or work-week.[16]

In addition to the above, there are now in the Wage-Hour Act numerous other specific provisions relating to the bases for computing overtime compensation that are not necessarily applicable to all employers or in all contracts or agreements with their employees. Hence, in case of doubt, personnel administrators would be well advised to examine the full text of the statute as well as the administrator's interpretations.

The law contains a number of special provisions with respect to overtime pay. These include: contracts for employees who necessarily work irregular hours but who are guaranteed a weekly wage including overtime for not more than 60 hours of work; commission pay arrangements for employees of retail or service establishments; averaging of equivalent straight-time rates for employees engaged in two or more jobs in the same workweek; computation of straight-time rates for overtime purposes of employees paid exclusively on a wage-incentive or piecework basis; and payments made for purposes other than the amount of time expended on the job or the volume of work performed, such as Christmas bonuses, holiday and vacation pay, and other fringe benefits, including employer contributions on behalf of individual employees for pensions or life or accident insurance.

---

[16]Quoted from Section 7 of the Wage Hour Act as amended on Sept. 23, 1966, effective Feb. 1, 1967.

The two administrative interpretations given below illustrate the situations sometimes encountered by management. These interpretations are generally consistent with official administrative rulings since the law was passed in 1938.

Shift Premium

Premiums for regularly scheduled hours of work outside of the normal daytime shift are considered part of an employee's regular rate for the purpose of computing overtime. Assume a factory operates three shifts: 8 a.m. to 4 p.m., 4 p.m. to midnight, and midnight to 8 a.m. For the first shift, only the straight-time rate is payable for persons scheduled to work and actually working on that shift. For the second shift, a shift premium of perhaps 10 cents an hour has been established, either by management or by union agreement. For the third shift, the premium might be 15 cents an hour.

The overtime rate for an employee working on the first shift who puts in some overtime after 4 p.m. is just one and one-half times his regular straight-time rate. Under the law, then, an employee who continues work after his regular shift into the second shift does not have to be paid a shift premium unless an applicable private contract or agreement requires it. But the picture is somewhat different with regard to the second-shift employee. When *he* works overtime beyond midnight, his overtime rate has to be calculated on the basis of his regular hourly rate plus his shift premium. In other words, a second-shift employee paid $2.65 per hour and a 10-cent shift premium has an effective rate for overtime purposes of $2.75 per hour. For work performed on an overtime basis after midnight, he would have to be paid one and one-half times $2.75, or $4.125 per hour.

The basis for such calculations of overtime payments has been explained officially in the administrators' *Interpretative Bulletin* and appear in the *Code of Federal Regulations* as follows:

> To qualify as an overtime premium under section 7 (e) (7) the premium must be paid because the work was performed during hours "outside of the hours established . . . as the basic . . . workday or workweek" and not for some other reason. Thus, if the basic workday is established in good faith as the hours from 8 A.M. to 5 P.M. a premium of time and one-half paid for hours between 5 P.M. and 8 A.M. would qualify as an overtime premium. However, where the contract does not provide for the payment of a premium except for work between midnight and six A.M. the premium would not qualify under this section since it is not a premium paid for work out-

side the established workday but only for certain special hours out-side the workday, in most instances because they are undesirable hours. Similarly, where payments of premium rates for work are made only if the employee has not had a meal period or rest period, they are not regarded as overtime premiums; they are premiums paid because of undesirable working conditions.[17]

Although this quotation may not seem precisely pertinent to the illustrations given above, the fact is that bona fide shift pre-miums cannot be used as a partial offset for statutory overtime, and, conversely, they must be counted as part of the regular rate in calculating statutory overtime.

Hours Not Worked

The second illustration of the rulings on the law seems self-explanatory. On the subject of payments for hours not worked, the administrator has stated that:

> Section 7(e) (2) of the Act provides that the term "regular rate" shall not be deemed to include "payments made for occasional periods when no work is performed due to vacation, holiday, illness, failure of the employer to provide sufficient work, or other similar cause; reasonable payments for traveling expenses, or other expenses, in-curred by an employee in the furtherance of his employer's interests and properly reimbursable by the employer; and other similar pay-ments to an employee which are not made as compensation for his hours of employment . . . ." However, since such payments are not made as compensation for the employee's hours worked in any work-week, no part of such payments can be credited toward overtime compensation due under the Act.[18]

Hours Worked

Questions concerning what constitutes time worked as distinct from time that must be compensated have given rise to many legal controversies. On most of these questions, the administrator and the courts have given definite answers over the past 30 years. For example, is an employee considered to have been working if his shift starts at eight in the morning but he punches in on his time clock at 7:35 a.m.? Not necessarily, the administrator has ruled. (A ques-tion such as this may arise in determining how much straight-time pay an employee is entitled to, as well as the amount of overtime, if any, due him.) As to the specific question, the correct answer may depend upon the location of the time clock in relation to the

---

[17]29 C.F.R. §778.204 (1975).
[18]*Ibid.*, §778.216 (1975).

employee's work station; whether or not the employee is permitted to do any work before the eight o'clock whistle blows; and whether or not other records besides time clocks are maintained to indicate the employee's actual starting time. In short, there is no single definitive answer.

The proper decision as to what constitutes time worked in a situation such as the one just outlined may depend not on the administrator's latest ruling but on what the federal district or circuit court of appeals having jurisdiction over the area in question has held to be the law.

The administrator's interpretations of the law, however, can usually be relied on as providing sound guidelines for compliance in most situations. Here are summaries of some of them:

> *Employees "Suffered or Permitted to Work."* Work not requested but suffered or permitted is work time. For example, an employee may voluntarily continue to work at the end of the shift. He may be a pieceworker, he may desire to finish an assigned task, or he may wish to correct errors, paste [sic] work tickets, prepare time reports or other records. The reason is immaterial. The employer knows or has reason to believe that he is continuing to work and the time is working time.[19]

> *Off Duty—General.* Periods during which an employee is completely relieved from duty and which are long enough to enable him to use the time effectively for his own purposes are not hours worked. He is not completely relieved from duty and cannot use the time effectively for his own purposes unless he is definitely told in advance that he may leave the job and that he will not have to commence work until a definitely specified hour has arrived. Whether the time is long enough to enable him to use the time effectively for his own purposes depends upon all the facts and circumstances of the case.[20]

> *On-Call Time.* An employee who is required to remain on call on the employer's premises or so close thereto that he cannot use the time effectively for his own purposes is working while "on call." An employee who is not required to remain on the premises but is merely required to leave word at his home or with company officials where he may be reached is not working while on call."[21]

> *Rest and Meal Periods.* Rest periods of short duration, running from about 5 minutes to about 20 minutes, are common in industry. They promote the efficiency of the employee and are customarily paid for as working time. They must be counted as time worked. Compensable time for rest periods may not be offset against other working time such as compensable waiting time or on-call time.

---

[19]*Ibid.*, §785.11 (1975).
[20]*Ibid.*, §785.16 (1975).
[21]*Ibid.*, §785.17 (1975).

> Bona fide meal periods are not work time. Bona fide meal periods do not include coffee breaks or time off for snacks. These are rest periods. The employee must be completely relieved from duty for the purpose of eating regular meals.[22]

This last section does not mean precisely what it seems to say. In fact, the Wage-Hour Act, unlike some state laws, has no requirement that employees be given any time off during their regular tour of duty for a meal period. The interpretative bulletin goes on to imply this when it further states that:

> The employee is not relieved if he is required to perform any duties, whether active or inactive, while eating. For example, an office employee who is required to eat at his desk or a factory worker who is required to be at his machine is working while he is eating.[23]

> *Training Programs.* Attendance at lectures, meetings, training programs and similar activities need not be counted as working time if the four following criteria are met:
> (a) Attendance is outside of the employee's regular working hours;
> (b) attendance is in fact voluntary;
> (c) the course, lecture, or meeting is not directly related to the employee's job; and
> (d) the employee does not perform any productive work during such attendance.

> Attendance is not voluntary of course, if it is required by the employer.[24]

This last statement appears in the interpretative bulletin, but, again, it apparently does not mean exactly what it says. For it is followed by this explanatory comment: "It is not voluntary if the employee is given to understand or led to believe that his present working conditions or the continuance of his employment would be adversely affected by non-atttendance."[25]

Preliminary and Postliminary Activities

Until the famous or infamous portal-to-portal case hit the courts, most employers subject to the Wage-Hour Act thought that time worked meant actual productive performance on the job. But an imaginative and militant union official thought otherwise. Or at least he and other union officials thought that they could persuade the administrator and the courts that time worked should be considered as including many activities of employees before reaching and after leaving their work stations. These activities, they con-

---

[22]*Ibid.*, §785.18 and §785.19 (1975).
[23]*Ibid.*, §785.19 (1975).
[24]*Ibid.*, §785.27 and §785.28 (1975).
[25]*Ibid.*, §785.28 (1975).

tended, should be compensable in calculating straight-time as well as overtime pay. They were partially successful. In the Supreme Court's awesome decision in the case of *Anderson v. Mt. Clemens Pottery Co.*,[26] the Court held that employees must be paid for the time before and after their regular shift that they were required to be on the company's premises. As the court put it:

> The employer required them to punch in, walk to their work benches and perform preliminary duties during the 14-minute periods preceding productive work; the same activities in reverse occurred in the 14-minute periods subsequent to the completion of productive work. Since the statutory workweek includes all time during which an employee is necessarily required to be on the employer's premises, on duty, or at a prescribed workplace, the time spent in these activities must be accorded appropriate compensation.

(Reference to 14-minute periods was occasioned by the company's established practice of using a 14-minute interval before the starting time and the lunch period for employees to punch time clocks and to proceed to workplaces and using the same interval at the end of the lunch period and workshift.)

One of the claims of the group of employees that instituted the proceedings leading to the Supreme Court's decision was that time-clock records showed four 14-minute periods more each day, or 56 minutes more of working time, than the total for which they had been paid. The Court did not hold in this case that the employees had necessarily been underpaid by 56 minutes per day, observing that "it is generally recognized that time clocks do not necessarily record the actual time worked by employees." It did decide on this issue that "compensable working time was limited to the minimum time necessarily spent in walking at an ordinary rate along the most direct route from time clock to work bench," and it sent the case back to the lower courts to make appropriate findings of fact on this question and on the related questions of what preliminary and "postliminary" activities were compensable. The word "postliminary" had not even been coined at the time and still is not to be found even in up-to-date unabridged dictionaries. According to present usage, the activities referred to include putting on and removing protective clothing, turning machinery off and on, opening and closing windows, etc.[27]

The portal-to-portal litigation initially generated a multibillion-dollar liability for companies subject to the Act. Only through hastily passed amendments to the law were employers relieved of

---

[26]Anderson v. Mt. Clemens Pottery Co., 6 WH Cases 83 (1946).
[27]*Ibid.*

much of their liability. The effects of the amendments now designated as the Portal-to-Portal Act have been summarized by the administrator as providing that no employer shall be liable for the failure to pay the minimum wage or overtime compensation for time spent in

> walking, riding, or traveling to and from the actual place of performance of the principal activity or activities which such employee is employed to perform either prior to the time on any particular workday at which such employee commences, or subsequent to the time at which he ceases, such particular activity or activities.[28]

But the law specifically states that:

> the employer shall not be relieved from liability if the activity is compensable by express contract or by custom or practice not inconsistent with an express contract. Thus travel time at the commencement or cessation of the workday which was originally considered as working time under the . . . Act (such as underground travel in mines or walking from time clock to work bench) need not be counted as working time unless it is compensable by contract, custom or practice. If compensable by express contract or by custom or practice not inconsistent with an express contract, such travel time must be counted in computing hours worked. However, ordinary travel from home to work need not be counted as hours worked even if the employer agrees to pay for it.[29]

In the same interpretative bulletin, the administrator cited two U. S. Supreme Court decisions, following by nearly 10 years its portal-to-portal decision, in which, the administrator pointed out, "the types of activities which are considered an integral part of the employees' jobs" are noted. In one decision, the administrator said:

> employees changed their clothes and took showers in a battery plant where the manufacturing process involved the extensive use of caustic and toxic materials (*Steiner* v. *Mitchell*, 350 U. S. 247 (1956).) In another case knifemen in a meatpacking plant sharpened their knives before and after their scheduled workday. (*Mitchell* v. *King Packing Co.*, 350 U. S. 260 (1956).) In both cases the Supreme Court held that these activities are an integral and indispensable part of the employees' principal activities.[30]

Special Exceptions

Innumerable special situations that have led to clarification of the law itself by the administrator's interpretations and court decisions have come down over the years and continue to prolifer-

---

[28]29 C.F.R. §785.34 (1975).
[29]*Ibid.*
[30]*Ibid.*, §785.28 (1975).

ate. Managers responsible for forming and administering company policies and practices bearing on the Wage-Hour Act would be well advised to subscribe to one of the several authoritative commercial reporting services that regularly publish new administrative rulings and significant court decisions on all phases of employment law. This statute, like others discussed in this volume, often means what the administrative agency and the courts say it means from day to day.

The validity of this last assertion can be demonstrated by citing developments involving a question of compliance with the law that still give rise to uncertainty and limitation some 20-odd years after the Supreme Court spoke authoritatively but not, as it turned out, with finality. These questions originally arose when the administrator challenged the legality of the so-called Belo plan. This plan guaranteed each employee it covered a stated weekly wage or salary which included both straight-time earnings and overtime pay for all hours worked up to 54½ per week, even though the actual time worked might have been considerably less than 54½ hours. The U. S. Supreme Court sustained the legality of the plan's basic principle—that the law permitted an employer to pay his employees a fixed weekly rate, provided that rate made allowance for the payment of the equivalent of at least the statutory minimum wage for straight-time hours and the equivalent of time and one-half for hours worked beyond 40 a week. In other words, the Court held in essence that, since Congress had failed to define the term "regular rate," there was nothing in the law to prevent an employer's establishing what amounted to variable hourly rates when working at irregular weekly schedules as long as the employee's total compensation, fixed and guaranteed as it was under the Belo plan, met the statutory provisions respecting minimum wages and maximum hours. The Court all but urged Congress to legislate further on this matter.[31]

Congress heeded the Supreme Court's suggestion in 1949. After the Wage-Hour administrator had taken the position that the Belo decision applied only to virtually the identical arrangement provided in the Belo plan and not to other plans with similar arrangements, Congress enacted clarifying amendments. These 1949 amendments expressly sanctioned Belo-type contracts. If a company considers irregular working schedules advisable (or the general provisions of the law relating to minimum wages or maximum hours onerous), its management might well

---

[31]Walling v. A.H. Belo Co., 2 WH Cases 39 (1942).

look into the feasibility of some type of Belo arrangement under the terms currently held permissible by the administrator. In this connection, the successive administrators apparently never viewed with enthusiasm either the Supreme Court decision or the congressional amendments stemming from the Belo Plan. To wit, the current "Rules and Regulations" relating to overtime compensation include a passage which declares that the Belo amendments were

> proposed and enacted in 1949 with the stated purpose of giving express statutory validity, subject to prescribed limitations, to a judicial "gloss on the Act" by which an exception to the usual rule as to the actual regular rate had been recognized by a closely divided Supreme Court as permissible with respect to employment in such situations under so-called Belo contracts.[32]

The present regulations caution employers that the type of special employment agreement now permissible under the law — constant pay for varying workweeks including overtime — may be utilized if "the nature of the employee's duties [are] such .that neither he or [sic] his employer can either control or anticipate with any degree of certainty the number of hours he must work from week to week."[33] The regulations say much more. Close scrutiny is therefore needed, and the administrator advises employers considering a Belo plan to submit it in advance for the administrator's judgment as to its legality.

Exemptions From Coverage by Occupation

The Wage-Hour Act explicitly excludes from coverage of its minimum-wage and maximum-hour provisions employees engaged in certain white collar occupations who are paid on *a salary basis.* Here there is an anomaly, if not a contradiction, in the law. There are minimum salary requirements for all of the occupational groups so excluded, and in all instances the minimum salary for exemption is materially in excess of the equivalent of the present statutory minimum of $2.65 per hour.

The principal salaried occupations that the law excludes are executive, administrative, professional, or outside sales jobs. These occupations are defined and delimited by the administrator. In significant contrast to the administrator's limited authority to apply and enforce other provisions of the statute, his powers to determine the basic occupational exemptions from coverage are unrestricted.

---

[32]29 C.F.R. §778.404 (1975).
[33]*Ibid.*, §778.405 (1975).

This means that his determinations stand as law unless the courts find them to be arbitrary or capricious. (The actual authority, as mentioned previously, is vested in the Secretary of Labor who, under the law, may delegate it to the Wage-Hour Administrator.)

Exempt Executives

Six separate tests or standards must be met for an employee to be considered as an executive. *All* of these must be met simultaneously. If an employee's job assignments fall short of meeting one or more of the standards in any workweek, he must be considered nonexempt that week.

The six precise tests delineated by the administrator are quoted in full below:

> The term "employee employed in a bona fide executive . . . capacity" . . . shall mean any employee
> (a) whose primary duty consists of the management of the enterprise by which he is employed or of a customarily recognized department or subdivision thereof; and
> (b) who customarily and regularly directs the work of two or more employees therein; and
> (c) who has the authority to hire and fire other employees or whose suggestions and recommendations as to the hiring or firing and as to the advancement or promotion or any change of status of other employees will be given particular weight; and
> (d) who customarily and regularly exercises discretionary powers; and
> (e) who does not devote more than 20 percent, or in the case of an employee of a retail or service establishment, who does not devote as much as 40 percent, of his hours of work in the workweek to activities which are not directly and closely related to the performance of the work described in paragraphs (a) through (d) of this section: Provided that this paragraph shall not apply in the case of an employee who is in sole charge of an independent establishment or a physically separated branch establishment or who owns at least a 20 percent interest in the enterprise in which he is employed; and
> (f) who is compensated for his services on a salary basis at a rate of not less than $155 per week (or $130 per week if employed in Puerto Rico, the Virgin Islands, or American Samoa) exclusive of board, lodging, or facilities.[34]

There is a different exemption for executives based primarily on a higher salary, namely, not less than the equivalent of at least $250 per week. Under this provision, an employee may be exempt without meeting continuously all of the six prescribed tests if he is

---

[34]*Ibid.*, §541.1 (1975).

paid not less than $250 a week (exclusive of board, lodging, or other facilities) *and if*

> "his primary duty consists of the management of the enterprise by which he is employed or if a customarily recognized department or subdivision thereof, and includes the customary and regular direction of the work of two or more employees therein by an employee in the management of his department or the supervision of the employees under him: Interviewing, selecting [sic] and training of employees; setting and adjusting their rates of pay and hours of work; directing their work; maintaining their production or sales records for use in supervision or contract; appraising their productivity and efficiency for the purpose of recommending promotions or other changes in their status; handling their complaints and grievances and disciplining them when necessary; determining the techniques to be used; apportioning the work among the workers; determining the type of materials, supplies, machinery or tools to be used or merchandise to be bought, stocked and sold; controlling the flow and distribution of materials or merchandise and supplies; providing for the safety of the men and the property.[35]

Authority to Hire and Fire

The administrator has given an explicit interpretation on the use of the power to hire and fire. To quote:

> Section 541.1 requires that an exempt executive employee have authority to hire or fire other employees or that his suggestions and recommendations as to hiring and firing and as to advancement and promotion or any other change of status of the employees whom he supervises will be given particular weight. Thus *no employee whether high or low in the hierarchy of management* [emphasis supplied] can be considered as employed in a bona fide executive capacity unless he is directly concerned either with the hiring or firing and other change of status of the employees under his supervision, whether by direct action or by recommendation to those to whom the hiring and firing functions are delegated.[36]

A few typical examples of the kinds of job duties that the administrator has deemed to be exempt or nonexempt under the "executive" definition are given below.

Supervisor of two or more employees.

If the "executive" supervises one full-time and two part-time employees, of whom one works mornings and one afternoons; or four part-time employees, two of whom work mornings and two afternoons, this requirement would be met.[37]

---

[35]*Ibid.*, §541.102 (1975).
[36]*Ibid.*, §541.106 (1975).
[37]*Ibid.*, §541.105 (1975).

Emergencies.

Under certain occasional emergency conditions, work which is normally performed by non-exempt employees and is non-exempt in nature will be directly and closely related to the performance of the exempt functions of management and supervision and will therefore be exempt work. In effect, this means that a bona fide executive who performs work of a normally non-exempt worker on rare occasions because of the existence of a real emergency will not, because of the performance of such emergency work, lose the exemption. Bona fide executives include among their responsibilities the safety of the men under their supervision, the preservation and protection of the machinery or other property of the department or subdivision in their charge from damage due to unforeseen circumstances, and the prevention of widespread break-down in production, sales or service operations. Consequently, when conditions beyond control arise which threaten the safety of the employees, or a cessation of operations, or serious damage to the employer's property, any manual or other normally non-exempt work performed in an effort to prevent such results is considered exempt work and is not included in the percentage limitation on non-exempt work. . . .

It is obvious that a mine superintendent who pitches in after an explosion and digs out the men who are trapped in the mine is still a bona fide executive during that week. On the other hand, the manager of a cleaning establishment who personally performs the cleaning operations on expensive garments because he fears damage to their fabrics if he allows his subordinates to handle them is not performing "emergency" work of the kind which can be considered exempt.[38]

Questionable Case

The rules and regulations for exemption of certain kinds of white collar or management employees are set forth in a document of some one hundred closely printed pages. This document includes but a fraction of the rulings and interpretations on these matters that have come from the administrator and from the courts, so these rulings obviously do not cover every situation that may arise. A court may, for example, issue a decision on a matter regarding which the administrator has taken no position. And many, if not most, of the administrator's rulings or opinions have not been challenged in the courts.

The administrator and the courts have ruled not only on how employees may qualify for exemption but how they may retain it while doing work normally classified as nonexempt. For example, what is the exempt or nonexempt status of foremen who engage in production work during a strike? If they are operating machines

---

[38]*Ibid.*, §541.109 (1975).

full-time and getting out orders, they are performing tasks normally done by nonexempt employees. If the foremen are so engaged for a workweek of forty hours or less, the question is academic. But suppose they do production work on an overtime basis, perhaps working 10 hours a day, six days a week. Do they lose their exempt status during the weeks or months when they are substituting for their own nonexempt employees? Are they accordingly entitled to overtime pay at time and one-half?

There have already been court decisions on these or related issues. In 1947 a Kentucky appellate court held that watchman duties performed by a section foreman (who was otherwise exempt) during a strike constituted exempt work for him regardless of how many hours he worked a week on this normally nonexempt task. On this point, the court declared:

> While it is true that ordinarily a watchman's job is nonexempt work, yet when a strike is in progress and a foreman undertakes a watchman's duties he is performing such duties in an executive capacity. In such circumstances it is only an executive employee who is not a member of the union on strike who can be depended upon to perform such duties. Indeed it is not unusual for higher executives than a section foreman to perform manual work in time of a strike but such are [sic] performed in their capacity of executives and they are not acting as laborers.[39]

Because the question was not before it, the Kentucky court did not rule on what would have been the status of administrative or professional employees had they been assigned watchman's work during a strike.

This case was directly cited as the precedent for a 1951 ruling by a federal appellate court that an exempt foreman did not lose that status by performing manual work during strike periods. Indeed the precedent was the only reason given by the second court in so ruling.[40]

Exempt Administrative Employees

The administrator's determination as to what employees are exempt, and when, based on their administrative duties, is as follows:

> The term "employee employed in a bona fide . . . administrative capacity" shall mean any employee
> (a) Whose primary duty consists of:

---

[39]Mafizola v. Hardy-Burlingham Co., 7 WH Cases 716 (1947).
[40]McReynolds v. Pocahontas Corp., 10 WH Cases 485 (1951).

(1) the performance of office or non-manual work directly related to management policies or general business operations of his employer or his employer's customers, . . . and

(b) who customarily and regularly exercises discretion and independent judgment;

(c) (1) who regularly and directly assists a proprietor or an employee employed in a bona fide executive or administrative capacity (as such terms are defined in the regulations of this sub-part) or

(2) who performs under only general supervision of work along specialized or technical lines requiring special training, experience or knowledge, or

(3) who executes under only general supervision special assignments and tasks; and

(d) who does not devote more than 20 percent, or in the case of a retail or service establishment, who does not devote as much as 40 per cent of his hours worked in the workweek to activities which are not directly and closely related to the performance of the work described in paragraphs (a) through (c) of this section; and

(e) (1) who is compensated for his services on a salary or fee basis at a rate of not less than $155 per week.[41]

Here, too, there is the same kind of special or high salary test as is applicable to exempt executives. Thus, an employee may be exempt by being classified as administrative if he is paid at least $250 per week *and if* his "primary duty consists of the performance of work described in paragraph (a) of this section, which includes work requiring the exercise of discretion and independent judgment."

Types of Administrative Employees

The administrator has provided in his regulations what amount to guidelines for determining the exempt or nonexempt status of administrative employees. The following are directly quoted or excerpted from his interpretations:

(1) Executive and administrative assistants. The first type is the assistant to a proprietor or to an executive or administrative employee. In modern industrial practice there has been a steady and increasing use of persons who assist an executive in the performance of his duties without themselves having executive authority. Typical titles of persons in this group are executive assistant to the president, confidential assistant, executive secretary, assistant to the general manager, and administrative assistant, and, in retail or service establishments, assistant manager and assistant buyer. Generally speaking such assistants are found in large establishments where the official assisted has duties of such scope and which require so much attention

---

[41]29 C.F.R. §541.2 (1975).

that the work of personal scrutiny, correspondence, and interviews must be delegated.

(2) Staff employees. (i) Employees included in the second alternative in the definition are those who can be described as staff rather than line employees, or as functional rather than department heads. They include among others employees who act as advisory specialists to the management. Typical examples of such advisory specialists are tax experts, insurance experts, sales research experts, wage rate analysts, investment consultants, foreign exchange consultants, and statisticians.

(ii) Also included are persons who are in charge of a so-called functional department, which frequently may be a one-man department. Typical examples of such employees are credit managers, purchasing agents, buyers, safety directors, personnel directors, and labor relations directors.

(3) Those who perform special assignments. (i) The third group consists of persons who perform special assignments. Among them are to be found a number of persons whose work is performed away from the employer's place of business. Typical titles of such persons are traveling auditors, lease buyers, field representatives of utility companies, location managers of motion picture companies, and district gaugers for oil companies. It should be particularly noted that this is a field which is rife with honorific titles that do not adequately portray the nature of the employee's duties. The field representative of a utility company, for example, may be a "glorified serviceman."

(ii) This classification also includes employees whose special assignments are performed entirely or partly inside their employer's place of business. Examples are special organization planners, customers' brokers in stock exchange firms, so-called account executives in advertising firms and contract or promotion men of various types.[42]

The foregoing illustrations describe by job title occupations of administrative employees that may be exempt if other requisite tests are met. But an employee is not necessarily an exempt accountant because his employer gives him the title of bookkeeper.

One rule-of-thumb test for determining the exempt or nonexempt status of an employee is to examine the work he does to decide if there can be more than one proper answer to the questions with which he copes. If the bookkeeper properly posts all the figures in the proper places, he is obviously not exercising independent discretion and must be held to be nonexempt. If there could be several different and presumably logical answers to an accounting problem, then the employee using independent judgment in reaching these answers could well be held exempt if he meets the other tests for exemption.

---

[42]*Ibid.*, §541.201 (1975).

As to job titles, the regulations make it explicit that titles in and of themselves provide little assistance in determining the status of employees engaged in administrative duties. "Titles can be had cheaply and are of no determinative value," says the administrator. He continues,

> Thus while there are supervisors of production control (whose decisions affect the welfare of large numbers of employees) who qualify for exemption . . . it is not hard to call a rate setter (whose functions are limited to timing certain operations and jotting down times on a standardized form) a "methods engineer" or "production control supervisor."[43]

Professional Employees

The administrator's definition of exempt professional employees is cited as follows:

> The term "employee employed in a bona fide . . . professional capacity" . . . shall mean an employee:
> (a) whose primary duty consists of the performance of:
>
> (1) work requiring knowledge of an advanced type in a field of science or learning customarily acquired by a prolonged course of specialized intellectual instruction and study, as distinguished from a general academic education and from an apprenticeship, and from training in the performance of routine mental, manual or physical processes. . .
>
> (2) work that is original and creative in character in a recognized field of artistic endeavor (as opposed to work that can be produced by a person endowed with general manual or intellectual ability and training), and the result of which depends primarily on the invention, imagination, or talent of the employee . . . or
>
> (b) whose work requires the consistent exercise of discretion or judgment in its performance; and
>
> (c) whose work is predominantly intellectual and varied in character (as opposed to routine mental, manual, mechanical, or physical work) and is of such character that the output produced or the result accomplished cannot be standardized in relation to a given period of time; and
>
> (d) who does not devote more than 20 per cent of his hours worked in the workweek to activities which are not an essential part of and necessarily incident to the work prescribed in paragraphs (a) through (c) of this section; and
>
> (e) who is compensated for his services on a salary or fee basis at a rate of not less than $170 per week . . . exclusive of board, lodging, or other facilities.[44]

---

[43]*Ibid.*
[44]*Ibid.*, §541.3 (1975).

There is also the special high salary provision for exemption of professionals that can be met by paying an otherwise qualified employee not less than $250 per week, if his work requires "the consistent exercise of discretion and judgment," or requires "invention, imagination, or talent in a recognized field of artistic endeavor."

The official regulations contain many explicit explanations of the tests for professional exemption. For instance:

> Generally speaking, the professions which meet the requirement for a prolonged course of specialized instruction include law, medicine, nursing, accountancy, actuarial computation, engineering, architecture, teaching, various types of physical, clinical and biological sciences, including pharmacy and registered or certified medical technology and so forth. The typical symbol of the professional training and the best prima facie evidence of its possession is, of course, the appropriate academic degree, and in these professions an advanced academic degree is a standard (if not universal) prerequisite.[45]

Similarly:

> accountants who are not certified public accountants may . . . be exempt as professional employees if they actually perform work which requires the consistent exercise of discretion and judgment and otherwise meet the tests prescribed in the definition of "professional employees."[46]

But:

> Accounting clerks, junior accountants, and other accountants, on the other hand, normally perform a great deal of routine work that is not an essential part of and not necessarily incident to any professional work that they may do. Where these facts are found such accountants are not exempt.[47]

For some inexplicable reason, employees who are licensed to practice law or medicine and are actually engaged in such practice are considered exempt regardless of their salary rate. These may be virtually meaningless exemptions since in today's labor market any practicing lawyer or physician who would be willing to work for any company at a salary rate of less than $170 per week would probably not be worth hiring. On the same semiserious note, it should be observed that personnel administrators are not regarded as professional employees *per se*. They may be so classified if they have learned their calling through graduate study and have an advanced degree in business administration.

---

[45]*Ibid.*, §541.302 (1975).
[46]*Ibid.*
[47]*Ibid.*

Outside Salesmen

For the purpose of defining the criteria for exemption, an outside salesman is declared by the regulations to mean any employee

(a) who is employed for the purpose of and is customarily and regularly engaged away from his employer's place or places of business in

(1) making sales within the meaning of section 3 (k) of the act [This section is officially interpreted to mean, generally speaking, to include the transfer of title to tangible property, and in certain cases, of tangible and valuable evidences of intangible property. Thus sales of automobiles, coffee, shoes, stocks, bonds, and insurance are construed as sales within the meaning of section 3 (k).], or

(2) obtaining orders or contracts for services or for the use of facilities for which a consideration will be paid by the client or customer; and

(b) whose hours of work of a nature other than that described in paragraph (a) (1) or (a) (2) of this section do not exceed 20 per cent of the hours worked in the workweek by non-exempt employees of the employer: Provided, that work performed incidental to and in conjunction with the employee's own outside sales or solicitations, including incidental deliveries and collections shall not be regarded as non-exempt work.[48]

Hundreds of explanatory comments and special rulings have been issued to clarify the exempt or nonexempt status of employees engaged in sales activities. For example, as already indicated, an "outside salesman" is construed as being an employee who is "customarily and regularly engaged 'away from his employer's place or places of business.' " Obviously, an outside salesman is the reverse of an inside salesman, and since there are no provisions to exempt inside salesmen, regardless of their functions, salary levels, etc., they must be considered nonexempt. An "Explanatory Statement" originally issued by the administrator in 1963 included this sage comment:

It would obviously lie beyond the scope of the Administrator's authority that "outside salesman" should be construed to include inside salesmen. Inside sales and other inside work (except such as is directly in conjunction with and incidental to outside sales and solicitation . . .) is nonexempt.[49]

How does one differentiate between outside and inside salesmen? Since the administrator has considered himself constrained from defining a type of position held nonexempt by nonreference in

---

[48]*Ibid.*, §541.500 (1975).
[49]*Ibid.*, §541.502 (1975).

the law, it is essential to regard closely the administrator's interpretations of what an outside salesman has to do to be designated as exempt.

"Characteristically," the administrator says,

> the outside salesman is one who makes his sales at his customer's place of business. This is the reverse of sales made by mail or telephone (except where the telephone is used merely as an adjunct to personal calls). Thus any fixed site, whether home or office, used by a salesman as a headquarters or for telephonic solicitation of sales must be construed as one of his employer's places of business, even though the employer is not in any formal sense the owner or tenant of the property. It should not be inferred from the foregoing that an outside salesman loses his exemption by displaying his samples in hotel sample rooms as he travels from city to city; these sample rooms should not be considered as his employer's place of business.[50]

Considerable latitude is given outside salesmen in determining what constitutes work that is "incidental to and in conjunction with the employee's own outside sales or solicitations." Such work "would include, among other things, the writing of his sales reports, the revision of his own catalogue, the planning of his itinerary and attendance at sales conferences."

Driver Salesmen

The exempt or nonexempt status of driver salesmen often presents borderline issues. Thus the administrator's explanatory statements include a caution to the effect that when drivers who deliver products to customers also perform some selling functions

> all the facts bearing on the content of the job as a whole must be scrutinized to determine whether such an employee is really employed for the purpose of making sales rather than for the service and delivery functions which he performs. . . . The employee may qualify as an employee employed in the capacity of outside salesman if, and only if, the facts clearly indicate that he is employed for the purpose of making sales and that he is customarily and regularly engaged in such activity within the meaning of the act.[51]

Court Cases on White Collar Exemptions

As already explained, the administrator's determinations of exempt status can be upset by the courts only if found arbitrary or capricious. Nevertheless, the courts have decided thousands of cases relating to the exemptibility of white collar employees. Not all of these challenged the propriety of the administrator's inter-

---

[50]*Ibid.*
[51]*Ibid.*, §541.505 (1975).

pretations. Many originated to resolve management, labor union, or individual doubts on how to apply the administrator's rulings in particular situations. The court cases present a kaleidoscopic picture: an employee may file suit, usually after he has been discharged, claiming substantial overtime pay due him. His employers may hold that the employee's functions have been those of an exempt executive. And the court may hold that the employee was exempt — not as an executive but as an administrative employee.

The court decisions on exempt questions virtually defy orderly classification. Some have resulted in modifications of the administrator's rulings on exempt white collar employees. Others, the administrator has concluded, were not good law, and he has therefore stuck to his guns. A random sample of court cases — both pro and con — on matters of white collar exemptions is presented below in order to re-emphasize the point that the law is what the administrator and the courts say it is from day to day and the law may be applied differently in different jurisdictions, unless some appellate court or the U. S. Supreme Court reconciles the differences and makes the ultimate decision. The statement in each case is taken from Wage and Hour Cases, published by The Bureau of National Affairs, Inc.

> Duties of buyers in purchasing department of ordnance plant of a cost-plus-fixed-fee contractor with Federal Government required "the exercise of discretion and independent judgment" within meaning of Administrator's regulations defining administrative employees exempt from Act, where buyers determined the selection and rotation of available bidders although buyers did not determine the kind of articles which should be purchased and the quality and the terms. — Austin v. Federal Cartridge Corp. (DC Minn, 1949) 6 WH Cases 188.

> Factory superintendent held an "administrative" employee exempt from Act under Section 13(a) (1), even though the time he spent on nonexempt activities exceeded 20 percent of the workweek of nonexempt employees, in view of absence of any 20 percent limitation in Administrator's definition of an administrative employee and the fact that superintendent's supervisory activities substantially predominated and his nonexempt activities were not wholly without relation to his primary responsibilities. — Sparks v. Pederson (DC Conn, 1949) 9 WH Cases 156.

> Work performed by section foreman in mine as watchman during strike constitutes exempt work for purpose of determining whether he exceeded nonexempt work allowance in Administrator's definition of exempt "executive" employee. When a strike is in progress, only executives who are not members of union can be depended upon to perform manual work, and at such time such work is performed in employee's capacity as an executive rather than as a

laborer. —*Mafizola* v. *Hardy-Burlingham Co.* (Ky CtApp, 1947) 7 WH Cases 716.

Master held justified in finding that the work of time-study men of electric company was "along technical lines requiring special training and experience" and that it involved "discretion and independent judgment" within meaning of Administrator's regulation defining an administrative employee who is exempt from Act. —*Hopkins* v. *General Electric Co.* (DC Mass, 1950) 9 WH Cases 391; see also 9 WH Cases 609.

Employee who is the sole full-time employee at employer's livestock sales yard, who exercises general supervision over part-time employees while weekly sales are in progress, and who is the only employee present at the yard during the remainder of the week, is not an executive or administrative employee exempt from FLSA under Section 13(a) (1). —*Mitchell* v. *Carter dba Home Base Auction Co.* (DC ND, 1958) 13 WH Cases 861.

Finding of trial court that assistants to personnel manager, assistants in purchasing department and certain employees in administrative department of construction company were not exempt administrative or executive employees under Act since they did not act independently of higher executive or administrative authority should not be disturbed on appeal where it is clear that none of such employees was regarded as exercising any important measure of discretion or independent judgment in performance of his duties. —*Lassiter* v. *Guy F. Atkinson Co.* (CA 9, 1947) 6 WH Cases 944; vacated and remanded (CA 9, 1947) 7 WH Cases 174; see also 7 WH Cases 816.

Safety inspectors and employee who was an administrative assistant to the manager of materials division of shipyard held exempt from Act. —*Baker* v. *California Shipbldg. Co.* (DC SCalif, 1947) 6 WH Cases 1004.

Analytical cost accountants, beef selector, the head of a branch office, the head of reclamation and accounts receivable department, the assistant head timekeeper, the assistant auditor of disbursements, a carload shipment coordinator, and time-study men employed by meat packing company are, in view of their type of work and duties actually performed by them, "administrative" employees exempt from Act. — *Walling* v. *Armour & Co.* (DC Kan. 1947) 6 WH Cases 886.

Employees of motor transportation company who calculate and audit shipping rates held not "administrative" employees exempt from Act under Section 13(a) (1). —*McComb* v. *New York & New Brunswick Auto Express Co., Inc.* (DC NJ, 1950) 9 WH Cases 379.

Bookkeeper is not an executive or administrative employee exempt from FLSA, even though bookkeeper was appointed custodian of pledged accounts under employer's contract with company that loaned employer money on such accounts. Bookkeeper's primary duties were routine bookkeeping and clerical work; the time spent on work as custodian was not segregated; the bookkeeper became custodian at behest of employer and his work in that capacity was for immediate and direct benefit of employer, the bookkeeper was not supervised by any person connected with lending company; and employer made full reimbursement to lending company of $100 monthly paid by lending company for bookkeeper's services as custodian. — *Mitchell* v. *Pan American Window Corp.* (DC SFla, 1960) 14 WH Cases 625.

Employee engaged by oil company as tabulating machine operator and later as head personnel clerk held not exempt administrative employee under Act since, although salary of $225 a month exceeded [then] salary requirement of Administrator's administrative employee definition, employee's work did not meet any of three remaining requirements of such definition, work being 90 percent manual in character and not requiring exercise of discretion and independent judgment. — *Donovan* v. *Shell Co., Inc.* (DC Md. 1947) 7 WH Cases 1036.

Chemists in No. 2 classification in ordnance plant held not exempt from Act as executive employees where, among other things, they spent more than 20 percent of workweek performing substantially same routine tasks as those performed by laboratory technicians. — *Anderson* v. *Federal Cartridge Corp.* (DC Minn, 1947) 7 WH Cases 58; see also 7 WH Cases 1,268.

Operating engineers in power plant of knitting company are not "executives" exempt from Act under Section 13(a)(1), their primary duty not having been supervision of other employees. — *McComb* v. *Utica Knitting Co.* (CA 2, 1947) 7 WH Cases 452; affirming in part and reversing in part 6 WH Cases 63; rehearing denied 7 WH Cases 452, 504.

"Process engineers" whose chief function was to determine most economical method of manufacture consistent with quality and quantity required and to specify sequence of production operations were "administrative employees" exempt from Act within meaning of Administrator's regulations. Facts that some of process engineers (1) worked in specialized fields so that there was certain amount of repetition and routine in their work or (2) spent a great deal of their time on production floor did not defeat employees' exempt status. — *Wells* v. *Radio Corp. of America* (DC SNY, 1948) 8 WH Cases 59; see also 7 WH Cases 892.

"Cost estimators" in electronics plant who worked under general supervision and with help of clerks in assembling, correlating and interpreting all data necessary to estimate costs were "administrative employees" exempt from Act within meaning of Administrator's regulations. — *Wells* v. *Radio Corp. of America (DC SNY, 1948)* 8 WH Cases 59; see also 7 WH Cases 892.

Field inspectors of casualty insurance company, who inspect steam boilers and other types of machinery to determine in the first instance on new risks and insurability and to determine periodically thereafter whether the objects are maintained in safe operating condition, are not administrative employees exempt from Act. — *Mitchell* v. *Hartford Steam Boiler Inspection and Insurance Co.* (DC Conn, 1955) 12 WH Cases 498; affirmed (CA 2, 1956) 12 WH Cases 930.

Equal Pay for Equal Work

The Equal Pay Act, passed by Congress in 1963, added a new and highly important chapter to the Wage-Hour Act. In fact, the 1963 law specifically amended the earlier statute and is now an integral part of it. The declared purpose of the new law was stated as being to correct "the existence in industries engaged in commerce or in the production of goods for commerce of wage differentials based on sex."

The essential provisions of the equal pay amendment are now found in Section 6 (d) of the Wage-Hour Act. They are:

> (1) No employer having employees subject to any provisions of this section shall discriminate, within any establishment in which such employees are employed, between employees on the basis of sex by paying wages to employees in such establishments at a rate less than the rate at which he pays wages to employees of the opposite sex in such establishment for equal work on jobs the performance of which requires equal skill, effort, and responsibility, and which are performed under similar working conditions, except where such payment is made pursuant to (i) a seniority system; (ii) a merit system; (iii) a system which measures earnings by quantity or quality of production; *or* (iv) a differential based on any other factor other than sex: Provided that an employer who is paying a wage differential in violation of this subsection shall not, in order to comply with the provisions of this subsection, reduce the wage rate of any employee.

> (2) No labor organization, or its agents representing employees of an employer having employees subject to any provisions of this section shall cause or attempt to cause such an employer to discriminate against an employee in violation of paragraph (1) of this subsection.[52]

Coverage of the equal pay provisions is identical to the coverage of the other main provisions of the Wage-Hour Act. That is, persons and establishments excluded by law or by administrative definition from minimum-wage or maximum-hour requirements are not subject to the equal pay controls.

This part of the law is administered, as are all other parts, by the Wage-Hour administrator. By what amounted to a mandate

---

[52]Equal Pay Act of 1963, as quoted in THE NEW WAGE AND HOUR LAW, Appendix, p. 7.

from the U. S. Supreme Court in the case of *Skidmore* v. *Swift,* [53] the administrator has issued official interpretations "to provide a practical guide to employers and employees as to how the office representing the public interest in its enforcement will apply it" and "constitute a body of experience and informed judgment to which courts and litigants may properly resort for guidance." The Court also declared: "Good administration of the Act and good judicial administration alike require that the standards of public enforcement and those for determining private rights shall be at variance only where justified by very good reasons."[54]

As a result, the administrator has come forth with a plethora of rulings which, in the minds of lawyers and laymen alike, are subject to a variety of constructions and interpretations. The administrator's task in interpreting the equal pay code is complicated by its interrelationship with the anti-sex-discrimination provisions of the Civil Rights Act (discussed in Chapter 3) and by the existence in more than 30 states of laws that bear directly or tangentially on the same issues. Compliance by employers is extremely complex for the same reason. The administrator has partially clarified the question of interrelationships by his declaration that where other federal or state legislation and equal pay provisions of the Wage-Hour Act both apply, the provisions of the statute providing superior advantage or protection shall govern. This is substantially the posture required by Section 18 (a) of the Wage-Hour Act.

Illustrative Rulings

Management's problems in assuring full compliance with equal pay requirements can possibly be best illustrated by reference to typical passages from the 1967 official interpretations. The following constitute direct quotations, excerpts, and summaries of explanatory comments from these interpretations, as published in the *Code of Federal Regulations.*

> It should be kept in mind, in determining an employer's obligations under the equal pay provisions, that "employer" and "establishment" as used in these and other provisions of the Act are not synonymous terms. An employer may have more than one establishment in which he employs employees within the meaning of the Act. In such cases, the legislative history makes clear that there shall be no comparison between wages paid to employees in different establishments.[55]

[53]Skidmore v. Swift & Co., 4 WH Cases 866 (1944).
[54]*Ibid.*
[55]29 C.F.R. §800.103 (1975).

The equal pay provisions apply to employees as follows:

> . . . in each distinct physical place of business where employees of an employer work (including but not limited to the employer's own establishments), the obligation of the employer to comply with the equal pay requirements must be determined separately with reference to those of his employees who are employed in that particular establishment. Accordingly, where there are a number of distinct physical places of business in which an employer's employees are employed, compliance with the equal pay provisions must be tested within each establishment by comparing the jobs in which employees are employed in that establishment and the wages paid for work on such jobs when performed by employees of opposite sexes.[56]

The administrator has defined wage "rate" as follows:

> The term wage "rate" . . . is considered to encompass all rates of wages whether calculated on a time, piece, job, incentive or other basis. The term includes the rate at which overtime compensation or other special remuneration is paid as well as the rate at which straight time compensation for ordinary work is paid.[57]

What wages are considered in determining compliance?

> . . . wages to be considered in determining compliance with the equal pay provisions include, in addition to such payments as hourly and daily wages, sums paid as weekly, monthly, or annual salaries; wages measured by pieces produced or tasks performed; commissions, bonuses or other payments measured by production, efficiency, attendance, or other job-related factors, or agreed to be paid under the employment contract; standby and on-call pay; and extra payments made for hazardous, disagreeable, or inconvenient working conditions . . . Study is still being given to some categories of payments made in connection with employment subject to the Act, to determine whether and to what extent such payments are remuneration for employment that must be counted as part of wages for equal pay purposes. These categories of payments include sums paid in recognition of services performed during a given period pursuant to a bona fide profit-sharing plan or trust meeting the requirements of Part 549 of this chapter or pursuant to a bona fide thrift or savings plan meeting the requirements of Part 547 of this chapter, and contributions irrevocably made by an employer to a trustee or third person pursuant to a bona fide plan for providing old-age, retirement, life, accident or health insurance or similar benefits for employees.[58]

Although study still continues on questions arising over employer contributions to pensions and other employee benefit plans in their relation to equal pay between the sexes, the administrator

---

[56]*Ibid.*, §800.104 (1975).
[57]*Ibid.*, §800.111 (1975).
[58]*Ibid.*, §800.113 (1975).

has already promulgated rulings on what appears to be the same issue. Thus, in phraseology not notable for its lucidity or reconcilability with the passage just cited, the administrator stated:

> If employer contributions to a plan providing insurance or similar benefits to employees are equal for both men and women, no wage differential prohibited by the equal pay provisions will result from such payments, even though the benefits which accrue to the employees in question are greater for one sex than for the other. The mere fact that an employer may make unequal contributions for employees in such a situation will not, however, be considered to indicate that the employer's payments are in violation of section 6 (d), if the resulting benefits are equal for such employees.[59]

The administrator has obviously shown knowledge of the realities of employer-employee relations, if not an unconscious sense of humor, in his treatment of maternity benefits. Despite the fact that almost all fringe benefits are construed as constituting wages for equal pay purposes, the administrator has solemnly decided that payments related to maternity do not constitute remuneration for employment.[60]

The administrator has made the following ruling on designation of jobs as "male" and "female":

> Wage classification systems which designate certain jobs as "male jobs" and other jobs as "female jobs" frequently specify markedly lower rates for the "female jobs". Because such a practice frequently indicates a pay practice of discrimination based on sex, where such systems exist a serious question would be raised as to whether prohibited wage differentials are involved . . . It should be further noted that wage classification systems which designate certain jobs as "male jobs" and other jobs as "female jobs" may contravene Title VI of the Civil Rights Act of 1964 except in those certain instances where sex is a bona fide occupational qualification reasonably necessary to the normal operation of that particular business or enterprise. . . .
>
> The statute is intended to eliminate sex as a basis for wage differentials between employees performing equal work on jobs within the establishment, and if the rates paid for the same jobs are lower when occupants of the jobs are of one sex than they are when the jobs are filled by employees of the opposite sex, such discrimination within the establishment is equally in violation of the statutory prohibition whether or not employees of both sexes are employed in such jobs at the same time. Accordingly, where an employee of one sex is hired or assigned to a particular job to replace an employee of the opposite sex, comparison of the newly assigned employee's wage rate with that of the replaced former employee is required for the

[59]*Ibid.*, §800.116(d) (1975).
[60]*Ibid.*, §800.110 (1975).

purpose of section 6 (d) (1), whether or not the job is performed concurrently by employees of both sexes. For example, if a particular job which in the past has been performed by a male employee becomes vacant and is then filled by a female employee, it would be contrary to the equal pay requirement to pay the female a lower wage than was paid for the same job when performed by the male employee, even though employees of both sexes may not be performing the job at the same time. Payment of the lower wage rate in such circumstances is a prohibited wage differential.[61]

What about wage differentials if certain employees are given special assignments?

The fact that an employee may be required to perform an additional task outside his regular working hours would not justify payment of a higher wage rate to that employee for all hours worked. However, employees who are assigned a different and unrelated task to be performed outside the regular work-day may under some circumstances be paid at a different rate of pay for the time spent in performing such additional duty provided such rate is commensurate with the task performed. For example, suppose a male employee is regularly employed in the same job with female employees in the same establishment in work which requires equal skill, effort, and responsibility, and is performed under similar working conditions, except that the male employee must carry money to a bank after the establishment closes at night. Such an employee may be paid at a different rate for the time spent in performing this unrelated task if the rate is appropriate to the task performed and the payment is bona fide and not simply used as a device to escape the equal pay requirements of the Act.[62]

How does the personnel administrator test the equality of jobs?

What constitutes equal skill, equal effort, or equal responsibility cannot be precisely defined. In interpreting these key terms of the statute, the broad remedial purpose of the statute must be taken into consideration. The terms are considered to constitute three separate tests, each of which must be met in order for the equal pay standard to apply. In applying the tests it should be kept in mind that "equal" does not mean "identical". Insubstantial or minor differences in the degree or amount of skill, or effort, or responsibility required for the performance of jobs will not render the equal pay standard inapplicable.[63]

The administrator has explained other laws that do not apply equally to employment of both sexes:

In making a determination as to the application of the equal pay provisions of . . . the Act, legal restrictions in state or other laws upon

---

[61]*Ibid.*, §800.114 (1975).
[62]*Ibid.*, §800.116 (1975).
[63]*Ibid.*, §800.122 (1975).

the employment of individuals of a specified sex, with respect to such matters as hours of work, weight-lifting, rest periods, or other conditions of such employment, will not be deemed to make otherwise equal work unequal or be considered per se as justification for an otherwise prohibited differential in wage rates. For example, under the Act, the fact that a state law limits the weights which women are permitted to lift would not justify a wage differential in favor of all men regardless of job content. The Act would not prohibit a wage differential paid to male employees whose weight-lifting activities required by the job invoke so significant a degree of extra effort as to warrant a finding that their jobs and those of female employees doing similar work do not involve equal work within the meaning of the Act. However, the fact that there is an upper limit set by state law on the weights that may be lifted by women would not justify a wage differential to male employees who are not regularly required to lift substantially greater weights or expend the extra effort necessary to make the jobs unequal. The requirement of equal pay in such situations depends on whether the employees involved are actually performing "equal work" as defined in the Act, rather than on legal restrictions which may vary from state to state.[64]

The administrator's interpretative bulletin from which the foregoing extracts have been drawn includes judgments or opinions on some sixty separate issues that may well confront management in a sizeable company. Personnel administrators charged with determining hiring and wage and salary policies would be well advised to heed the entire publication. They also should be aware that the administrator's opinions are subject to review and modification by the courts and are also subject to change on short notice. This, no doubt, is why the administrator declared that his interpretations

provide statements of general principles applicable to the subjects discussed and illustrations of the application of these principles to situations that frequently arise. They do not and cannot refer specifically to every problem which may be met in the consideration of the provisions discussed. . . . Questions on matters not fully covered by this part may be addressed to the Administrator of the Wage and Hour and Public Contract Divisions, United States Department of Labor, Washington, D.C. 20210, or to any Regional Office of the Divisions.[65]

The administrator's interpretations on equal pay manifestly have been drafted with meticulous care and an attempt at legal precision. Nevertheless, differences of opinion as to their meaning and effect have developed, most of them in recent years. One result has been that from the year of enactment, 1963, until the end of the

[64]*Ibid.*, §800.163 (1975).
[65]*Ibid.*, §800.4 (1975).

fiscal year 1974 more than five hundred court suits were instituted. In the fiscal year 1974, nearly 33,000 employees were found to have been underpaid in a total amount exceeding twenty million dollars. Doubtless most of this money became due in back pay as a result of honest disagreements as to the proper application of the law. Without any question it was a difference of interpretation only that led the American Telephone and Telegraph Company to pay out in 1974 almost seven million dollars to about 7,000 employees.

In all fairness the official position of AT&T as to the reasons for this settlement merits direct reference. The company's annual report for 1974 contained this explanation:

> In 1974 we instituted a new promotion pay policy for first and second level Bell management employees. Under an agreement reached with the Federal government, approximately 25,000 employees at these levels, — about 60 per cent of them women and minority employees—received salary increases. The agreement also provided for back pay awards of about $7 million to some 7,000 management people.[66]

An issue involving equal pay that had tremendous significance was resolved by the United States Supreme Court in 1974. It arose from cases involving plants of the Corning Glass Company in New York and Pennsylvania. These were the first equal-pay-law cases to be reviewed by the Supreme Court. The Court's decision was summarized in a Labor Department report to Congress as follows:

> Concluding that Corning's pay practices ". . . though phrased in terms of a neutral factor other than sex, nevertheless operated to perpetuate the effects of the company's prior illegal practice of paying women less than men for equal work," this historic decision confirmed a number of principles which had previously been stated by the lower courts. Specifically, the Court held that shift differences (with the men working at night and the women during the day) did not make the "working conditions" of the men and women "dissimilar" and thus would not justify a larger rate for men (over and above their plantwide night differential); the Court also approved the "substantially equal" (as opposed to "substantially identical") test adopted by the several courts of appeals. In addition, the Court held that Corning did not cure the equal pay violation by integrating the formerly all male and all female jobs, and paying the higher rate to the women who transferred to the male or night job and the lower rate to the men who transferred to or were hired for the female or day job. The only way a violation can be remedied under the Act, said the Court, is for the lower rates to be raised to the

---

[66]American Telephone and Telegiaph Company, 1974 ANNUAL REPORT (New York, 1975), pp. 27, 28. For more on the government settlement that involved the Civil Rights Act as well as the Equal Pay Act, see below, Chapter 3, p. 74.

higher. Nor could the company equalize the wages, and then grant an additional increase to the men and women on the night job (as a "red circle" rate, since this rate perpetuated the effects of past discrimination). As a result of this decision, Corning paid out approximately $1 million in back wages.[67]

THE WALSH-HEALEY ACT

Frequently characterized by its critics as an unnecessary anachronism, the Walsh-Healey Act, officially known as the Public Contracts Act, no longer exerts a potent influence on the wage scales of thousands of enterprises holding government contracts. It does have an important influence on practices in relation to overtime pay. For, unlike the Wage-Hour Act which specifies that time and one-half must be paid for hours worked beyond 40 in any workweek, the Walsh-Healey Act requires covered employers to pay time and one-half for all time worked beyond eight hours in any workday.

When this statute was enacted in 1936, its sponsors considered it a stop-gap remedy for the loss of federal controls and wages in private industry resulting from the decision of the U.S. Supreme Court the previous year denying the constitutionality of the National Industrial Recovery Act (NIRA) of 1933. The NIRA had provided for promulgation by federal edict of enforceable standards for minimum wages and maximum hours—industry by industry—after such standards had been proposed by representatives of the dominant companies in each industry. After this law was stricken down by the Supreme Court, Congress sought to establish an unchallengeable substitute. It found a partially effective substitute by enacting a law applicable only to enterprises entering into contracts to supply the Federal Government with goods or services. There was no serious question as to the constitutional right of Congress to pass a law that would enable the Federal Government to exercise its "sovereign powers" to determine the working conditions required of its own suppliers. Acceptance of government-imposed standards for wages and hours is considered voluntary in that no enterprise is forced to bid on government contracts.

The main thrust of the Walsh-Healey Act, apart from requiring daily overtime beyond eight hours (and requiring conformance to special safety and health regulations), has been in the

---

[67]U.S. Department of Labor, Employment Standards Administration, MINIMUM WAGE AND MAXIMUM HOURS STANDARDS UNDER THE FAIR LABOR STANDARDS ACT: AN ECONOMIC EFFECTS STUDY SUBMITTED TO CONGRESS 1975, p. 25.

setting of differing minimum-wage rates for specific industries. As anticipated, these minimum rates markedly influenced the general wage levels of industries that supply substantial quantities of products to all branches and departments of the government. In addition, the establishment of minimum rates at levels considerably higher than many government contractors had previously paid generated corresponding increases for semi-skilled and skilled workmen, thus preserving pre-existing relative wage differentials.

Coverage

The Walsh-Healey Act applies to all enterprises which, by contracts with the government, furnish materials, supplies, and articles (including, especially, naval vessels) whenever any separate contract involves amounts of $10,000 or more. As the coverage extends directly to the contracting supplier, the application of the law's minimum-wage and maximum-hour standards is confined only to employees actually engaged in performing work connected with such contracts. But as a practical matter, it is quite often difficult to segregate and properly identify the particular employees handling government work. Therefore, unless this can be accurately done with accurate records kept to substantiate the separation of work between government contracts and private orders, most employees in establishments having Walsh-Healey contracts are considered to be covered by its wage and hour rules. There are two specific categories of exceptions. One is the broad group of executive, administrative, and professional employees who are exempt from the Wage-Hour Act. The other is a more sweeping exemption of all employees who perform only office or custodial work.

Minimum Wages

The criteria used by the Secretary of Labor in fixing minimum wages for particular industries involved in Walsh-Healey contracts have long been controversial. Much of this controversy is now academic since the Secretary's latest ruling overrode past decisions and set the current rate for all establishments in all industries covered by the law as not less than the basic minimum ($2.30 per hour) fixed by the Wage-Hour Act in 1974.

To put previous and current decisions of the Secretary of Labor in proper perspective, however, prior determinations, and the apparent reasoning behind them, must be considered briefly. The need for the Walsh-Healey Act and the methods of interpreting it are still bitterly disputed among influential management and labor groups.

By its own terms, the Walsh-Healey Act as passed by Congress in 1936 authorized the Secretary of Labor to determine what were the

> prevailing minimum wages for persons employed on similar work or in the particular or similar industries or groups of industries currently operating in the locality in which the materials, supplies, articles, or equipment are to be furnished [i.e., the type of contract covered by the law itself].

The language of the statute was obviously ambiguous. And successive Secretaries of Labor have used their own unfettered discretion in fixing minimum wage rates applicable to industries and enterprises affected by the law at such levels as they thought would best carry out the objectives of the law as they saw them. The net result was a potpourri of almost inexplicable rate determinations, each of which, nonetheless, could be substantiated as meeting at least one of the ambiguous standards set in the statute.

A bench mark or two must be used to explain the Secretary's early decisions, unrealistic as they may seem to those too young to recall prevailing wage levels in the era before World War II. The Wage-Hour Act of 1938 fixed the immediate minimum wage at 25 cents an hour. From October 1939 to October 1945, the rate was set at 30 cents an hour. Thereafter, the statutory rate was fixed at 40 cents per hour. When the legal minimum was 30 cents per hour, the Secretary of Labor set the Walsh-Healey minimum for the seamless hosiery industry at 35 cents per hour, for the photographic supply industry at 40 cents per hour, and for the die casting industry at 50 cents per hour. In a critical analysis of the Secretary's wage determinations published in 1945, it was pointed out that "On occasion the prevailing minimum wage seems to have been based almost entirely on the average wage paid in the industry" and that "in at least eleven instances the minimum union rate was used as the basis of decision."[68]

Minimum Wage Rates Fixed Prior to 1974

The statutory minimum wage under the Wage-Hour Act was fixed at $1.60 per hour as of February 1, 1968. While all minimum rates under the Walsh-Healey Act were increased to at least that

---

[68]Harold W. Metz, LABOR POLICY OF THE FEDERAL GOVERNMENT (Washington: The Brookings Institution, 1945), p. 202.

amount as of the same date, rates higher than that minimum were left unchanged. The Secretary had promulgated minimums exceeding $1.60 per hour for particular industries. Some of the highest were $1.80 for miscellaneous chemicals and the battery industry and $1.90 for conveyors and conveying equipment.

The relatively meager list of industries covered by minimum rates higher than those imposed by the all-inclusive Wage-Hour Act would make it appear that the mountainous labors of the U.S. Labor Department in administering the Walsh-Healey Act have produced only a molehill. But the Department's activities, limited as they have been, have not been accepted without resistance from some companies and some trade associations representing their industries. For example, the National Machine Tool Builders Association challenged the statistical techniques used in a Labor Department survey on the grounds that the types of employees covered by the Act were not adequately defined and that many employers failed to report the wages paid to all covered employees. Partially as a result of this criticism, the Secretary's original minimum-wage determination was modified, making blueprint machine operators' and draftsmen's rates lower than those of other employees of the industry. The two rates were $1.65 and $1.80 respectively. Two years after these rates were promulgated, the U. S. Court of Appeals of the District of Columbia held that the Secretary's action could not be sustained because one rate resulted from a Labor Department survey of the industry and the other from a study by the trade association for the industry. The two wage orders that were set aside were not replaced by any new determination by the Secretary.[69]

With the increase in the generally applicable minimum wage to $2.30 under the 1974 amendments to the Wage-Hour Act, the impact on Walsh-Healey special minimum rates for particular industries became almost negligible. All the rates higher than the premium Wage-Hour minimum of $1.60 were automatically increased to $2.30. The only minimum rates previously imposed under the Walsh-Healey Act that exceeded this figure were those promulgated in 1968 for various segments of the bituminous coal industry. The still applicable minimum rates for government contractors in this industry range on a geographical area basis from $2.45 in the Appalachian region to $2.846 in Montana.[70]

---

[69]Industrial Union Department v. Barber Colman Co., 17 WH Cases 1 (1965).
[70]41 C.F.R. §50-202.16 (1975).

The Davis-Bacon Act

First enacted in 1931 and subsequently much broadened in scope and benefits through various amendments, the Davis-Bacon Act is designed to authorize the United States Secretary of Labor to determine and enforce minimum wages for employees of private contractors engaged in public works construction for the Federal Government. It also applies to public construction projects financed in part with federal funds. This law is much more than a minimum-wage statute for the construction industry, since it requires the Secretary to ascertain the *prevailing* wage rates and fringe benefits for laborers and mechanics working on public construction projects subject thereto. The term "prevailing wage" as defined in the law means whatever wage rate the Secretary of Labor finds to be the current rate paid to the majority of the construction employees in each craft in the area where the contract is let. The term "area" is defined narrowly as the city, town, or other governmental subdivision within a state. "Prevailing" fringe benefits are deemed to include pensions, life and other types of insurance, vacation and holiday pay, as well as medical and hospital care.

Most of the wage and fringe benefit determinations of the Secretary are effective for no more than 90 days. They have been so numerous that when printed they fill some 10 thick volumes. They may embody the going union rate for a given occupation or area or both. They may exceed the craft rate fixed in a local union contract for a particular occupation. In practice the going rate has often been determined to be the top scale payable under a current union contract in a given city or in a nearby city if no union contract is in effect in the immediate area where the covered construction work is to be performed. Typical rates so determined may range in localities where craft unions are well established from $5.00 an hour to $10.00 an hour or more.

Suspension of Davis-Bacon Act in 1971

The impact of this law on current wage and benefit levels in the building trades had been so great that its temporary suspension by President Nixon in February 1971 caused a tremendous furor in organized labor circles. The President acted after attempts to induce the construction unions to accept voluntary restraints on wage improvements in contracts up for renegotiation in 1971 had proved fruitless. The suspension was ordered under the President's general authority to cope with national emergencies. Only once previously had there been such a suspension. This was in 1941 when President Roosevelt issued a suspension order that he terminated within a month.

The 1971 suspension also lasted barely one month. It was instituted as part of the Administration's domestic economic program to combat inflation. In 1970, first-year increases in wage rates under new union contracts in the construction industry had averaged about 18 percent. The trend early in 1971 was still higher.

Opposition to the suspension of the Davis-Bacon Act in February 1971 was not confined to organized labor. Management spokesmen for the construction industry criticized it as inadequate and futile. William E. Dunn, executive director of the Associated General Contractors' Association, quickly issued a statement declaring that it "would not help in any way to stop the demand for huge wage increases with 1,368 construction agreements set to expire each year."

Federal authorities insisted that the suspension automatically negated the somewhat similar terms of "little Davis-Bacon Acts" in effect in a number of states where there was a substantial volume of federally aided construction projects. Some state officials disagreed, holding their own laws still were operative.

STATE WAGE AND HOUR LEGISLATION

State laws affecting wages and hours have in the past been about as important as the federal statutes, particularly for enterprises fully subject to the federal Wage-Hour and Walsh-Healey acts. The Wage-Hour Act is specific on this point:

> No provision of this Act or any order thereunder shall excuse noncompliance with any Federal or State law or municipal ordinance establishing a minimum wage higher than the minimum wage established under this Act or a maximum workweek lower than the maximum workweek established under this Act, and no provision relating to the employment of child labor shall justify noncompliance with any Federal or State law or municipal ordinance establishing a higher standard than the standard established under this Act. No provision of this Act shall justify any employer in reducing a wage which is in excess of the applicable minimum wage under this Act, or justify any employer in increasing hours of employment maintained by him which are shorter than the maximum hours applicable under this Act.[71]

---

[71]Section 18(a), Fair Labor Standards Act, as amended.

Minimum Wages

As of 1977 only one state had in effect generally applicable minimum-wage rates higher than the new federal minimum of $2.65 per hour. This state was Alaska, where the present rate is $2.80.

Some states have not yet attempted to revise their minimum wage statutes for women to avoid conflict with Title VII of the Civil Rights Act of 1964 (see Chapter 3 for detailed review of this statute) which prohibits sex discrimination in employment. As the U. S. Department of Labor has continually pointed out in its manifold publications, "where there is dual coverage by both State and Federal law, the higher standard prevails."[72]

At the risk of subjectivity, this query comes to mind: If a minimum wage is set by statute or administrative decree at a level that inhibits employment of persons the prospective employer considers incapable of actually earning the requisite amount, what valid legal or social purpose is served by a law that results in lessening the employment of persons who might have been hired at a rate considered advantageous both by themselves and their employers?

For example, the U. S. Labor Department constantly stresses that current minimum-wage rates are inadequate to enable an employee to support a typical family of four. Slight consideration seems to be given to the fact that probably most employees or prospective employees that would be hired for jobs subject to state minimum wages are youths just entering the labor market or are members of families with more than one wage-earner. Never in either federal or state minimum-wage legislation has there been any provision that the head of a family must receive a higher rate than a single employee without dependents. Instead, the U. S. Supreme Court has upheld the theory that a state can decide what is the absolute minimum at which any person can be employed. But, if not considered productively employable at that rate by a prospective employer, what, if any, alternative may be used to support such an individual and his dependents? This question was still being debated by Congress as late as 1977.

---

[72]U.S. Department of Labor, EMPLOYMENT STANDARDS ADMINISTRATION, STATE MINIMUM WAGE LAWS: A CHARTBOOK ON BASIC PROVISIONS (Labor Law Series No. 4-A, May 1974).

Maximum Hours

Originally most state laws regulating hours of work were confined to limiting the working time of women and children. Now, following the pattern of the Wage-Hour Act, such statutes usually specify maximum hours that can be worked by employees in any category without payment of overtime. There are, however, stringent restrictions in some states against using certain employees (primarily women) beyond a fixed limit of working time in a given workday or workweek. As for male employees, the state laws usually restrict total weekly hours unless overtime is paid at legally prescribed rates. Supreme Court sanction for such legislation was given as early as 1917 when the Court upheld an Oregon law that prohibited factory employees from working more than 13 hours in any one day and prescribed overtime pay at time and a half their regular rates for the last three of the 13 hours.

The Supreme Court decided in the case of *Bunting* v. *Oregon*[73] that the State of Oregon had the constitutional authority to enact a law utilizing its "police power" to protect the health of citizens by restricting their hours of work. A portent of future legislative permissiveness was indicated by the Supreme Court in 1917 when it said:

> It is enough for our decision if the legislation under review was passed in the exercise of an admitted power of government; and that it is not as complete as it might be, not as rigid in its prohibitions as it might be, gives, perhaps, evasion too much play, is lighter in its penalties than it might be, is no impeachment of its legality. This may be a blemish, giving opportunity for criticism and difference in characterization, but the constitutional validity of legislation cannot be determined by the degree of exactness of its provisions or remedies. New policies are usually tentative in their beginnings, advance in firmness as they advance in acceptance. They do not at a particular moment of time spring full-perfect in extent or means from the legislative brain. Time may be necessary to fashion them to precedent customs and conditions, and as they justify themselves or otherwise they pass from militancy to triumph or from question to repeal.
>
> But passing from general considerations and coming back to our immediate concern, which is the validity of the particular exertion of power in the Oregon law, our judgment of it is that it does not transcend constitutional limits.[74]

By 1976 most state legislatures had long since gone far beyond the limited purposes of state regulation of hours sanctioned by the Court in the landmark Oregon decision of 1917. But present maximum-hour laws for men generally follow the pattern of the

---

[73]Bunting v. Oregon, 243 U.S. 426 (1917).
[74]*Ibid.*

federal Wage-Hour Act and permit unlimited overtime beyond 40 hours in a workweek, so long as overtime pay at time and one-half is given for such work. There are some exceptions relating to hazardous occupations such as mining, working with compressed air, etc., the details of which have to be searched out, usually in fine print of state regulations. For all practical purposes, personnel administrators of typical commercial and industrial firms may safely assume that by complete compliance with the maximum-hour provisions of the Wage-Hour Act, and the more stringent provisions of the Walsh-Healey Act (if their companies are subject to it), they will also be complying with state laws regulating hours of work for men.

Special Working-Time Restrictions for Women

As already indicated, state laws providing special limitations on hours and terms of employment have been all but completely nullified by the terms of the 1964 Civil Rights Act prohibiting discrimination in employment on account of sex. But before and after the enactment of the sweeping civil rights legislation, most states had so-called protective legislation for working women with accompanying regulations much too encyclopedic to warrant detailed review here. To cite only a few extreme illustrations: Arizona had prohibited females under 21 from engaging in night messenger service, and Ohio had prohibited employment of women as taxicab drivers on the night shift. In both North Dakota and Washington State, women could not work nights as elevator operators. As for lunch periods, about one-half of the states required by statute from 20 minutes to one hour off. And at least 20 states had either prohibited employment of women after specified evening hours or provided working-time standards different from those applicable to day workers.

Continuing Special Working Rights of Women

Sharply reduced as they have been by the Civil Rights Act, there are still sufficient special statutory protective regulations for women to justify the publication in 1975 of a manual prepared by the Women's Bureau, Employment Standards Administration, United States Department of Labor. Captioned *A Working Woman's Guide to Her Job Rights* (Leaflet 55), this manual sets forth in substantial detail the special rights and privileges of female industrial employees that have not been abridged by any federal or state legislation.

Among the permutations and combinations of the state laws

and regulations, the Department of Labor has observed certain patterns relating both to coverages and exceptions. These are summarized here.

Overtime and Permitted Variations. Maximum-hour laws in most states permit some variation from the maximum daily and/or weekly hours beyond the maximum for specified reasons or under certain conditions. In general, such variations fall into two categories: (1) adjustments in daily hours without an extension of the workweek, and (2) overtime work beyond the established weekly maximum.

*   *   *   *   *

In most of the 24 states that permit adjustments in daily hours, hours in excess of the weekly maximum are prohibited. The conditions under which adjustments in daily hours are permitted vary from state to state. Among the more usual ones are: to make one short workday in the week; to make up lost time due to the breakdown of machinery, accident, or illness; to meet needs arising from emergencies, seasonal processing, or unusual events; or to alleviate hardships which might otherwise result from strict application of the law. The majority [of the 36 states that permit overtime on a weekly basis] allow women to be employed longer hours in seasonal industries to prevent spoilage of perishable products; in mercantile or retail trade prior to or following holiday seasons; or during emergencies which may endanger life, health, or the welfare of the community.[75]

Day of Rest. The Labor Department finds that almost half of the states and the District of Columbia establish a six-day week for women in some or all industries. Of the 28 states and Puerto Rico with no laws limiting the workweek to 6 days, 8 states have laws applicable to both men and women which prohibit employment on Sunday with specified exceptions. Eight other states have Sunday "blue laws" which prohibit the performance of work by an individual on that day.[76]

Meal and Rest Periods. Regarding state requirements, the Department notes that in 25 jurisdictions meal periods varying from one third to one hour must be allowed to employed women in some or all industries, mainly in manufacturing, mechanical, and mercantile establishments. . . . Twelve states and Puerto Rico require rest periods as distinct from meal periods for women workers in one or more industries. Most of the provisions provide for a 10-minute rest period within each half-day of work.[77]

GENERAL OBSERVATIONS

It cannot be said too often that no one statute stands on its own feet. Hence, personnel administrators responsible for form-

---

[75]U.S. Department of Labor, GROWTH OF LABOR LAW IN THE UNITED STATES (Washington: U.S. Government Printing Office, 1967), pp. 125-126.

[76]*Ibid.*, p. 126.

[77]*Ibid.*

ing policies or assuring compliance with all applicable laws have to review the entire complex of federal and state statutes. Federal and state wage and hour legislation must be considered in relation to other laws dealing with equal pay and civil rights. Moreover, where enterprises are unionized or potentially subject to unionization, the Taft-Hartley Act's requirements as to bargaining about terms and conditions of employment must always be taken into account. At the same time, it must be emphasized that management's problems in compliance with all applicable laws are not insuperable. Diligent research into the laws and regulations under which enterprises in any state must operate should enable every management to comply fully.

CHAPTER 3

Equal Employment Opportunity
and Civil Rights

The maze of federal civil rights legislation, often complicated by state laws and municipal ordinances, presents constant problems for employers striving to comply in good faith. The emphasis of such legislation has progressively changed in recent years from antidiscrimination measures relating to hire and tenure of employment to much more stringent regulations requiring "affirmative action" to assure adequate employment and promotional opportunities for minority groups.

Most antidiscrimination laws provide no clear-cut definitions of the minority groups for whom protection is intended. When New York State enacted the first comprehensive law of this sort in 1945, the initial thrust of its administrators was to protect Jewish people who were being discriminated against by certain establishments in the greater New York area. When the Federal Government first attempted to proscribe racial discrimination through regulations promulgated in World War II and applicable to defense contractors, the main objective was to assure employment opportunities for Negroes. At the same time other minority groups, such as Nisei on the West Coast and refugees from Axis nations or countries overcome by the Nazis, were overlooked. Indeed, there was affirmative discrimination against nationals of or emigrants from some countries at both federal and state levels.

As an historical footnote, the U.S. Department of Labor has pointed out in a review of civil rights developments that

> During the period up to 1921 when successive waves of immigrants were arriving on American shores, new arrivals, particularly those from certain countries, had difficulty finding suitable work. These and other groups, including American Indians, Catholics, Jews, Mexican-Americans, Orientals, and especially Negroes, have been the victims of discrimination, varying in intensity from one part of the country to another, and from one period of history to another.[1]

---

[1]U.S. Department of Labor, GROWTH OF LABOR LAW IN THE UNITED STATES (Washington: U.S. Government Printing Office, 1967), p. 221.

Today's picture is much different, although not entirely clear. Discrimination against *any* and *every* minority racial group is now prohibited by statute. However, present guidelines are not all-inclusive. For instance, the concepts of what one agency of the Federal Government considers to constitute protected minorities are to be found in the regulations requiring companies with government contracts to file annual reports disclosing certain racial components of their work forces. The companies that have to file the *Employer Information Report* (EEO-1) must provide specific statistics as to the number of employees classified as Negro, Oriental, American Indian, and Spanish-surnamed Americans. (All persons of Mexican, Puerto Rican, and Spanish origin are included in the last category.) In Alaska, only, Eskimos and Aleuts are considered to be American Indians.

Paradoxically, perhaps, the agencies administering the federal statutes concentrate on protecting the job rights of the largest rather than the smallest minorities. This is apparently because the former often file their complaints and pursue their possible remedies on an organized or collective basis. A WASH, for instance, could presumably have little chance of winning a court suit charging a prospective employer with religious discrimination.[2]

NONDISCRIMINATION UNDER CIVIL RIGHTS ACT OF 1964

The keystone of the structure of antidiscrimination legislation is to be found in Title VII of the federal Civil Rights Act of 1964. Section 703 (a) of that statute provides:

It shall be an unlawful employment practice for an employer —

(1) to fail or refuse to hire or to discharge any individual, or otherwise to discriminate against any individual with respect to his compensation, terms, conditions, or privileges of employment, because of such individual's race, color, religion, sex, or national origin; or

(2) to limit, segregate, or classify his employees in any way which would deprive or tend to deprive any individual of employment opportunities or otherwise adversely affect his status as an employee, because of such individual's race, color, religion, sex, or national origin.

An ancillary provision, Section 704 (b), also specifies that it shall be an unlawful practice for an employer "to print or cause to

---

[2]For the benefit of any reader who might not be up on the latest popular acronym, the term "WASH" may require definition. The term applies to a person who might have been or who some day might become a "WASP." It refers to a "White Anglo-Saxon Heathen."

be printed or published any notice or advertisement relating to employment by such employer . . . indicating any preference, limitation, specification, or discrimination, based on race, color, religion, sex or national origin."

Coverage of Employers

As defined in the statue, the term "employer" is given the broadest scope of any federal law regulating the personnel practices of employers in private enterprise. For the purpose of this law an employer was declared to be any person, or corporation, or virtually any type of enterprise engaged in business activities affecting commerce that has 25 or more employees for each working day in each of 20 or more calendar weeks in the current or preceding calendar year. There are none of the exclusions from coverage as *employees* which are found, for example, in the Wage-Hour Act or the Taft-Hartley Act. A 1972 amendment extended coverage to establishments with 15 or more employees. Everyone from president to sweeper is now counted as an employee.

Exceptions From Unlawful Employment Practices

As in most legislation, the Civil Rights Act provides certain exceptions to its sweeping prohibitions against conduct by employers that would otherwise be deemed unlawful by its express provisions. Section 703 (e) of Title VII provides that

> Notwithstanding any other provision of this title, (1) it shall not be an unlawful employment practice for an employer to hire and employ employees . . . in those certain instances where religion, sex, or national origin is a bona fide occupational qualification reasonably necessary to the normal operation of that particular business or enterprise.

The same exception applies to the requirements of Section 704 (b) relating to employment advertisements. It must be particularly noted, however, that the exception conspicuously omits the terms "race" and "color." Hence, the general prohibition against discrimination or preference with respect to these categories remains absolute.

Obvious illustrations of permissible exceptions for religion, sex, or national origin would be the employment of Orthodox Jews to perform prescribed ritualistic functions in Kosher meat-processing establishments, female and male restroom attendants, and culinary staffs in, for example, Chinese restaurants operated by a distinct national group and catering to a special trade.

Another general exception cannot be summarized without the risk of oversimplification or inadvertent misinterpretation. Hence it is quoted in full. This is Section 703 (h), which states:

> Notwithstanding any other provision of this title, it shall not be an unlawful employment practice for an employer to apply different standards of compensation, or different terms, conditions, or privileges of employment pursuant to a bona fide seniority or merit system, or a system which measures earnings by quantity or quality of production or to employees who work in different locations, provided that such differences are not the result of an intention to discriminate because of race, color, religion, sex, or national origin; nor shall it be an unlawful employment practice for an employer to give and to act upon the results of any professionally developed ability test provided that such test, its administration or action upon the results is not designed, intended, or used to discriminate because of race, color, religion, sex, or national origin. It shall not be an unlawful employment practice under this title for any employer to differentiate upon the basis of sex in determining the amount of the wages or compensation paid to employees of such employer if such differentiation is authorized by the provisions of Section 6(d) of the Fair Labor Standards Act of 1938 as amended (29 USC 206(d)).

Never can a reference in one statute to a provision in another statute be ignored with prudence. Such a reference always has some significance in construing and attempting to comply with both laws. Hence, the above citation of Section 6(d) of the Fair Labor Standards Act, as amended, has to be taken into account by personnel administrators responsible for assuring their companies' compliance with civil rights legislation in its totality. Even though that section — which amounts to an entirely separate set of provisions to prevent sex discrimination in employment — has been reviewed in Chapter II, a portion of the text of the Equal Pay Act of 1963, which added a new amendatory section to the Fair Labor Standards Act, warrants quotation again. It reads:

> Section 6(d) (1). No employer having employees subject to any provisions of this section shall discriminate, within any establishment in which such employees are employed between employees on the basis of sex by paying wages to employees at a rate less than the rate at which he pays wages to employees of the opposite sex in such establishments for equal work on jobs the performance of which requires equal skill, effort, and responsibility, and which are performed under similar working conditions, except where such payment is made pursuant to (i) a seniority system; (ii) a merit system; (iii) a system which measures earnings by quantity or quality of production; or (iv) a differential based on any other factor other than sex: *Provided, that an employer who is paying a wage rate differential in violation of this subsection shall not, in order to*

comply with the provisions of this subsection, reduce the wage rate of any employee. [Italics supplied]

But this is not by any means the only other legislation that impinges on management's responsibilities in the selection and retention of employees. The federal law known as the Age Discrimination in Employment Act of 1967 always must also be considered in personnel decisions. (This statute is discussed briefly later in this chapter.) Then, too, there are the special and more exacting federal regulations applicable to defense contractors, as well as the numerous state laws and city ordinances, some of which may override the federal statutes when their requirements set more rigid standards for nondiscrimination in employment for any reason.

COMPLIANCE PROBLEMS FOR EMPLOYERS

At this juncture it would be impracticable, if not impossible, to set out specific guidelines supported by landmark decisions of administrative agencies and the courts that would enable employers to be certain of full compliance with all the civil rights regulations that may be applicable to their own personnel practices. Ten plus years of experience under the Civil Rights Act and auxiliary legislation is too short a period for employers in the private sector to obtain a full grasp of their rights and obligations under these laws. After all, more than 40 years has elapsed since the passage of the Wagner Act. Yet the National Labor Relations Board and the courts still wrestle with new issues arising out of the sets of government controls established by that law, as amended and supplemented by the Taft-Hartley Act of 1947 and the Landrum-Griffin Act of 1959. No wonder then that many issues involved in civil rights statutes are not now fully predictable or well-settled.

Facts are perishable. So declared Alvin Toffler in his mind-jolting book, *Future Shock.* Writing in 1970, Toffler observed:

> Today the whole world is a fast breaking story. It is inevitable therefore, in a book written over the course of several years that some of its facts will have been superseded between the time of research and writing and the time of publication. Professors identified with University A move, in the interim, to University B. Politicians identified with Position X shift, in the meantime, to Position Y.[3]

---

[3]Alvin Toffler, FUTURE SHOCK (New York: Random House, 1970), p. 6.

Toffler could well have been reflecting on the changing tides of political thought on civil rights in Washington administrative circles, and possibly in the federal appellate courts as well, when he wrote as he did. The present authors are acutely aware, as we repeatedly stress throughout this book, that federal courts with different jurisdictions sometimes come out with diametrically opposite decisions on virtually identical questions of statutory interpretation.

As already indicated briefly in Chapter 1 and as further discussed in Chapter 8, the United States Supreme Court came out with a tremendously important decision in 1974 which, according to knowledgeable attorneys specializing in labor relations problems, leaves some loose ends that no doubt will give rise to further litigation. More specifically, the Court held that resort by an employee to the final and binding grievance arbitration procedure of an applicable union agreement could not preclude the aggrieved from seeking redress through court action after an arbitrator had decided against him. In the Court's view, by passage of the Civil Rights Act, Congress intended to guarantee to individuals all the rights and remedies they might pursue with that statute, regardless of prior rejection of a claim of illegal discrimination in another forum.[4]

The case specifically referred to is Alexander v. Gardner-Denver. The full impact of this true landmark decision has yet to be fully felt. (cf. Chapter 1 and Chapter 8.) The decision is so significant as to warrant reproduction below of the summary that the High Court calls a Syllabus:

> Following discharge by his employer, respondent company, petitioner, a black, filed a grievance under the collective-bargaining agreement between respondent and petitioner's union, which contained a broad arbitration clause, petitioner ultimately claiming that his discharge resulted from racial discrimination. Upon rejection by the company of petitioner's claims, an arbitration hearing was held, prior to which petitioner filed with the Colorado Civil Rights Commission a racial discrimination complaint which was referred to the Equal Employment Opportunity Commission (EEOC). The arbitrator ruled that petitioner's discharge was for cause. Following the EEOC's subsequent determination that there was not reasonable ground to believe that a violation of Title VII of the Civil Rights Act of 1964 had occurred, petitioner brought this action in District Court, alleging that his discharge resulted from a racially discriminatory employment practice in violation of the Act.

---

[4]Alexander v. Gardner-Denver, 346 F.Supp. 1012 (1971), *aff'd per curiam*, 466 F.2d 1209 (10th Cir. 1972), *rev'd*, 415 U.S. 36, 7 FEP 81 (1974).

The District Court granted respondent's motion for summary judgment, holding that petitioner was bound by the prior arbitral decision and had no right to sue under Title VII. The Court of Appeals affirmed. *Held:* An employee's statutory right to trial *de novo* under Title VII of the Civil Rights Act of 1964 is not foreclosed by prior submission of his claim to final arbitration under the nondiscrimination clause of a collective-bargaining agreement.

(a) Title VII was designed to supplement, rather than supplant, existing laws and institutions relating to employment discrimination, as may be inferred from the legislative history of Title VII, which manifests a congressional intent to allow an individual to pursue rights under Title VII and other applicable state and federal statutes.

(b) The doctrine of election of remedies is inapplicable in the present context, which involves statutory rights distinctly separate from the employee's contractual rights, regardless of the fact that violation of both rights may have resulted from the same factual occurrence.

(c) By merely resorting to the arbitral forum petitioner did not waive his cause of action under Title VII; the rights conferred thereby cannot be prospectively waived and form no part of the collective-bargaining process.

(d) The arbitrator's authority is confined to resolution of questions of contractual rights, regardless of whether they resemble or duplicate Title VII rights.

(e) In instituting a Title VII action, the employee is not seeking review of the arbitrator's decision and thus getting (as the District Court put it) "two strings to his bow when the employer has only one," but is asserting a right independent of the arbitration process that the statute gives to employees, the only possible victims of discriminatory employment practices.

(f) Permitting an employee to resort to the judicial forum after arbitration procedures have been followed does not undermine the employer's incentive to arbitrate, as most employers will regard the benefits from a no-strike pledge in the arbitration agreement as outweighing any costs resulting from giving employees an arbitral antidiscrimination remedy in addition to their Title VII judicial remedy.

(g) A policy of deferral by federal courts to arbitral decisions (as opposed to adoption of a preclusion rule), would not comport with the congressional objective that federal courts should exercise the final responsibility for enforcement of Title VII and would lead to: the arbitrator's emphasis on the law of the shop rather than the law of the land; factfinding and other procedures less complete than those followed in a judicial forum; and perhaps employees bypassing arbitration in favor of litigation.

(h) In considering an employee's claim, the federal court may admit the arbitral decision as evidence and accord it such weight as may be appropriate under the facts and circumstances of each case.[5]

---

[5] 415 U.S. 36 (1974).

Later herein specific illustrative cases will be cited to indicate the types of employer conduct considered by federal administrative agencies and the judiciary to constitute illegal infringement on employees' civil rights. To keep the whole problem in proper perspective, however, at least a cursory review of the scope of the statutory controls on employer conduct in this general field seems indicated.

Multiplicity of Federal Administration and Enforcement Agencies

Much of the uncertainty about management's obligation enters the equal employment opportunity provisions of the Civil Rights Act and related laws because there are several different federal agencies with their fingers in the administration and enforcement pie. First, if not foremost, is the Equal Employment Opportunity Commission (EEOC) itself. We say "if not foremost" advisedly. Of course, the law administered by the EEOC has by far the greatest coverage, reaching nearly all employees of consequence throughout the United States. But the U.S. Department of Labor has the most fingers in the pie.

The Labor Department's Wage-Hour Division administers the Equal Pay Act (as related in Chapter 2). And in addition, various branches of the Department are responsible for administering the Age Discrimination in Employment Act of 1967, the Rehabilitation Act of 1973, and the Viet Nam War Veterans Readjustment Act of 1974.

It is not a specific federal law, however, but a set of federal regulations stemming from an executive order of the President that provides the Labor Department with its most potent weapon in enforcing employers' employment opportunity obligations in the tens of thousands of enterprises doing business with the Federal Government. This is Executive Order 11246. It was originally promulgated by the late President Johnson in 1965. Sharp teeth were added by subsequent amendments in 1967 (E.O. 11375) and by administrative interpretations in 1971. What makes E.O. 11246 so potent is its mandate to require government contractors and subcontractors to adopt explicit affirmative action programs which, among other things, have to minimize the effects of previous discriminatory practices toward minority groups and women.[6]

---

[6]Major affirmative action programs are described in the CODE OF FEDERAL REGULATIONS (C.F.R.), Title 41, *Public Contracts and Property Management,* Chapter 60.

The Office of Federal Contract Compliance is the agency of the Department of Labor that administers and interprets the executive order. But that agency has compounded confusion among large companies holding government contracts by delegating partial authority for interpretation and administration to 16 other federal bureaus and independent agencies. One such is the strife torn Federal Communications Commission (FCC).

As recently as July 1975 the FCC announced that "our Equal Employment Opportunity Program guidelines as embodied in Section VI of our various broadcast application forms fail to adequately describe and exemplify the measures which broadcasters should undertake to promote the full realization of equal opportunity in employment for all qualified individuals." So it proposed to "clarify" its policy to assure that "equal employment programs must be active and affirmative, not merely passive or *nondiscriminatory.*" One of the proposed clarifications would require an applicant for a broadcast license to "examine the effectiveness of its recruitment sources to determine whether sufficient qualified minority and female applicants are being referred. *Those sources which are not providing the needed service should be eliminated and new sources developed.*" [Emphasis supplied][7]

Extreme example? Perhaps. Yet it could be that bureaucratic doublespeak of this sort over recent years has given rise to acute dissatisfaction with administration of equal employment programs.

The dissatisfaction is not confined to management folks, bewildered and perplexed as they have reason to be. Even John T. Dunlop when still Secretary of Labor expressed his sympathy for employers when his department was criticized for its enforcement performance. Referring to the "plethora" of enforcement agencies, Dunlop made the comment at a congressional hearing in June 1975 that "One might question whether there is not a redundancy of authority, administration and forums creating confusion among both those seeking to comply with the law and those attempting to secure enforcement."[8]

A month later the United States Commission on Civil Rights was even more critical. A New York Times editorial observed that the Commission had "assessed the Federal programs designed to achieve equal opportunities for women and minorities and has found them to be floundering and ineffectual. As a result the Commission has proposed a stiff remedy: the establishment of a single new agency possessing strong enforcement powers to take

---

[7]40 FED. REG. 31,627 (1975).
[8]NEW YORK TIMES, June 20, 1975, p. 38.

over the morass of programs now spread through a plethora of Federal agencies."[9]

The Civil Rights Commission is no Johnny-come-lately branch of the federal bureaucracy. It was created by statute in 1957 (71 Stat 734) and its functions were enlarged in a government manual as follows:

> The Commission investigates complaints alleging that citizens are being deprived of their right to vote by reason of their race, color, religion, sex, or national origin; or in the case of Federal elections, by fraudulent practices. It appraises the laws and policies of the Federal Government with respect to denials of equal protection of laws under the Constitution and collects and studies information concerning legal developments constituting the same. The Commission serves as a national clearinghouse for civil rights information, and in turn submits reports of its activities, findings and recommendations to the President and the Congress.[10]

Some progress toward adoption of uniform guidelines on employee selection procedures was made in 1975. An interdepartmental committee known as the Equal Employment Opportunity Coordinating Council drafted the proposed new rules.

Then, on Nov. 18, 1976, the U.S. Department of Labor, the Civil Service Commission, and the Department of Justice promulgated the Federal Executive Agency Guidelines on Employee Selection Procedures after prolonged debate with the EEOC. A bureaucratic donnybrook promptly ensued. The very next day, the EEOC reissued its own highly controversial set of guidelines in the identical form originally published in 1970.[11]

Uniform Guidelines on Employee Selection Procedures

The original EEOC guidelines had been bitterly criticized by knowledgeable employers and business organizations as being quite unrealistic and virtually impossible to comply with. Under new administrative direction in 1977 the EEOC agreed, however, to participate in the formulation of a new and uniform set of guidelines. The proposed new guidelines were published in the *Federal Register* on Dec. 30, 1977, with the joint endorsements of the EEOC, the Departments of Justice and Labor, and the Civil Service Commission. However, it was not until August 22, 1978, that they were approved by all four agencies. Issuance was delayed pending re-

---

[9]*Ibid.*, July 21, 1975, p. 20.
[10]UNITED STATES GOVERNMENT MANUAL, 1975/1976 (rev. May 1, 1975; Washington: U.S. Government Printing Office).
[11]35 Fed. Reg. 12,333 (1970).

lease of the Supreme Court's long delayed decision in the celebrated Bakke case referred to at some length below. In television interviews on "Issues and Answers" and "Meet the Press" respectively, on July 2, 1978, both HEW Secretary Joseph A. Califano and EEOC Chairman Eleanor Holmes Norton expressed their opinions that the Bakke decision would not necessitate any drastic revision of the guidelines for employers' affirmative action programs.

In giving notice of the proposed new rules, their sponsors explained the rationale for obtaining uniformity. They wrote:

> The undersigned found the existence of different, and possibly conflicting, interpretations of Federal law on this important subject to be intolerable. They strongly believe that the Federal government should speak with one voice on this important subject; and that the Federal government ought to impose upon itself obligations for equal employment opportunity which are at least as high as those it seeks to impose on others. . . .
>
> The draft guidelines are intended to assert a uniform Federal position on this subject, and to protect the rights created by Title VII, Executive Order 11246 and other provisions of Federal law. The guidelines are also intended to represent "professionally acceptable methods"of the psychological profession for demonstrating whether a selection procedure validly predicts or measures performance for a particular job. . . . They are also intended to be consistent with the decisions of the Supreme Court and authoritative decisions of other appellate courts.[12]

And in the statement of purpose of the final guidelines they said:

> These guidelines do not require a user to conduct validity studies of selection procedures where no adverse impact results. However, all users are encouraged to use selection procedures which are valid, especially users operating under merit principles.[13]

SPECIAL OBLIGATIONS OF
GOVERNMENT CONTRACTORS

Ever since 1942 most private corporations providing goods or services to federal agencies have been subject to various executive orders designed to prevent employment discrimination against minority groups. Such orders have usually been promulgated under the general authority of the President to administer and set the rules for the operations of the Executive Branch of the Federal Government. Without doubt the most sweeping order is Executive Order 11246 promulgated by President Johnson in 1965. Under this order the Secretary of Labor was delegated responsibility for achieving equal employment opportunity by contractors and

[12]42 Fed. Reg. 65,542 (1977).
[13]43 Fed. Reg. 38,296 (1978).

subcontractors in their work forces engaged in government contracts regardless of employees' race, color, creed, national origin, or sex. The obligations of government contractors go beyond the requirements of the Civil Rights Act in that the executive order mandates them to take affirmative action to assure nondiscrimination.

The most important provision of the equal-opportunity clause in Executive Order 11246 reads as follows:

> (1) The contractor will not discriminate against any employee or applicant for employment because of race, color, religion, sex, or national origin. The contractor will take affirmative action to ensure that applicants are employed, and that employees are treated during employment without regard to their race, color, religion, sex or national origin. Such action shall include, but not be limited to the following: employment, upgrading, demotion or transfer, recruitment or recruitment advertising; layoff or termination; rates of pay or other forms of compensation; and selection for training; including apprenticeship. The contractor agrees to post in conspicuous places, available to employees and applicants for employment, notices to be provided by the contracting officer setting forth the provisions of this non-discrimination clause.

Meaning of "Affirmative Action"

It is this specific phrase that has given rise to the most contentions and litigation between the office of Federal Contract Compliance (OFCC) of the Department of Labor as the enforcement agency and the government contractors affected thereby.

The Office of Federal Contract Compliance provided in its official regulations issued in 1969 the following capsulized version of what it then considered affirmative action to entail:

> A necessary prerequisite to the development of a satisfactory affirmative action program is the identification and analysis of problem areas inherent in minority employment and an evaluation of opportunities for minority group personnel. The contractor's program shall provide in detail for specific steps to guarantee equal employment opportunity keyed to the problems and needs of members of minority groups, including, when there are deficiencies, the development of specific goals and time tables for the prompt achievement of full and equal employment opportunity. Each contractor shall include in his affirmative action compliance program a table of job classifications. This table should include but need not be limited to job titles, principal duties (and auxiliary duties, if any), rates of pay, and where more than one rate of pay applies (because of lengths of time in the job or other factors), the applicable rates.[14]

---

[14]See 41 C.F.R. §60-1.40.

Compliance Through Conciliation and Consent Decree

Judged solely from the vast sums involved, the agreements entered into by the Bell system companies since 1973 constitute by far the most important of all Civil Rights Act cases settled through voluntary compliance. It is not, however, the magnitude of the payments to minority groups and women but, rather, the Bell system management's long record of fostering equal employment opportunities that warrants much more than cursory attention here. True, AT&T and its affiliates committed themselves to payments of more than $75 million in back pay or future wage and salary adjustments to "aggrieved" groups of employees. This aggregate figure includes the sum of approximately $38 million payable under the initial agreement consummated in 1973. Subsequent unofficial estimates indicated that further increases in Bell system payroll costs attributable to this agreement may run as high as $35 million per year at least until 1978. The EEOC chairman in 1973, William H. Brown, III, declared that he considered "our AT&T settlement to be the most significant legal settlement in civil rights employment history." Brown summarized some of the salient features of this agreement as follows:

> The agreement was signed in January of this year by the EEOC, the Department of Labor and the American Telephone and Telegraph Company and its 24 operating companies. Under this agreement AT&T will make one-time payments totaling approximately $15 million dollars to some 15,000 present employees whom [sic] the government claims have been injured by the companies' employment practices. In addition to the one-time payments, a new promotion pay policy and wage adjustments resulting from the agreement will increase wages for many women, minorities and other employees by an estimated $23 million a year. The plan that AT&T agreed to follow contained three major points:
>
> *First* the companies will develop goals for increasing the utilization of women and minorities in each job classification of all 700 establishments within the Bell system and will set specific hiring and promotion targets.
>
> *Second* the plan included an 'unusual provision' for the establishment of goals for the employment of males in previously all female job categories.
>
> *Third* the companies will take the necessary steps to assure that their transfer and promotion policies are in compliance with the Equal Pay Act, the Civil Rights Act of 1964, and Executive Order 11246.[15]

---

[15]William H. Brown, III, *Voluntarism and EEOC*, THE CONFERENCE BOARD RECORD, Aug. 1973, p. 54.

On the same day that the parties executed the agreement, that is, Jan. 18, 1973, judicial approval in the form of a consent decree was sought and obtained forthwith from the U.S. District Court in Philadelphia.

Needless to say this agreement was not consummated without almost every conceivable kind of accusation, threat, law suit, and propaganda device being aimed at the Bell system by government agencies and a few private organizations which for years had been accusing Bell-system management of flagrant discrimination in employment policies. But the top management had a different story to tell and has related it with considerable support in the business community. Significantly, neither in the agreement itself nor in the consent decree ratifying it were the signatory companies declared guilty of any unlawful employment practices.

At the same forum where Chairman Brown made the remarks, as condensed above, an assistant vice president of AT&T, John W. Kingsbury, also spoke. He said, in part:

> There is no secret that we at AT&T were genuinely hurt back in Dec. 1970 when the Equal Employment Opportunity Commission first filed its charges of discrimination against the Bell Telephone Companies. Like many other businesses, we felt we had done a good job—by any objective standard—of providing employment opportunities for both women and minorities.
>
> According to societal expectations, as we understood them at the time, we had the top management commitment; we had the program needed to help the disadvantaged and our numbers were not out of line with those of other companies. But perhaps because we had done such a good job in telling people, including our own managers, of the progress we had actually made, we were not sufficiently sensitive to the change in expectations. It was not until a year later, when revised Order no. 4 was issued and after we had provided the EEOC's evaluation of our record. With that and the emergence of new guide lines and their interpretation, we immediately recognized new or additional weak spots.
>
> Frankly, I think we reacted with dispatch. We set about developing comprehensive and definitive affirmative action programs and an interdepartmental upgrade and transfer plan to help individuals select their own career path and advance as far in the business as their talents and aspirations warranted.[16]

But quite obviously the governmental *dei ex machinis* thought that the Bell system empire could and should be rebuilt in a day. Anyhow, the EEOC considered two more years to be too long a period for full achievement of the goals toward which the management had ordered all-out efforts. Hence, the Bell system

---

[16]*Ibid.*, p. 55.

management was constrained to enter into a supplementary equal employment agreement which, among other things, required back pay awards to an indeterminate number of employees—mostly women—whose promotions into certain job classifications, named as special EEO targets, may have been delayed. One of the vexatious problems that arose in fulfilling the original commitment for promotion of women to higher rated positions was, as explained in an AT&T news bulletin, that "experience showed a considerable lack of interest in jobs" formerly held almost exclusively by members of the opposite sex, despite company efforts to attract employees to nontraditional jobs.[17]

Personnel administrators concerned with their own companies' problems should dig deeper into the implications of the AT&T consent decree and review elements not expressly included in the three major points referred to above by EEOC Chairman Brown. One especially perplexing segment of the agreement relates to the controversial issue of the continued validity of seniority systems as the determining factor in layoffs from and promotions to any supervisory positions. Answering a hypothetical question about the effect of the 1973 agreement in current union agreements, AT&T management announced with some ambiguity that "The federal government has said that the *need* to make changes in our procedures takes preference. We have notified all unions representing our employees and are discussing the agreement with them." Another passage in AT&T's news bulletin summarizing the terms of the agreement read: "Women and minorities in non-management, non-craft jobs will compete for entry-level craft jobs on the basis of basic qualifications and seniority. Competition for higher paying craft jobs will also be facilitated." Are these just weasel words? To get some insight into their significance, one has to turn to the text of the "Model Affirmative Action Program" embodied by reference in the 1973 settlement and resultant consent decree. Section (B) of this program reads:

> It is the policy of the — — —[operating affiliate] Telephone Company to hire well qualified people to perform the tasks necessary in providing high quality telephone service at reasonable costs. An integral part of this policy is to provide equal employment opportunity for all persons for employment and to recruit and administer hiring, working conditions, benefits and privileges of employment, compensation, training, appointment for advancement including upgrading and promotion, transfers, and *terminations of employment including layoffs and recalls* [emphasis

---

[17] AT&T News Bulletin, May 13, 1975.

supplied] for all employees without discrimination because of race, color, religion, national origin, sex or age.

To many laymen and, manifestly, to the unions representing Bell system employees, the policy declaration just quoted implies the right to deviate markedly from rigid seniority rules, provided the purpose is to avoid discriminatory action toward minorities and women.

No wonder, then, that the unions immediately instituted proceedings to block judicial approval of the revised agreement executed in May 1975. (In August 1976 a federal district court judge signed the order as filed.) Meanwhile, some additional monetary settlements had to be deferred, and individuals claiming unlawful discrimination were free to file claims in court for back pay or other restitution.

Why Ma Bell Was the Leading EEOC Target

The term "Ma Bell" coincidentally is an apt sobriquet. Among the Bell system's force of over 900,000, women make up almost a majority. Abundant documentary evidence can be adduced to support the thesis that sex discrimination rather than racial discrimination in employment practices was the main concern of the EEOC in focusing its attack on the nation's largest employer.[18]

The fiercest onslaught against the Bell system's alleged discrimination against women was conceived in a brainstorm by a young EEOC attorney, David Copus, ex-Harvard Law and a former Peace Corps volunteer. He had read in 1970, so he says, that the Federal Communications Commission (FCC) was considering an AT&T petition for an increase in long distance telephone rates. (That commission had proper jurisdiction to determine whether any utility subject to its regulation was guilty of any form of unlawful employment discrimination.)

Copus' first maneuvers have been verbally described in a lengthy feature article by Harvey D. Shapiro—in 1970 a fellow at the ultraliberal Russell Sage Foundation. Copus caused to be presented to the FCC on behalf of his own agency some 30,000 pages of documents intended to demonstrate that the Bell system had persistently underutilized minorities and had deprived most women of chances to move up into skilled blue collar work or into managerial positions.[19]

---

[18]Jerolyn R. Lyle, AFFIRMATIVE ACTION PROGRAMS FOR WOMEN, Equal Opportunity Employment Commission monograph, 1973.

[19]Harvey D. Shapiro, *Women on the Line, Men at the Switchboard*, NEW YORK TIMES, May 20, 1973, pp. 73, 75-76.

If Copus failed to convince the FCC that the Bell system was deliberately grinding into the faces of helpless women, he did come forth with enough plausible statistics to instill some doubts as to the adequacy of the system's treatment of women in the job force. But when AT&T made its initial settlement for women of $15 million, the National Organization for Women referred to this sum as "chicken feed." NOW's president, Wilma Scott Heide, was quoted by Shapiro as saying, "$4 billion is the amount actually owed female employees of the Bell System."[20]

To be sure, the Federal Communication Commission gave the AT&T management a figurative day in court. It set up a separate docket and proceeded with the so-called discovery process. That exploration continued throughout the entire year 1971. During these proceedings the management filed about 100,000 pages of documents, including expert testimony and elaborate statistical tabulations showing current and prospective distribution of its personnel among both sexes and among minority groups. There followed in 1972 sporadic public hearings over a six-month period. The management did not attempt in any of these proceedings to hide its light under a bushel. On the contrary, it built up for itself an impressive record to demonstrate its signal accomplishments toward achievement of its goal to make equal employment opportunity a viable reality throughout the Bell system.

It's almost inconceivable that any other American corporation, no matter how huge, will ever have to undergo almost a full two years of the kinds of harassment that developed during the FCC's investigation of the Bell system employment policies. But the personnel administrators and legal counsel of almost every company, regardless of size, would find it profitable to take a look at a summary of the AT&T management's presentation to the FCC. Such a summary is to be found in an impressive 100-page document titled "The Bell Companies as Equal Opportunity Employers—a Record of Achievement—a Commitment to Progress." This impressive document was prepared in memorandum form by a special team of attorneys that represented AT&T in the FCC hearings. It dramatically summarizes the Bell system's current policies, accomplishments, and commitments for future progress. No punches are pulled in the report. As its introduction states:

> (1) The Bell companies are fully and firmly committed to the national goal of equal opportunity and have been so committed as that policy has evolved over the years;

---

[20]*Ibid.*, p. 85.

(2) their commitment has produced results—good, substantial results;

(3) these results are being produced by employment practices that are, contrary to the assertions of the EEOC, progressive and lawful and nondiscriminatory;

(4) the Bell companies are nevertheless fully cognizant that much remains to be done, and they are continuing to work at the task. Their employment policies are constantly being reviewed and updated to keep them abreast of changing employment conditions as well as legal decisions and regulations.[21]

Small businessmen, who are the supposed perennial favorites of politicians and bureaucrats, cannot expect to get preferential treatment on issues within the purview of the EEOC. The long arms of the law reach far down, even if they produce only a futile scratch. An actual case: There could be no doubt that a small New Jersey plant had gone overboard in complying with the law. By 1965 a majority of its production workers were black women. There were also blacks in other plant jobs. Then came an EEOC inspector to investigate a complaint of what was tantamount to reverse discrimination. Black men, according to the complaint, were being discriminated against in favor of black women. How? In the maintenance crew of eight men there was not a single black. Why? Just a few weeks before the complaint was filed, the single black maintenance mechanic had been promoted to a foremanship.

The management, fearful of its impeccable record of affirmative action, retained a high-powered lawyer. It took him the better part of a day to convince the inspector to drop action on the complaint. End of incident—an unrecorded case that erudite attorneys would classify only as *de minimus* or *reductio ad absurdum*.

Required Contents for Affirmative Action Programs

Present obligations of enterprises required to maintain affirmative action programs were summarized in the Office of Federal Contract Compliance (OFCC) document designated as "Revised Order No. 4" issued in Dec. 1971. This order stated, in part:

An affirmative action program is a set of specific and result-oriented procedures to which a contractor commits himself to apply every good faith effort. The objective of those procedures plus such effort is equal employment opportunity. Procedures without effort to

---

[21]Memorandum accompanying the Aug. 1, 1972, submission of the Bell Companies before the Federal Communications Commission, Docket No. 19143, Aug. 1, 1972, pp. 1, 2.

make them work are meaningless, and effort, undirected by specific and meaningful procedures, is inadequate. An acceptable affirmative action program must include an analysis of areas within which the contractor is deficient in the utilization of minority groups and women, and further, goals and timetables to which the contractor's good faith efforts must be directed to correct the deficiencies and thus to achieve prompt and full utilization of minorities and women, at all levels and in all segments of his work force where deficiences exist.[22]

Underutilization of Minorities and Women

There is much more to Revised Order No. 4 than the passage just cited. Two other passages are explicitly set out as musts and so necessitate direct quotation:

> 1. In determining whether minorities are being underutilized in any job group, the contractor will consider at least all of the following factors:
>
> (i) The minority population of the labor area surrounding the facility;
> (ii) The size of the minority unemployment force in the labor area surrounding the facility;
> (iii) the percentage of the minority work force as compared with the labor work force in the immediate labor area;
> (iv) The general availability of minorities having requisite skills in the immediate labor area;
> (v) The availability of minorities having requisite skills in an area in which the contractor can reasonably recruit;
> (vi) The availability of promotable and transferable minorities within the contractor's organization;
> (vii) The existence of training institutions capable of training persons in the requisite skills; and
> (viii) The degree of training which the contractor is reasonably able to undertake as a means of making all job classes available to minorities.

There is a second section to this passage in which the only change consists of the substitution of the term "women" for the term "minorities."[23]

---

[22]Office of Federal Contract Compliance, Revised Order No. 4, 36 FED. REG. 23,152 (1971), as amended at 39 FED. REG. 5,630 (1974). See 41 C.F.R. §60-2.11.
[23]41 C.F.R. §60-2.11 (1976).

Management Implementation Responsibilities

One set of directives embodied in OFCC's revised Order No. 4 is of particularly direct concern to personnel administrators. This set declares that:

> An executive of the contractor should be appointed as director or manager of company Equal Opportunity Programs. Depending on the size and geographical alignment of the company this may be his or her sole responsibility. He or she should be given the necessary top management support and staffing to execute the assignment. His or her identity should appear on all internal and external communications on the company's Equal Opportunity Programs.[24]

Following this declaration the order lists some 20 different types of activity for which the company compliance manager should assume responsibility.

RACIAL DISCRIMINATION UNDER TAFT-HARTLEY

An employer's unjustified racial discrimination against employees can constitute an unfair labor practice in violation of the Taft-Hartley Act. So the National Labor Relations Board has ruled, and its findings have been upheld by the U.S. Court of Appeals for the District of Columbia. The Board held that Farmers' Cooperative Compress, a Texas corporation engaged in processing cotton, had illegally refused to bargain with the union representing its production and maintenance employees over alleged discrimination against Negro and Latin American workers. The court decided that the Civil Rights Act does not deprive the National Labor Relations Board of jurisdiction in the area of racial discrimination. Nothing in that statute, the court ruled, indicates that the Board is ousted from jurisdiction in such matters. Rather, its legislative history demonstrates that the Board has concurrent jurisdiction with the Equal Employment Opportunity Commission. The court went further. It stated that if, besides refusing to bargain about the correction of alleged racial discriminatory employment practices, the company was in fact discriminating against a minority group, this in itself would involve illegal infringement on employees' right of self-organization under Taft-Hartley.[25]

---

[24]*Ibid.*, §60-2.22 (1976).
[25]Packinghouse Workers v. NLRB, 70 LRRM 2489 (D.C. Cir. 1969).

AGE DISCRIMINATION

Coverage of employers is limited by the Age Discrimination in Employment Act to those with 20 or more persons in their regular work forces. The law authorizes the Secretary of Labor to issue rules and regulations and to make reasonable exceptions. The Secretary has assigned administration of the Act to the Labor Department's Wage and Hour and Public Contracts Division.

There is one feature of the Act that differs markedly from other laws administered in the U.S. Labor Department and other federal agencies regulating management-employee relations: This Act is explicit in requiring "that before any legal proceeding can be instituted, attempts must be made to eliminate discriminatory practices through informal methods of conference, conciliation and persuasion."[26]

Occupational Exceptions to Age Discrimination in Employment Act

Through interpretative bulletins the administrator of the Act has attempted to define and delineate the occupational functions permissible to persons in the age group from 40 to 65, who may be excluded from the general ban on age discrimination. Examples of a bona fide occupational qualification based on age that can be deemed "reasonably necessary" to the operation of the particular business include: "actors required for youthful or elderly characterization of roles, and persons used to advertise or promote the sale of products designed for and directed to appeal exclusively to either youthful or elderly consumers."[27]

Another set of possible occupational differentiations considered to be lawful is explained as follows:

> A differentiation based on a physical examination, but not one based on age, may be recognized as reasonable in certain job situations which necessitate stringent physical requirements due to inherent occupational factors such as the safety of individual employees or of other persons in their charge or those occupations which by nature are particularly hazardous. For example, iron workers, bridge builders, sandhogs, underwater demolition men, and other similar job classifications which require rapid reflexes or a high degree of speed, coordination, dexterity, endurance, or strength.

---

[26]U.S. Department of Labor, Employment Standards Administration, DISCRIMINATION IN EMPLOYMENT ACT OF 1967: A REPORT COVERING ACTIVITIES UNDER THE ACT IN 1974, Jan. 31, 1975, p. 3.

[27]29 C.F.R. §860.102 (1976).

Then comes a *caveat*

> However, a claim for a differentiation will not be permitted on the basis of an employer's assumption that every employee over a certain age in a particular type of job usually becomes physically unable to perform the duties of the job. There is medical evidence, for example, to support the contention that such is generally not the case. In many instances, an individual at age 60 may be physically capable of performing heavy lifting on a job, where as [*sic*] another individual of age 30 may be physically incapable of doing so.[28]

Variable Terms and Conditions of Employment

Apart from occupational bases for the statutory ban on age discrimination, there are rigorous rules for determining what may constitute unlawful discrimination against employees in the 40-65 age bracket. As an interpretive bulletin phrases it, job-related factors include, but are not limited to:

> job security, advancement, status, and benefits. The following are some examples of the more common terms, conditions, or privileges of employment: The many and varied employee advantages generally regarded as being within the phrase, 'fringe benefits,' promotion, demotion or other disciplinary action, hours of work (including overtime), leave policy (including sick leave, vacation, holidays), career development programs, and seniority or merit systems (which govern such conditions as transfer, assignment, job retention and recall).[29]

Possibly Unlawful Seniority Systems

There is one passage in the official interpretative bulletin that has given rise to much uncertainty among employers and a multiplicity of claims by employees allegedly discriminated against. Some seniority systems, it would appear, can be held by the Labor Department to have become unlawful *retroactively*. The passage in question asserts:

> Seniority systems not only distinguish between employees on the basis of their length of service, they normally afford greater rights to those who have longer service. Therefore adoption of a purported seniority system which gives those with longer service lesser rights and results in discharge or less favored treatment to those within the protection of the Act, may, depending upon the circumstances, be a 'subterfuge to evade the purposes' of the Act. Furthermore a seniority system which has the effect of *perpetuating discrimination which*

---

[28]*Ibid.*, §860.103 (1976).
[29]*Ibid.*, §860.50 (1976).

may have existed on the basis of age prior to the effective date of the Act will not be recognized as 'bona fide.'[30]

Intensified Enforcement Programs

Most employers paid little heed to this Act's rather nebulous requirements for some years after its enactment in 1967. The Labor Department enforcement staff initially concentrated primarily upon elimination of job-wanted ads with apparent bias against older workers. It also made some not-too-successful passes at recalcitrant companies, hoping to cajole them into voluntary compliance.

One veteran commentator on government regulation of labor-management relations, Lawrence Stessin, wrote in 1974 that the law had been "little known, and until recently, limply enforced."[31]

Whether or not with any political motive, a massive publicity campaign was launched by the Labor Department in 1973 to familiarize the nearly 40 million older workers covered by the Act about their statutory rights and how to get redress for management mistakes. The campaign still continues and has been a howling success. As Stessin commented, the Wage-Hour Administrator "pulled out all the publicity stops to spread the word about its recent consent decree with the Standard Oil Company of California, in which the company agreed to ante up $2 million in back pay to workers let out because of age." The elderly beneficiaries of the SOCAL consent decree included some managers earning up to $40,000 a year who had to be reinstated with back pay.

There was still more to come. On the heels of the oil company settlement, Labor Department Solicitor William J. Kilberg reportedly announced that his department had in preparation another suit on age discrimination "that will make the Standard Oil settlement look small."[32] Large suits against the Baltimore and Ohio and the Chesapeake and Ohio railways were also pending.[33]

The largest sum yet awarded against a company by way of damages resulting from age discrimination was engendered by a U.S. district court decision in February 1975. This was truly a landmark case. The court held that an Exxon Company research chemist was, in effect, forced to retire at age 60 when after 30 years of service with the company he was transferred to menial "laboratory duties." His prior position was taken over by a much younger em-

---

[30]*Ibid.*, §860, 105 (1976).
[31]Lawrence Stessin, *The Ax and Older Workers*, NEW YORK TIMES, June 23, 1974, p. F3.
[32]NEWSWEEK, June 17, 1974, p. 26.
[33]*Ibid.*, p. 14.

ployee. Thereupon he became seriously ill and died. The district court handed down a judgment in the staggering sum of $775,000 in favor of his widow and daughter. The judgment assessed court costs against Exxon.[34]

Changes in the Act

In April 1978 Congress enacted and President Carter signed into law a measure, effective Jan. 1, 1979, that raised the permissible retirement age from 65 to 70 for most private-sector employees. An exception is that those employed in a "bona fide executive position or a high policy-making position" for two years before reaching 65 and entitled to an immediate nonforfeitable pension of at least $27,000 per year may be forced to retire at 65.

Seniority Versus Job Rights of Women and Minorities

From the welter of often conflicting guidelines it has taken scores of court cases to develop meaningful and lasting interpretations of civil rights legislation on management practices. Judges are expected—and usually do—call them as they see them. That is to say, they construe the law as they think its framers intended it to be construed, within constitutional bounds. There is at least some room for agreement, however, that the several administrative agencies might be influenced by the views of what could be regarded as their natural constituencies. The Labor Department, for instance, might be swayed by strong stances taken by organized labor. Or the EEOC by feminist organizations and associations speaking for racial minorities.

To generalize thus is not to impugn the good faith of any agency heads. They have just been doing what comes naturally, as has long been the custom in the executive branch of the Federal Government. Of course, whichever way they rule, a lot of folks in the nation's work force are bound to be hurt, either in their job, earnings, or occupational outlook.

Many vexatious issues confronting the courts have come up over conflicting claims about the legitimacy of seniority rights as measured against the rights of racial and ethnic minorities and of women.

A fairly recent case on seniority produced a district court decision in favor of black employees who had been displaced by whites with greater seniority when wholesale layoffs became necessary.

---

[34]NEW YORK TIMES, Feb. 6, 1975, p. 72.

The layoffs had been effectuated in conformity with the seniority provisions of the then current labor agreement at a southern plant of Continental Can Company.[35]

There was no dispute in ensuing litigation about management adherence to the standard clause of "last in first out" in making lay-offs and the reverse in making recalls. As stipulated in the agreement, seniority was observed on a plantwide basis — a system in which length of service anywhere in the plant rather than in a single department or occupation was controlling.

Black employees who were laid off because of low seniority charged the company with unlawful discrimination in violation of Section 703(h) of the Civil Rights Act (quoted earlier in this chapter). Why could any charge of improper discrimination arise in a situation where the seniority clauses of the current agreement were faithfully adhered to? Why should there be a lawsuit challenging the validity of the agreement when the statute has an explicit proviso that it shall not be an unlawful employment practice for an employer to differentiate in terms and conditions of employment *pursuant to a bona fide seniority system?*

Summarized below are some facts considered most relevant by the federal district judge who ruled that some laid-off black employees had been subject to unlawful discrimination:

> Until 1965 the only blacks who had been hired at the employer's plant were two who had been hired during World War II. The company hired one black in 1966, some in 1967 and 1968, and more thereafter. Beginning in 1971, the company cut back employment pursuant to a contract requiring layoffs to take place in the reverse order of seniority. . . . The layoffs reached employees who were hired as early as 1956. As a result, all the blacks but the two hired during the war were laid off and the first 138 persons on the recall list were white.[36]

The court observed that if the recall procedures established by the contract were valid, the company could not be expected to employ another black man for many years.

The gist of the court's finding in this case was that the company's current seniority system perpetuated the effects of pre-Act discrimination against blacks. As one remedy, the court directed the company "without laying off any incumbent employee," to recall enough blacks to restore the racial percentage of the work force that existed as of the date that the last new

---

[35]Watkins v. Steelworkers, Local 2369, 369 F. Supp. 1221, 7 FEP 90 (Dist. Ct. La. 1974).

[36]*Laying Off Employees Pursuant to a Seniority System,* a special report in DAILY LAB. REP. (BNA), No. 36, Feb. 21, 1975, p. 3.

employee was hired. As a second remedy, the court directed that in the future, layoffs had to be allocated between white and black employees so that the ratio of blacks to whites would remain unchanged.[37]

The company appealed. A year or so later the Fifth Circuit Court of Appeals reversed the district court's decision. In so doing it upheld the constitutionality of the seniority system as applied to layoffs, the same system that, it had been charged, fostered unlawful discrimination.[38]

In explaining the rationale of its decision the circuit court stated:

> We hold that, regardless of an earlier history of employment discrimination when present hiring practices are nondiscriminatory and have been for over ten years, an employer's use of a long-established seniority system for determining who will be laid off, and who will be rehired, adopted without intent to discriminate is not a violation of Title VII or §1981 [§1981 refers to a civil rights act enacted in 1866 after the adoption of the Thirteenth Amendment], even though the use of the seniority system results in the discharge of more blacks than whites to the point of eliminating blacks from the workforce, where the individual employees who suffer layoff under the system have not themselves been the subject of prior discrimination.

Then to some court watchers there was something like an ambiguous "straddle" in the circuit court's decision. This appeared in the following passage:

> We specially do not decide the rights of a laid-off employee who could show that but for the discriminatory refusal to hire him at an earlier time than the date of his actual employment, or but for his failure to obtain earlier employment because of exclusion of minority employees from the work force, he would have sufficient seniority to insulate him against layoff.

Legal scholars are quick to point out that no federal circuit court is bound to follow the dictate of a district court when the substance seems to the former to constitute bad law. Conversely, a circuit court frequently will cite from another circuit court decision that meets with its approval to buttress his own reasoning in a case involving a comparable issue. In the *Watkins* case the Fifth Circuit Court used exactly this tactic in citing the decision the Seventh Circuit Court handed down a bit earlier. As related by the Fifth Circuit Court, the case, known as *Waters* v. *Wisconsin Steel Works* involved a law suit brought into a federal district court by two indi-

---

[37]*Ibid.*, p. 14.
[38]Watkins v. Steelworkers, Local 2369, 516 F.2d 41, 10 FEP 1297 (5th Cir. 1975).

vidual employees. Their contention was that their employer's observance of the seniority principle of "last hired, first fired" was in violation of their rights under both Section 1981 and Title VII in that
it allegedly perpetuated the company's "prior discrimination policies and hiring practice decision."

To quote from a pertinent passage in the appellate court's
Watkins decision referring to the *Waters* case: "The district court in
Waters held that the seniority system had its genesis in a period of
racial discrimination and was thus violative of §1981 and not a
bona fide seniority system under Title VII."

On appeal, the Seventh Circuit reversed. Distinguishing a departmental seniority system from the employment seniority system
in the *Waters* case, the court held that it did not have the effect of
perpetuating prior racial discrimination in violation of the strictures of Title VII.

Then the Fifth Circuit Court quoted the Seventh Circuit Court
as follows:

> Title VII speaks only to the future. Its backward gaze is found
> only on a present practice which may perpetuate past discrimination.
> An employment seniority system embodying the "last hired, first
> fired" principle does not of itself perpetuate past discrimination. To
> hold otherwise would be tantamount to shackling white employees
> with a burden of a past discrimination created not by them but by
> their employer. Title VII was not designed to nurture such reverse
> discrimination preferences.

Thus, the Fifth Circuit Court ruled in the *Watkins* case that "the
use of employment seniority to determine the layoff of employees
does not violate Title VII of the Civil Rights Act of 1964."

In combination the *Watkins* and *Waters* decisions in the two
federal appellate courts gave much encouragement to management
and organized labor to continue to honor their contractual commitments to protect employees with seniority when layoffs become necessary. One basis for their encouragement was that the Supreme
Court denied certiorari in the *Waters* case. But such encouragement was rather short lived. The U.S. Supreme Court granted certiorari in a case that may set the precedent for cases on seniority versus employment rights of minorities for the next several years at
least. The case in question was *Jersey Central Power and Light Co.*
v. *IBEW*.[39]

Important developments in the *Jersey Central* litigation are
discussed below. But what amounted to a severe limitation of the ef-

---

[39]508 F.2d 687, 9 FEP 117 (3d Cir. 1975), *vac'd*, 425 U.S. 998, 12 FEP 1335 (1976).

fects on the Supreme Court's action in the *Waters* case transpired before the Court had to determine whether to hear and decide on its own the tremendously complicated issues presented in the *Jersey Central* law suits. The case affecting the *Waters* decision was *Franks v. Bowman Transportation Company*. In a unanimous decision the Supreme Court held that identifiable job applicants who were denied employment after the effective date and in violation of Title VII may be awarded seniority status retroactive to the dates of their employment applications.

The underlying facts, as summarized in the High Court decision, were that the employer, Bowman Transportation Company, had been held by a federal district court to have engaged in a pattern of racial discrimination in various company policies, including the hiring, transfer, and discharge of employees. It was also found that the discriminatory practices were perpetuated in Bowman's collective bargaining agreement with the unions. The district court directed the company to divide the class of blacks allegedly discriminated against into two groups: (1) those then-employed applicants who had applied for the jobs that they did not get prior to Jan. 1, 1972; and (2) those who had applied for jobs they were denied because of lack of seniority prior to the same date. Then the court denied retroactive seniority status or back pay before the date when they applied for the jobs they did not get. The Fifth Circuit Court of Appeals sustained in part and reversed in part the lower court verdict. On final review by the Supreme Court only the one aspect of the circuit court's judgment came up for review. This was the affirmation by the circuit court of the district court's denial of retroactive seniority to non-employee applicants who claimed sex discrimination as the reason for their rejection. In the briefest of brief summaries, subject of course to qualifications expressed in footnotes and in the partially concurring and dissenting opinions, the verdict of the Supreme Court was that victims of illegal hiring discrimination may be under many circumstances entitled to retroactive seniority rights.[40]

A Leading Seniority Court Case of the Decade

The Jersey Central Power and Light Company's involvement in litigation respecting seniority rights versus minority group employment rights could well have been characterized as one of the most

---

[40]Franks v. Bowman Transportation Co., 495 F.2d 398, 8 FEP 66 (8th Cir. 1974), *rev'd on other grounds*, 424 U.S. 747, 12 FEP 549 (1976).

important Title VII cases of the 1970s. It has been in and out of the courts for several years.

For proper perspective it seems imperative to review at some length Jersey Central's problems of compliance with the terms of its labor agreement and with the requirements' of Title VII. Early developments are succinctly summarized below.

> The employer and the unions negotiated a company-wide seniority system. After they entered into their latest collective bargaining contract, which provided that layoffs would occur in the reverse order of seniority, they signed a conciliation agreement with the EEOC designed to settle certain claims of discrimination. The agreement obligated the employer to use its "best efforts" to increase the percentages of minority-group and female employees in its workforce over a five-year period to the percentages that these groups represent in the relevant labor market. The agreement did not affect the operation of the contract, although the EEOC had tried unsuccessfully to negotiate a seniority system that would have given minority-group and female employees greater seniority than they would be entitled to under the contract.
>
> Some months thereafter, the employer determined that economic conditions required it to lay off 200 employees, which figure was later raised to 400. The unions demanded that the contractual seniority system be followed in selecting the employees to be laid off. The EEOC and other U.S. Government agencies warned that if the newly hired minority-group and female employees were laid off, the employer would be violating the conciliation agreement and Title VII. The employer then went to arbitration with the union for a ruling as to whether it would be a violation of the anti-discrimination provision of the contract to lay off employees in the reverse order of their seniority. The arbitrator said no.[41]

When the arbitrator gave the green light to make layoffs as required by the contract's seniority provisions, the Jersey Central management proceeded with great caution and astuteness before go ahead with the requisite layoffs by requesting from a federal district court a declaratory judgment to determine which of its seemingly conflicting agreements had to be honored. The judgment sought by management would have applied to the local unions concerned, as well as the EEOC, the Labor Department's Office of Federal Contract Compliance, the General Services Administration, and also the Division on Civil Rights of the New Jersey Department of Law and Public Safety. The New Jersey agency apparently had some concern as to enforcement of the state anti-discrimination statute but did not intervene in the federal court proceedings.

---

[41] *Laying Off Employees Pursuant to a Seniority System*, p. 6.

During the pendency of the court proceedings it [the management] began its layoff pursuant to the contract. The district court ruled that the conciliation agreement would be violated if the employer followed the seniority provision on the contract in making the layoffs. The court explained that doing so would substantially reduce the relative percentages of those whose hiring was the purpose of the conciliation agreement. To the extent that the conciliation agreement conflicted with the contract, the court ruled, the agreement was to prevail. It told the employer to set up three seniority lists—one for minority group workers, one for females, and one for "all others"—and to lay off employees in such a way that the relative percentage of each group prior to the start of the layoff would be preserved. The employer then began to lay off employees pursuant to this method. Thereafter the unions obtained a stay from the Third Circuit Federal Appellate Court and the employer completed the layoff by once again following the seniority provision of the contract.

The appeals court vacated the district court's decision. The conciliation agreement and the collective bargaining agreement were not in conflict, the court ruled. It pointed out the thrust of the conciliation agreement was in increasing the proportions of minority group and female employees through new hiring, not through displacement of incumbent employees. The court observed that the conciliation agreement incorporated the contractual seniority system; once hired, the minority group and female employees were to be treated like other employees.[42]

A relevant passage from the circuit court's finding as to the effect of compliance with the applicable union agreement is quoted below:

> We believe that Congress intended to bar proof of the perpetuating effect of a plant-wide seniority system as it regarded such systems as 'bona fide.' Congress, while recognizing that a bona fide seniority system might well perpetuate past discriminatory practices, nevertheless chose between upsetting all collective bargaining agreements with such provisions and permitting them despite the perpetuating effect that they might have. We believe that Congress intended a plantwide seniority system, facially neutral but having a disproportionate impact on female and minority group workers, to be a bona fide, seniority system within the meaning of Section 703(h) of the Act.[43]

The U.S. Supreme Court put off the burden of further consideration of the law and the facts when in 1976 it refused to hear the complex issues on appeals for certiorari and remanded the case back to the Third Circuit Court of Appeals.[44]

---

[42]*Ibid.*

[43]Jersey Central Power and Light Co. v. IBEW, 508 F.2d 687, 9 FEP 117 (3d Cir. 1975).

[44]425 U.S. 998, 12 FEP 1335 (1976).

That court, in turn, sent the whole complicated controversy back to a New Jersey federal district court for a trial on the merits and the obvious conflicts in applicable contracts, agreements, and federal and state statutes. As of August 1, 1978, the district court had not scheduled a trial de novo. Quite probably the whole case will be settled by agreement among the litigants without ever going to trial. But it may yet be reviewed by the circuit court of appeals and perhaps several years hence it will be the subject of final adjudication by the U.S. Supreme Court.

There is no proper place in this book for quoting the odds on future High Court decisions. That speculation should be left to the professional bookmakers. Prudent personnel administrators perhaps already in the middle would do well to heed the advice of outside counsel. But they have to remember that even the most sagacious lawyers sometimes have been wrong in predicting the outcomes of difficult issues that have to be resolved by the judiciary. Finley Peter Dunne may have been partly right when he wrote — three quarters of a century ago — that "the Supreme Court follows the election returns."

It might be logical to assume that Congress would act to amend the law at the behest of organized labor should the Supreme Court ultimately rule that minority group protection against discrimination must take precedence over seniority provisions in union agreements. Those who so assume, however, may be just engaged in wishful thinking. Members of Congress occasionally surprise some of those who have most vigorously campaigned for them at election time. One such big surprise occurred in March 1977.

The election of a Democratic President and an overwhelming majority of Democrats in the House of Representatives did not enable Big Labor to win out in its No. 1 legislative goal, that is, the passage of the so-called common situs picketing bill. This is the measure that would enable just one of a number of unions engaged in a construction project to seek a contractor's compliance with its demands by picketing and thus presumably shutting down all union work on the project. A bill for the same purpose had been passed by both the Senate and the House in 1976 but had been vetoed by President Ford. Much to the indignation of the AFL-CIO hierarchy, the House defeated the proposed new law in March 1977 by a vote of 205 for to 317 against.

At first glance there might seem to be no relevancy in the House rebuke to organized labor and what it might do sooner or later to amend the Civil Rights Act, either to give further sanction to the principle of seniority in labor contracts or to nullify seniority clauses if they limit job retention rights for minorities and/or women. Manifestly, most labor unions believe in the paramount importance of seniority as the basis for determining who stays and who gets let out when force curtailment is imperative. It could well be, however, that Civil Rights activists have enough clout with Congress to induce it to enact amendments to the present statute that could virtually nullify contract clauses embodying the last-in-first-out formula.

A Brand New Ball Game on the Seniority Issue

The Supreme Court handed down a crucial decision that may presage how it might finally adjudicate the Jersey Central Case when and if that case comes back to the Court before the end of the decade. The Court's decision sustaining a union agreement that obviously permitted some perpetuation of pre-Civil Rights Act discrimination in the matter of seniority will doubtless produce a spate of learned articles and editorials supporting or castigating the Court. Meanwhile, it is anyone's guess as to whether the High Court has instigated a brand new ball game for the litigants still struggling with the basic issue of seniority rights versus minority group employment rights.

The essence of the Court verdict mentioned above is to be found in the syllabus accompanying its decision of May 31, 1977, in the case involving the Teamsters Union and a nationwide common carrier of motor freight. The Federal Government was a direct respondent in this case. The Supreme Court held:

1. The Government sustained its burden of proving that the company engaged in a systemwide pattern or practice of employment discrimination against minority members in violation of Title VII by regularly and purposefully treating such members less favorably than white persons. The evidence, showing pervasive statistical disparities in line-driver positions between employment of the minority members and whites, and bolstered by considerable testimony of specific instances of discrimination, was not adequately rebutted by the company and supported the findings of the courts below.

2. Since the Government proved that the company engaged in a post-Act pattern of discriminatory employment policies, retroactive seniority may be awarded as relief for post-Act discriminatees even if the seniority system agreement makes no provision for such relief. *Franks v. Bowman Transportation Co.,* 424 U.S. 747, 778-779.

3. The seniority system was protected by §703(h) and therefore the union's conduct in agreeing to and maintaining the system did not violate Title VII. Employees who suffered only a pre-Act discrimina-

tion are not entitled to relief, and no person may be given retroactive seniority to a date earlier than the Act's effective date. The District Court's injunction against the union must consequently be vacated.

(a) By virtue of §703(h) a bona fide seniority system does not become unlawful simply because it may perpetuate pre-Title VII discrimination, for Congress (as is manifest from the language and legislative history of the Act) did not intend to make it illegal for employees with vested seniority rights to continue to exercise those rights, even at the expense of pre-Act discriminatees. Thus here because of the company's intentional pre-Act discrimination the disproportionate advantage given by the seniority system to the white line drivers with the longest tenure over the minority member employees who might by now have enjoyed those advantages were it not for the pre-Act discrimination is sanctioned by §703(h).

(b) *The seniority system at issue here is entirely bona fide, applying to all races and ethnic groups, and was negotiated and is maintained free from any discriminatory purpose.* [Emphasis supplied][45]

The Court's opinion was delivered by Mr. Justice Stewart with six other Justices concurring (Burger, C.J., and White, Blackmun, Powell, Rehnquist, and Stevens). Mr. Justice Marshall filed a sharply worded separate opinion concurring in part and dissenting in part. Mr. Justice Brennan joined in the Marshall opinion. Commenting on the majority opinion that the case at bar could be decided on the basis of imputed legislative intent, Marshall raised the question of which choice was it more likely that Congress would have made: Would it have validated or invalidated seniority systems that perpetuate pre-Act discrimination? The Justice Marshall pulled no punches when he wrote:

To answer that question the devastating impact on today's holding validating such systems must be fully understood. Prior to 1965 blacks and Spanish-speaking Americans who were able to find employment were assigned the lowest paid, most menial jobs in many industries throughout the Nation but especially in the South. In many factories, blacks were hired as laborers while whites were trained and given skilled positions; in the transportation industry blacks could only become porters; and in steel plants blacks were assigned to the coke ovens and blasting furnaces, "the hotter and dirtier" places of employment. The Court holds, in essence, that while after 1965 these incumbent employees are entitled to an equal opportunity, they must pay a price: they must surrender the seniority they have accumulated in their old jobs. For many, the price will be too high, and they will be locked-in to their previous positions. Even those willing to pay the price will have to reconcile themselves to being forever behind subsequently hired whites who were not discrimi-

---

[45]Teamsters v. U.S. (75-636) and T.I.M.E.-D.C., Inc. v. U.S. (75-672), 45 U.S. LAW WEEK (BNA) 4506 (1977).

natorily assigned. Thus equal opportunity will remain a distant dream for all incumbent employees.

I am aware of nothing in the legislative history of the 1964 Civil Rights Act to suggest that if Congress had focused on this fact it nonetheless would have decided to write off an entire generation of minority group employees.[46]

The Continuing Dilemma on Seniority

Minority organizations and feminine activists are still hoping for the best for their constituencies. Of course, they have the EEOC firmly on their side. The National Association for the Advancement of Colored People (NAACP) is in the forefront of those looking for judicial indication of their advocacy of the supremacy of minority rights over seniority rights. Herbert Hill, the chief spokesman for the NAACP on labor relations issues, has pointed out that prevailing seniority systems give job expectations to whites "that are largely based on the systematic denial of the rights of black workers."[47]

Vernon E. Jordan, Executive Director of the National Urban League, has spoken out even more bluntly. Referring in 1975 to the dilemma of recession-struck companies, Jordan announced:

> If they lay off blacks who have less seniority, thanks to the earlier refusal to hire, the company reverts back to its lily white work force and violates affirmative action agreements with the government, as well as the Civil Rights Act.
>
> Caught in the middle are workers of both races who face layoffs in a job market that offers no opportunity for alternative employment. There are already some signs of deepening racial bitterness as some workers are victims of layoffs that don't affect the other race as much. If this situation continues we would see a lethal combination of racial conflict and economic hardship, an explosive mix.[48]

A partial middle-of-the-road solution has been proposed by Stephen I. Schlossberg, general counsel of the United Automobile Workers. The UAW has been a zealous supporter of equal employment opportunity. But as Schlossberg has observed, "layoffs are too volatile an issue to be controlled by EEOC guidelines. In his view, "Remedying past discrimination is hard enough without pitting worker against worker during a recession. That's not the way you make progress. You have to do it when the economy is expanding."[49]

---

[46]*Ibid.*, at 4523.
[47]NEW YORK TIMES, Jan. 29, 1975, p. 17.
[48]National Urban League Communications Department Release, Feb. 26, 1975.
[49]BUSINESS WEEK, May 5, 1975, p. 67.

More than a few cents' worth of suggestions as to how to reconcile differences between unions and minority groups in layoff situations has been volunteered in a *New York Times* editorial. It was
commenting on the budget squeeze confronted by the New York
Telephone Company in 1975 and by the union representing nearly
6,000 of its operators in New York City. "Faced with the prospect of
a layoff of 400 operators for economic reasons," the editorial said,
"the union agreed to have its members go on a four-day week at
four days' pay. The International Ladies Garment Workers Union,
the city's biggest union, has long taken the same share-the-work
view when business is slack in its volatile industry."[50]

STATE FAIR EMPLOYMENT PRACTICE LEGISLATION

Even though a company is manifestly subject to all provisions
of the federal Civil Rights Act and may be also a government
contractor subject to E.O. 11246, its management cannot with
impunity ignore state laws. Some state statutes impose more rigorous requirements for fair employment practices than do their
federal counterparts. What's more, the Civil Rights Act was
designed to encourage the adoption of complementary legislation
by the states and to stimulate increased enforcement activity among
those states already having antidiscriminatory statutes. And the
methods of operation under the state laws may determine whether
the primary enforcement of equal employment opportunity rules
will be by federal or state agencies.

Thirty-two states have laws with teeth. That is, they provide
both for administrative hearings on alleged violations and then for
judicial enforcement. These states are: Alaska, California,
Colorado, Connecticut, Delaware, Hawaii, Illinois, Indiana, Iowa,
Kansas, Kentucky, Maryland, Massachusetts, Michigan, Minne-
sota, Missouri, Nebraska, Nevada, New Hampshire, New Jersey,
New Mexico, New York, Ohio, Oklahoma, Oregon, Pennsylvania,
Rhode Island, Utah, Washington, West Virginia, Wisconsin and
Wyoming. The District of Columbia and Puerto Rico also have
such statutes.

There are four states that have fair employment practice laws
that make discrimination a misdemeanor but provide no special
enforcement machinery. These are: Idaho, Maine, Montana, and
Vermont. Two other states, Arizona and Tennessee, have laws that
constitute little more than pious protestation of legislative intent.

---

[50]NEW YORK TIMES, May 20, 1975, p. 35.

With respect to jurisdictional issues, the state laws in general apply equally to enterprises engaged in or affecting interstate commerce, and to enterprises operating exclusively in intrastate commerce. The U.S. Supreme Court has spoken on this issue. The Court has explicitly decided that federal law does not preclude the states from enacting fair employment legislation on their own that applies to companies also subject to the federal legislation.[51]

Deferral to State Agencies

Why the emphasis on state laws when most employers are subject to federal statutes as well? It is a virtual impossibility to set forth guidelines for fair employment practices that would be applicable to a company doing multistate business without giving heed to the laws of each state in which they operate. The Civil Rights Act, through Section 706 (b), requires the Equal Employment Opportunity Commission to defer to the states for a reasonable time when a charge of job discrimination is filed within a state that has a state or local law prohibiting the practice alleged, *if* such non-federal law grants the state or local authority power to grant or seek relief from the possible discriminatory practice or to institute criminal proceedings against an apparent employer-offender. All the 32 states having enforceable laws of any real substance have been designated by the EEOC to take original jurisdiction in the investigation and, when warranted, litigation of job discrimination charges.

Unusual Requirements in Particular State Laws

While the state laws, as already mentioned, followed substantially the same pattern as the Civil Rights Act, there are variations and anomalies both in the statutes themselves and in judicial construction. Only a few specifics need be cited to illustrate this point.

In Wisconsin, the state law makes it illegal to discriminate in employment against a handicapped person. No prohibition of this sort is to be found in any other state fair employment practice law. The Wisconsin law rather narrows its prohibition against the handicapped by providing in the section on definitions that this ban "does not apply to failure of an employer to employ or to retain as an employee any person who because of a handicap is physically or otherwise unable to efficiently perform, at the standards set by the

---

[51]Colorado Antidiscrimination Commission v. Continental Airlines, 372 U.S. 714, 52 LRRM 2889 (1963).

employer, the duties required in that job." There is another restrictive proviso. It states: "An employer's exclusion of a handicapped employee from life or disability insurance coverage, or reasonable restrictions of such coverage, shall not constitute discrimination."

The New Jersey law is unique in prohibiting employment discrimination on account of any individual's liability for military service. This law is also unusual in that it has been officially construed by its administrators as precluding an employer from including on employment application forms such seemingly innocuous data as the residence of the applicant or the name of the closest relative to be notified in case of an emergency. Such interpretations have presumably been based on the assumption that disclosure of a home address might indicate that the applicant lived in a minority group "ghetto" or that the name of a close relative might disclose a minority ethnic background.

On the basis of the reported facts, an objective analyst could scarcely quarrel with a 1968 decision of the Missouri Human Rights Commission involving two Negro women employed in a manufacturing company's mail room. They charged that their employer had illegally discriminated against them by failing to give them promotions. It developed that a white woman had been promoted to the position of assistant mail room supervisor. Three Negro women in the department had more seniority. The two complainants had a high school education, while the white woman did not. This was presumably considered at least circumstantial evidence of discriminatory intent on the part of the employer. In any event, after the complaint was filed with the Missouri Commission, the two Negro women were promoted to better jobs and, without litigation, the company entered into a so-called conciliation agreement with the Commission under which it agreed to offer the complainants the chance to be trained as assistant mail room supervisors and to reimburse them for wages lost because of the initial refusal to promote either of them.

It might be expected that New York State's experience in civil rights legislation would provide the most fruitful examples of logical interpretations of employers' statutory obligations. But administrative and judicial interpretations have ranged from one extreme to the other. For instance, a Negro girl was rejected for employment as a model for beachwear way back in 1951. The State Commission on Human Rights dismissed her complaint of racial discrimination on the finding that her body measurements did not meet the prospective employer's specifications.[52]

---

[52]29 LRRM 52.

Conversely, and much more importantly perhaps, a Puerto Rican applicant was refused employment in the same year by a luncheonette in Harlem. (For the benefit of readers who may be unfamiliar with colloquially designated areas in the Greater New York Metropolitan Area, Harlem is a section of Manhattan in New York City predominantly inhabited by Negroes.) The Harlem luncheonette admittedly had employed Negroes only. The employer was informed by the Commission that it would not condone "discrimination inside or outside of Harlem." Two years later, in response to a specific question propounded at a widely publicized interview, the chairman of the New York State Commission declared that his agency would by no means institute proceedings against another Manhattan restaurant because this employer insisted on employing *only* Negroes as its waiters.

Still more importantly, a decision of the highest New York state court has permanent significance. That court had to determine the legality of the action of an oil company with international operations in requiring job applicants to fill out passport visa applications for travel in Saudi Arabia. These applications included an inquiry into the applicant's religion. In support of its position, when challenged as to its legality by an influential racial and religious organization of the Jewish faith, the oil company noted that the King of Saudi Arabia not only prohibited the employment of Jews in his domain but also strenuously objected to the employment of Jews in any segment of this great company's operations.

The New York State Commission decided that the inquiry of the company related to a bona fide occupational qualification. The highest court of New York State, the Court of Appeals, ruled however, that the Commission could not subordinate state law "to the dictates of a foreign state which violated our own public policy."[53]

By no means the latest or most important case, but still indicative of a possible trend in judicial thinking, was the decision of New York State's high court, handed down in December 1970 on the controversial question of an employer's beard ban. To be sure, the New York Court of Appeals did not give unfettered license to conservative employers committed to a policy of beardlessness among their employees. As is its wont, the court ruled specifically on the narrow issue before it. Thus, in the case of Abdullah Ibrahim, an Orthodox Moslem residing in Brooklyn, the court decided that he was not illegally denied employment as a baggage clerk by Eastern Greyhound Lines because he was not clean-shaven.

---

[53]173 N.E. 2d 7888, 47 LRRM 2949 (N.Y. Ct. App. 1961).

Ibrahim, a job applicant, had been told by the company that though otherwise apparently qualified to be a baggage smasher he did not and would not comply with an explicit company regulation. This regulation stated, "A good clean appearance must be presented at all times when dealing with the public. The men will be freshly shaven and with reasonable haircuts." His religion, Ibrahim argued before the State Division of Human Rights, required him to wear his beard. Hence he was being unlawfully discriminated against because of his creed. The Court of Appeals thought otherwise. On the record it was disclosed that the company rejecting him for the job in question had employed a number of Moslems. There was no conclusive evidence that he had in fact been denied a job because of his religion. The court first raised and then answered this question: "Whether an employer must accommodate his general pattern of employment to the special requirements of each individual's religion." Such an accommodation, the court observed, assuming, as it might, many variations, would not be compelled to avoid violation of a prospective employee's civil rights.[54]

Once again the interrelationship between federal and state fair employment practice legislation assumed significance in the decision just summarized. The New York high court referred in support of its conclusion to the *Reynolds Metal Company* case decided by the U.S. Court of Appeals for the Sixth Circuit.[55] The *Reynolds* case produced a decision that a collective agreement making occasional Sunday work mandatory did not involve illegal religious discrimination against a church member whose faith inhibited him from working on Sunday. But the validity of the New York high court decision still hung in the balance, for in January 1971 the U.S. Supreme Court decided to review the *Reynolds* case, on which the New York court's conclusion in the *Ibrahim* case was largely grounded. Nevertheless, the Supreme Court finally sustained the circuit court's *Reynolds* decision.

Deferral to Municipal Agencies

Some cities have fair employment ordinances that are much more stringent than their own state laws. Where such ordinances applicable to employers having establishments in, or selling goods or services to, these municipalities are in effect, the EEOC normally defers to the state rather than to the cities for compliance. But the Pennsylvania Human Relations Commission defers to the local fair

---

[54]Eastern Greyhound Lines, 2 FEP 710 (N.Y. Ct. App. 1970).
[55]Dewey v. Reynolds Metals Co., 71 LRRM 2406 (6th Cir. 1970).

employment agencies of Philadelphia and Pittsburgh. So the EEOC does likewise.

SEX DISCRIMINATION IN EMPLOYMENT

Many of the biggest and best managed corporations in the United States have encountered grievous problems in attempting to adjust their personnel policies to comply with the ban against sex discrimination in the Civil Rights Act. The problems of most companies have not been finally resolved either through unilateral management action, conciliation agreements with federal enforcement agencies, or litigation.

It was not any overwhelmingly compassionate desire on the part of Congress to enhance the job status and opportunities of women that led to the inclusion of the anti-sex-bias provision in the 1964 law. The influential conservative Senate group that succeeded in ramming through a sex amendment to the bill, as originally proposed by the Johnson Administration, had a totally different objective. Its leaders hoped to scuttle the bill in its entirety because of their violent objections to the provisions banning racial discrimination in private-sector employment. To be sure, they failed utterly. Instead of blocking enactment of a law to cope with racial and ethnic discrimination in employment, the anti-sex-ban begat what some of the most extreme southern Senators later came to regard as a legislative creature of Frankensteinian monstrosity.

No wonder, then, that the original EEOC staff proceeded gingerly for some years in interpreting and trying to enforce the sex provisions of the law. In later years, the Commission repeatedly reversed initially "soft" rulings that did little to improve women's chances of ultimately attaining realistic job equality. By 1975, the Commission under new leadership had gone all out for anti-sexism in the job market. Indeed in that year it published a monograph written by a pro-feminist staff consultant who went so far as to assert that:

> the statute's position is that sex is a bona fide occupational qualification for only a few jobs in the American economy. *Positions of sperm donor or wet nurse* [emphasis supplied] or actor and actress are perhaps the only good examples of jobs within the Equal Employment Opportunity Commission's interpretation of Title VII. Along with this narrow definition of bona fide occupational qualification the Commission has held that when Title VII is in conflict with state laws [i.e. laws that provide special protection for women against onerous terms and hazardous conditions of employment] state laws are invalid as defenses for employment discrimination.[56]

[56]Lyle, p. 43.

FEDERAL ANTIDISCRIMINATION GUIDELINES AND SIGNIFICANT COURT RULINGS

Sex Discrimination

None of the sets of guidelines promulgated by the EEOC has the force of law. Guidelines almost by definition indicate recommended courses of action or approved routes to follow in general, hypothesized situations. In this light, the Commission's sex guidelines can be an invaluable aid in determining how companies' policies can be kept within the law.

It is traditional in both the executive and judicial branches of the Federal Government for the special exceptions to statutory coverage to be interpreted narrowly. The Commission has followed the tradition by holding that "Labels, — 'Men's jobs' and 'Women's jobs' tend to deny employment opportunities unnecessarily to one sex or the other."[57]

Several examples of guidelines are provided to illustrate those things in the Commission's view which do *not* constitute bona fide occupational qualification exceptions. About one of these there can be little dispute. If a stage role requires portrayal of a male character, a man can be hired to fill it — and obviously the opposite is true for feminine roles.[58]

Another seems to have less solid bottoming. It insists on the presumption of unlawful sex discrimination when a refusal to hire a woman because of her sex is based "on assumptions of the comparative employment characteristics of women in general. For example the assumption that the turnover rate among women is higher than among men."[59]

The stark truth is that labor turnover rates for women in general and for women in many particular occupations are much higher than are men's rates. Why should management be forced to shut its eyes to any number of U.S. Labor Department studies?[60] Can anyone deny that continuity of employment over an extended period can be a prime requisite for successful performance in a supervisory job and also imperative for promotion to managerial ranks?

---

[57] 29 C.F.R. §1604.2(a) (1976).
[58] *Ibid.*, §1604.2(a)(2) (1976).
[59] *Ibid.*, §1604.2(a)(1)(i) (1976).
[60] See, for example, Paul A. Armknecht and John F. Early, *Quits in Manufacturing: A Study of Their Causes*, MONTHLY LABOR REVIEW, U.S. Department of Labor, Bureau of Labor Statistics, Nov. 1972, *95*(No. 11), 31-37.

Exclusion of Disability Benefits for Pregnancy Held Not Discriminatory

A 1976 U.S. Supreme Court decision on the benefit rights of pregnant women generated massive outbursts of indignation from feminists and other crusaders in the civil rights movement. The case, *General Electric Co.* v. *Gilbert,* was bitterly contested; and shortly after the Court ruling was handed down representatives of unions and of women's and civil rights groups formed the Coalition to End Discrimination Against Pregnant Workers and began to map strategy for overturning the decision in Congress.

The case in question concerned the constitutional validity of General Electric's disability benefits plan. What the majority (6-3) of the Supreme Court held in this volatile case was that the exclusion of benefit rights for women temporarily disabled because of pregnancy violates neither the Equal Protection Clause of the Fourteenth Amendment nor the anti-sex-discrimination provisions of Title VII of the Civil Rights Act. The majority decision declared that the exclusion of pregnancy from a disability benefits plan providing general coverage for all other kinds of non-occupational temporary disability and job absence did not result in gender-based discrimination as such. The Court majority further held that this exclusion was not for the pretext or purpose of discrimination against women since pregnancy, though confined to women, is in other ways significantly different from the typically covered diseases or ailments.

To quote from the Court's official syllabus, "Gender-based discrimination does not result simply because an employer's disability benefits plan is less than all-inclusive. Petitioner's plan [General Electric Company] is no more than an insurance package covering some risks but excluding others, and there has been no showing that the selection of included risks creates a gender-based discriminatory effect."[61]

Feminist organizations, and, indeed, the minority of the Supreme Court Justices, found it difficult to accept some of the dicta in the majority opinion. Take the following passage, for instance:

> "Normal pregnancy is an objectively identifiable physical condition with unique characteristics. Absent a showing that distinctions involving pregnancy are more pretexts designed to effect an invidious discrimination against the members of one sex or the other, lawmakers are constitutionally free to include or exclude pregnancy

---

[61]General Electric Co. v. Gilbert et al., 429 U.S. 126 (1976).

from the coverage of legislation such as this on any reasonable basis, just as with respect to any other physical condition."

*   *   *   *   *

. . . But we have here no question of excluding a disease or disability comparable in all other respects to covered diseases or disabilities and yet confined to the members of one race or sex. Pregnancy is of course confined to women, but it is in other ways significantly different from the typical covered disease or disability. The District Court found that it is not a "disease" at all, and is often a voluntarily undertaken and desired condition, 375 F Supp at 375, 377. We do not therefore infer that exclusion of pregnancy disability benefits from the petitioner's plan is a simple pretext for discriminating against women. . . .[62]

And here is a portion of another passage that continues to create outbursts of righteous or self-righteous indignation from spokespersons for activist groups.

The "package" going to relevant identifiable groups we are presently concerned with—General Electric's male and female employees—covers exactly the same categories of risk, and is facially nondiscriminatory in the sense that "[t]here is no risk from which men are protected and women are not. Likewise, there is no risk from which women are protected and men are not." Geduldig, 417 U.S., at 496-497. As there is no proof that the package is in fact worth more to men than to women, it is impossible to find any gender-based discriminatory effect in this scheme simply because women disabled as a result of pregnancy do not receive benefits; that is to say, gender-based discrimination does not result simply because an employer's disability benefits plan is less than all inclusive. For all that appears, pregnancy-related disabilities constitute an *additional* risk, unique to women, and the failure to compensate them for this risk does not destroy the presumed parity of the benefits, accruing to men and women alike, which results from the facially evenhanded *inclusion* of risks. To hold otherwise would endanger the common-sense notion that an employer who has no disability benefits program at all does not violate Title VII even though the "underinclusion" of risks impacts, as a result of pregnancy-related disabilities, more heavily upon one gender than upon the other. Just as there is no facial gender-based discrimination in that case, so, too, there is none here.[63]

Significant Passages in Dissenting Opinions

While six Justices concurred in the result with one only doing so in part, there were two separate dissenting opinions, both couched in language critical of the majority judgment.

Mr. Justice Brennan, with whom Mr. Justice Marshall concurred, seemed to pull out all the stops when he wrote:

The Court [majority opinion] argues that pregnancy is not

---

[62]*Ibid.*, at 134, 136.
[63]*Ibid.*, at 138.

"comparable" to other disabilities since it is a "voluntary" condition rather than a "disease." The fallacy of this argument is that even if "non-voluntariness" and "disease" are to be construed as the operational criteria for inclusion of a disability in General Electric's program, application of these criteria is inconsistent with the Court's gender-neutral interpretation of the company's policy.

For example, the characterization of pregnancy as "voluntary" is not a persuasive factor, for as the Court of Appeals correctly noted, "other than for childbirth disability, [General Electric] has never construed its plan as eliminating *all* so-called 'voluntary' disabilities," including sport injuries, attempted suicides, veneral disease, disabilities incurred in the commission of a crime or during a fight, and elective cosmetic surgery. 519 F. 2d, at 665. Similarly, the label "disease" rather than "disability" cannot be deemed determinative since General Electric's pregnancy disqualification also excludes the 10% of pregnancies that end in debilitating miscarriages, 375 F. Supp. at 377, the 10% of cases where pregnancies are complicated by "diseases" in the intuitive sense of the word, *ibid.*, and cases where women recovering from childbirth are stricken by severe diseases unrelated to pregnancy. . . . In fostering the impression that it is faced with a mere underinclusive assignment of risks in a gender-neutral fashion—that is, all other disabilities are insured irrespective of gender—the Court's analysis proves to be simplistic and misleading. For although all mutually contractible risks are covered irrespective of gender, . . . the plan also insures risks such as prostatectomies, vasectomies, and circumcisions that are specific to the reproductive system of men and for which there exist no female counterparts covered by the plan. Again, pregnancy affords the only disability, sex-specific or otherwise, that is excluded from coverage.[64]

The separate dissenting opinion of Mr. Justice Stevens warrants more than passing attention. This is so because this Justice implied that Congress could do what the majority of the High Court would not do, i.e., write into the Civil Rights Act a more specific provision declaring disparate treatment in disability leaves on account of sex to constitute illegal discrimination. Mr. Justice Stevens' dissent read in part:

Does a contract between a company and its employees which treats the risk of absenteeism caused by pregnancy differently from any other kind of absence discriminate against certain individuals because of their sex?

An affirmative answer to that question would not necessarily lead to a conclusion of illegality, because a statutory affirmative defense might justify the disparate treatment of pregnant women in certain situations. In this case, however, the company has not established any such justification. On the other hand, a negative answer to the threshold question would not necessarily defeat plaintiffs' claim because facially neutral criteria may be illegal if they have a discriminatory effect. An analysis of the effect of a company's rules relating

---

[64]*Ibid.*, at 151.

to absenteeism would be appropriate if those rules referred only to neutral criteria, such as whether an absence was voluntary or involuntary, or perhaps particularly costly. This case, however, does not involve rules of that kind.

Rather, the rule at issue places the risk of absence caused by pregnancy in a class by itself. By definition, such a rule discriminates on account of sex; for it is the capacity to become pregnant which primarily differentiates the female from the male. The analysis is the same whether the rule relates to hiring, promotion, the acceptability of an excuse for absence, or an exclusion from a disability insurance plan.[65]

Disability for Pregnancy Compensable (in New York State)

Laymen do not always easily understand why some high state court decrees cannot be appealed to or reversed by the U.S. Supreme Court. But the fact is that if a case decided by an appellate state court does not involve any issue arising under the United States Constitution, it cannot be appealed to the U.S. Supreme Court.

Such a case came before the New York State Court of Appeals shortly after the G.E. decision was handed down by the Federal High Court. New York's highest court took cognizance of the Supreme Court's holding that exclusion of pregnancy-related disability from eligibility to disability insurance benefits did not constitute a violation of Title VII of the federal Civil Rights Act. But the majority opinion subscribed to by five of the seven members of the highest New York court declared that while the pertinent provisions of the federal statute were substantially identical to those of the New York Human Rights Law, "the determination of the Supreme Court, while instructive, is not binding on our court as we now confront the contention of private employers that the provisions of our state's Disability Benefits Law excuse their failure to conform to the standard that we have held our Human Rights Law demands of public employers."

The New York State Court of Appeals had ruled in cases involving public employers that an employment policy which singles out pregnancy for treatment different from that afforded other physical impairments violates the state's Human Rights Law.[66] Two different New York State laws were invoked by the litigants in the case in point. Since 1965 the Human Rights Law has proscribed employment discrimination on account of sex by private employers as well as public employers. The Disability Benefits Law, enacted in 1949, provided that "no employee shall be entitled to benefits under

---

[65]*Ibid.*, at 161.
[66]DAILY LAB. REP. (BNA), No. 248, Dec. 23, 1976, pp. A-8, A-9.

this article . . . for any period of disability caused by or arising in connection with a pregnancy."

The successful litigants were three pregnant women who had been denied disability benefits by their private-sector employers. They, at least, and feminist crusaders for abolition of any form of sex bias in employment, would no doubt regard the majority opinion in their favor as indeed Solomonic in its reasoning. After conceding the "evident incongruity" between the two laws invoked by the claimants and their employer, the majority opinion stated: "[T]he DBL and the HRL each lay down minimum demands on employers. Whichever statute imposes the greater obligation is the one which becomes operative. In the cases before us it is in the Human Rights Law."[67]

Pregnancy Disability Amendment to Title VII

The outcries of activists over *Gilbert* and other rulings finally resulted in the passage of a pregnancy disability amendment to Title VII of the Civil Rights Act of 1964. Signed into law (P.L. 95-555) on Oct. 31, 1978, the amendment enlarged the definition of sex discrimination in the Civil Rights Act to include "pregnancy, childbirth, or related medical conditions." Henceforth pregnancy and childbirth must be treated the same as other disabilities covered in fringe-benefit plans. The amendment prohibits refusal to hire or termination on the grounds of pregnancy, bars mandatory leaves for pregnant women arbitrarily set at a certain time in pregnancy, and protects job rights of women on pregnancy leave.

Sex Equality for Pension Plan Contributors

It is a violation of Title VII of the Civil Rights Act for any employer, public or private, to require female employees to make larger contributions than male employees for an equal amount of pension benefits. The U.S. Supreme Court so ruled in a 6-2 decision handed down on April 25, 1978.[68] As to the facts, the pension plan under review compelled female employees to contribute from their wages to a compulsory retirement fund 15 percent more than men to receive the same benefits. Their employer's contention was

---

[67]Brooklyn Union Gas Company v. New York State Human Rights Appeal Board, et al.: American Airlines, Inc. v. New York State Human Rights Appeal Board, et al.; State Division of Human Rights v. Crouse-Irving Memorial Hospital, N.Y. Ct. App., Nos. 495, 496, and 497, Dec. 20, 1976, as cited in DAILY LAB. REP., No. 248, pp. A-8, A-9.

[68]City of Los Angeles v. Manhart, U.S. Sup. Ct., No. 76-1810.

that since women as a class live about five years longer than men, their higher contribution rate was justified on actuarial grounds.

Writing the majority opinion, Mr. Justice Stevens declared that the Act "precludes treatment of individuals as simply components of a racial, religious, sexual or national class." He went on to remark that "many women do not live as long as the average man and many women outlive the average man." But Justice Stevens' majority opinion stated that while they were working, "women received smaller paychecks because of their sex, but they will receive no compensating advantage when they retire."

Discretionary Authority of Congress

At the close of 1976 the Supreme Court provided a fuller indication of how it might construe present anti-sex-discrimination legislation or whatever new legislation might soon be enacted by Congress as a result of pressure from vociferous critics of its G.E. decision. The case here summarized presented a fairly narrow issue for the Court's judgment. It concerned the eligibility of divorcees who are mothers of young or disabled children for certain types of social security benefits. The Court's unanimous decision was notable, *not* for its findings of fact in the narrow issue it had to adjudicate, but for its dicta as to constitutional questions respecting congressional powers. For proper perspective of the facts, the official syllabus accompanying the full text of the case in point is quoted below.[69]

As often occurs, it is essential to examine the footnotes as well as the text of a Supreme Court decision to ascertain the full impact of the Court's rationale. Hence, it is clear that the Court did not rule out any and all eligibility of divorcees for social security benefits for any of their children. In fact, the Court noted in a footnote, the Social Security Act defines the qualification for a wife's insurance benefits as relating to a person who has been divorced but before attaining age 62 had been married to her former husband for at least 20 years. With this proviso, the Court observed that the law enables a divorced woman to receive Social Security payments for child support if she is aged 62 or over and her ex-husband retires or becomes disabled, but if she is under 62 she receives no benefits even if she has a young or disabled child in her care.

The appellee in the case had been divorced from her husband after more than 20 years of marriage, and at age 56 had applied for

---

[69]Mathews, Secretary of Health, Education, and Welfare v. DeCastro, 429 U.S. 181 (1976).

child's insurance benefits. Her application was denied by HEW pursuant to the express language of the law. She filed suit in federal district court contending a violation of the Due-Process Clause of the Fifth Amendment. The court found in her favor. But the Supreme Court reversed and did so unanimously when HEW appealed directly to it.

The Supreme Court's decision is significant primarily for its dicta connoting probable holdings in future cases involving possible violations of individuals' Fifth-Amendment rights. Some of these dicta are quoted below:

> The basic principle that must govern an assessment of any constitutional challenge to a law providing for governmental payment of monetary benefits is well established. Governmental decisions to spend money to improve the general public welfare in one way and not another are "not confined to the courts. The discretion belongs to Congress, unless the choice is clearly wrong, a display of arbitrary power, not an exercise of judgment." (Helvering v. Davis, 301 U.S. 619, 640) In enacting legislation of this kind a government does not deny equal protection "merely because the classifications made by its laws are imperfect. If the classification has some 'reasonable basis,' it does not offend the Constitution simply because the classification 'is not made with mathematical nicety or because in practice it results in some inequity.' " Dandridge v. Williams, 397 U.S. 471, 485)[70]

Most assuredly, despite caustic comments to the contrary, all nine of the Justices of the Supreme Court were not concertedly thinking like male chauvinists when they handed down their judgment in *Mathews* v. *De Castro*. They were construing a law as it was written — not how some of them may have thought it could have better coverage within constitutional boundaries. Justice Stewart virtually said as much when he explained that:

> Section 202(b)(1)(B) of the Act addresses the particular consequences for his family of a wage earner's old age or disability. Congress could rationally have decided that the resultant loss of family income, the extra expense that often attends illness and old age, and the consequent disruption of the family's economic well-being that may occur when the husband stops working justify monthly payments to a wife who together with her husband must still care for a dependent child.[71]

One does not have to accept in toto Mr. Justice Stewart's views as to the financial effects of divorce to accept the reasonableness of the following passage in his opinion:

---

[70]*Ibid.*, at 185.
[71]*Ibid.*, at 187.

Divorce by its nature works a drastic change in the economic and personal relationship between a husband and wife. Ordinarily it means that they will go their separate ways. Congress could have rationally assumed that divorced husbands and wives depend less on each other for financial and other support than do couples who stay married. The problems that a divorced wife may encounter when her former husband becomes old or disabled may well differ in kind and degree from those that a woman married to a retired or disabled husband must face. For instance, a divorced wife need not forego work in order to stay at home to care for her disabled husband. She may not feel the pinch of the extra expenses accompanying her former husband's old age or disability. In short, divorced couples typically live separate lives. It was not irrational for Congress to recognize this basic fact in deciding to defer monthly payments to divorced wives or retired or disabled wage earners until they reach the age of 62.

This is not to say that a husband's old age or disability may never affect his divorced wife. Many women receive alimony or child-support that their former husbands might not be able to pay when they stop work. But even for this group—which does not include the appellee in the present case—Congress was not constitutionally obligated to use the Social Security Act to subsidize support payments. It could rationally decide that the problems created for divorced women remained less pressing than those faced by women who continue to live with their husbands. . . . We conclude, accordingly, that the statutory classifications involved in this case are not of such an order as to infringe upon the Due Process Clause of the Fifth Amendment.[72]

Why such a comparatively lengthy review of a case that at most affects only a minuscule number of American citizens? The implications of the Court's judgment are what made it appear of great significance. It should be considered especially significant by those individuals in management, politics, or education—and private citizens—who may be inclined to believe that federal bureaucracies have the prime goal of discovering new ways to increase their authority to spend more and more for the benefit of almost every *deserving* class of citizens. Note full well that it was the U.S. Health, Education, and Welfare Department that appealed an adverse decision of a lower federal court to the High Court. And HEW won its case, thereby saving money and reducing the number of beneficiaries of government largesse.

It's entirely true, to be sure, that the number of recipients of federal funds for private purposes has multiplied for several years and so has the volume of federal litigation. According to one source, HEW employs twice as many lawyers as it did in 1970 to handle four times as many cases, with 10,000 currently pending.

---

[72]*Ibid.*, at 189.

Further, in 1976 the Labor Department had the responsibility for enforcing 134 federal statutes, compared to only about 40 in 1960. And note the following pungent and pertinent quote of a statement by Labor Department Solicitor William Kilberg: "We are so busy defending the department for what we have failed to do that we haven't gotten time to enforce what we are supposed to. At the same time we are being told we do too much."[73]

Kilberg's statement most certainly should be given heed by those who vociferously criticize the U.S. Labor Department's activities in pursuing its manifold functions as one of the several enforcement agencies not only of the Civil Rights Act but of ERISA (see Chapter 4) and OSHA (see Chapter 5) as well.

Reverse Discrimination Under Review

In June 1978 the U.S. Supreme Court came out with an extraordinarily important decision relating to affirmative action. The question at issue was, "When do affirmative action programs on behalf of women and minorities produce an end result of reverse discrimination?"

On Feb. 22, 1977, the Supreme Court announced that it would review the constitutionality of certain admission programs in a California graduate school of medicine. In 1976 the California Supreme Court held unconstitutional provisions of a preferential selection program that had resulted in rejection of a white man for admission to the school. The rejectee, Allan Bakke, instituted a court proceeding charging that he had been illegally discriminated against on account of his race. The California High Court ruled in his favor and issued a decree requiring his admission to the medical school despite the presumption that the result might be to exclude most minority groups from admission to California medical schools.

The U.S. Supreme Court's decision to review the California court's conclusion was made at the behest of the regents of the University of California. They were supported by arguments advanced by four deans of law schools affiliated with the University on the grounds that if special admission programs for minorities were declared unconstitutional, there could be virtually no admissions of minorities to their schools.

According to *New York Times* correspondent Lesley Oelsner, "The issue is one of the most controversial and difficult in civil rights today. The Court's decision to consider it sets the stage for a landmark ruling — both on the permissibility of preferential univer-

---

[73]NEWSWEEK, Jan. 10, 1977, p. 44.

sity admissions policies and also, perhaps, on the broader issue of voluntary affirmative actions in general."[74]

Not directly related to employment discrimination but still indicative of the Supreme Court's shifting views on improper racial discrimination in general was a Court ruling in March 1977 at least partially striking down one form of apparent reverse discrimination in the Social Security Act. A 5-to-4 majority of the Court held unconstitutional the portion of the Act that has been construed as precluding widowers from receiving survivors' old-age insurance benefits attributable to many of the earnings of their deceased spouses. Up to now the Act has been officially interpreted as requiring widowers to prove they had depended for a substantial part of their own incomes on their spouses' earnings in covered employment. Not so any longer, the Court now declares. This would constitute discrimination against men and women. Four of the Justices representing the majority held that the law was discriminatory against women by providing them with less protection for families than men could get with the same earnings. The fifth Justice construed the law simply as reverse discrimination against male wage earners.[75]

The Bakke Case and Its Implications for Affirmative Action

It was not until Oct. 12, 1977 that the U.S. Supreme Court proceeded to hear oral arguments in the *Bakke* case. Basic facts involved in the *Bakke* case have been summarized in a highly condensed form in *United States Law Week*. Here is what the allegations of reverse discrimination were all about:

> The University of California established its medical school at Davis in 1968. Concerned with the need to boost minority enrollment, the faculty resolved in 1968 to set up a special Task Force to fill 16 seats. The regular admissions committee continued to select 84 regular candidates. The Task Force Committee, composed mostly of minority faculty members and students, was empowered to select 16 "economically and educationally disadvantaged" applicants. In 1974, application forms were changed to add questions asking students to identify themselves by race and whether they wished to be considered as minority applicants.
>
> Allan Bakke, a civil engineer of Norwegian ancestry applied under the regular admissions procedure in 1973 and again in 1974. He was rejected on both occasions, despite high undergraduate grades and high scores in the Medical College Admissions Test.

---

[74]NEW YORK TIMES, Feb. 23, 1977, p. A12.
[75]*Ibid.*, March 3, 1977, p. 19.

Bakke also had received a favorable "benchmark" rating from the regular admissions committee, which included such factors as community involvement and character, as revealed by recommendations and a personal interview.

Bakke filed suit shortly after the second rejection. The Supreme Court of California sustained his claim, and ordered that Bakke be admitted after the school stipulated that he probably would have been admitted had the 16-seat admissions program not been in effect. The state court declared that Bakke's constitutional rights were violated by the grant of a "preference on the basis of race to persons who, by the university's own standards, are not as qualified to the study of medicine as nonminority applicants denied admission." 45 LW 2179.[76]

Presented below is an editorial summary by the *Law Week* staff. In beginning his two-hour argument Archibald Cox (representing the petitioner, the University of California Board of Regents) declared that the outcome of the case would determine "perhaps for decades" whether minorities would have equal opportunity in education. Affirmation of the state court ruling would mark a return to virtually all-white professional schools, he asserted.

Cox: "This case . . . presents a single vital question: whether a state university, which is forced by limited resources to select a relatively small number of students from a much larger number of well-qualified applicants, is free, voluntarily, to take into account the fact that a qualified applicant is black, Chicano, Asian or native American in order to increase the number of qualified members of those minority groups trained for the educated professions and participating in them — professions from which minorities were long excluded because of generations of pervasive racial discrimination. . . .

"There are three facts, realities, which dominated the situation that the Medical School at Davis had before it, and which I think must control the decision of this Court.

"The first is that the number of qualified applicants for the nation's professional schools is vastly greater than the number of places available. That is a fact and an inescapable fact. In 1975-76, for example, there were roughly 30,000 qualified applicants for admission to medical school, a much greater number of actual applicants, and there were only about 14,000 places. . . .

"The second fact, on which there is no need for me to elaborate, but it is a fact, for generations racial discrimination in the United States, much of it stimulated by unconstitutional state action, isolated certain minorities, condemned them to inferior education, and shut them out of the most important and satisfying aspects of American life, including higher education and the professions. . . .

"And then there is one third fact. There is no racially blind

---

[76]46 U.S.L.W. (BNA) 3249.

method of selection, which will enroll today more than a trickle of minority students in the nation's colleges and professions. These are the realities which the University of California at Davis Medical School faced in 1968, and which, I say, I think the Court must face when it comes to its decision.

"Until 1969, the applicants at Davis, as at most other medical schools, were chosen on the basis of scores on the medical aptitude test, their college grades, and other personal experiences and qualifications, as revealed in the application.

"The process excluded, virtually, almost all members of minority groups, even when they were fully qualified for places, because their scores, by and large, were lower on the competitive test and in college grade point averages."[77]

United States Solicitor General Wade McCree participated in the oral arguments as *amicus curiae*. So did Bakke's attorney, Reynold H. Colvin. Both were less persistently questioned by several Justices than was Cox. According to McCree, the United States entered as *amicus curiae* because Congress and the Executive Branch had many "minority-sensitive" programs which took races into account to equalize the effect of past discrimination.[78]

Allan Bakke's attorney, emphasized in his argument that the single question at issue was "the plea of an individual — Bakke — and not the broader issue of affirmative action." He said,

"It seems to me that the first thing that I ought to say to this Honorable Court is that I am Allan Bakke's lawyer and Allan Bakke is my client. And I do not say that in any formal or perfunctory way. I say that because this is a lawsuit. It was a lawsuit brought by Allan Bakke up at Woodland in Yolo county, California, in which Allan Bakke from the very beginning of this lawsuit in the first paper we ever filed stated the case. And he stated the case in terms of his individual right. He stated the case in terms of the fact that he had twice applied for admission to the Medical School at Davis and twice he had been refused, both in the year 1973 and the year 1974. And he stated in that complaint what now, some three-and-a-half years later, proves to be the very heart of the thing that we are talking about at this juncture. He stated that he was excluded from that school because that school had adopted a racial quota which deprived him of the opportunity for admission into the school. And that's where the case started. It started with a suit against the University.

"He stated three grounds upon which he felt that he had been deprived of the right to admission to that school: the Equal Protection Clause of the Fourteenth Amendment, the Privileges and Immunities portion of the California Constitution, and Title VI, 42 United

---

[77]*Ibid.*, 3249-3250.
[78]*Ibid.*, 3253.

States Code 2000(d). And those were the three grounds upon which he placed his complaint from the very beginning."[79]

On Oct. 17, 1977 the Court directed the parties in the case to file supplemental briefs discussing Title VI of the Civil Rights Act of 1964 as it applied to this case. As explained earlier in this chapter, it is Title VII of the 1964 statute that makes it unlawful for employers to engage in any form of discrimination in terms of employment because of an individual's race, color, religion, sex, or national origin. Title VI prohibits such discrimination in all programs or activities which receive federal financial aid.

The Court's directive respecting the application of Title VI seemed to imply that some of the Justices were concerned with more than the basic constitutional question of whether the university's denial of Bakke's admission to medical school had violated the Equal Protection clause of the Fourteenth Amendment. As asserted in the Justice Department's supplemental brief: "The threshold question here is whether this Court could or should decide whether Title VI either prohibits or authorizes the special admissions program." The brief's concluding statement was that Title VI "does not prohibit petitioner from voluntarily adopting any minority-sensitive admissions program that is consistent with the Fourteenth Amendment." The petitioner's supplemental brief supported the same conclusion. As was inevitable, Bakke's counsel stood pat on his original position.

Presumably after many months of agonized reflection and research the Supreme Court in six separate opinions finally reached a verdict on the Bakke case on June 28, 1978. Bakke was ordered to be admitted to the Davis Medical School.

Now for the verdict in the Bakke case: Who won and who lost? It may be many months or years before we know for sure.

A Box-Score Summary

Forty thousand words that encompass the six separate opinions of the Supreme Court as promulgated in the decisions of June 28, 1978, leave open many questions which have to be answered through further litigation. For those in personnel management or with educational responsibilities in the public and private sector who desperately need to know, *Newsweek* provided an illuminating box-score summary:

---

[79]*Ibid.*, 3253-3254.

Summary*

In a complicated split decision, the nine Justices of the Supreme Court issued six separate opinions that dealt with three main issues.

How They Voted

	Yes	No	Not Relevant In This Case
Should Bakke be admitted to medical school?	5 Powell, Burger, Stevens, Rehnquist, Stewart	4 Brennan, White, Marshall Blackmun	—
Was the racial "quota" system at Davis Medical School acceptable in deciding who should be admitted?	4 Brennan, White, Marshall Blackmun	5 Powell, Burger, Stevens, Rehnquist, Stewart	
Can an applicant's race ever be considered in deciding who should be admitted?	5 Powell,** Brennan, White, Marshall, Blackmun		4 Burger, Stevens, Rehnquist, Stewart

*Newsweek, July 10, 1978, p. 21. Chart by Fenga & Freyer, N.Y., N.Y.

**Powell said race can be considered if a school is seeking a diverse student body. The other four said race can be considered to redress past discrimination or to increase the number of minority doctors.

Immediately following the Supreme Court's landmark decision on Bakke, there were numerous commentaries on television and in the press by legal scholars and constitutional lawyers, including protagonists for and against civil rights. It is too soon to separate the wheat from the chaff. Nevertheless here is a brief summary of the views of a legal authority of impeccable standing, Paul Freund, emeritus professor of law at Harvard Law School, which appeared in the *New York Times* on July 9, 1978 (p. E 17):

> Hard cases often make fuzzy law. We do know that Mr. Bakke is entitled to enroll for his medical course, but beyond that the Court has given us little definitive guidance in the field of racial preference. Indeed the very judgment in favor of Mr. Bakke rested on a kind of minority preference: A minority of four (Justices Stevens, Stewart, and Rehnquist, and Chief Justice Burger), who thought that Title VI of the Civil Rights Act protected Mr. Bakke, joining a minority of one, Justice Powell, who thought that the Constitution protected him against the special features of the admissions system of the University of California at Davis.

But Justice Powell was prepared to accept a system that takes race into account as a factor in selection, and apparently even numerical goals where there has been prior illegal discrimination. The other four Justices — Brennan, White, Marshall and Blackmun — who fully accepted the Davis plan, undertook to summarize the composite position of themselves and Justice Powell: "Government may take race into account when it acts not to demean or insult any racial group, but to remedy disadvantages cast on minorities by past racial prejudice, at least when appropriate findings have been made by judicial, legislative, or administrative bodies with competence to act in this area."

By not specifying the nature of the "remedy" or the "appropriate findings" this statement might appear incontestable. Nevertheless, Justice Stevens warned that only a majority can rightly interpret the meaning of a decision. Fortunately, clarification of the law is not the only mission of the Supreme Court.

What does the case portend for the future? The degree race will continue to be decisive in admissions depends on the weight actually given to this factor. On that crucial point there is no mandate from the Court, nor could there well be, given the nuances and complexities of the selection process and the ambiguities of the moral issue. Aside from education, in the employment field for example, the standards set by the composite majority should be satisfied by the prevalence of past discrimination, the urgency of reducing inner-city unemployment, and the presence of legislative or administrative findings on these issues.

Of course four members of the Court have not spoken on those questions. For them, Justice Stevens explained that only if the University prevailed on the statutory issue (Title VI) would it be necessary to address the ultimate issue of the equal-protection clause of the 14th Amendment. But the University did in fact prevail on the statutory issue, and still four members declined to commit themselves.

In future cases, if even one of the four uncommitted Justices were to adopt the broadly-permissive position of the four for whom Justice Brennan spoke, the reservations in Justice Powell's opinion would no longer be crucial.

But all of this parsing, patching and predicting really misses the significance of the Bakke case. Its real meaning is that we are dealing with a complex problem whose outer contours can be drawn by judges but whose resolution lies within a wide spectrum of moral and practical choices to be made by ourselves, choices that must consider not only individual rights but the health of the society within which those rights are asserted.

Nearly a month went by after the Bakke verdict before the Department of Justice came out with an official interpretation. What it thought the Supreme Court meant was to sanction affirmative action programs where apparently essential to counteract results of prior discrimination. As noted on page one of the July 26 *New York Times,* the Justice Department announced that the Bakke decision did not require a public agency to be "color blind" and did not disturb previous rulings that require such agencies to take positive steps to remedy the effects of past discrimination.

At this juncture the co-authors are constrained to depart from their prior posture of objectivity. Call it anarchistic, if you will, to say that perhaps less legislation and less government control are necessary to achieve genuine equal employment opportunity rather than more. To quote Scripture, "God loveth a cheerful giver" (II Cor. 9:7). Society's proper goal of unrestricted equal educational and employment opportunity will never be fully realized until top management, personnel administrators, and others in authority decide of their own volition to do what is morally and ethically right.

Religion and National Origin

Neither the EEOC nor the OFCC administrators have considered it necessary to expatiate on how they have chosen to interpret the law's barriers on employment discrimination on account of religion or national origin. The OFCC in fact confines the subjects of both religion and national origin to a single brief policy pronouncement.

On the issue of religious discrimination, the most significant passage in the EEOC's guideline, which can be found in the Code of Federal Regulations (C.F.R.), 1605.1(b), simply reads:

> The Commission believes that the duty not to discriminate on religious grounds . . . includes an obligation on the part of the employer to make reasonable accommodations to the religious needs of employees and prospective employees where such accommodations can be made without undue hardship on the conduct of the employer's business. Such undue hardship, for example, may exist where the employee's work cannot be performed by another employee of substantially similar qualifications during the period of absence of the Sabbath observer [or of some other day of the week or special religious holidays]

With respect to discrimination because of national origin, the EEOC gives as an example of unlawful employment practices the following passage at C.F.R., §1606.1(b):

> The use of tests in the English language where the English language is not that person's first language or mother tongue, and where English language is not a requirement of the work to be performed; denial of equal opportunity to persons married to or associated with persons of a specific national origin; denial of equal opportunity because of membership in lawful organizations identified with or seeking to promote the interests of national groups; denial of equal opportunity because of attendance at schools or churches com-

monly utilized by persons of a given national origin; denial of equal opportunity because their name or that of their spouse reflects a certain national origin, and denial of equal opportunity to persons who as a class of persons tend to fall outside of national norms for height and weight where such height and weight specifications are not necessary for the performance of the work involved.

In its condensed guideline on both religious and ethnic discrimination, C.F.R. §60.50.1(b), the OFCC singles out the main categories for which protection against unlawful discrimination is needed:

> Members of various religious and ethnic groups, primarily but not exclusively of Eastern, Middle and Southern European ancestry, such as Jews, Catholics, Italians, Greeks, and Slavic groups [who] continue to be excluded from executive, middle-management, and other job levels because of discrimination based upon their religion and/or national origin.

The OFCC guideline goes further in delineating employers' obligations to adjust their operations to the needs of members of particular religious sects. It does so by stating at C.F.R. §60.50.3 that:

> an employer must make reasonable accommodations to the religious observances and practices of an employee or prospective employee who regularly observes Friday evening and Saturday, or some other day of the week as his Sabbath and/or who observes certain religious holidays during the year and who is conscientiously opposed to performing work or engaging in similar activity on such days, when such accommodations can be made without undue hardship on the conduct of the employer's business.

Note well: The guideline just quoted ends with a sentence giving grounds for exculpatory considerations. It reads: "In determining the extent of an employer's obligations under this section, at least the following factors shall be considered: (a) business necessity, (b) financial costs and expenses, and (c) resulting personnel problems."

In November 1976, the Supreme Court for the second time in five years split in a vote on Sabbath observance, thus affirming the Sixth Circuit's ruling that Parker Seal Company, in discharging a foreman for refusing Saturday work, had violated Title VII of the Civil Rights Act (*Parker Seal Company* v. *Cummins,* 429 U.S. 65).

According to the 1972 amendments to Title VII of the Civil Rights Act of 1964, an employer must within reason accommodate employee religious practices unless this would cause the company undue hardship. Parker Seal claimed that for over a year it had attempted to accommodate the religious practices of the foreman in question, a member of the World Wide Church of God. The Sixth Circuit held that the company had failed to establish the "undue hardship" principle. In dissent, Judge Celebrezze objected that the 1972 amendment to Title VII was unconstitutional since it established preferential treatment for certain individuals on the basis of religion.

The Supreme Court tie vote affirming the Sixth Circuit decision sets no precedent and leaves the present law unclear. Still before the Court in late 1976 was the Eighth Circuit decision in *Hardison* v. *Trans World Airlines, Inc.* (11 FEP Cases 1121, 527 F.2d 33). In *Hardison*, the joint union/employer position was that allowing the plaintiff's Sabbath practices violated the seniority clause of the collective bargaining agreement. In June 1977 the Supreme Court affirmed this position, holding that the employer had made a reasonable attempt to provide for the plaintiff's beliefs.[80]

Employment Testing Guidelines

Section 703(h) of the Civil Rights Act declares that it shall *not* be an unlawful employment practice for an employer

> to give and act upon the result of any professionally developed ability test provided that such test, its administration or action upon the results is not designed, intended or used to discriminate because of race, color, religion, sex or national origin.

The meaning of this section has constantly been subjected to administrative interpretation or judicial review with disparate results.

It was not so much the extremely broad EEOC interpretation of what have to be deemed as selection tests as it was the extraordinarily rigorous specifications for validation of tests that engendered the most complaints about the EEOC selection guidelines.[81]

Consider the views on this issue as expressed by the joint authors of an exhaustive and impartial compendium covering in some 1400 pages about every consequential aspect of the employment discrimination law. The authors are Barbara L. Schlei, formerly counsel, Los Angeles District Office, EEOC, and Paul Grossman, a partner in California law firm who specializes in representing management on all aspects of labor law, with emphasis on employment discrimination matters. Here quoted are some of their comments:

---

[80]Trans World Airlines v. Hardison, U.S. SupCt, Nos. 75-1126 and 75-1385, June 16, 1977.

[81]See the E.E.O.C. guidelines reissued in Nov. 1976, 41 Fed. Reg. 51,984 (1976).

The Supreme Court's holdings in *Griggs* and *Moody* with respect to the application of the EEOC testing guidelines to scored tests, and the Supreme Court's holding in *Griggs* with respect to objective criteria, may induce many employers to rely more heavily on subjective criteria for employment decisions. There is a serious question as to whether such a trend is to the benefit of the groups supposedly protected by the Supreme Court decisions. There is a further question as to whether or not the use of subjective criteria, no matter how structured, puts the employer in a more defensible position. In short, the employer's quandary has become exceedingly difficult. Validating a test in accordance with the EEOC's guidelines is extremely expensive at best and, in many cases, economically prohibitive. Expense aside, such validation may well be practically or technically impossible. The then chief of the Research Studies Division of the EEOC, who was principally responsible for drafting the EEOC selection guidelines, has testified that he is aware of only two or three instances where criterion-related validation studies have been made which met all the requirements of the guidelines. For most employers, validation in accordance with the EEOC guidelines is impossible.

A possible result is that employers will be led to make employment decisions primarily utilizing ratios of minority female and Caucasian male employees. Whether this is desirable is, of course, a serious question. The only possible solution would appear to be a relaxation of the requirements with respect to demonstrating job-relatedness (be it with respect to scored tests, unscored objective criteria, or the utilization of subjective criteria), so that the utilization of such criteria will withstand attack if structured in a professional manner to predict job capabilities to the extent practicably feasible within the limits of our knowledge, about selection procedures. The Supreme Court seems to be moving in this direction, based on its decision in *Washington* v. *Davis* [12 FEP 1415 (1976)].[82]

Now that the uniform guidelines have actually been adopted, the debate over validity may very well cool down. The following passages from the uniform guidelines are of particular concern to private-sector employers: §2, *Scope;* §3, *Discrimination Defined;* §5, *General Standards for Validity Studies,* §7, *Use of Other Validity Studies;* §13, *Affirmative Action.* [83]

The EEOC "Mess"

The liberal *New York Times* editorial writers have joined the claque of conservative corporate spokesmen who have been deploring for some years what a *Times* editorial recently characterized as

---

[82]Barbara Schlei and Paul Grossman, EMPLOYMENT DISCRIMINATION LAW (Washington: The Bureau of National Affairs, Inc., 1976), p. 181. The reference in the quote to *Griggs* relates to the Supreme Court decision cited elsewhere in this chapter as the *Duke Power Company* case. The *Moody* case is more familiarly known as *Albemarle Paper Co.* v. *Moody,* decided by the Supreme Court in 1975 (10 FEP 1181).

[83]43 Fed. Reg. 38,296 – 38,300 (1978).

"The Equal Employment Mess." Excerpts from the editorial as quoted below may give to unbiased analysts a good idea of the manifold problems confronted by the most conscientious corporate executives in striving for full compliance with the Civil Rights Act and related statutes:

> The E.E.O.C. was created by the Civil Rights Act of 1964 and charged with wiping out discrimination in employment. Orginally it was given the authority to investigate and conciliate individual complaints of discrimination. It had no enforcement power. Later it began to look for patterns of discrimination and still later, in 1972, it was finally given the power to sue employers to end discrimination and to obtain relief for past discrimination.
>
> The initial failure to give it enforcement powers, and the creation of five presidentially appointed commissioners instead of one, have been compounded by subsequent bumbling, bureaucratic tragedies and the inattention of three Presidents. E.E.O.C. has become a mess. The most celebrated measure of its failure is its Everest-like backlog of cases. In 1970 it stood at 25,000, by 1974 it had climbed to 98,000 and it is now about 130,000.
>
> One of the major problems has been an incredible turnover in chairmen — there have been six in twelve years. The other commissioners, nominally high Federal officials, have so little to do that bickering and backbiting have become common. All of this has had its effects on the ag ncy staff: administrative chaos and an ugly lack of professionalism. Black and Spanish-speaking employees are said to attribute racial and ethnic motives to policy disagreements; the investigative and legal staffs are so unsympathetic to each other that it is extraordinarily difficult properly to prepare cases for trial.
>
> However the restructuring turns out, the new chairman will need help. Larger, rather than diminished responsibilities would seem to be the logical result of any reorganization. There must be a commitment from the Administration to keep the agency's personnel out of politics and to restructure radically its internal workings. There must also be enough funds and staff to clean up the backlog and to develop a rational program.
>
> Most of all, what is needed is serious and sustained Presidential attention. Social distress is nowhere more clear than in dollars lost and hopes dashed from job discrimination. It is an evil the President [Carter] wishes to combat. But until he reforms E.E.O.C. he will be doing so with a wooden sword.[84]

The "reformation" of EEOC commenced in early 1977 with the appointment of a new chairman, Eleanor Holmes Norton of New York. If anything, Mrs. Norton is most likely to bear down more heavily on management and to seek more stringent enforcement of EEOC policies and guidelines, announced in previous years but often more honored during the Nixon administration in the

---

[84]NEW YORK TIMES, Feb. 13, 1977, p. 20.

breach than in the observance. As for Mrs. Norton's outstanding record as a public servant and civil rights crusader (see Chapter 8, p. 437), the probabilities are that Chairman Norton will reaffirm and diligently endeavor to get observance of the guidelines for the thousands of employers subject to the requirements of Executive Orders 11246 and 11375 prescribing that they make affirmative action commitments.

The proposed new uniform guidelines on employee selection procedures represent a giant step toward wiping out the EEOC mess referred to above. And the new head, Eleanor Holmes Norton has additional plans for reform, some of which were summarized in a Jan. 16, 1978, *Newsweek* article. The article noted Norton's plans to shift the agency's over-all emphasis. It went on to report that "the EEOC is abandoning the practice of expanding individual complaints into class-action suits—a frequent nuisance to business. Instead, Norton hopes to root out 'systematic patterns and practices' of discrimination by monitoring corporate behavior. Then, without waiting for individual complaints, the EEOC will file a carefully formulated class-action suit against a company or industry. 'I am convinced,' [said Norton,] 'that only by an effective attack on entire systems that discriminate can we have any significant impact.' "

A Question for Private-Sector Management

How in the light of the confusing and conflicting dicta of the courts, the EEOC, and other agencies can employers make certain that their work force can be maintained and built up to provide a proper heterogeneous composition? Thus far there is no certain answer to this question. In fact, the clouded crystal ball became even more murky when the National Labor Relations Board in February 1977 departed from the side of the EEOC "angels." The Board, like other government institutions, has often been thought to keep a finger in the dike of the great silent majority of American citizenry. Thus, the Board by a 4-to-1 vote abandoned the position it had taken in 1974 that it could and would evaluate contentions of union discrimination on account of race or sex prior to certifying a union as the bargaining agent for an appropriate bargaining unit. The latest ruling of the Board would delay action on charges of illegal discrimination by a unit until unfair labor practice charges were dealt with *after* certification. It was the conclusion of the Board majority in February 1977 that neither the Fifth Amendment nor the Taft-Hartley Act mandated the Board to adjudicate discrimination issues before certification of a union as the bargaining agent for an appropriate unit.

This ruling is not the only one in which the Board has been at cross-purposes with the EEOC. Although the Board has the exclusive authority to decide what constitute appropriate bargaining units, the EEOC has urged employers to defy Board certification rulings when considered essential to enlarge job openings for minority groups. Indeed, EEOC in one of its official publications has gone so far as to suggest that individuals expressly excluded from a bargaining unit, and thus from coverage by a union contract, be offered positions covered by the contract. For other specific illustrations of the manifest determination by the EEOC to assert its superior authority over employment practices that conceivably could be held discriminatory, see the passage headed "Continuing Dilemmas for Management" in Chapter 8 (p. 437).

Some Aids for Determining EEO Obligations

Should personnel administrators and their legal counsel desire to research the administrative and court decisions involving their affirmative action obligations, we recommend use of the exhaustive work by Schlei and Grossman, *Employment Discrimination Law,* which has drawn on the views of outstanding EEO specialists throughout the country. [85] For EEOC official advice, not yet, if ever to be repudiated by the present board members of this agency, there can be no substitute for continued references to the two-volume guidebook for employers entitled, *Affirmative Action and Equal Employment,* widely distributed when first issued in January 1974.[86] It is Volume I of the guidebook that enumerates in detail what the Commission then construed as management's obligations to comply with each of the various federal and state laws "requiring equal employment and affirmative action." Volume II contains appendices and tables.

For starters, we suggest, however, a highly compressed manual, *Equal Employment Opportunity, An Executive's Guide to Compliance,* written by authorities in EEO compliance, one of them an attorney who specializes in labor and equal opportunity law. In 1976 the authors wrote, "A series of multi-million-dollar awards, out-of-court settlements and related agreements setting

---

[85]See Schlei and Grossman.

[86]Equal Employment Opportunity Commission, AFFIRMATIVE ACTION AND EQUAL EMPLOYMENT: A GUIDEBOOK FOR EMPLOYERS (2 volumes; Washington: U.S. Government Printing Office, 1974).

new patterns for future employment, training and promotion have made EEO considerations a major factor in corporate performance. Still to be decisively tested in the courts are interpretations of the law that may profoundly alter fringe benefit arrangements."[87]

The authors of the guidebook get down to brass tacks when they note:

> Various government agencies cannot be expected to give much actual help, so it is important for the executive to become familiar with the fundamental requirements of the applicable statutes, executive orders and regulations. Responsibility for implementing EEO policies and especially the development of an affirmative action program is the employer's *alone*. [Here the authors seem to disagree with the EEOC itself, which has charged labor unions with the duty to assure that their contracts conform to the nondiscriminatory mandates of the Civil Rights Act and related statutes.] With respect to affirmative action programs, the government has published eight basic considerations and EEOC has prepared a model plan.
>
> But this plan is still far from being tailored to a specific company's needs.[88]

The authors suggest some sources of outside assistance that personnel officers may contact in developing a company's affirmative action program. For instance, they point out that:

> If the company's selection criteria have not yet been professionally validated the American Psychological Association can supply a list of experts to help insure that criteria are non-discriminatory and job-related. Organizations such as the National Urban League and the American Association of University Women can assist in identifying schools and other institutions that can provide minority and female job applicants.[89]

Among the more sagacious advice offered by the authors is the following, which merits italicizing herein:

> *Remember: before approaching a government compliance agency for help that there is no guarantee of confidentiality for the information supplied voluntarily. The best course of action is to work with managers, counsel and outside specialists as needed in solving EEO problems.*[90]

DISCRIMINATORY MANAGEMENT-UNION AGREEMENT

Pitfalls to be avoided by employers in adapting personnel policies to the often vague requirements of the Civil Rights Act can be

[87]EQUAL EMPLOYMENT OPPORTUNITY: AN EXECUTIVE'S GUIDE TO COMPLIANCE (New York: Management/Employee Relations Council, a Division of Hill and Knowlton, 1976).
[88]*Ibid.*
[89]*Ibid.*
[90]*Ibid.*

further illustrated by one more important case example. It was the *effect* in actual operation, rather than the purpose of the departmental seniority provisions, in the union contract of one of Continental Can Company's plants in Virginia that caused a U.S. district court to hold both the company and the union in violation of the statute. There was no contention that the seniority arrangement in the contract was in itself violative of the law. It was, however, the contention of the Department of Justice, in prosecuting the case against the company and the union, that because both parties to the contract had applied its provisions for departmental seniority in such a way *before* the passage of the Civil Rights Act as to produce discrimination against Negroes, the continued adherence to the specific terms of the seniority provisions was illegal. It ordered the company and the union to replace department seniority with a plant-wide seniority system that imposed an obligation on both parties to give full credit for total length of service at the plant "in all areas where Negro employees have been denied the opportunity to accumulate department seniority by the Company's past discriminatory assignment practices."

Then the district court proceeded drastically to limit the sweep of its ruling by stating:

> However, the Company is not required to forego its legitimate interest in maintaining the skill and efficiency of its labor force and the safety of its operations. Title VII merely requires the removal of any procedures, standards or other structural impediments which are not required by overriding business necessity, but which serve to delay the attainment by Negroes of jobs, generally as good as held by white contemporaries, or which force Negroes to pay a price for those opportunities.[91]

The reference to the payment of a price necessitates a brief comment. Prior to the enactment of the Civil Rights Act, Negroes at this plant had been virtually excluded from employment in traditional all-white production lines. And upon being granted the right of transfer to these lines, they were required by the applicable contract to suffer a reduction in pay and a loss of accumulated department seniority. This was what the court held to be a violation of the Act.

COMPANY CIVIL RIGHTS POLICIES OVER AND ABOVE THE LAW

Admittedly what follows does not constitute a strictly objective exposition of how civil rights legislation affects nearly all American

---

[91]U.S. v. Continental Can Co., 2 FEP 1044 (Dist. Ct. E. Va. 1970).

employers. Were the present authors to come out foursquare in favor of the platform of the more militant women's organizations, it would be less than honest. We think that management should concentrate on obliteration of racial discrimination. That's a hard enough task. It in our view should not be subordinated to desperate attempts to match up all jobs for men and women on virtually a one-to-one basis. What can and should employers seek to accomplish over and above the law to obliterate racial prejudices? An influential, distinguished spokesman for the NAACP, Jack Greenberg, has identified the biggest problems in an idealistic statement fraught with some pessimism.

Greenberg wrote in 1976:

> The moral legitimacy of affirmative action and quotas favoring racial minorities must be assessed in a social and historical context, in the light of the many conflicting values that our society holds.
>
> Traditionally, we profess reliance upon grades, scores and experience as bases upon which to assign jobs or admit to schools those who by these prevailing measures of competence are said to be most qualified.

> *   *   *   *   *

> Seniority rights advance individual security, worker satisfaction and job loyalty by promoting older workers although younger persons may be objectively more qualified, while, paradoxically, compulsory retirement favors younger persons over older, experienced, and perhaps more competent workers.

> *   *   *   *   *

> The mere assertion of new policy with respect to black citizens has not adequately changed the social situation. To select someone for employment or school on the basis of race, as a means of breaking the cycle of inferior education, poverty, unemployment, and damaged families, has at least as great moral justification as the many criteria we use other than so-called merit. [92]

As the late Whitney M. Young, Jr., wrote in 1969:

> Many corporations are now willing to become involved in social problems and to step up hiring of black workers. Some do so for "fire insurance" — they don't want to be hit by riots. . . . Some know that the only way they can attract the bright college graduates who will be their future managers is to give them a chance to participate in social change. . . .
>
> Whatever the reason, the business community is beginning to accept the responsibilities that go with its power and status. . . .
>
> Even with this new-found concern, however, business' involvement in social issues is not on a scale commensurate with its

---

[92]NEW YORK TIMES, Feb. 7, 1976, p. 21.

enormous stake in their solution. Too often the reason for this is not the lack of will or even a failure to understand the depth of the problem; it is simply not knowing what to do.

Whitney Young, Jr., was not a black extremist. He was the highly respected Executive Director of the National Urban League, advisor to and confidant of Presidents of the United States and to hundreds of leading corporation officials. Young's sage advice to corporate management he has summarized pungently as follows:

The obvious place to start is in hiring and personnel practices. HIRE NEGROES should replace the traditional THINK signs in executive offices. It should be the credo of every personnel department that spent such time and energy in *not* hiring black workers in the past. Hire Negroes—not just the Phi Beta Kappa from the Harvard Business School, and not just the beautiful secretary who looks like Lena Horne. Hire dumb Negroes; hire mediocre Negroes. I run into dumb white people and mediocre white people every day; they have jobs, sometimes pretty good ones. There is no reason why average and below-average Negroes shouldn't have jobs too. So long as a company is just looking for a couple of not-too-black "Exhibit A's," it's not being serious about changing its hiring policies—and it isn't fooling anybody either. If every large employer were to hire two new black workers for every hundred men it now employs—whether it "needed" these new men or not—the burden would be small for each company, and they would end unemployment while coming closer to the goal of a racially balanced work force.[93]

As for gratuitous advice, we would not presume to urge any employer to hire unneeded workmen. We would suggest, however, that heeding Young's advice about racial nondiscrimination in employment practices makes good economic and social sense and would go far to assume good-faith compliance with civil rights legislation.

---

[93]Whitney M. Young, Jr., BEYOND RACISM (New York: McGraw-Hill Book Co., 1969), p. 207. Copyright © 1969, by Whitney M. Young, Jr. Used with permission of McGraw-Hill Book Co.

CHAPTER 4

Employee Benefits and Insurance

"With 20 to 35 percent of total employee compensation going into benefits, [benefits] have become a major business cost." So stated E. S. Willis, General Electric Company's Benefits Manager, in 1968. He also pointed out that employee benefits in the aggregate "generally exceed the costs of annual plant and equipment additions, or taxes, or dividends to shareholders. Next to direct pay and cost of materials, benefits will undoubtedly represent a larger expenditure year in and year out than any other cost of doing business."[1]

Willis was so right. By 1977 employee benefit costs, particularly in large, unionized companies, had increased by 25 percent or more. A 1975 survey instituted by the Chamber of Commerce of the United States disclosed that for the 761 reporting companies, benefit payments averaged 35.4 percent of payroll. The average benefit payment per employee was nearly $4,000.

To be sure, the figures just cited were obtained from a relatively small cross-section of American business. It is to be presumed that the companies were big companies with advanced and liberal personnel policies and, typically, ones that had contractual relations with unions representing hourly workers. In the primary metal industries, which would include steel companies, the amount of employee benefits expressed as a percentage of payroll was 40.6 percent. For companies making chemicals and allied products, the percentage was 42.2 percent.

With respect to the breakdown of benefit payments the 1975 survey showed the following:

Benefit Payments	Percent of Total
Employer's share only of legally required payments	8.0
Pension, insurance, and other agreed-upon payments (employer's share only)	11.6

---

[1] E. S. Willis, *The Job of the Benefits Manager,* in EMPLOYEE BENEFIT PLAN REVIEW (Chicago: Charles D. Spencer and Associates, 1968), p. 3.

Benefit Payments	Percent of Total
Paid rest period, lunch period, etc.	3.6
Vacations, holidays, sick leave, etc.	10.1
Profit sharing, bonuses, etc.	2.1
Total	35.4

Nearly all types of benefits available to employees of American business enterprises are subject to some form of government regulation. Even plans that have been developed voluntarily and are administered privately by management may be subject to public regulation, at least for tax purposes. Additionally, there are the benefit programs that are either made mandatory through federal or state legislation or that have been established and are administered directly by federal or state agencies as a result of legislative enactments.

Employee benefit plans affected or controlled by legislation include those providing payments to employees, their dependents, or survivors for such purposes as pensions, life insurance, hospital and medical expenses, nonoccupational accidents and illnesses, and unemployment insurance. Then, too, there is workers' compensation insurance for job-related accidents and occupational ailments. Workers' compensation insurance constitutes such a separate and complex category of the type of benefits required by law that this subject is dealt with separately and at length in Chapter 5.

THE SOCIAL SECURITY ACT

It would be utterly unrealistic for employers engaged in private enterprises to develop employee pension plans or plans for unemployment and disability benefits without taking into account the elaborate programs for mitigating the financial risks of old age, death, unemployment, and disability fostered under the Social Security Act.

Management has to concern itself primarily with the social insurance features of the law applicable to employees generally rather than with the Act's provisions relating to aid to the indigent, the aged, the blind, and dependent children. From the inception of the government programs instituted upon the passage of the Act in 1935, these noninsurance plans went far to cope with the distress of millions of Depression victims. They have for the most part been expanded over the years and still represent a major portion of the direct cost of the entire system.

Old-Age Assistance Distinguished From Old-Age Insurance

To the extent that employers in the private sector maintain pension plans for their own employees, which in conjunction with the old-age insurance benefits payable under the Act provide adequate incomes for the employees upon retirement, the governmental old-age assistance program may seem to be of small concern to management. There should, however, be an awareness of what this program encompasses. Over the years it has provided many billions of dollars that have been allocated to the states for disbursement to indigent residents aged 65 or older, in the form of regular monthly allotments to aid such residents in meeting their minimum subsistence needs. Old-age assistance benefits are payable by the states to recipients regardless of whether they have ever had gainful employment in private enterprise or the public sector. The precise amounts are set by the staffs of the state agencies who are delegated to administer this part of the Social Security Act (Title I). Currently the monthly old-age assistance payments range from about $50 to more than $300. There is nothing in the federal law that precludes state agencies, upon determination of need, from paying to retired employees receiving old-age insurance benefits monthly supplemental payments as old-age assistance in amounts substantially greater than the insurance benefits to which they have a statutory right.

Long-Range Objectives of Old-Age Insurance

One of the original objectives of the Act's old-age insurance provisions was to provide ultimately some mitigation for the catastrophic unemployment situation prevailing at the time of its enactment. This obviously was a long-range objective, for the statute stipulated that no benefits would be payable before 1942, nearly seven years after the passage of the law. In any event, sponsors of the Act thought that unemployment would be markedly reduced by the withdrawal from the labor market of large numbers of workers upon reaching age 65 and thus becoming eligible for old-age insurance benefits. In 1939 the law was amended to permit benefits to be payable in 1940 rather than in 1942. Nevertheless, barely 100,000 employees eligible for these benefits actually retired in 1940. One obvious reason for the paucity of retirees was that the average monthly benefit paid in 1940 was only $22.60. The maximum monthly benefit payable under the law as first enacted was $85, and this could be received only by persons who had been covered by the Act for more than 40 years.

The concept that federal old-age insurance benefits afford a means for curtailing the nation's work force and thus presumably alleviating unemployment still remains as one of the basic rationales of the Act. Hence, the law as it stands in 1978 still prohibits persons of retirement age who are eligible for old-age insurance benefits financed in part by their taxes, from collecting all their benefits if they continue in private employment or self-employment and receive substantial earnings therefrom. Not until covered employees have attained the age of 72 do they become entitled to their full benefits if they have stayed on their jobs or engaged in any other fairly remunerative occupation while between the ages of 65 and 72.

The second and much more important objective of the old-age insurance provisions of the Act was to minimize the need for public or private assistance to elderly persons by providing the great bulk of the previously employed population with an assured, albeit small, regular income on retirement. The framers of the original law and the sponsors of repeated amendments have always assumed that employees of private enterprises would have to continue to rely on, as major sources of income after retirement, their own savings and investments, augmented by pensions paid under privately administered company or union pension plans, or participation in other types of long-range joint or individual thrift programs. In other words, when the benefit scales were first fixed and then recurrently raised — with or without corresponding increases in the employer and employee taxes to support the system — there was never any realistic expectation that the levels of old-age insurance benefits would be sufficient in and of themselves adequately to support wage earners and their dependents after retirement. (Nothing in the law, incidentally, either supports or negates the old world tradition or the erstwhile American principle of rugged individualism which contemplated that gainfully employed adults should bear some responsibility for supporting their aged and indigent relatives.)

Present Old-Age Insurance Rates

Accepted actuarial principles have been observed generally in the formulation of the benefit structure and the combined employer-employee federal taxes levied to finance the old-age insurance system. Other considerations nevertheless have assumed much importance to the Act's framers and administrators. Indubitably, sociological and political issues have influenced Congress in making numerous changes in the law year after year. Major changes have included expansion of the coverage of wage-earner groups and the self-employed, provisions for additional benefits for spouses and dependents, very substantial increases in benefit rates to keep them at least partially attuned to inflation, and, likewise, very substantial upward adjustments in employer-employee tax rates.

The Social Security Administration has given this brief but by no means complete explanation of the rationale of the benefit structure:

> Benefits are based on the worker's average monthly earnings as computed under the law, except for the special fixed-rate benefits payable to certain age-72 persons. The amount of the worker's average monthly earnings is affected by the worker's level of earnings (up to the maximum creditable in a year) and, over the long run, the proportion of his potential lifetime that he spent in covered employment. In the interest of social adequacy, the worker with low earnings gets a larger cash benefit in relation to his earnings than the higher paid worker, and dependents' and survivors' protection is provided without additional cost to the worker with dependents.[2]

The term "maximum creditable earnings" as used by the Social Security Administration is something less than unambiguous. Actually, it is the employee's taxable earnings rather than his total earnings in his years of covered employment that control the amount of his old-age insurance benefits. The maximum annual earnings of any wage earner that are creditable for the purpose of computing his benefits have been repeatedly upped. So have the maximum earnings that are subject to the federal taxes on employers and employees for social security financing purposes.

The Social Security Administration has quite properly given a lucid explanation as to why newly retired workers usually cannot receive the maximum benefits payable under the law. Quoted below is the official explanation:

> Some people think that if they've always earned the maximum amount covered by social security they will get the highest benefits shown on the chart. This isn't so. For people reaching 65 in 1977, maximum monthly benefits are $437.10 for a man and $447.40 for a woman. The reason is that the maximum amount of earnings covered by social security was lower in past years than it is now. Those

---

[2]U.S. Department of Health, Education, and Welfare, Social Security Administration, SOCIAL SECURITY PROBLEMS IN THE UNITED STATES, 1968, pp. 31-32.

years of lower limits must be counted in with the higher ones of recent years to figure your *average* earnings and thus the amount of your monthly retirement check.[3]

The 1977 Old-Age Insurance Law

After months of deliberation and controversial debate Congress passed a bill that substantially changed the tax and benefit structures of the old-age insurance provisions of the Social Security Act. The bill was signed into law by President Carter in Dec. 1977.

To paraphrase lamely several proverbial metaphors, cynical critics of the new legislation might well say that a mountainous — if not mutinous — Congress labored long and hard to gestate an elephant but finally delivered only an unwholesome, mouselike creature. This is not written just in jest. As finally signed into law, the amended statute embodies compromises that were not at all satisfactory to well-informed groups of employees and employers subject to the law, or to the taxpaying public in general.

The major changes effected by the 1977 amendments up the tax rate equally for covered employers and employees. With these increased rates the maximum benefits payable henceforth to retirees would have corresponding upward adjustments. The 1978 tax rate for both employers and employees was set at 6.05 percent. The maximum earnings on which the tax must be paid were advanced to $17,700.

Further increases in taxes levied at the same rate on employers and employees are due to become effective for the years 1979 and 1980, when the common rate will be 6.13 percent. For 1981 the rate will be advanced to 6.65 percent. As for the maximum taxable wage and salary bases, those are due to become $22,900 in 1979, $25,900 in 1980 and $29,700 in 1981.

The tax rate for self-employed persons was increased for 1978 to 8.1 percent from the previous levy of 7.9 percent. This higher rate will stay the same until 1981. For that year the self-employed tax rate will become 9.3 percent.

Cost-of-Living Adjustments in Benefits and Taxable Earnings

The Social Security Act now provides for automatic adjustments in retirement benefits geared to rises in the U.S. Labor Department's consumer price index or CPI (more often but inac-

[3]U.S. Department of Health, Education, and Welfare, Social Security Administration, HEW Publication No. (SSA) 77-10047, June, 1977.

curately referred to as the cost-of-living index). Thus, there was a general benefit increase of 8 percent in July 1975. In 1976 it was 6.4 percent; in 1977, 5.9 percent; and in 1978, 6.5 percent. Whenever the CPI rises 3 percent or more between the first quarter of the preceding year and the first quarter of the current year, all benefits are to be increased by the same percentage in June of the current year.

Early Versus Delayed Retirement

Personnel administrators may often be called upon to advise employees about the pros and cons of retirement before age 65 or about deferred retirement beyond age 65 if company policy permits. On this matter they would be smart to get the aid of their company's insurance advisor or consulting actuary. A man who retires and begins to collect Social Security benefits at age 62 can get in monthly payments only 80 percent of what he could obtain by waiting until the normal retirement age of 65. And the 80 percent applies throughout the remainder of his lifetime. (Before 1973 men retiring early received somewhat lower benefits than women. The present law has corrected this inequity, and now men and women receive the same benefits.)

As is the case in buying life insurance or individual annuities, the purchaser has to gamble, in a sense, about how long he can expect to live. The longer he lives the more an ordinary life insurance policy will cost him. And the less it will cost the insurance carrier in making the ultimate death settlement. On the other hand, the sooner an individual dies after buying an annuity, the less will be the return to him or to his estate. This, the actuaries and insurance experts could well say, amounts to gross oversimplification. There may be much less inaccuracy in the explanation provided by BNA in its latest *Social Security and Medicare Fact Sheet* for employees. Referring specifically to the possible gains and losses of early as against deferred retirement, BNA has noted: "As it works out, a person who retires at 62 and starts drawing benefits is generally ahead of the game for the first 15 years. But if he lives to be more than 77, the total benefits he gets during retirement will not be so large as if he had waited until 65."[4]

A lot more could be said about what other considerations besides Social Security benefits might properly determine an individual's decision to retire at a certain age when there are options

---

[4]Your New Social Security and Medicare Fact Sheet (Washington: The Bureau of National Affairs, Inc., 1978).

open to him. Manifestly a person who could continue to earn good wages while still in the 60s would be financially ahead by staying on the job as long as company policy permitted. The Social Security Act itself, while originally intended to encourage, if not require, retirement by age 65, now provides a sort of financial inducement for continued employment beyond that age. It's not a gimmick. It's a fact. The law permits, or indeed requires, that there be an increase in monthly retirement benefits of a small percentage per year for every year that a person engages in gainful employment beyond the age of 65 until, and only until, reaching age 72. That statutory right accrues to all persons who by reason of staying on a job after age 65 and before reaching age 72, forfeit some or all of their retirement benefits because their annual earnings exceed the minimums, requiring reduction or temporary elimination of benefits. On this issue the law was unequivocal. For example, if in 1976 any employee or self-employed person earned more than $2,760 in any calendar year, he would forfeit $1 in benefits for each $2 earned above $2,760. The 1977 amendments changed the limit on permissible earnings without deduction of benefits to become $4000 in 1978. The limit will be further increased to $4500 in 1979, $5000 in 1980, $5500 in 1981 and $6000 in 1982. Over-age workers are scheduled to get another break in 1982 when the age at which they can keep all their earnings without forfeiting benefits will be reduced to 70 years instead of 72.

But this partial or complete forfeiture of benefits applies only when individuals continue in gainful employment or self-employment after reaching age 65 and before reaching age 72. For those age 72 or older there is no deduction from benefits on account of job earnings, regardless of how high the monthly or annual amounts may be.

There is another exception for persons continuing to work beyond 65, but only in the year of retirement. This is the proviso in the law that requires no reduction in benefits for any month in which a person did not earn at least $375 (for 1979) or render "substantial services in self employment." What constitutes substantial services is something that the Social Security Administration may have to decide on its own. The term may seem unambiguous, but as officially construed it contains an exception to the exception.

A company pensioner eligible for old-age insurance might earn much less than $375 a month or nothing at all and still be disqualified from old-age insurance benefits for months at a time. This could occur if the retired employee enters into a contractual relation as a real estate salesman or an insurance agent on a commission basis. Or perhaps he becomes a management consultant to be paid "finder's fees" plus per diem rates for professional engagements he might generate for his firm. Or he might begin writing articles or books for prospective publication. Even if an individual doing any of these things does not receive a single dollar in remuneration for such work in the month in which he performed it, he will be disqualified from receipt of old-age insurance benefits for that month should the Social Security Administration decide that he has devoted a substantial amount of time to such efforts with a good prospect of ultimately receiving more than $375 in the form of commissions, fees, royalties or other compensation.

The decision is likely to be determined by the narrow issue as to whether the self-employed individual spent 45 hours or more in a particular month on work that did not produce immediate remuneration. While 45 hours is the usual break-off point in such cases, a high-level retired executive could be disqualified from old-age insurance benefits for any month in which he devoted more than a few hours doing specialized consulting work that might months later bring in a sizable fee.

Formulas for Calculating Old-Age Insurance Benefits

The Social Security Administration properly informs employees about to retire and to collect old-age insurance benefits that the Administration's staff has to calculate the precise amount that will be payable. This can be done only at the time application for benefits is made.

Benefits for Purposes Other Than Retirement

Even the most cursory review of the old-age insurance provisions of the Social Security Act would be inadequate without some reference to the terms under which benefits are payable for purposes other than retirement for age. The other kinds of benefits payable to employees and/or to their dependent relatives *as a matter of right* accrue only by reason of the coverage of the employees themselves and the payment of social security taxes by them and their employers. Auxiliary benefits payable under the diverse provisions of the Act include monthly cash payments to disabled persons and their dependents, and to dependent spouses, dependent divorced wives, dependent children, widows, and dependent widowers. In general terms it is the status of the covered employee in relation to age, earnings, and length of employment which determines his eligibility or that of his relatives and which fixes the amounts of these types of benefits.

Special Situations

The Social Security Act is almost unique among the federal statutes that regulate various phases of employer-employee relations in that by and large the law itself spells out in meticulous detail the basic rights of its beneficiaries. Comparatively few issues are left to administrative determination or discretion. This is in sharp contrast to other laws dealt with in this volume, such as the federal Fair Labor Standards Act, which delegates to its administrator authority to define the categories of employees who are held to be "exempt" and "nonexempt" from its mandatory overtime provisions, or the Taft-Hartley Act, which authorizes the National Labor Relations Board to decide what constitute appropriate bargaining units and what constitute broadly stated types of conduct by employers and labor organizations that may be held to involve "unfair labor practices." Even so, there are some gaps and ambiguities in the Social Security Act that its administrator has authority to deal with in specific regulations or rulings. Some of these are here referred to in brief summary.

Self-Employment Tax Rates

Persons who in the same year are both employed and engaged in self-employment, get a slight break in the assessment of their taxes. As explained in a Social Security Administration leaflet:

> If you have income from wages as well as self-employment, the wages count first for social security. You pay a lower contribution rate on wages and your employer pays a matching amount. If your wages total less than the maximum covered by social security, you pay the self-employment contribution only on the difference between the amount of wages and the maximum covered by social security.[5]

Disability Pensions

Disability pensions may be granted to employees under age 65 who have ailments that have lasted or are expected to last more than 12 months, or which are presumed to result in death, even though persons with such serious afflictions are still able to perform some remunerative work. Employees as young as age 24 may be

---

[5]U.S. Department of Health, Education, and Welfare, Social Security Administration, HEW Publication No. (SSA) 75-10071, July 1975.

entitled to disability pensions if they have obtained credit for at least one and one-half years of covered employment before becoming afflicted.

Family Benefits

Family benefits may be granted to dependents of employees who are or have been recipients of old-age insurance or disability benefits, provided such dependents are, by way of example, unmarried children under 18, or under 22 and full-time students; children who become disabled before reaching age 18 and who continue to be disabled thereafter regardless of age; widows who become disabled not later than seven years after the demise of their husbands; dependent parents aged 62 or over upon the death of a covered employee providing substantially for their support; and divorced wives under special and limited circumstances.

A Dubious Plus for the Newly Retired

Believe it or not—it is possible under the law for a newly retired individual aged 62 or over simultaneously to collect a company pension, Social Security benefits, and unemployment insurance too. Personnel administrators may properly question whether this is as it should be. If in their judgment such a combination of payments to one of their own retirees represents a miscarriage of justice, at least there is something they can try to do about it. They can contest in a state tribunal the payment of unemployment insurance to an ex-employee who on retiring files for unemployment benefits without realistic expectation of taking any sort of suitable employment. More often than not they may not succeed.

Benefit payments made pursuant to the terms of state unemployment insurance laws are not considered as wages for either the purpose of determining possible disqualification from or temporary reduction of retirement benefits. Correspondingly, under some state laws a recipient of Social Security benefits, with or without getting a company pension at the same time, is not automatically disqualified from eligibility for unemployment insurance. If, however, there is a rational basis for concluding that a retiree collecting a company pension and Social Security, has not tried sincerely to obtain post-retirement employment at a salary or wage rate close to his pre-retirement earnings, his former employer can challenge his claim for unemployment compensation. If the challenge is unsuccessful the retiree could continue, under the terms of state law, to be the recipient of his company pension, regular old-age insurance benefits, and unemployment benefits for at least six months and possibly as long as one year.

Litigation

The constitutional validity of the Social Security Act was upheld by the United States Supreme Court within two years after its enactment. The Court dealt simultaneously with the old-age insurance and payroll tax features of the law and with its unemployment insurance provisions in three landmark cases all announced at the same time in May 1937. The cases were *Seward Machine Company* v. *Davis*, 301 US 548; *Helvering* v. *Davis*, 301 US 619; and *Carmichael* v. *Southern Coal Company*, 301 US 495. Four of the nine Supreme Court Justices filed vigorous dissenting opinions. But the majority of the Court sustained the validity of the Act primarily on the bases of the powers of Congress to enact tax legislation and to appropriate the revenues therefrom, together with its right to use general tax revenues for any reasonable purposes that would serve the public welfare.

Much subsequent litigation has involved disputes over the coverage of a specific individual or specific groups of workers — that is to say, over whether or not an employer-employee relationship actually existed. In 1947 the Supreme Court came to grips with major disputed issues relating to employee status. In doing so it set out basic criteria for determining when an individual might be classified as an independent contractor and when he should be considered as an employee covered by old-age insurance. One case involved a group of coal unloaders. Holding that in the light of the particular arrangements under which they worked, these workmen were in fact employees, the Court declared:

> . . . The unloaders provided only picks and shovels. They had no opportunity to gain or lose except from the work of their hands and these simple tools. That the unloaders did not work regularly is not significant. . . . They are of the group that the Social Security Act was intended to aid. Silk [the employer] was in a position to exercise all necessary supervision over their simple tasks. Unloaders have often been held to be employees.

Conversely, the Court ruled in divided opinions that certain coal truck drivers (and moving van drivers who were involved in a different case) were in fact independent contractors. The majority opinion concluded that:

> These driver-owners are small business men. They own their own trucks. They hire their own helpers. In one instance they haul for a

single business, in another for any customer. The distinction, though important, is not controlling. It is the total situation, including the risk undertaken, the control exercised, the opportunity for profit from sound management, that marks these driver-owners as independent contractors.

Finally, the majority opinion enunciated these dicta:

> The Social Security Agency and the courts will find that degrees of control, opportunities for profit or loss, investment in facilities, permanency of relation and skill required in the claimed independent operation are important for decision. No one is controlling nor is the list complete. These unloaders and truckers and their assistants are from one standpoint an integral part of the business of retailing coal or transporting freight. Their energy, care and judgment may conserve their equipment but Grey Van [one of the employers] and Silk [the other] are the directors of their businesses. On the other hand, the truckmen hire their own assistants, own their own trucks, pay their own expenses, with minor exceptions, and depend upon their own initiative, judgment and energy for a large part of their success.[6]

Successive amendments to the Social Security Act passed almost biennially by Congress have made moot many of the initial court decisions interpreting the coverage and terms of eligibility for old-age insurance. The Social Security Administration has, of course, adapted its administrative rulings to the progressively liberalized amendments and to conform to unchallenged court decisions construing the statute and its multifarious amendments. One useful source of information on current official determinations is the compendium issued periodically by the Social Security Administration under the title, *Social Security Rulings—On Federal Old-Age, Survivors, Disability and Health Insurance.*[7]

Medicare

Special taxes for financing of the Medicare program established under the Social Security Act in 1965 are officially designated as insurance premiums. Whether Medicare is now a viable, actuarially sound system is for this reference beside the point. The facts are that in 1976-1977 every employer and employee covered by Social Security became subject to the tax otherwise known as hospital insurance at the rate of .9 percent each on the employee's annual

---

[6]United States v. Silk and Harrison v. Greyvan Lines, 331 U.S. 704 (1947). The excerpts quoted are selections appearing in Thomas F. Broden, LAW OF SOCIAL SECURITY AND UNEMPLOYMENT INSURANCE (Chicago: Callaghan and Co., 1962).

[7]For example, see U.S. Department of Health, Education, and Welfare, Social Security Administration, Cumulative Bulletin, 1967, SSR-67-1 to SSR-67-63.

earnings to the maximum of $16,500. For the years 1978 to 1980 this tax rate is now scheduled to increase to 1.10 percent; for the years 1981 to 1985, to 1.35 percent; and from 1986 thereafter indefinitely to 1.50 percent. It would be utterly futile to attempt to estimate how much of a bite out of any individual employee's earnings might be taken by this tax in the remote future.

However the Social Security Administration may describe it, Medicare involves a mandatory tax on employers and employees. This part of Medicare is otherwise characterized as "hospital *insurance*." "Medical insurance" is something quite different and differently financed. It is financed by monthly premiums paid by the individual, with at least an equal amount contributed by the Federal Government. As of July 1978 the hospital insurance premium for each eligible person was $8.20 a month.[8]

Personnel administrators have reason to give much more than tangential attention to the hospital insurance and medical insurance features of Medicare. These programs go a long way toward absorbing the bulk of hospital and doctors' bills for their beneficiaries. And persons aged 65 or older who have been covered by social security are entitled to Medicare protection even though continuing to work after reaching age 65. Companies that have established or are considering the adoption of health insurance programs that are applicable to their own pensioners and/or the employees not subject to compulsory retirement after 65 can usually adapt their own plans to provide higher benefits or lower costs, if these plans are correlated with the government insurance schemes.

In a government document written for prospective Medicare beneficiaries perhaps in a form much too condensed to be entirely accurate, the coverage of hospital insurance benefits is summarized as follows:

Hospital insurance benefits

Your hospital insurance helps pay the cost of medically necessary covered services for the following care:

Up to 90 days of inpatient care in any participating hospital in each benefit period. For the first 60 days, it pays for all covered services after the first [$160. For each day over 60 days you pay an additional $40.].

What services are covered?

Covered services in a hospital or skilled nursing facility include the cost of room and meals (including special diets) in semiprivate accommodations (2 to 4 beds), regular nursing services, and services

---

[8]YOUR NEW SOCIAL SECURITY AND MEDICARE FACT SHEET.

in an intensive care unit of a hospital. They also include the cost of drugs, supplies, appliances, equipment, and any other services ordinarily furnished to inpatients of the hospital or skilled nursing facility in which you are treated.

What services are not covered?

Hospital insurance is basic protection against the high cost of illness after you are 65 or while you are severely disabled, but it will not pay all of your health care bills. No payment will be made for:

Services or supplies that are not necessary for the diagnosis or treatment of an illness or injury.

Doctor bills. (They are, however, covered if you have medical insurance.)

Private duty nurses.

Cost of the first 3 pints of blood needed during a benefit period while you are an inpatient in a hospital or skilled nursing facility.[9]

Medical Expense Benefits

The same government document that summarized salient points about hospital expense benefits also provides a highly condensed summary of the principal types of medical expenses payable under Medicare to those who elect to participate by paying the requisite insurance premiums. Addressed to those presently or prospectively covered, the document states:

Medical insurance will help pay for the following services:

Physicians' services no matter where you receive them in the United States—in the doctor's office, the hospital, your home, or elsewhere—including medical supplies usually furnished by a doctor in his office, services of his office nurse, and drugs he administers as part of his treatment which you cannot administer yourself. There is a limit on payment for covered psychiatric services furnished outside a hospital. . . .

Outpatient hospital services in an emergency room or an outpatient clinic of a hospital for both diagnosis and treatment. . . .

What services are not covered?

Medical insurance does not cover some services or supplies. For example, the insurance does not cover:

Services or supplies that are not necessary for the diagnosis or treatment of an illness or injury.

Routine physical checkups.

Prescription drugs and patent medicines.

Glasses and eye examinations to fit glasses.

Hearing aids and examinations for hearing aids.

Immunizations.

Dentures and routine dental care.

---

[9]U.S. Department of Health, Education, and Welfare, Social Security Administration, A BRIEF EXPLANATION OF MEDICARE, HEW Publication No. (SSA) 75-10043, Jan. 1975. The bracketed material indicates a 1979 change.

Orthopedic shoes.

Personal comfort items.

The first 3 pints of blood you receive in each calendar year. . . .[10]

THE EMPLOYEE RETIREMENT INCOME SECURITY ACT

Prior to the passage of the Employee Retirement Income Security Act of 1974,[11] nothing in the Social Security Act, or indeed in any other federal statute, precluded any private enterprise from instituting on its own a retirement benefit program in whatever form management considered properly adaptable to the needs of its own employees and its own financial situation.

To be sure, in most instances it would have been the height of folly for a company to ignore U.S. Treasury Department regulations controlling company payments into pension funds as tax deductible business expenses. Nor could enterprises with employees covered by union agreements prudently ignore the requirements of the Taft-Hartley Act. Moreover, such enterprises could not fail to give due heed to the provisions of the Landrum-Griffin Act prohibiting certain types of contributions to benefit plans that might be construed as involving illegal payments to union representatives. (These tangential matters are discussed briefly in Chapter 7.)

ERISA, as the 1974 law is now almost always referred to, is probably the most complex and far-reaching single statute regulating employer-employee relations in the private sector ever to be enacted by Congress. Its text runs to more than two hundred closely printed pages. Three different federal agencies are assigned to administer, interpret, and enforce it. One of these is the newly created Pension Benefit Guaranty Corporation (hereafter referred to by its unpronounceable acronym PBGC). The two others are the Labor and Treasury Departments. Singly or in combination they are authorized by ERISA to formulate initially over 150 regulations and a lot more later, if and when deemed advisable.

The main thrust of ERISA is the regulation of employees' retirement plans, including those maintained independently by employers, or those maintained independently by labor organizations, or those maintained jointly by employers and unions. Additionally, ERISA prescribes federal regulations for every "employee welfare benefit plan" and every "welfare plan" maintained by an employer or by an employee organization or both for the purpose of

---

[10]*Ibid.*, pp. 9-11.

[11]P.L. 93-406, effective Sept. 2, 1974.

providing for its participants or beneficiaries through the purchase of insurance or otherwise. Among such plans are:

Medical, surgical, or hospital benefits
Sickness, disability, death, unemployment, or vacation benefits
Apprenticeship or other training programs
Day care centers
Scholarship funds
Prepaid legal services.

Background Developments

Pension reform bills had been in the congressional hopper for seven years before the passage of the 1974 law. Active investigation and study and public hearings by the Senate Committee on Labor and Public Welfare and the House Committee on Education and Labor preceded the enactment of the law by some three years. Hence its ultimate enactment came as no surprise to the enterprises directly affected. Moreover, the Internal Revenue Service of the U.S. Treasury Department had also been intensively reviewing its regulations for so-called qualified pension plans and had originally scheduled major changes to become effective in 1972.

The term "qualified" when used in connection with private company pension plans has a special and technical meaning. A qualified plan is one that provides such retirement benefits and is so financed and administered as to enable the enterprise maintaining it for some or all of its employees to deduct as business expense its own contributions in computing the enterprise's federal income taxes. With these taxes approaching 50 percent of most companies' net income, the cost of financing a pension plan could almost be doubled if the plan does not meet all of the tests for qualification.

The Internal Revenue Service had proposed tighter regulations to qualify, some especially designed to lessen discriminating differences between benefits creditable to highly paid employees and rank and file workers. These regulation changes were put on ice when the IRS denied the enactment of a new and much more comprehensive law to be in the early offing.

The congressional committees considering new legislation adduced much evidence tending to support their conclusion that innumerable workers had failed to get any of the retirement benefits supposed to have been provided. The basic purpose of ERISA was, therefore, to protect the interests of workers and their beneficiaries depending on benefits from employee pension and welfare plans.

To effectuate this purpose, as stated by the U.S. Labor Department in a concise summary:

The law requires disclosure of plan provisions and financial information and establishes standards for conduct for trustees and administrators of welfare and pension plans. It sets up funding, participation, and vesting requirements for pension plans and makes termination insurance available for most pension plans.[12]

In the light of the continuing criticism of the law by business organizations, the Labor Department's explanation (no doubt oversimplifed) of what the law does not do seems pertinent:

The Act does not require employers to offer pension plans. . . .

The Act does not guarantee a pension to every worker — only to workers who have satisfied plan requirements which are consistent with the minimum standards of the law.

It does not set specific amounts of money to be paid out as pensions and it does not deal with the adequacy of pension benefits — although it does require that a survivor benefit be at least 50 percent of the retirement benefit.

The Act does not guarantee benefits to all widows(ers). . . .

Termination insurance does not cover all pension plans — only those defined benefit pension plans . . . which terminate after July 1, 1974.

The law does not provide that an employee can automatically transfer his pension if he changes jobs.

With few exceptions the Act does not restore rights and benefits lost before enactment.[13]

Potent business groups have not ceased putting intensive pressure on Congress in the hope of mitigating what their leaders consider to be unwarranted restrictions and excessive expense. But the Act has its staunch supporters. The two co-authors of the law spoke out vigorously in its defense in a prepared statement made public as recently as February 1976. The co-authors were Senators Jacob K. Javits (R-NY) and Harrison A. Williams (D-NJ). They still are proud of their legislative brain child and minced few words in so indicating. They said:

ERISA established a comprehensive framework of safeguards guaranteeing the private pension rights of 35 million workers. Now it is under attack from a vocal group, one which has opposed the legislation from its inception.

There have been allegations recently that pension plan terminations were attributable to ERISA and the alleged bureaucratic logjam of executive agencies responsible for its administration. The loudest critics of the Act are those consulting firms, actuaries and other members of the pension industry who fought reform in the first

---

[12]U.S. Department of Labor, Labor-Management Service Administration, OFTEN-ASKED QUESTIONS ABOUT THE EMPLOYEE RETIREMENT INCOME SECURITY ACT OF 1974, 1975, p. 3.
[13]*Ibid.*, p. 26.

place and now may think they have found a new way to undermine its·credibility.

The vital interests of so many millions of Americans in this fundamental reform do not deserve a renewal of past hostilities but an objective analysis of the performance of the law.[14]

The Senators then proceed to cite figures indicating that in the year before ERISA became law, some 4,000 private pension plans had been terminated and that the terminated plans in 1975 numbered fewer than commonly reported. To quote them further:

> While less than 1 percent of the 600,000 pension plans affected by ERISA in 1975 were terminated, more than 33,000 applications for new plans were received by the Internal Revenue Service during the same period. It must be noted that the terminations of 1975 occurred during the largest and deepest of the post war recessions.[15]

Resources for Understanding ERISA

Here too, as was done in Chapter 3, both short and long commentaries on ERISA are recommended for laymen who want or need to understand some of the almost inexplicable passages in the law itself. First, there is a 365-page paperback rushed to print by the Bureau of National Affairs within a week after then-President Ford signed the measure. This book, entitled *Highlights of the New Pension Reform Law,* is of special value to laymen and lawyers concerned about the nationale for the law's enactment. It not only reproduces the full text of the statute; but it also has a succinct summary of the major provisions and a 100-page summary of what was issued as the "Joint Explanatory Statement of the Committee of Conference." The Conference Committee report is the joint statement of the House and Senate managers of the bill, in which the managers sought to reconcile House and Senate disagreement over amendments by the Senate to the original House bill.

Neophyte personnel administrators now charged with some responsibility for their companies' compliance with ERISA (as well as students of federal labor law) could profit initially by a highly condensed overview of the law. One of the most understandable and informative for nonprofessionals is the short monograph prepared in late 1974, no doubt for its customers or potential customers, by the Personal Trust Division of the Irving Trust Company, New York. Presented in wholly outline form, some of the points made in the monograph are quoted below.

---

[14]Jacob K. Javits and Harrison A. Williams, *In Defense of the Pension Reform Act,* NEW YORK TIMES, Feb. 29, 1976, p. F14.
[15]*Ibid.*

Participation and Coverage of Existing Pension Plans

A. Permissible minimum participation requirements:
   1. Not later than age 25 and completion of 1 year's service
   2. Not later than age 25 and completion of 3 years' service if plan provides full and immediate vesting of accrued benefits.
   3. One year of service, generally defined as at least 1,000 hours worked over a 12-month period

B. Permissible exclusion from participation:
   1. Part-time (less than 1,000 hours employment in a year)
   2. *[Note especially]* Employees hired 5 years or less before *normal retirement age* (defined benefit plans only)

C. Coverage requirements:
   1. Not to discriminate in favor of higher-paid employees
      a. as determined on a case-by-case method or
      b. plan covers 70% of all employees or 80% of all eligible employees if 70% are eligible
      c. employees not eligible because of age or service may be excluded under the 70% test

Vesting

A. Employee contributions: vesting will always be full and immediate

B. Employer contributions:
   1. Three alternative tests:
      a. 100% after 10 years service (For vesting purposes only, service after age 22 will be taken into account)
      b. 25% after first 5 years service, 5% for each of next 5 years, 10% for next 5 years
      c. Rule of 45: 50% vested when age + service = 45, 10% per year thereafter (provided at least 5 years' service)
   2. Under any of above tests, 10 years service must be 50% vested (regardless of age) and vest 10% per year thereafter . . .
   6. Employee must be 100% vested at normal retirement date . . .
   11. On plan termination, all accrued benefits become fully vested.[16]

At this point it must be noted that ERISA, as detailed and explicit as it was on some issues, gave unprecedented authority to the several agencies administering it to fill in the gaps, to interpret and even to expand the terms of the law. It was pursuant to that authority that the Internal Revenue Service in November 1975

---

[16]EMPLOYMENT RETIREMENT INCOME SECURITY ACT OF 1974 — OUTLINE OF SELECTED PROVISIONS (New York: Irving Trust Company, 1974).

added a fourth possible schedule for vesting pension plans. One prominent consulting firm in the field described this schedule as follows:

A Fourth Vesting Schedule

On November 3rd [1975], the Internal Revenue Service published Revenue Procedure 75-49 which provides guidelines for advance determination or vesting schedules for pension plans. The reason for the creation of this procedure is that the IRS feels that pension plans, given the choice of three ERISA vesting schedules, would select a schedule which might discriminate in favor of the highly compensated. In effect what the procedure says is if a plan cannot pass a key employee test or a turnover test, it cannot use one of three ERISA schedules but must use a schedule created by the IRS. This fourth schedule provides 40% vesting after four years' service and incrementally produces 100% vesting after 11 years' service. To give you an idea of the likelihood of having to use the 4 - 40 schedule, many, if not most, plans will have to demonstrate a rank-and-file turnover rate of less than 6% in order to pass the test and avoid the 4 - 40 schedule.[17]

The following items continue the outline of ERISA prepared by the Irving Trust Company.

Funding

A. Minimum annual contribution will be actuarially determined amount necessary to fund formal costs plus:

1. Past service liability over not more than 40 years, existing plans

2. 30 years for new plans

3. Contributions are based on accrued liabilities

Additional Requirements for Qualified Retirement Plans

A. Plan must provide for joint and survivor annuity [J & S]

1. J & S can be waived in writing by employee within a reasonable time before annuity starting date

2. Plans with early retirement provision must permit election to have J & S in event of death during employment after early retirement date

B. Plan must provide that retirement benefits are nonassignable

1. However, loan to employee in amount of vested interest, not deemed an assignment

C. Plan must provide for commencement of benefits at normal retirement date

---

[17]ERISA INFORMATION, Vol. 1, Special Edition, Nov. 1975, p. 1. Copyright © 1975, Alexander & Alexander, New York, N.Y.

1. Normal retirement date will in no case be at a time beyond the later of:
   a. age 65 or earlier prescribed normal retirement date
   b. 10 years participation
   c. termination of employment

D. *Benefits with respect to retirees and vested terminees may not be reduced by increase in OAS benefits* [Emphasis supplied][18]

Many, if not most of the ERISA requirements for management, as outlined above, were embodied in the elaborate set of what was captioned "Rules and Regulations for Minimum Standards for Employee Pension Benefit Plans." Management personnel responsible for compliance with ERISA cannot properly find any short-cuts to intensive study of these rules and regulations. They were published in the *Federal Register* for Dec. 28, 1976. In fine print they took up 34 pages of that issue (pp. 56462-56496). It must be remembered, moreover, that what was published represented only those portions of ERISA administered by the U.S. Department of Labor. Consequently, the partial explanation (or expiation) of that department's participation in ERISA interpretation and enforcement may be somewhat revelatory.

James D. Hutchison retired in October 1976 as the administrator of Pension and Welfare Benefit Programs of the Labor Department. Just before his resignation from that post he delivered what could be considered his swan song and apologia. Some of his observations are quoted below:

> In pursuing our policy of voluntary compliance, *so long as full and effective compliance is achieved,* the Department has found that a significant majority of plans are both willing and anxious to meet the Act's standards. . . . At the same time, the Department has shown, and will continue to show, its willingness to initiate formal enforcement proceedings where necessary to achieve compliance.

Hutchison referred to what he described as "some of ERISA's problem areas which have become apparent during the past two years." These he suggested would have to be handled through legislation "if ERISA is to accomplish its underlying purposes without causing widespread disruption or elimination of private employee benefit plans."

Issues in ERISA's problem areas mentioned by Hutchison included, among others:

---

[18]EMPLOYMENT RETIREMENT INCOME SECURITY ACT OF 1974 — OUTLINE OF SELECTED PROVISIONS.

- The numerous, diverse practices which are swept within the coverage provisions of the Act
- General problems inherent in dual/overlapping jurisdiction, particularly the processing of administration exemptions from the prohibited transaction rules.
- The potential widespread preemption of many state laws which are only tangentially related to ERISA.

Hutchison further remarked:

> In the area of dual jurisdiction, almost all knowledgeable observers in the private sector, as well as the Congress and Executive departments, have reached the conclusion that jurisdiction divided among the Department of Labor, the IRS, and the PBGC [Pension Benefit Guaranty Corp.] has resulted in both delay and confusion on regulatory and compliance matters, and duplicative reporting and administrative costs. . . .
>
> A final issue which is becoming the subject of increasing concern is the broad reaching preemption principles contained in section 514 of ERISA, which with minor exceptions supersede "any and all state laws insofar as they . . . *relate to* any" covered employe benefit plan. This has caused significant concern for many states which have strongly supported state standards affecting community property, escheat provisions, sex discrimination and other practices not uniquely tied to employe benefit plans and their operation. . . .[19]

Temporary Regulations Made Permanent

In general, the rules and regulations published in the *Federal Register* on Dec. 28, 1976, explain in bureaucratic phraseology and supplement rather than supplant previous temporary ones. No useful purpose would here be served by citation of any of the recently issued rules and regulations, which now have the presumption of permanency—unless and until there are amendments to the law itself.

ERISA Regulations

Bad and/or Good News for Tycoons

Virtually all published summaries of the key features of ERISA fail to refer to some of the special exceptions. It is often essential to delve into the fine print of the regulations to disclose the sleepers.

---

[19]Quoted passages appear in a two-part article in the Oct. 9 and Oct. 16, 1976, issues of the NATIONAL UNDERWRITER—LIFE AND HEALTH EDITION (Chicago, Ill.), and in turn cite and summarize passages from two of Hutchison's addresses shortly before he retired from government service. The first of the two addresses was delivered at the American Bar Association's annual meeting in August 1976. The second address was made at the Mountain States Pension Conference in Salt Lake City on Oct. 1, 1976.

One such is the requirement that every qualified company pension plan must fix a ceiling on the maximum benefits payable to the highest salaried beneficiaries. The original prescribed maximum in 1974 was $75,000 per year or 100 percent of the participant's highest three consecutive years of contribution — *whichever is less.* By 1976 the maximum had been raised to $84,525.

Here is the exception, or sleeper. The venerable "grandfather clause" — that is, a clause which creates an exception or exemption on the basis of prior circumstances — has been invoked to enable some tycoons to get pensions in excess of annual maximum. Now ERISA has officially ruled that pension benefits in excess of the maximum may be paid but only to recipients whose salary levels, length of service, and special perquisites qualified them prior to October 1973.

How high annual pension benefits may rise under unqualified plans is still undetermined. Conceivably the sky is the limit if a company does not wish to claim tax deductions for the amounts of accrued liability or actual payments to its most highly paid executives.

Employee Rights

Quite apart from the standards fixing minimum benefits, service requirements, etc., ERISA grants some new rights to pension plan participants. Possibly the most important is "the right to know." In this respect the new law goes far beyond the provisions of the Landrum-Griffin Act (see Chapter 7) and the relatively ineffective law designated as the "Labor-Management Reporting Act" of 1959 (amended in 1965). Actually, the employer reporting mandates of these statutes have been all but nullified by ERISA.

The present law assures pension plan participants and beneficiaries that they are entitled:

- To receive a written explanation, revised every five years, if there are any amendments, describing their pension plan in language they can understand. [This proviso might assume all employees have been high school graduates with A + marks in English.] . . .
- To be informed of any material change in the plan within 210 days after the plan year.
- To receive parts of the plan's annual reports showing its financial condition. . . .
- To receive a statement of accrued benefits and vesting status on request to the plan administrator but not oftener than once a year. . . .
- To receive a statement of vested benefits from the plan administrator on leaving the employment covered by a plan. . . .

- To receive Labor Department assistance in determining whether appropriate benefits are provided by a new employer for money transferred from an individual retirement account established with the money received for vested pension benefits from a previous employer. . . .
- To see the application for approval of a pension plan filed with IRS by an employer and to see the supporting documents.
- To intervene in Treasury Department suits in the Tax Court over qualification of pension plan for tax deductions.
- To sue in state or federal courts to collect benefits they believe due them. . . .
- To be free from discharge, fine, discrimination or other punitive treatment for exercising any right . . . under the Act or for giving information, testifying, or planning to testify in an investigation or proceeding relating to the Act.[20]

Joint and Survivor Annuities

Most pension plans covered by ERISA must henceforth provide employee participants with the right to exercise an option regarding so-called joint and survivor annuities. There is nothing new about company plans providing for options of this kind. But now they must be available to active employees nearing retirement.

A lucid explanation of what the joint and survivor annuity requirements involve was included in the Conference Committee report of the Senate and House of Representatives explaining ERISA as recommended for final passage. The report stated . at:

[W]hen a plan provides for a retirement benefit in the form of an annuity, and the participant has been married for the one year period ending on the annuity starting date, the plan must provide for a joint and survivor annuity. The survivor annuity must be not less than half of the annuity payable to the participant during the joint lives of the participant and his spouse.

In the case of an employee who retires or who attains the normal retirement age, the joint and survivor provision is to apply unless the employee elects otherwise.

In the case of an employee who is eligible to retire prior to the normal retirement age under the plan, and who does not retire, the joint and survivor provisions need not be applicable under the plan, unless the employee made an affirmative election. Moreover the plan need not make this option available until the employee is within ten years of normal retirement age. (Of course, a plan may provide that a joint and survivor annuity is to be the only form of benefit payable under the plan, and in this case no election need be provided.) . . .

The employee is to be afforded reasonable opportunity, in accordance with regulations, to exercise his election, out of (or before normal retirement age, possibly into) the joint and survivor

---

[20]Highlights of the New Pension Reform Law (Washington: The Bureau of National Affairs, Inc., 1974), pp. 6-7.

provision before the annuity starting date (or before he becomes eligible for early retirement). The employee is to be supplied with a written explanation of the joint and survivor provision, explained in layman's language, as well as the practical (dollar and cents) effect on him (and his or her spouse) of making an election either to take or not to take the provision. . . .

To prevent adverse selection the plan may provide that any election, or revocation of an election, is not to become effective if the participant dies within some period of time (not in excess of two years) of the election or revocation (except in the case of accidental death where the accident which causes death occurs after the election).[21]

Benefits Payable Under Insolvent or Discontinued Plans

ERISA provides for the creation of a governmentally operated nonprofit corporation to assure a fair measure of insurance protection against loss of benefits by employee participants. This is the Pension Benefit Guaranty Corporation that functions under the U.S. Department of Labor.[22] The Corporation is authorized to assess all enterprises with covered pension plans what amount to insurance premiums to generate funds to make partial payments to retirees whose plans have been discontinued. Individuals who have been employed by companies which have terminated their plans are eligible to receive up to a maximum of $750 if the plan goes broke or the firm goes out of business.

The foregoing generalization is subject to a number of exceptions. For instance, the discontinued plan must have been one that had met IRS regulations for at least five years, in order to qualify for tax credits. As for the precise amount payable to any person, the legalistically phrased formula amounts to something like the following:

> The amount of monthly basic benefits insured by the corporation that a participant may receive from the corporation cannot have an actuarial value that exceeds the actuarial value of a monthly benefit in the form of a life annuity beginning at age 65, equal to the lesser of:
>
> 1. His average monthly income during the five year period in which he received the highest wages, or if less, during the number of calendar years in the five year period during which he participated in the plan; or
>
> 2. $750 a month, adjusted to reflect changes in social security contribution and the benefit base.[23]

---

[21]*Ibid.*, pp. 87-88.
[22]*Ibid.*, pp. 38, 158, 336.
[23]*Ibid.*, pp. 21-22.

In February 1976 the Corporation issued its "final regulations" that raise the maximum insured private pension benefits to make allowance for these changes. For plans terminating in 1975 the adjusted figure is $801.14; for plans with 1976 terminations, the figure is $869.32. According to the regulation, the guaranteed maximum monthly benefit must be the same at age 65 and beyond. There is no permissible adjustment because of impaired health of the participant.[24]

The PBGC is authorized by law to set the annual premium for all single-employer plans at $1 per employee for the first three years. The initial rate for multiple-employer plans is 50 cents for each participant.

Self-Financed Retirement Income Plans

In its foray into the field of pension reform, Congress made certain not to neglect the interests of the large segment of the American work force representing the self-employed or those who work for firms without any type of retirement programs. The number of individuals without such protection is not too reliably estimated at from 40 to 50 percent of those gainfully employed in the private sector.[25]

Congress took two major steps through ERISA to facilitate accumulation of retirement incomes for the major groups not covered by company pension programs: (1) It raised the annual tax-deductible contribution permissible under a Keogh plan from 10 to 15 percent of earned income with the maximums lifted from $2,500 to $7,500. (2) It created a personal tax-sheltered retirement program available for anyone not a potential beneficiary of a private pension plan.

Under this program eligible individuals may establish Individual Retirement Accounts with tax deferral advantages.

Keogh Plans

In essence, a Keogh plan is one that enables self-employed individuals to make tax-deductible contributions to a savings or insurance plan, with no federal income taxes payable until they reach retirement age. These plans were authorized in 1962 by an Act of Congress still known as H.R. 10.

---

[24]DAILY LAB. REP. (BNA), No. 29, Feb. 11, 1976.

[25]The U.S. Bureau of Labor Statistics' estimate for the latest year on which data were available showed that 65 percent of all private nonfarm workers were covered. Private-source estimates put the total not covered in 1976 at from 30 to 40 million people.

A Keogh plan can also cover employees of independent propri-
etorships, but only if they provide benefits for all participants on a
non-integrated basis, i.e., without taking social security benefits
into account.[26]

If an entrepreneur with high income takes full advantage of
the tax shelter afforded by a Keogh plan and sets aside $7,500 of the
first $100,000 of his business income, he also would have to contrib-
ute 7½ percent of the total compensation of his employees for their
retirement income.

Individual Retirement Accounts

These accounts have been quite accurately described as "do-it-
yourself pension plans." The originator of any such account may
invest annually up to $1,500 a year in bank savings, insurance
annuities, savings-and-loan associations and credit unions, trust
funds investing in stocks and bonds, or mutual funds. No federal
income tax has to be paid on the investment until the owner begins
to withdraw some or all of the accumulated principal. Except in a
case of permanent disability, no one can make withdrawals before
attaining age 59½ and must start withdrawals before reaching age
70½.

No doubt representatives of financial institutions that are
having a field day in selling IRAs to customers have done a better
job in explaining the financial rewards they present than could be
detailed by a purely objective analysis. So with the cheerful permission of the noncopyright owner we include below some practical
answers to a few pertinent questions formulated by a major New
Jersey bank:

- Can you establish an IRA?
  IRA's are available to any wage earner. The only requirement is
  that you not currently be a participant in any other retirement
  plan.
- Can your spouse also establish one?
  Yes, working spouses may establish a separate IRA, too, provided
  they are not currently a participant in a plan sponsored by their
  own employers.
- How much can you contribute to your IRA?
  Federal law allows a maximum annual contribution of $1,500 or
  15% of wages, whichever is less. Of course, you can contribute
  smaller amounts each year.

---

[26]U.S. House of Representatives, House Report 2411, 87th Congress — HR 10 Conference
Committee Report, Title II, Subtitle 3. HR 10 was officially known as the Self-Employed
Individuals Tax Retirement Act of 1962.

- Are your contributions tax deductible?
  Yes. For federal income tax purposes your contributions are fully deductible from gross income up to the maximum allowed by law. Contributions can be deducted even though you don't itemize deductions.
- Do you pay taxes on the income earned by your account?
  The earnings of your account are not currently taxable. Each dollar of earnings produces additional dollars which also escape current income taxation. This tax-free compounding continues until retirement.
- When do you pay taxes on your account?
  Your account, including principal and earnings, is not taxed until you receive payment from it. If you receive your account in a lump sum, you must include the entire amount as ordinary income on the return filed for the year of receipt. However you may be eligible to use the five-year income averaging provision available to all taxpayers.

  If funds from your account are paid to you periodically, you will pay taxes only on the amount you receive each year.

  Whichever way you receive your account, however, you will probably pay less in taxes than you would have if the amount put away each year, and the earnings from them, had been included in your income during your working years. The reason: an employee in retirement generally receives less income, and pays taxes at lower rates, than he did while he was working. And if he is 65 or older he qualifies for a double exemption on his income tax return. If he is married he and his wife will have four exemptions once she also reaches 65.[27]

Cautionary Notes

It cannot be gainsaid that both the Keogh and IRA plans present favorable investment opportunities for those eligible to subscribe to either of them. Yet there is certainly no guarantee of a pot of gold at the end of the rainbow.

Each type of plan has its limitations. Under the Keogh plan, for instance, the self-employed entrepreneur must include his employees and contribute at the same relative rate as he makes his own tax-deferred payments. His status in a firm must be more than just that of the principal owner. And all those working for him with three or more years of service and partners with less than 10 percent interest are deemed employees for whom participation is mandatory.

Then under neither type of plan can there be any guarantee that current relatively high rates of interest will prevail until the

---

[27]Excerpted from promotional leaflets published by the American National Bank & Trust of New Jersey.

cash-in times come. Moreover, the plans cannot give participants any option to borrow from the savings credited to their accounts.

Qualified Pension Plans

The term "qualified" when used in connection with private company pension plans has a special and technical meaning. A qualified plan is one that provides such benefits and is so financed and administered as to enable the enterprise maintaining the plan for some or all of its employees to deduct as business expense its own contributions for the support of the plan in computing the enterprise's federal income taxes. With federal income taxes usually amounting to almost 50 percent of a company's net income it is obvious that the cost of financing a pension plan practically may be doubled if the plan does not meet all the tests for qualification.

The Internal Revenue Service of the United States Treasury Department establishes the rules for determining what plans qualify for tax deductibility. Unlike the "immutable" laws of the Medes and the Persians, these rules are subject to change with due advance notice.

ERISA established substantially identical requirements as those mandated by the Internal Revenue Code of 1954 to enable employer contributions to a pension plan to qualify as business expense deductions for federal income tax purposes. These requirements are imposed by Subchapter D of Chapter 1 of the 1954 Code. They are much too technical to be subject to summary without grave risk of oversimplification or misinterpretation. The Internal Revenue Service has repeatedly revised its own regulations interpreting the standards to which a company pension plan must conform to be entitled to tax credits. Present Code standards are regarded as merely setting minimums. There is no ban on plans providing more liberal benefits. There is, however, one absolute prohibition in the latest version of the IRS Code. While an enterprise in the private sector may maintain a pension for a specific classification of employees, such a plan *cannot* discriminate in favor of its officers, shareholders, or highly compensated employees.

Pensions Under Union Agreements

All of the terms of a company pension plan that covers any group of its employees in a recognized or certified bargaining unit may be subject to collective bargaining. This is a requirement of the Taft-Hartley Act regardless of whether or not the plan was first established by management unilaterally and whether or not it applies to all employees of the company or just to a small segment of the work force in one plant of a multiplant enterprise. And since 1972 advance approval of the Internal Revenue Service has to be obtained for a plan adopted or modified through collective negotiations. This requirement is just one of many instances of the interrelationship between federal statutes and regulations impinging on management decisions in the field of employee relationships.

There are no ifs, ands, or buts about management's obligation to bargain with any and all unions over pension plans when the unions represent employees of bargaining units covered or to be covered by the plans. This has been held an obligation under Taft-Hartley since 1949. In that year the United States Supreme Court by indirection placed all types of retirement plans covering unionized employees in the arena. It did not specifically rule on the issue of the "bargainability" of pension plans. Instead, by refusing to grant certiorari in a circuit court case, it in effect sustained the federal circuit court decision which in turn had upheld and enforced a decision of the National Labor Relations Board directing a company to bargain with a union concerning the question of the age of forcible retirement.

The case in point, which stemmed from a controversy between the Inland Steel Company and the United Steelworkers of America, resulted in a true landmark decision with far-reaching consequences for management and unions. Its origins occurred when Inland Steel's management, shortly after the end of World War II, reinstated the provisions of its pension plan requiring retirement of employees at age 65. (During the war the company had suspended its mandatory retirement rules because of the severe manpower shortage.) In 1946 the company retired some two hundred employees who were then 65 or older. By this time the Steel Workers' union had gained recognition for production and maintenance employees in two of the company's mills. When this union filed a grievance protesting the company's action, the company refused to discuss the grievance with the union. Its stated reason was that no law compelled it to do so. Moreover, the company took the position, so the National Labor Relations Board asserted, that the then-applicable Wagner Act did not require management to bargain over any of the provisions of its pension plan, more specifically, to bargain over the issue of compulsory retirement. The Board flatly rejected the validity of the company's position.

Apparently the rationale behind the Board's decision in the Inland Steel case has been generally accepted as valid doctrine applicable in all management-union bargaining situations where pension questions arise. Perhaps this rationale can be best clarified by citing pertinent passages from the majority opinion of the federal circuit court that sustained the Board's findings and reinforced them as a matter of law. The court quoted the Board as stating:

> With due regard for the aims and purposes of the Act, and the evils which it sought to correct, we [the Board] are convinced and find that the term "wages" as used in Section 9(a) must be construed to include emoluments of value, like pension and insurance benefits, which may accrue to employees out of their employment relationship. . . . Realistically viewed this type of wage enhancement or increase, no less than any other, becomes an integral part of the entire wage structure, and the character of the employee representative's interest in it, and the terms of its grant, is no different than in any other case where a change in the wage structure is effected.

Thereafter in its own words the court went on to say:

> We are unable to differentiate between the conceded right of a union to bargain about a discharge, and particularly a non-discriminatory discharge, of an employee and its right to bargain about the age at which he is compelled to retire. In either case the employee loses his job at the command of the employer. . . . A termination by discharge is concededly a matter of collective bargaining. To say that termination by retirement is not amenable to the same process could not, in our judgment, be supported by logic, reason or common sense. . . . A unilateral retirement and pension plan has as its main objective not job security for older workers but their retirement at an age predetermined by the company, and we think the latter is as much included in "conditions of employment" as the former. What would be the purpose of protecting senior employees against lay-off when an employer could arbitrarily and unilaterally place the compulsory retirement age at any level that would suit its purpose. If the company may fix an age at 65, there is nothing to prevent it from deciding that 50 or 45 is the age at which employees are no longer employable, and in this manner wholly frustrate the seniority provisions for which the union has bargained.[28]

The National Labor Relations Board has consistently followed the lead given it by the courts in the Inland Steel decision. In 1969 the Board ruled that the obligation of an employer to negotiate over the benefits to be paid on retirement to its employees included the further obligation to negotiate changes in benefits payable to employees who had already retired even though such individuals were no longer included in any bargaining unit.

---

[28]Inland Steel Company v. NLRB, et al. United Steelworkers of America, CIO, et al. v. NLRB, 170 F.2d 247, 22 LRRM 2506 (7th Cir. 1948).

The Board held: (1) that the term "employee" includes retired employees; (2) that the employer had the duty to bargain with the union about the benefits payable to retired employees because (3) wages, hours, and other terms and conditions of employment must be the subject of collective bargaining. The Board grounded its decision in this case on the theory that it was the original employment of the retired individuals which gave rise to their rights to have postretirement benefits negotiated.[29]

But the Supreme Court decided two years later that the Board had gone too far. As related in Chapter 7, the Court pronounced a categorical ruling to the effect that retirees could not be considered as employees at all and that, therefore, employers did not have to bargain about any changes in their pension rights. (See page 336 for a summary of this later decision.)[30]

UNEMPLOYMENT INSURANCE

Legislative history is doubtless of much less concern to personnel administrators and to students of social insurance than are the present provisions of federal and state laws. Still, the original concepts which led to the enactment of the intricate, partially integrated federal-state unemployment compensation system covering at least 75 percent of the nation's work force warrant some passing review. Though no longer well known and perhaps already forgotten among the older generation in the industrial relations field, privately conceived and administered unemployment compensation plans antedated governmental schemes in the United States by many years. Indeed, the congressional sponsors of the present federal-state system argued persuasively that what had been good for the employees of Eastman Kodak, General Electric, and a handful of other companies should, perforce, be made mandatory for the employees of all private enterprises of any consequence. Moreover, the first unemployment benefit system was established by a local trade union more than a hundred years ago. By the end of 1930 some 35,000 members of labor unions were entitled to participate in the benefits derived from plans set up by their own contributions from earnings, and during the same period, at least 65,000 trade union members were eligible to participate in unemployment benefits payable from funds set up jointly by manufacturers and

[29]Pittsburgh Plate Glass Company, 177 NLRB No. 114, 71 LRRM 1433 (1969).
[30]Allied Chemical and Alkali Workers, Local 1 v. Pittsburgh Plate Glass Co., 404 U.S. 157, 78 LRRM 2784 (1971).

unions. These funds were created primarily in the garment industries.

The General Electric plan that might have been called unemployment insurance "without more" was put into effect in 1930 on a
contributory basis. Before that year only 13 American corporations
were known to have been maintaining formal unemployment benefit plans, and all of these were noncontributory. There were, in
addition, a few so-called guaranteed employment plans such as the
one established by Procter and Gamble in 1923. Procter and Gamble had so regularized its operations by 1923 as to enable its management to guarantee 48 weeks of continuous employment for its
regular working force.[31]

In its monumental study *Growth of Labor Law in the United
States,* frequently referred to in these pages, the United States
Department of Labor used a curious euphemism. The explanation
of the origin of the 1935 unemployment insurance legislation reads,
"The Federal Social Security Act of 1935 *helped* inaugurate a
federal-state system of unemployment insurance." [Italics supplied.] In reality, the Social Security Act used federal taxing powers
so ingeniously to bring pressure on all the states that complementary state legislation setting up state taxes and state unemployment benefit plans was virtually inevitable. Congress succeeded in
doing this at a time when, despite the continued prevalence of devastating unemployment, there was anything but enthusiastic support for such legislation on the part of organized business, organized labor, or the general public.

The ingenious tax device embodied in what was then known as
Title IX of the Social Security Act (now the Federal Unemployment
Tax Act) was the imposition of a federal payroll tax on employers at
the rate of 3 percent of the first $3,000 of each of their employees'
annual earnings from wages or salaries. At the same time employers
were automatically entitled to a credit or offset against that tax of
all but three tenths of 1 percent of the total federal levy, provided
they were assessed and paid taxes of substantially the equivalent
amount, i.e., 2.7 percent to a state under the terms of a state
unemployment compensation law meeting prescribed federal standards. In short, unless each state promptly enacted its own unemployment compensation law conforming to the federal standards,
the proceeds from the federal taxes imposed on the employers
having operations in the state would go into general federal

---

[31]An extensive review of company plans for minimizing unemployment appears in the
monograph by Russell L. Greenman, EMPLOYMENT REGULARIZATION IN THE UNITED STATES
(Washington: International Chamber of Commerce, 1931).

revenues, and their employees could gain none of the benefits of a state unemployment compension system. To record this legislative history is neither to extol nor to criticize the unique legislative device used by Congress in 1935. It worked. It worked so effectively that within the next two years all the states and the District of Columbia had adopted conforming unemployment compensation plans, and the constitutionality of the federal-state system was sustained by the United States Supreme Court without great ado. (Prior to 1935 Wisconsin was the only state that had enacted unemployment insurance legislation of any sort.)

As already indicated, the federal statute set certain standards that had to be incorporated in each state law to enable the employers of that state to receive credit for the offset against the federal tax of 3 percent on their employees' earnings up to $3,000 per year. In a most highly condensed summary of the conditions fixed by federal law for state compliance, the Social Security Administration has explained that no state "can deny benefits to a claimant if he refuses to accept a new job under substandard labor conditions, where a labor dispute is involved, or if he would be required to join a company union or resign from or refrain from joining any bona fide labor organization." These conditions have been embodied in the law since its original enactment. They have given rise to the necessity of much interpretation by state administrative agencies and much review by the courts. Some of the significant rulings are summarized later in this chapter.

Tax Rates (Employer and Employee "Contributions")

Now that all states have long since enacted statutes of their own as the result of the ingenious strategem used by Congress in 1935 to make adoption of state unemployment insurance laws a practical necessity, there is no logical basis for precluding the states from levying taxes on employees' earnings in excess of $3,000 or, indeed, of limiting their tax rate to 2.7 percent. As indicated in footnote (b) to the tabulation appearing on page 165, all states fix the maximum amount of employees' annual earnings subject to employees' taxes at at least $4,200. Nine states presently have higher maximums, ranging from Missouri's $4,500 to Alaska's $10,000.

The Social Security Act leaves entirely to the discretion of the states whether to finance their own unemployment compensation programs with taxes levied exclusively on employers or with compulsory contributions by employees as well as employers. By 1976 only three states had laws requiring such contributions. These were

SIGNIFICANT PROVISIONS OF STATE UNEMPLOYMENT INSURANCE LAWS*

| State | *Benefits* | | *Taxes* | |
	Maximum weekly benefit amount for total unemployment	Normal maximum benefit weeks for total unemployment[a]	1976 Tax rates (percent of wages)[b] Minimum	Maximum
Ala.	$ 90	26	0.5[b]	4.0[b]
Alaska	90-120	28	2.3[b]	4.8[b]
Ariz.	85	26	0.1	2.9
Ark.	100	26	0.5	4.4
Calif.	104	26[a]	1.4[b]	4.9[b]
Colo.	116	26	0	3.6
Conn.	116-174	26[a]	1.6[b]	4.5[b]
Del.	125	26	1.6	4.5
D.C.	148	34	2.7	2.7
Fla.	82	26	0.7	4.5
Ga.	90	26	0.05[b]	4.03[b]
Hawaii	120	26[a]	3.0[b]	3.0[b]
Idaho	99	26	0.5[b]	3.6[b]
Ill.	110-135	26	0.1	4.0
Ind.	69-115	26	0.3	3.3
Iowa	116	39	0.7[b]	4.7[b]
Kans.	101	26	0	3.6
Ky.	87	26	0.4	4.2
La.	120	28	0.7	3.3
Maine	79-119	26	2.4	5.0
Md.	89	26	2.8	3.6
Mass.	108-162	30	3.9	5.1
Mich.	97-136	26	0.8[b]	6.6[b]
Minn.	113	26	0.9[b]	6.0[b]
Miss.	80	26	1.3	2.7
Mo.	85	26	0.5[b]	3.2[b]
Mont.	97	26	1.5[b]	3.1[b]
Neb.	80	26	0.1	3.7
Nev.	94	26	1.1[b]	3.5[b]
N.H.	95	26	2.4	4.15
N.J.	104	26	1.2[b]	6.2[b]
N. Mex.	83	30	0.6	3.6
N.Y.	95	26	1.5	5.2
N.C.	105	26	0.3	4.7
N. Dak	107	26	0.9	4.2
Ohio	102-161	26	0.6	4.3
Okla.	93	26	1.2	2.7
Oreg.	102	26	2.6[b]	4.0[b]
Pa.	133-141	30	1.0	4.0
P.R.	60	20[a]	2.95	3.45
R.I.	100-120	26	3.2[b]	5.0[b]

| | Benefits | | Taxes | |
| | Maximum weekly benefit amount for total | Normal maximum benefit weeks for total | 1976 Tax rates (per-cent of wages)[b] | |
State	unemployment	unemployment[a]	Minimum	Maximum
S.C.	103	26	1.3	4.1
S. Dak.	89	26	0	2.7
Tenn.	85	26	0.4	4.0
Tex.	63	26	0.1	4.0
Utah	110	36	1.3[b]	2.8[b]
Vt.	96	26	1.0	5.0
Va.	103	26	0.55	2.7
Wash.	102	30	3.0[b]	3.0[b]
W. Va.	128	26	0	3.3
Wisc.	126	34	0.5	5.2
Wyo.	95	26	1.16	3.86

[a]Benefits extended under State program when unemployment in State reaches specified levels: *Calif., Hawaii,* by 50%; *Conn.* by 13 weeks. . . Benefits also may be extended during periods of high unemployment by 50%, up to 13 weeks, under Federal-State Extended Compensation Program and up to 26 additional weeks under the Federal Supplemental Benefits program.

[b]Represents min.-max. rates assigned employers in CY 1975. *Ala., Alaska, N.J.* require employee taxes. Contributions required on wages up to $4,200 in all States except *Mo.,* $4,500; *Ala., Mont., R.I.,* $4,800; *Mich.,* $5,400; *N.J.,* $5,800; *Ariz., Ark., Conn., Ga., Iowa, Wis.,* $6,000; *Minn., Nev.,* $6,500; *Calif.,* $7,000; *Wash.,* $7,800; *Oreg.,* $8,000; *Idaho,* $8,400; *Utah,* $8,800; *Hawaii,* $9,300; *Alaska,* $10,000; *P.R.,* all wages.

*Adapted from U.S. Department of Labor, Employment and Training Administration, SIGNIFICANT PROVISIONS OF STATE UNEMPLOYMENT INSURANCE LAWS, January 3, 1977. This table sets forth benefit and tax rate data by states as these numbers were applicable in 1976. No later complete official data applicable to all states have been put out in any official government publication. There has been some upping of rates since 1976 in a number of states. For instance the maximum benefit rate in New Jersey has been set for 1978 at $110. For New York the maximum which had been $95 a week in 1977 is due to be advanced to $125 in Sept. 1978.

Personnel administrators needing to know current rates applicable to employees whose unemployment benefits are determined by the benefit schedule in various states are advised periodically to consult the area unemployment insurance offices in the state where they make their headquarters. Such offices are able to obtain the requisite data from other states even though there is no one single reliable document that sets out the present benefit and tax rates for all states.

Alabama, Alaska, and New Jersey. For Alabama the employees' tax amounts to .5 percent of the first $4,200 in annual earnings. For New Jersey it is also .5 percent but on the first $4,800. For Alaska the rate can vary from .3 to .8 percent.

Unemployment Benefit Rates

For the first 20 years or so after the enactment of state unemployment compensation laws, typical benefits authorized thereby amounted to about 50 percent of the recipients' prior earnings. In every state, however, maximum benefits were fixed by statute. By 1968 the upper limits had ranged in different states from $30 to $68 per week. Slightly higher maximums were payable nevertheless in 11 states providing additional allowances to claimants with dependents. Since 1968, most states have rapidly increased the average and maximum amounts payable in benefits. Legislative developments in New Jersey might be considered as indicative of the trend. The New Jersey law provides for automatic adjustment of maximum benefits to fix them at levels equivalent to about one-half the average weekly earnings of all employees in the state covered by the unemployment insurance system. In 1971 that state set a new maximum of $72 per week, upping it from the 1968 figure of $68. In 1972 it was raised to $76. By 1976 this limit became $96. That increase was put into effect even though the New Jersey system reached the point of bankruptcy as early as January 1975. Aggregate benefits paid out in New Jersey during the entire year amounted to $1.2 billion. But employer and employee tax payments totaled only $380 million. By the end of 1976 New Jersey authorities anticipated that the system would owe the Federal Government about $700 million as a result of federal loans to enable the state to continue to meet its benefit obligations.[32]

Federal loans to the state unemployment compensation fund were made possible by emergency legislation enacted by Congress in 1974. The nation's generally worsening economic conditions in 1975 induced further congressional action, this time in the form of monetary grants to the states having especially high unemployment rates to enable them to extend benefit payments to individuals for as long as 65 weeks.

The volume of unemployment rose to a new peak of 8.5 million persons, or 9.2 percent of the labor force, by May 1975. In a hindsight article published in January 1976, a U.S. Department of Labor economist made some pungent (and wholly nonpolitical) observations about the crucial economic situation in the final half of 1975. She wrote:

> The unemployment compensation system served as an important automatic stabilizer in early 1975, paying out much more money as the economy fell into a decline and helping to prevent the development of a cumulative downturn. Preliminary figures indicate the unemployment compensation system paid out $9.2 billion from January to June 1975, compared with approximately $3.3 billion during the same period of the previous year.[33]

---

[32]THE DAILY RECORD, Morristown, N.J., March 15, 1976, p. 1.
[33]Catherine C. Define, *Labor and the Economy During 1975*, MONTHLY LABOR REVIEW, U.S. Department of Labor, Bureau of Labor Statistics, Jan. 1976, *99* (No. 1), 5.

A footnote to the article just cited merits, we think, more than secondary reference. It reads:

> Federal legislation (The Emergency Unemployment Compensation Act of 1974, Public Law 93-572) enacted in December 1974 had extended unemployment compensation for covered workers an additional 13 weeks. Thus, fully covered workers were entitled to a maximum of 52 weeks of benefits; 26 weeks from the regular State programs, 13 weeks from the combined Federal-State program, and 13 weeks under the 1974 law's "Federal Supplemental Benefits" program. Another program, "Special Unemployment Assistance," also passed in December 1974 as part of The Emergency Jobs and Unemployment Assistance Act of 1974 (Public Law 93-567), had provided—for a maximum of 26 weeks—benefits to workers not covered by the unemployment compensation program. These included State and local government employees, farmworkers, domestic workers, and others.
>
> The Tax Reduction Act extended benefits for covered employees for an additional 13 weeks. Thus, covered employees were entitled to 65 weeks of benefits. However, the 65-week maximum was effective only through June 30, 1975. Legislation passed in mid-1975 extended the 65-week maximum through March 1977. This legislation also extended Special Unemployment Assistance by another 13 weeks to total 39, and renewed the program for 1 year.[34]

Experience Rating Under State Laws

The states have been permitted under the terms of the Federal Unemployment Tax Act to include merit rating devices in their own unemployment compensation systems. Merit rating contemplates a sliding scale of payroll taxes for employers with the lowest tax rates assessed on employers with relatively favorable labor turnover experience, i.e., the lower the rate of layoffs and job terminations, the lower the tax rate for the particular enterprise.

Merit rating, or experience rating as the Social Security Administration chooses to call it, is not viewed by the administrators as any sort of panacea for unemployment. And with good reason. Establishments in industries which are of a seasonal nature or are subject to unpredictable fluctuations in their volume of business and employment are effectively penalized under experience rating by having to pay higher taxes than establishments with a more stable volume of business. Small as it may seem to be, the higher tax cost for the unstable business contributes at least slightly to its further instability.

The laws of all 50 states make some provision for adjusting employees' taxes on the basis of the relative stability or instability of

---

[34]*Ibid.*, p. 15.

their employment record. In most states companies with relatively low labor turnover and consequently with relatively small claims for unemployment benefits originating from their own work force can be permitted a reduction in their state tax rate to as low as 1 percent or less of applicable payrolls. In most states employers must have been covered by the state law and have had at least three years of contribution experience before qualifying for a reduced tax rate.

The Labor Department has attempted to explain in non-technical language what an experience rating can mean. Of course, the generalizations are subject to qualification. Hence an examination of the current statutory provisions and administrative interpretations must be made before any employer can be certain how to get the greatest tax advantage. The Labor Department's summary, in the broadest of strokes, includes the following:

> Under the general federal requirements, the experience-rating provisions of state laws vary greatly and the number of variations increases with each legislative year. The most significant variations grow out of the differences in the formulas used for rate determinations. The factor used to measure experience with unemployment is the basic variable which makes it possible to establish the relative incidence of unemployment among the workers of different employers. Differences in such experience represent the major justification for differences in tax rates, either to provide incentive for stabilization of employment or to allocate the cost of unemployment. At present there are five distinct systems, usually identified as reserve-ratio, benefit-ratio, benefit-wage-ratio, compensable separations, and payroll-decline formulas. A few states have combinations of the systems. . . .
>
> All formulas are devised to establish the relative experience of individual employers with unemployment or with benefit costs. To this end, all have factors for measuring each employer's experience with unemployment or benefit expenditures, and all compare this experience with a measure of exposure—usually payrolls—to establish the relative experience of large and small employers. . . .
>
> The reserve ratio was the earliest of the experience-rating formulas and continues to be the most popular. It is now used in 32 states. The system is essentially cost accounting. On each employer's record are entered the amount of his payroll, his contributions and the benefits paid to his workers. The benefits are subtracted from the contributions, and the resulting balance is divided by the payroll to determine the size of the balance in terms of the potential liability for benefits inherent in wage payments. The balance carried forward each year under the reserve-ratio plan is ordinarily the difference between the employer's total contributions and the total benefits received by his workers since the law became effective. . . .
>
> The employer must accumulate and maintain a specified reserve before his rate is reduced; then rates are assigned according to a schedule of rates for specified ranges of reserve ratios; the higher the

ratio the lower the rate. The formula is designed to make sure that no employer will be granted a rate reduction unless over the years he contributes more to the fund than his workers draw in benefits. Also, fluctuations in the state fund balance affect the rate that an employer will pay for a given reserve; an increase in the state fund may signal the application of an alternate rate schedule in which a lower rate is assigned for a given reserve and conversely, a decrease in the fund balance may signal the application of an alternate tax schedule which requires a higher rate.[35]

Effectiveness of Merit Rating

A savings of 2 percent or more in payroll costs that can be achieved in most states by employers through reduction in involuntary labor turnover is obviously worthwhile if this is obtainable without offsetting additional higher costs of operations.

Personnel administrators have many factors to weigh in considering the relationship of experience-rating to advantages vis-à-vis other company policies. As one illustration, how about the relative costs of overtime work compared with the costs of hiring new employees for uncertain tenure? Presumably the new employees will cost the company plenty in the way of fringe benefits if they stay and work long enough to meet eligibility standards. And when they are laid off after meeting minimum requirements to collect unemployment insurance, will the resultant reduction in the company's experience-rating tax be enough to more than offset the costs of retaining a stable work force and utilizing overtime to meet temporary increases in output? Manifestly there are no pat answers to this question. Nor are there any conclusive answers to the question of whether the stabilizing effect on employment of experience-rating taxation formulas tends to increase rather than diminish the general level of unemployment in recession periods.

Nevertheless, as might be expected, the "pros" in the Labor Department continue to cite authoritative research studies to bulwark their contentions as to the economic values of the present unemployment insurance system. One such study stated:

> Neither the boosters of unemployment insurance, who deny that it offers any disincentive, nor the attackers, who blame it for a large amount of unemployment, are persuasive. The study demonstrates that the existing system causes a perceptible, but small, amount of unemployment in the United States—between 0.2 and 0.3 percent of the labor force—that is not a figure that supports the notion of armies of unemployed malingerers and chiselers. . . . Among the

---

[35]U.S. Department of Labor, Manpower Administration, Unemployment Insurance Service, COMPARISON OF STATE UNEMPLOYMENT INSURANCE LAWS, JAN. 1972. This publication is periodically updated.

various forms of income support for the unemployed, unemployment insurance stands out as the most successful and the least controversial. The experience-rating method of financing the system has helped to make it self-policing and relatively free of scandal. The system provides income support with dignity, without a humiliating means test. It should not now be attacked by exaggerated claims of work disincentives.[36]

The author of the study went on to state that if additional research, warranted it, administration of the "work test" might be made stricter or the experience-rating system improved. Then he concluded, "otherwise, the unemployment insurance system can be left intact without severely prejudicing the Nation's chances for full employment."[37]

Conditions for Benefit Eligibility

Like any other type of insurance, every state unemployment insurance plan has to apply certain elements of co-insurance. Otherwise the costs would be utterly prohibitive. A waiting period before becoming eligible to receive benefits is one of the fundamentals. In nearly all state laws the prescribed waiting period is one week. There have to be many other conditions for eligibility. These are too diversified to permit precise summary. A few of them, however, are of almost universal application in state laws.

One basic condition for eligibility is expressed in negative form in the Federal Unemployment Tax Act. This condition was a carryover from a set of stipulations embodied in the Social Security Act and without these the New Deal Administration of the 1930s could not have gained enough support from organized labor to assure the passage of the law. The "negatives" are explicitly stated in the proviso of the federal law enabling employers to credit most of their state taxes against the federal tax. This proviso states:

> Compensation shall not be denied [by any state] to any otherwise eligible individual for refusing to accept work under any of the following conditions:
> (A) If the position offered is vacant due directly to a strike, lockout, or other labor dispute;
> (B) if the wages, hours or other conditions of the work offered are substantially less favorable to the individual than those prevailing for similar work in the locality;

---

[36]Stephen T. Marston, *The Impact of Unemployment Insurance on Job Search*, BROOKINGS PAPERS ON ECONOMIC ACTIVITY (No. 1; Washington: The Brookings Institution, 1975), pp. 40-41.
[37]*Ibid.*

(C) if as a condition of being employed the individual would be required to join a company union or to resign from or refrain from joining any bona fide labor organization.

Criteria for Suitable Work

Among typical provisions of state laws implementing the federal proviso are those that permit acceptance of a worker's claim when there is a substantial risk to a claimant's health, safety, and morals; or the prospects for obtaining a job in the worker's customary occupation are remote *and* suitable work is available only at an unreasonable distance from the worker's residence.

Minimum Length of Employment and Minimum Earnings for Eligibility

There is no common pattern among state laws with respect to minimum length of time on a job or minimum earnings to qualify for any unemployment compensation. Some state laws specify the minimum duration of employment. Some have combinations of minimum service and minimum earnings. On the high side is the law of Washington State, which specifies at least 16 weeks of work and $1,300 in earnings to qualify. Some states, such as Ohio, require at least 20 weeks of prior employment but specify minimum earnings as low as $400.[38]

Potential Bases for Disqualification

In a typically bureaucratic glossing over of the restrictive aspects of social welfare legislation, the Labor Department has said the following about basic conditions that *could* disqualify a previously employed worker from receiving unemployment compensation:

> All state laws provide that, to receive benefits, a claimant must be able to work and must be available for work; i.e., he must be in the labor force, and his unemployment must be caused by lack of work. Also, he must be free from disqualification for such acts as voluntary leaving without good cause, discharge for misconduct connected with the work, and refusal of suitable work. These eligibility and disqualification provisions delineate the risk which the laws cover: the able-and-available tests as positive conditions for the receipt of benefits week by week, and disqualification as a negative expression of conditions under which benefits are denied. The pur-

---

[38]The permutations and combinations of state employment and wage eligibility conditions are summarized in tabular form with copius footnotes in the looseleaf manual, COMPARISONS OF STATE UNEMPLOYMENT INSURANCE LAWS.

pose of these provisions is to limit payments to workers unemployed primarily as a result of economic causes.[39]

Some state administrative agencies are not notable for strict enforcement of the law in accepting claims for persons who have left their jobs for any reason, even as a result of discharge for good cause. The state laws are supposed to provide unemployment benefits for individuals who have been idled for reasons beyond their own control. And once workers have been involuntarily separated from their jobs, eligibility for unemployment benefits is supposed to be conditioned on their bona fide but unsuccessful efforts to obtain other "suitable" employment. What constitutes such employment, to say nothing about the original cause of loss of job, depends not only on the views of state hearing officers and administrators but also ultimately on the decisions of state appellate courts when initial determinations as to eligibility or ineligibility have been challenged by the employer or a former employee.

The possibilities of evasion by workers of the latest requirements of an applicable state law are endless. Employees can deliberately soldier on the job or engage in other tactics to cause their layoff or dismissal in such ingenious ways that they are not disqualified. They may court severance from the payroll when they have no intent immediately thereafter to seek other employment of any sort.

Then there is also almost no limit to the apparently legitimate reasons benefit claimants may assert for their inability to obtain other suitable positions. Here summarized is what admittedly was an extreme case:

A professional personnel woman resigned from her position on the personnel staff of a large corporation in New York City to accompany her husband, who had been assigned as an Air Force Reserve officer to a two-year tour of duty at a military base in Massachusetts. This base was close to one of the largest industrial centers in that state. When she resigned, her employer volunteered to assist her in obtaining comparable employment in her new community. She declined any offer of such aid. Instead, after what was obviously only a casual hunt for a new position that would pay her as much as her salary in New York City, she filed for and collected full unemployment benefits for a six-month period. The amount of her benefits was charged against the experience rating account of her New York employer. Its management challenged the propriety of the claim, not because she had resigned to join her husband, but because this former estimable employee had manifestly made no

---

[39]*Ibid.*, Section 4-1, revised Sept. 1973.

realistic attempt to obtain any position comparable to the one she had held in New York. After reviewing the matter the New York State authorities informed her employer that the corporation had no case and advised it not to appeal.

A second case, on a dissimilar issue, produced an entirely different result. An employee of a New Jersey plant was laid off for lack of work and no other reasons. He obviously was entitled to unemployment benefits and forthwith began to collect. After some weeks the employment manager of the company from which he had been laid off received a reference inquiry about him from a concern in another town. In giving an oral answer to this inquiry by telephone the employment manager learned that this individual was already working for the other establishment, while still collecting unemployment benefits. The state authorities were promptly notified, with the result that benefits were cancelled at once and the man was hauled into court and prosecuted for fraud.

Litigation

Few cases that center about questions of fact rather than questions of law reach the courts for final adjudication. Most disputed claims are disposed of within state administrative agencies on appeals by the employers of the claimants. This is because when questions of fact are paramount, the courts usually uphold the agency with jurisdiction to find the facts in the absence of persuasive testimony to controvert them.

There have been, however, some landmark court decisions. One such case was decided by the Superior Court of Pennsylvania in 1946 in the case of *Bliley Electric Co.* v. *Unemployment Compensation Board of Review.*[40] Here the court had to decide the same sort of question that led some years later to the administrative ruling in New York State granting unemployment benefits to the wife of an Air Force officer assigned to duty in a different state from that in which his spouse had held a responsible management position. Declaring, in substance, that a wife who followed her husband to another state upon his assignment to military service had good cause to do so and hence was eligible *per se* for unemployment benefits if unable to find an acceptable job, the Pennsylvania court stated, "Registration for work is the first requirement, and ordinarily it will be presumed that a claimant who registered is able and available for work. By registering the claimant makes out a prima facie case of availability, which is of course rebuttable by counter-

[40]158 Pa. Super. Ct. 548, 45 A.2d 898.

vailing evidence, e.g., refusal of referred work, illness, inability due to superannuation, and other conditions."

In more detail and with more specific delineation, the Pennsylvania court went on to say:

> There is no requirement in the quoted section, nor elsewhere in the act, that a claimant shall be available for work in any particular place, such as the locality in which he earned his wage credits or where he last worked or resided. The mere fact that a claimant has moved from one locality to another does not create a basis for holding him unavailable for work. If he registers for work in the new locality and labor-market conditions there afford reasonable opportunities for work he is available for work. Even if it appears that he might more readily have been employed had he remained in his former locality, he is nevertheless available for work if he is willing to take work for which opportunities exist in the new locality. . . .

Among the issues that have been the subject of countless controversies with resultant administrative and judicial rulings have been those involving determination of the eligibility for benefits of pregnant women, aged individuals of both sexes, persons unwilling to work on their Sabbath, professional people refusing nonprofessional job offers, craftsmen insisting on staying in their own crafts, no matter how obsolete the crafts might have become, and even craftsmen who have refused to accept new job offers in their own craft. Several of the most significant court decisions pertaining to these issues have been summarized by Dr. Thomas F. Broden, Professor of Law, University of Notre Dame, as follows:

> The Appellate Division of the New York Supreme Court held that personal restriction of work to that of an actress where clerk-typist jobs were available and acting jobs were extremely scarce rendered one unavailable. [Austen v. Carsi, 285 App Div 577, 139 NYS2d 690 (1955)]. However, later in In re Tucker, the New York Court of Appeals sustained an agency finding that a typist job was not suitable for a budding actress even though she could type. She had gotten parts before [8 NY2d 1145, 209 NYS2d 829 (1960)]. A California court has held that a personal preference and work restriction to extra work in movies paying $10.50/day thus excluding extra work of $5.50/day and all other work renders one unavailable where extra work is by its very nature irregular and intermittent. [Loew's Inc. v. California Employment Stabilization Commission, 76 Cal App2d, 231, 172, P2d 938 (1946)]. . . .
>
> In Miles v. Review Board, claimant retired from Indiana to Florida and offered himself for only well-paying managerial or white-collar work. The Appellate Court of Indiana denied benefits because of the restrictions placed on the work claimant would do and the fact that he had moved to a labor market which did not afford a

reasonable opportunity for him to find work he would do. [120 Ind App 685, 96 NE2d 128 (1951)].[41]

The United States Supreme Court handed down a truly landmark decision in 1975 in the *Mary Ann Turner* v. *Department of Employment Security and Board of Review of the Industrial Commission of Utah* when it reversed a Utah Supreme Court decision that had held a woman to be ineligible for unemployment benefits when her discontinuance of work was attributable to her pregnancy. In the *Turner* case, the Court came out four square for feminine individuality and hardihood. In so doing, the Court in its "per curiam" claim asserted:

> The petitioner, Mary Ann Turner, challenged the constitutionality of a provision of Utah law that makes pregnant women ineligible for unemployment benefits for a period extending from 12 weeks before the expected date of childbirth until a date six weeks after childbirth.
>
> The petitioner was separated involuntarily from her employment . . . for reasons unrelated to her pregnancy [she received unemployment benefits up to 12 weeks before the expected date of the birth of her baby]. Thereafter Mrs. Turner worked intermittently as a temporary clerical worker.
>
> It cannot be doubted that a substantial number of women are fully capable of working well into their third trimester of pregnancy and resuming employment shortly after childbirth. The Fourteenth Amendment requires that unemployment compensation boards no less than school boards (an earlier case originated in a restrictive rule by an Ohio school board) must achieve state ends through more individualized means when basic human liberties are at stake.

The Supreme Court concluded:

> The Utah unemployment compensation statute's incorporation of conclusive presumption of incapacity during so long a period before and after childbirth is constitutionally invalid.[42]

By no means all the issues that might reach the courts and give rise to landmark decisions ultimately reach that point. One tremendously significant issue, from the standpoint of management, was settled without court review. In this instance the union that instigated the developments accepted the decision of a state hearing officer and did not appeal to the courts. In the case in point employees of a plant being picketed by employees of another plant claimed unemployment benefits on the grounds that the picketing effectively prevented them from remaining on their jobs. Both

---

[41]Broden, pp. 334-335.
[42]Turner v. Dept. of Employment Security, 423 U.S. 44, 11 FEP 721 (1975).

plants were located in New Jersey. Under New Jersey state laws, as under the laws of many other states, employees who participate in a labor dispute are precluded from collecting unemployment insurance while so engaged. (The New York law and the laws of several other states disqualify strikers, but only for a limited period such as seven weeks.)

Some of the matters that brought about the New Jersey case were not in dispute. One of two plants operated in the state by the same corporation was shut down as a result of a legitimate economic strike. That is to say, the strike was authorized at one plant by an international union after the expiration of a contract and after an impasse had been reached in negotiations for a new contract. A different local of the same international union represented employees of the second plant. At the time the claims for unemployment compensation arose, this local's contract had almost six more months to run. When pickets representing the union local of the plant engaged in the legal strike appeared at the second plant, none of the unionized employees of that plant crossed the picket line and reported for work. After the usual one-week waiting period they all filed for unemployment compensation. They did so on the grounds, as later argued by their union counsel, that they were not in fact engaged in a strike or any form of concerted work stoppage but rather that all of them had been forced to refrain from working because of the presence of a formidable and menacing picket line maintained by the members of their sister local.

The claims of the employees of the second plant were initially denied by the New Jersey unemployment compensation agency. On appeal there was a formal hearing before a deputy state labor commissioner at which the company's management challenged its employees' claims. The main basis of the challenge was that the local union asserting the right of its members to collect unemployment compensation because they were "afraid to cross the picket line of a sister local" had in fact collaborated with the striking local in an attempt to induce the company to enter into joint agreements with uniform terms for both locals and with a common expiration date despite the fact that the agreement with the nonstriking local had many more months to run. Finding the company's position to represent the essential facts, the state hearing officer sustained it, thereby holding that the employees of the picketed plant were themselves voluntarily engaged in a labor dispute and thus ineligible for unemployment benefits.

Another type of labor controversy wherein both the Taft-Hartley Act and a state unemployment compensation law were involved reached the U.S. Supreme Court. This was the case of *Nash v. Florida Industrial Commission*. The Supreme Court held in substance that a claimant who filed an unfair labor practice charge against his employer with the National Labor Relations Board could not be denied benefits under the labor dispute qualification of the state law. It reasoned that the Labor Management Relations Act, which prohibits coercive acts by employers or unions against employees, also safeguards employees from coercive acts by the states. The denial of unemployment compensation benefits is a coercive act by a state and contravenes the supremacy clause of the Federal Constitution by impeding the execution of a congressional act, the Court said. Stripped of its legal verbiage, the Supreme Court's position was, in substance, that a state could not refuse to grant unemployment insurance to an employee laid off from work solely because he had filed an unfair labor practice charge against his employer alleging the impropriety of his layoff.[43]

Benefits Payable During Lockout

Some 15 states specifically have authorized the payment of unemployment benefits to employees who are idled because of a lockout. But what is a lockout? Here, again, there is an interplay, as was stressed in Chapter 1, between the rights and obligations of employers and employees under different statutes. Generally, the term "lockout" means a "shutdown of a plant by an employer to discourage union membership or activity." But whether a suspension of work actually constitutes a lockout is a question that may have to be decided, and perhaps decided otherwise, by entirely different tribunals and under quite dissimilar circumstances.

California and New York are two of the states that sanction unemployment benefits for employees who have been temporarily idled by lockouts. In the case here summarized, however, it was not the state administrative agency or a court that determined whether a lockout occurred. It was, rather, an *arbitrator*.

This case involved the simultaneous shutdown by the management of two of its plants in California and one in New York State. The shutdown in question occurred when an impasse had been reached after the provisions of the current contract had expired and while negotiations for a new master contract (one with local supplements) were in progress. Instead of striking any of the three plants, as it obviously had a legal right to do, the union proceeded to engage in whipsaw tactics. These tactics took the form of action by

---

[43]Nash v. Florida Industrial Commission, et al., 389 U.S. 235, 66 LRRM 2625 (1967).

the three local unions in alternately calling off the job all shop
stewards for "strategy sessions" or holding membership meetings for
all employees for an hour or two at the beginning or toward the end
of their shifts. After futile protests and due notice of their intended
action, the management of each of the plants informed the local
unions and the international representatives that the plants would
be shut down and remain closed either until a new contract was
negotiated and ratified or until the union notified management
that the daily disruption of working schedules would end. The
plants were then closed and kept closed until a new master contract
was ratified.

Immediately thereafter the union filed grievances at all three
plants charging their managements with lockouts in violation of the
express terms of the master agreement that was still in effect. When
no settlement was reached through the grievance procedure at any
of the plants, the three separate grievances were consolidated into
one arbitration proceeding involving all three plants, and a single
arbitrator was designated to decide the issues. Because of some
apparent disparities between the factual situations incident to the
plant shutdowns, separate hearings were held on the grievance of
each plant, and the arbitrator was thus free to decide whether an
improper lockout had occurred in one or more plants but not at all
three together. The arbitrator sustained the company's position in
its entirety. He found, in effect, that the plant shutdowns were for
legitimate economic reasons, permissible under the terms of the
then-applicable agreement. The principal reason for the management's actions was declared to be that the company could not
expect to keep these three plants running when work schedules were
subject to sudden, crippling, and intermittent interruptions.

The arbitrator, in holding that the company had not engaged
in lockouts, produced his own definition of the term. The arbitrator, incidentally, was James J. Healy, long distinguished in the field
of arbitration and also a professor of industrial relations on the
faculty of the Harvard Graduate School of Business Administration. Arbitrator Healy said:

> Both parties have supplied various definitions of the term "lock-
> out." The union highlights the element of "labor dispute context"
> and it must be admitted that a lockout is used invariably at a time
> when a labor dispute exists. However, it does not follow that the
> action of closing a plant at the time of a labor dispute is necessarily a
> lockout. In general the dictionary approach is unsatisfactory.
> In the arbitrator's judgment, three characteristics are indis-
> pensable in a lockout situation:

    a. the place of employment is closed in part or in whole by the employer,

    b. it is an action on the offense,

    c. its purpose is to use such deprivation of employment as an economic weapon to gain concessions from the employees.[44]

The union did not file for unemployment compensation for its members after Arbitrator Healy's decision was handed down. Nor did any of its members as individuals. The master contract under which the arbitration proceedings were instituted explicitly provided that the grievance procedure was the sole mechanism for adjudicating disputes over the meaning and application of all terms of the contract and that neither party would or could resort to any other tribunal to seek remedies for alleged violations.

Pertinent but not on all fours with the previous case are two others that did undergo judicial review. Both arose as a result of decisions by the management of Westinghouse Electric Company. In both instances management decisions were upheld by the state courts as not involving lockouts. The employees affected were thus ruled ineligible for unemployment benefits. These two cases and their implications have been summarized by Dr. Willard A. Lewis as follows:

> In one situation the company undertook a work survey to institute a cost-saving change unilaterally with notice to the union. This led to a strike of 2,000 day workers and the consequent furloughing of some 7,000 incentive workers. In another case the company, over the local union's protest, put a new promotion program into effect in accordance with the master agreement. When employees walked off, the company refused to allow them to return unless they accepted the new program. In both cases the (state) board of review found a lockout and granted benefits. Each time, upon appeal, the Board's finding was reversed by the courts and employees were denied unemployment benefits.
>
> The courts ruled that if a contract is in force, a strike does not become a lockout by reason of unilateral action by the employer where there are such other ways open for employees to defend themselves as grievance procedures, actions to compel arbitration, or law suits for breach of contract. Such unilateral action must have the effect of coercing employees into accepting onerous and disadvantageous terms of employment so that they could not be reasonably expected to continue in their jobs under such circumstances. Only then would the employees be considered as "locked out" and, therefore, eligible for benefits.[45]

---

[44]General Cable Corporation, 18 LA 741 (1952).

[45]Willard A. Lewis, *Strikes and Unemployment Insurance*, PREPARING FOR COLLECTIVE BARGAINING, II (New York: National Industrial Conference Board, 1961), p. 59.

Contesting Dubious Claims

Management must always be wary in considering whether or not to contest an individual employee's unemployment benefit claims that might seem dubious or worse. Assume, for instance, that a supervisor is found *flagrante delicto* or *pante pendente* with one of his female subordinates on company time and company premises. Assume further that, instead of being discharged forthwith, he is allowed to resign because of "unsatisfactory working conditions" or "lack of suitable work." Failing to find other suitable employment within the next few weeks, the ex-supervisor files for unemployment benefits and claims that he was summarily discharged without good cause. What then is management's responsibility in protecting its own company's experience rating and what is its obligation to the state agency processing this sort of claim? Can or should management talk out of both sides of its mouth? Obviously, from an ethical and legal standpoint, these questions have to be decided on the basis of telling the truth. Management can have no valid basis for challenging a former employee's right to claim unemployment benefits if the reason for his separation as given to him and recorded on the company's records was one that would not constitute a disqualification even though the real reason for termination was one that would make the former employee patently ineligible.

Privileged Communications

There is little uniformity in state unemployment compensation laws with respect to the delicate question of what constitutes privileged communications. Such communications relate, of course, to the types of information the employer supplies to state administrative agencies that process the claims of laid-off or discharged employees for benefits, as well as the claims of workers who have left their jobs voluntarily and seemingly for reasons that would not disqualify them from receiving unemployment benefits.

On this set of issues The Bureau of National Affairs, Inc., has provided the following information and advice:

> In many states it is assumed that a claim is valid if no information pointing to a contrary conclusion is supplied by the employer. It is therefore up to the individual employer to protect himself by furnishing relevant information regarding separations in reports or other communications to the state UC officials. A question which then arises is this: Does a frank statement of the reasons for the discharge or other termination lay the employer open to a charge of slander or libel by a former employee?

Many state laws provide that letters, reports, oral statements and other communications related to or required for the administration of the UC law are absolutely privileged and cannot be used as the basis for a suit for libel or slander. In a few other states the employer's immunity is not so sweeping but is limited to reasonable statements made without malicious intent.

Where the state law is silent on the point, the question of privilege is for the courts to decide. In Idaho, for example, a state court has ruled that relevant statements supplied by an employer in the "Wage and Separation Report" are absolutely privileged and cannot be used as a basis for a suit for defamation.

Virtually all state laws provide that reports and other information supplied by an employer to the UC agency are to be kept confidential and that the details may be disclosed only to the extent necessary for proper presentation of a claim or protest. This affords a measure of protection to the employer.[46]

Temporary Disability Insurance

Five states now have statutes requiring payments to employees for time lost on account of illness or nonoccupational disability. These states are California, Hawaii, New Jersey, New York, and Rhode Island. The Rhode Island law establishes the terms under which benefits are payable to employees under an exclusive state-administered plan financed by payroll taxes levied solely on employees. The laws of the other states permit employers to set up their own plans and to administer such plans themselves (or through insurance carriers), provided that the benefits payable are at least equal to, if not in excess of, those required under the state-administered systems.

Although currently in effect in only the five states previously mentioned, temporary disability laws have exerted a tremendous impact on employers' fringe benefit plans and policies. The industrial population of these five states represents nearly one quarter of the nation's entire work force. Plans set up in these states by companies with nation-wide multiplant or multifacility operations have set precedents and provided benefits difficult or impossible to ignore in both unionized and nonunion operations in other states.

Nonoccupational disability benefits required to be paid by state laws are usually fixed on the same scale as unemployment compensation. Current weekly maximum benefits range from $72 per week in Rhode Island to $119 in California. There is the customary one-week waiting period before any benefits are payable for

---

[46]BNA POLICY AND PRACTICE SERIES FOR EMPLOYEE RELATIONS EXECUTIVES, Payroll Section, Chapter 356.

the original disability. Often close questions arise as to the distinction between occupationally connected disability and nonoccupational disability. Some of these questions are reviewed in the next chapter. More often than not, an employee who has been injured in a situation where some company connection is established or even arguable will seek coverage under the applicable workmen's compensation law. This is quite understandable. If an occupational connection can be proved, the injured employee can usually collect for medical expenses as well as lost time and frequently will obtain an award for permanent partial disability as well.

CHAPTER 5

Workers' Compensation, Safety, and Health

The states rather than the Federal Government have been for more than a half century the prime movers in enacting legislation to indemnify employees for disability caused by occupational injuries or ailments. They still are. Except for workers in certain industries subject to special federal legislation, such as railroads and maritime transportation, nearly all employees of private establishments are covered by workers' compensation laws enacted and administered by the states themselves. As for railroad and maritime employees, the applicable statute, the Federal Employers' Liability Act, does not actually provide a system for paying benefits for occupational disability. Rather, it sets the conditions under which workers can sue their employers for negligence resulting in injuries. It also prevents employers from avoiding liability by invoking the common law defenses of contributory negligence by the employees themselves or by their fellow workers.

Occupational safety and health is, of course, quite a different matter. The states have had and still have almost complete jurisdiction to determine what benefits will be payable for occupational disability. But in 1970 Congress took a gigantic step towards establishing federal controls over safety and health hazards in nearly all fields of business and industry by the passage of the Federal Occupational Safety and Health Act. By its own terms, this federal law cannot be construed to supersede any state workers' compensation law. (Its modus operandi and objectives are dealt with later in this chapter.) Should there be anything like full realization of its objectives, which are to minimize unsafe and unhealthful conditions at the workplaces of private employers, compliance with state workers' compensation laws by employers would ultimately present far fewer problems than now prevail. But these objectives are far from attainable in the next few years. Accordingly, workers' compensation legislation still holds major problems for management throughout the private sector.

THE NATIONAL COMMISSION ON
STATE WORKMEN'S COMPENSATION LAWS

When it enacted the Occupational Safety and Health Act of 1970, Congress was evidently not convinced that the passage of this statute alone would provide sufficient impetus to prod private-sector employers to take speedy action to develop more satisfactory safety and health programs. So Congress included in the law a special provision (Section 27) establishing the National Commission on State Workmen's Compensation Laws. That Commission was directed to report to the President and Congress by July 1, 1972, its findings as to whether existing state laws provided "an adequate, prompt and equitable system of compensation." The basic conclusion of the Commission was that the present state system was essentially sound but the protection furnished to American workers was generally inadequate and inequitable. In its report the Commission set forth its views as to the proper objectives of state workers' compensation programs. The four basic objectives were declared to be:

> *Broad coverage of employees and of work-related injuries and diseases.*
> Protection should be extended to as many workers as feasible and all work-related injuries and diseases should be covered.
> *Substantial protection against interruption of income.*
> A high proportion of a disabled worker's lost earnings should be replaced by workmen's compensation benefits.
> *Provision of sufficient medical care and rehabilitation services.*
> The injured worker's physical condition and earning capacity should be promptly restored.
> *Encouragement of Safety.*
> Economic incentives in the program should reduce the number of work-related injuries and diseases.

The Commission's concluding observation was that "achievement of these four basic objectives is dependent on a fifth objective: *An effective system for delivery of the benefits and services. . . .*"

Most state legislatures were quick to amend their workers' compensation laws to go part way toward adopting some of the more important recommendations of the National Commission. As noted in a report issued by the United States Chamber of Commerce:

> The constructive criticism rendered by the Commission gave new impetus to the development and growth of workmen's compensation laws and these laws now enjoy a more prominent role within the social insurance system of the United States. . . .

[During 1973] in all over two hundred laws were enacted covering almost every phase of workmen's compensation, such as increasing benefits, reducing waiting periods, increasing medical care and improving administration of the laws. Undoubtedly much of the legislation enacted was a result of the recommendations of the National Commission accompanied by the caveat that in the event the states failed to improve their laws so as to insure an adequate, prompt and equitable workmen's compensation system, it may become necessary to enact federal legislation requiring minimum standards.[1]

Then in 1974 "in a continuing effort to update their laws and bring them into conformity with recommendations of the National Commission on State Workmen's Compensation Laws, the legislatures of 46 states enacted over 200 amendments. . . ." This was so reported in the January 1975 issue of the Bureau of Labor Statistics publication, *The Monthly Labor Review*. But as the report indicated, no state had yet fully met the Commission's essential recommendations.[2]

Possible Federalization of Workers' Compensation

Pending in the Senate at the close of its 1975 session was a bill (S.2018) that would superimpose a federal workers' compensation statute on existing state laws. If enacted by Congress, so the Chamber of Commerce of the United States has charged, the estimated annual cost of $6 billion for the total aggregate workers' compensation programs might rise more than sixfold to $40 billion, weaken our ability to compete in the world economic market, and remove strong incentives for accident prevention built into the current state programs.[3]

Significant Recent Changes in State Laws

No doubt it was the willingness of many state legislatures convening in 1974 to make substantial increases in benefit rates that has all but eliminated the possibility of easy passage of a federal law to supersede state compensation statutes. Nearly three fourths of the states increased the maximum weekly benefits pay-

---

[1]Chamber of Commerce of the United States, ANALYSIS OF WORKMEN'S COMPENSATION LAWS (Washington: Chamber of Commerce of the United States, 1974), pp. 3-4.

[2]Florence C. Johnson, *Workers' Compensation Laws—Changes in 1974*, MONTHLY LABOR REVIEW, U.S. Department of Labor, Bureau of Labor Statistics, Jan. 1975, 98(No. 1), p. 30.

[3]BEST'S INSURANCE DIGEST, as cited in PUBLIC AFFAIRS NEWSLETTER, Kemper Insurance Companies, 1975, 5(No. 21). There is no realistic indication that S. 2018, which could increase workers' compensation costs so drastically, has any chance of passage. No action was taken in the 94th Congress, and the bill died. There are plans, however, to reintroduce the measure in the 95th Congress.

able for temporary disability. But only nine states have thus far gone all the way in accepting the National Commission's recommendation that maximum benefits should be fixed at 100 percent of the average weekly wages for the state's private-sector employees.

Quite obviously, there have been other forces that induced state legislatures to raise benefit rates to unprecedented levels in the past 10 years. The greatest force could well have been the inflationary rises in industrial workers' earnings in the past five or six years. Whatever the causes, the facts as disclosed in the following table speak for themselves. The maximum benefit rate for temporary disability is the standard by which progress in attaining more equitable workmen's compensation allowances is commonly judged. As the tabular analysis discloses, 16 states had by 1975 increased the maximum weekly benefits for temporary total disability to rates more than 100 percent higher than those prevailing in 1970. For example, the percentage increase from 1971 to 1975 for some of these states ranged from 102 percent in Colorado and Maryland to 152 percent in North Carolina, 172 percent in Idaho, and 230 percent in Utah.

STATE PROGRESS IN WORKERS' COMPENSATION[*]

	Temporary total disability (Maximum Weekly Payment)		
State	1970	July 1975	Percentage Increase
Alabama	$ 50.00	$ 75.00	50
Alaska †	127.00	198.40	56
Arizona	154.04	154.04	0
Arkansas	49.00	66.50	38
California	87.50	119.00	70
Colorado †	59.50	120.17	102
Connecticut †	84.00	119.00	43
Delaware †	75.00	125.40	67
District of Columbia	70.00	210.60	200
Florida	56.00	80.00	43
Georgia	50.00	95.00	90
Hawaii †	112.50	232.50	107
Idaho †	43.00	117.00	172
Illinois †	91.00	205.00	125
Indiana	57.00	90.00	57
Iowa †	61.00	160.09	125
Kansas †	56.00	103.10	84
Kentucky †	56.00	88.00	57
Louisiana	49.00	65.00	33
Maine †	73.00	141.41	94

Temporary total disability
(Maximum Weekly Payment)

State	1970	July 1975	Percentage Increase
Maryland †	81.50	164.50	102
Massachusetts	70.00	80.00	14
Michigan †	75.00	136.00	81
Minnesota	70.00	135.00	93
Mississippi	40.00	63.00	58
Missouri	63.50	95.00	50
Montana †	60.00	147.00	145
Nebraska	55.00	100.00	82
Nevada †	79.96	176.86	121
New Hampshire †	67.00	147.00	119
New Jersey †	91.00	119.00	31
New Mexico	48.00	90.00	88
New York	95.00	125.00	32
North Carolina †	50.00	126.14	152
North Dakota †	59.00	142.80	142
Ohio †	56.00	119.00	113
Oklahoma	49.00	60.00	16
Oregon †	80.00	120.17	50
Pennsylvania †	60.00	154.61	158
Rhode Island †	70.33	97.00	38
South Carolina †	50.00	91.16	82
South Dakota †	50.00	88.00	76
Tennessee	47.00	85.00	81
Texas †	49.00	70.00	43
Utah †	47.00	155.00	230
Vermont †	61.00	91.00	49
Virginia †	62.00	149.00	140
Washington †	81.23	138.92	71
West Virginia †	65.50	173.00	164
Wisconsin †	79.00	108.00	37
Wyoming †	63.46	111.03	75

*Compiled as of July 1, 1975, by the American Mutual Insurance Alliance and condensed in *Public Affairs Newsletter,* Kemper Insurance and Finance Companies.

†Automatic maximum benefit increases based on state gross average weekly wage (for death and temporary and total disability).

It must be explained that as shown in the footnote to this table, 31 states have acted between 1970 and 1975 to increase maximum benefits payable for *death and total disability* as well as for temporary disability. It has become common practice for the state legislatures that have adopted automatically operative formulas for modifying benefit rates — based essentially on changes in average earnings of the state's work force — to adjust death and total disability benefits to the same degree as benefits for temporary disability.

BASIC PROVISIONS OF STATE WORKERS' COMPENSATION LAWS

All states now have viable workers' compensation laws. These are usually characterized as "elective" or "compulsory." Under an elective law an employer has the option of insuring or self-insuring his compensation risks or of subjecting himself to employees' suits arising out of their claimed occupational disabilities.

If an employer chooses to reject coverage under an elective law, he forfeits his right to defend himself in employee suits for compensation awards through invoking the common-law defenses known technically as assumption of risk, fellow servant rule, and contributory negligence. Such forfeiture means, in layman's terms, that when an employee sues to recover damages attributable to occupational injuries from an employer who has decided not to be bound by the determination of a state agency as to his compensation liability, the employer may not assert that he is exposed legally only to proof of his actual or imputed negligence. Employers now have this dubious right in only five states. Moreover, in some of these states such rights are subject to the qualification that employees filing claims for occupational disability have themselves the right to reject the nonapplicability of the compensation law.

In the 45 states where full compliance is compulsory for employees covered, the laws apply to virtually all businesses engaged in industry or commerce, regardless of the number of their employees. There are a few minor exceptions such as in Missouri, where the law applies only to firms with at least six employees; South Carolina, to firms with four or more employees; and Georgia, to firms with three or more employees. The laws of 39 states with compulsory coverage permit employers to exercise limited options as to how their compensation risks can be financed. There are, however, six states that make it mandatory for employers to participate in an exclusive state-administered insurance fund. Except in these states, the employers covered mandatorily by workmen's compensation can choose to meet their liabilities through self-insurance plans, or through insurance policies purchased from casualty insurance companies, or through payment of premiums to state-managed plans or funds.

The Co-Insurance Principle

Whether or not a state law permits employers to self-insure their workers' compensation risks, all the laws contemplate that the principle of co-insurance should generally prevail in determination of the benefits payable for occupational disability. This principle was not negated but, rather, was emphasized by the National Commission in proposing that a *high* proportion of a disabled worker's lost earnings should be replaced by workers' compensation benefits. But not usually *total earnings*. For the laws are predicated on the theory that employees themselves should assume some responsibility for minimizing the chances of getting disabled on the job. That is to say, most state laws have a built-in deterrent factor akin to the principle of co-insurance in homeowners' insurance policies. No one is able normally to buy a fire insurance policy that will pay him the full current value, or more, of his home should it be destroyed by fire. Seventy-five or perhaps 80 percent of the value of the house is the most he could reasonably expect to collect.

It's true that the amendments to state laws from 1973 on have been narrowing the gap between employees' regular weekly pay and the benefits receivable under workers' compensation laws. According to an American Mutual Alliance study reported in 1975, "state workers' compensation benefits replaced 73 percent of the average worker's spendable earnings as compared with 54 percent in 1960 and 64 percent in 1972."[4]

Nevertheless, the majority of the state laws still have in effect what amount to guidelines establishing flexible maximums equivalent generally to about two thirds of the average weekly wages of the state's own workers. There are now such provisions in 29 state laws as well as in the law for the District of Columbia. It is quite manifestly the wage earners in the highest brackets whose compensation benefits do not now and will not in the immediately forseeable future come close to approximating their weekly take-home pay.

The term "self-insurance," connoting a method of financing workmen's compensation and many other types of employee benefits, for 50 years and more has given rise to much controversy. A standard argument advanced by insurance company executives and salesmen is that a widget manufacturing company should stick to making widgets and stay out of the insurance business. A standard response among advocates of self-insurance

---

[4]PUBLIC AFFAIRS NEWSLETTER, p. 3.

is that if a company can do a good job in providing professional safety engineering and benefit administration, as well as in earning an adequate return on the funds it set aside to meet its actuarially determined benefit liabilities, self-insurance can save it much money.

Occupational Hazards Covered by Workers' Compensation

Under most state workers' compensation laws employers subject thereto are liable for providing monetary benefits or reimbursement of medical and hospital expenses for employees who become involved in the following types of job-connected occurrences:

- *Non-lost-time accidents,* for which an employee needs only medical attention, even though subsequent benefits for permanent partial disability, such as a crippled finger or minor facial disfigurement, may be payable.
- *Lost-time accidents,* which compel an employee to be absent from work, with or without medical or hospital expense.
- *Temporary partial disability,* where a minor physical impairment prevents an employee from continuing full-time on his regular job or from earning normal wages for a limited period, in which event cash benefits may be payable for a stated period or in a lump sum.
- *Permanent partial or total disability,* where an employee's injury involves serious disfigurement, partial or complete loss of an essential function (sight in one or both eyes, crippling or dismemberment of hands, legs, etc.), or other incapacity that prevents an employee from resuming his previous job or, in extreme cases, any gainful employment. There have been numerous instances, however, in which awards for permanent total disability have been made and then after skillful occupational rehabilitation and retraining, employees officially declared to be totally disabled have returned to work—usually in different occupations—but not necessarily at lower rates of pay.
- *Death,* which usually entitles the deceased employee's surviving dependent relatives (widowed spouse, minor children, or parents) to periodic benefits over a large number of weeks or years.
- *Occupational disease,* such as silicosis, because of which an employee may be entitled to benefits cumulatively over a long period of time after continued exposure to toxic substances or unhealthy working conditions.

- *Noncrippling physical impairments,* such as deafness, that an employee may gradually suffer after protracted exposure to excessive noise in his workplace.

- *Other job-connected impairments* suffered by an employee while not doing his regular work and often developing away from the workplace but with employer sanction or sponsorship, such as during athletic or social activities or during travel related to company business.

- *Injuries or disabilities attributable to an employer's gross negligence,* in which event additional penalties may be imposed, ranging from additional benefits of 10 percent to the equivalent of double damages.

All of these potential liabilities and contingencies have to be taken into account by management in determining how to finance its workers' compensation risks. And their scope and possibly great costs make it equally or more important for management to maintain effective preventive safety and health programs in addition to compensation insurance. Mere compilation of statistics on lost-time and non-lost-time accidents usually does not reveal the magnitude of a company's safety and health problems. Trivial accidents that might go unreported may produce complications developing into major claims. "Near misses" involving damage to equipment or products without causing injuries to any workmen may represent major safety hazards to both men and machinery. A trivial scratch, bump, or bruise resulting from inadequately guarded equipment or careless work habits can lead to serious infections or require complicated surgery at a cost of thousands of dollars, or can even result in a claim for double indemnity on account of management's alleged negligence. And an undetected and untreated pulmonary condition of an employee exposed to excessive dust could develop into months or years of hospitalization, with the employer paying the bill plus partial wages.

Selected Illustrative and Leading Compensation Cases

In citing herein specific cases our purpose is not to provide a manual or casebook on workers' compensation law. To be reasonably complete and authoritative this treatment would require a work of several volumes and many thousand pages. Such is *Larson's Workmen's Compensation Law,* published in five volumes with periodic supplements. As its distinguished author, Professor Arthur Larson, has so succinctly put it: "Compensation law is so prolific that sooner or later it provides an actual case to fill any gap."[5]

The cases summarized in this chapter have been chosen, therefore, for their value in indicating to management — and especially to personnel administrators having responsibilities extending beyond compensation and safety functions — the urgency of integrating accident prevention activities into a well-rounded set of personnel practices. It may well be true that compensation benefits are often awarded employees because of their carelessness, stupidity, or cupidity. Almost as often claims have to be paid because of seemingly unrelated management decisions in formulating policies on pre-employment and periodic physical examinations, in determining the calibre of individuals selected to perform or supervise particular jobs, and in determining what constitute adequate first aid and other medical facilities.

Some misguided employers still have the belief that industrial accidents and resultant compensation claims are largely unavoidable. This is just not true. Some of the most hazardous industries have by far the best safety records.

"Acts of God"

Countless cases have been litigated on the issue of what constitutes a job-connected injury as distinguished from an "Act of God." The published decisions by no means all reach the same conclusions. If there is any pattern, it is generally in favor of the theory that any disability sustained while in the course of employment has an occupational connection and is thus compensable.

One leading case required a Texas court to determine whether an employee's death was due to an occupational injury or to a noncompensable Act of God. To evaluate the significance of this case, the essential facts must be summarized. The widow and minor children of a deceased employee of a road construction company filed claims for death benefits under the state workmen's compensation law on the ground that the deceased had lost his life as a result of a heat stroke received in the course of his employment. The deceased employee had been a common laborer working for a road construction firm. He was 39 years old and apparently in good health. On the day he died, he was shoveling sand into a wheelbarrow and emptying the sand into a concrete

---

[5]Arthur Larson, LARSON'S WORKMEN'S COMPENSATION LAW (New York: Matthew Bender and Co., Inc.), Sections 12, 14, p. 192.20.

mixer some distance away. While doing so, he complained to a fellow workman of feeling sick and went to a water barrel to get a drink. After pushing two more barrows of sand, he stopped and was taken to the company office in a car. When he arrived he was unconscious. Shortly thereafter he died. The maximum temperature on the day in question was 97 degrees, a factor considered significant in the court's decision. There were many allegations as to what had caused this laborer's death: heat prostration, drinking foul water, heart disease associated with acute gastritis. The dependents' claim for death benefits was originally decided by a jury, whose verdict was that the man had died of heat stroke in the course of his employment.

This case was then reviewed by the Texas Court of Civil Appeals, which ruled as follows:

> Our compensation statute . . . in defining the term "injury" excludes an injury caused by the act of God "unless the employee is at the time engaged in the performance of duties that subject him to a greater hazard from the act of God responsible for the injury than ordinarily applies to the general public." The interpretation given to the provision by the practical application of it in adjudicated cases by the courts of our state is to exclude injuries caused by storms, lightning, heatstroke, and other acts of God which do not have their origin in the employment. But where the work or employment of the employee is a contributing factor in bringing about the injury, it is compensable. *In the case before us the very work which the deceased was doing for his employer exposed him to greater hazard from heatstroke than the general public was exposed to for the simple reason that the general public were not pushing wheelbarrow loads of sand in the hot sun on that day.* [Italics supplied][6]

Perhaps the most extreme case that produced a result directly contrary to the one just cited was decided by an Illinois court in 1926. Denying compensation to a workman whose hands had been frozen while he was shoveling coal, the court declared:

> Of the six men who shoveled coal in the same yard at the same time, defendant in error was the only person who experienced the frostbite of his hands. . . . The fact that the other workmen did not suffer the injury of which he complains, although they were engaged in the same work at the same place and time, shows that he was not, by reason of his occupation, exposed to a special or peculiar danger from freezing greater than that shared by other persons in the same locality.[7]

---

[6] American General Insurance Co. v. Webster, 118 S.W.2d 1082 (1938).
[7] Consumers Co. v. Industrial Commission, 324 Ill. 152, 154 N.E. (1926).

When a disabling or fatal injury is suffered by an employee, invocation of the Deity as a defense against compensation liability is often futile. The Texas Court of Civil Appeals so indicated in a case involving a widow's claim for death benefits when her husband died within 24 hours after having been stung by a wasp. There was no dispute about the fact that the victim received the wasp sting while working on his regular job. The basic issue the court had to decide was whether the sting was or was not an Act of God. The court ruled that in this particular case, it was not. In so ruling, the court had this to say:

> If the wasp sting can be said to be an act of God, then in order to effect recovery it is incumbent upon deceased's beneficiaries to show deceased was "engaged in the performance of duties that subject him to a greater hazard from an act of God responsible for the injury than ordinarily applies to the general public." . . . We are of the opinion, and so hold, a wasp sting is not an act of God. Although an act of God is not defined in the workmen's compensation act, the phrase has been considered by our courts. Even though it is not susceptible of an accurate and comprehensive definition, the courts use such language as "the act must be occasioned exclusively by the violence of nature," and such injury "is due directly and exclusively to natural causes, without human intervention, where no amount of foresight or care which could have been reasonably required . . . could have prevented the injury."

Although partially out of context, another case involving an alleged insect bite points up the essentiality of adequate safety precautions and medical treatment of real or fancied injuries. From management's standpoint, this specific case was more closely akin to the machinations of the devil than to an Act of God. The basic facts were these. A night-shift factory workman went to the plant dispensary complaining of an irritation in his eye. He asserted no occupational cause. The irritation persisted despite the first aid treatment he had received from the plant nurse.

A few days later the employee rubbed his eye so vigorously — at least he later said he did — that he suffered a detached retina. After a serious and expensive eye operation the employee belatedly filed a compensation claim, contending that on the night he went for treatment at the plant dispensary a mosquito had bitten him in the eye. The attending nurse who treated him had seen no indication of a bite of any sort on his eye. Nor did the employee say anything about a bite before or during the casual first aid treatment with an eye wash.

When the employee's compensation claim was scheduled for a hearing and the basis for his claim first became known to the plant management, a belated examination of his workplace disclosed a screen missing from a window near a bright overhead light fixture. Because the factory where he worked was in a New Jersey town in an area notorious for the prevalence of mosquitoes, the plant management was advised by its compensation counsel that the indisputable absence of a screen on a window near a light would be considered as *prima facie* evidence to support the employee's allegation that a mosquito had in fact flown into the plant and bitten him on the eye. It is not inconceivable that this employee, or one of his friends, or perhaps one of his legal advisors, had heard of completely credible accounts of actual injuries from insect stings or bites that culminated in substantial compensation awards. Despite a lingering doubt as to the truth of the employee's contentions and the actuality of a causal connection between the alleged mosquito bite and the detached retina, his employer did not contest the case. The result was a substantial award for partial loss of vision, plus, of course, an additional award for surgical fees and hospital expenses running into many thousands of dollars.

Cumulative Disability

It is by no means required by law that an employee has to suffer a specific one-shot injury in order to be entitled to workmen's compensation benefits. Similarly, dependents of deceased employees can be awarded death benefits for progressive or cumulative long-term disabilities leading ultimately to death. Progressively increased deafness, for example, if demonstrably connected with constant exposure to excessive noise at the employee's workplace, is usually held to be compensable as partial permanent disability. The administrative and court rulings on this issue are too numerous and too consistently in favor of employees with hearing impairments to warrant extensive review or discussion. One landmark decision of a Georgia court, which, incidentally, included citation of comparable decisions in other states, resulted in an award for an airline mechanic who had suffered progressive impairment of hearing while working in close proximity to jet aircraft engines, even though he was unable to pinpoint any particular time or incident that precipitated the onset of his deafness.[8]

It is the more unusual cases that cause personnel administrators to become concerned about preventive action and to establish

---

[8]Shipman v. Employers Mutual Liability Insurance Company, 125 S.E.2d 72 (1962).

bases for defense against dubious claims. The following is one of the most unusual decisions. In March 1969, a New York State appellate court held that a judge of a lower court in the same state had worked himself to death while trying to clear up a logjam of cases. Representatives of the state itself challenged the widow's claim for death benefits, taking the position that the judge's duties did not involve circumstances beyond the stress and strain of ordinary life. But the appellate court ruled otherwise. That court considered as highly relevant testimony the fact that the deceased judge had foregone a normal two-week break and in so doing had expressed anxiety that his cases be promptly decided. In support of its award to the judge's widow the court declared that "it had been held that undue anxiety, strain and mental stress from work are frequently more devastating than a mere physical injury."[9]

There are also leading cases which establish the principle that an apparently minor injury may touch off dire consequences months or years later and culminate in a major award for death benefits or permanent total disability. One such case was decided by the then (as now) prestigious U.S. Circuit Court of Appeals for the District of Columbia. Briefly, an occupationally connected bruised toe turned eventually into a court decision holding that a restaurant employee whose last illness was diagnosed as pneumonia while he was a hospital patient, but whose actual cause of death was certified as being due to "diabetes mellitus," had nevertheless had his death hastened because he had stubbed his toe while at work the previous year.

The deceased employee had been a known diabetic. After he had accidentally bruised one of his toes the toenail came off. Then, as the court stated, "infection and gangrene developed and spread to the foot and leg, and the toe was amputated; two weeks later the metatarsal bone; five weeks later the foot, and another two weeks later the leg just below the knee. The stump never completely healed and the man never returned to work." Unquestionably this employee had incurred an occupationally connected accident and the court so ruled.

But what about the actual cause of this unfortunate man's death. Here, as so often happens in compensation litigation, the medical experts disagreed. After mentioning that the death certificate gave the cause as diabetes mellitus the court went on to say:

---

[9]NEW YORK TIMES, March 13, 1969.

An attending physician testified that "the immediate cause of death was due to the particular hemorrhage present at the brain and the death was entirely respiratory . . ." A pathologist performed an autopsy and testified that "This man died as a result of a chronic glomerulonephritis," a pathological condition of the kidney, "with considerable other complications."

Two attending physicians said that there was no "causal connection" or "causal relation" between the injury, with its consequent series of operations, and the man's death. The pathologist said that "the injury is not a part and parcel of the nephritis that killed him. . . . I cannot draw a direct causal effect between this injury to his foot and the cause of death as a result of the nephritis."

But the same pathologist testified that "the nephritis, of course, and the diabetes and the arteriosclerosis all going along together with the injury resulted in his death." . . .

A physician who had not seen the patient testified that an injury which breaks the continuity of the skin is "potentially" dangerous to a diabetic; that four successive operations would "weaken his resistance" more than that of a person in good health; and that if the four successive wounds failed to heal, and the final one remained open at the time of death, the original injury "had a relation to his death as a cause."

The court decided in this case that there was substantial evidence to support the common-sense conclusion that "an injury to a diabetic, which resulted in infection, gangrene, four amputations, and a permanently unhealed stump, probably hastened his death from disease. *To hasten death is to cause it.* [Italics supplied.] There was abundant evidence that such an injury to such a man, with such consequences, might cause death, and some testimony that it did so." Thus the court ruled that a compensable injury having occurred, the widow was entitled to death benefits.[10]

Aggravation of Preexisting Disability

Frequently employers are obligated to pay compensation benefits for aggravated disabilities that may have originally developed a long time prior to an actual employment relationship. Thus, it has been held by a New Jersey appellate court that an occupationally connected injury to an employee's back contributed to and hastened his death from a malignant tumor that presumably had been metastasizing, i.e., spreading to other parts of his body, for an undetermined period before the accident happened. Little else except the meaning of the term "metastasizing" was agreed upon by the medical specialists who testified at the

---

[10] Avignone Freres, Inc. v. Carillo, 117 F.2d 385 (1940).

protracted hearings on the cause of death of the employee whose widow claimed compensation benefits.

No dispute arose over the fact that the deceased employee, an "operator and beamer" in a textile mill, had complained to a fellow worker that his back hurt just as he and the other man had lifted a roll of dress material into place on a machine. He promptly told the mill superintendent of his complaint. At the compensation hearing, a fellow worker testified that the decedent was walking in slouched position although he apparently worked through the end of his shift. The next day, as instructed by the superintendent, the employee reported to the company physician. The initial diagnosis was that the patient had suffered strain of his lower back muscles. He returned to work, but approximately a month later left his job and never resumed employment. The appellate court that finally decided the case concluded:

> The County Court judge determined that Celeste [the deceased] suffered a stress or strain to his lumbosacral area which already had a metastatic lesion; that the trauma caused the hastening of the disease in his body with a rapid retrogression. It has been well settled that a work-connected aggravation of a preexisting cancerous condition is compensable. . . .
>
> The burden of proof is on the petitioner [the widow] to justify an award for compensation. In determining whether petitioner has sustained the burden of proof the quality of the evidence required is probability rather than certainty. The burden is sustained if the tendered hypothesis is based on the preponderance of probabilities. . . .
>
> The testimony presented revealed that Celeste was in apparent good health prior to the accident, had worked regularly, suffered only an occasional cold. He was unaware that he was a victim of cancer. Nevertheless the employer takes his employees with their mental and physical defects or disabilities. . . . While it is true that he might and probably would have died of the disease in the normal course of events, nevertheless his serious physical impairment soon after the accident and the rapid progress of the disease makes a finding of cause and effect between trauma and acceleration of death a reasonable probability. . . .
>
> From our review of the entire evidence and exhibits, especially in view of the enhanced weight which must be accorded petitioner's medical witnesses as treating physicians we conclude that the burden of proving that Celeste's death arose out of and in the course of employment has been established by the preponderance of the probabilities.[11]

---

[11]Celeste v. Progressive Silk Finishing Co., 72 N.J. Super. Ct. 125 (1962).

Smoking the Cause of Disability?

Here is another capsulized case summary. A mechanic went to a doctor with a skin problem, a discoloration of the skin on his hands. The cause of the discoloration was determined to be Raynaud's Disease, which is due to a lessening of blood in the capillaries. The mechanic believed that the disease was related to his work and therefore compensable.

He filed a claim with the Arizona Industrial Commission; it was denied. He next took his case to the state court of appeals *(Nelson v. Industrial Commission of Arizona)*, asserting that his skin problems resulted from use of tools that vibrated. The court noted that according to the principle of causation work-related accidents that aggravate a pre-existing problem and produce additional injuries are compensable. But the mechanic had not shown evidence to link his skin problem and his work. He was, however, a smoker; and doctors stated that smoking could have caused his skin problem. The court denied benefits, asserting that smoking was more likely to be the cause of his disability than vibrating tools.[12]

Another leading case in New York State went in the same direction as the one just cited. The New York State Court of Appeals decided, in an action for death benefits, that the presumption in the state law that there had been a compensable injury was not a substitute for actual proof. The facts given here were summarized in the court's decision.

An elevator operator in a bank building had been helping a mechanic repair one of the elevators. The repairs had been almost finished when the mechanic left the scene to get a special wrench to complete the job. He left the operator standing in the corridor with nothing to do. A few minutes later, the operator was found lying on the floor unconscious. No one saw him fall, and when he regained consciousness he said he did not know what had happened. He died about two weeks later. An autopsy revealed no marks on his body, no scars on his face, and no fracture of his skull. The cause of his death was declared to be a cerebral hemorrhage resulting from the rupture of a preexisting aneurism at the base of his brain. The state Workmen's Compensation Board had made an award to the operator's dependents on the grounds that he had been the victim of an industrial accident, and that the fall had not been caused by "underlying pathological condition." In rejecting this finding and conclusion, the New York State Court

[12]*Right Off the Docket*, OCCUPATIONAL HAZARDS, Oct. 1975, 37 (No. 10), 56.

of Appeals pointed out that the sole item in the record to support
the claim of an accident was the testimony of one physician who
had made a "casual examination" of the operator after his collapse. This doctor had noticed a slight skin abrasion on the man's
forehead and expressed the opinion that the rupture of the brain
aneurism might have been caused by a blow if there had been such
a blow. The court noted that there was no proof of any sort of a
blow, and the statement of a possibility, "founded as it was upon
a hypothesis having no support in the record, is a far cry from any
fact. . . ."[13]

Injuries Arising Out of *and* in the Course of Employment

The workers' compensation statutes of more than 40 states
and the District of Columbia hold employers responsible for
indemnifying their employees for injuries "arising out of *and* in
the course of their employment." An employee may be injured in
a situation arising out of his employment and still not be entitled
to compensation. An obvious illustration would be an instance in
which a worker made an unprovoked attack on his foreman and
in self-defense the foreman threw a counter-blow that broke the
worker's jaw. Conversely, an entirely reverse type of situation
may be encountered wherein an employee may be engaged in an
activity off the employer's premises and presumably in a private
pursuit and still can hold his employer liable for an injury while so
engaged.

Disability Attributable to Union Negotiations

How far can the law be stretched to cover disabilities originating when an employee has not been working on his own job? One
answer given by a New Jersey appellate court was, in effect,
"plenty far." The case in question is presented here in highly
condensed summary:

> Salierno, a union steward, suffered a heart attack during a
> heated debate in contract talks with the company negotiator. After
> recovering, Salierno had another attack and had to quit his job.
> When Salierno won benefits for permanent total disability the
> company appealed to the New Jersey Superior Court, Appellate Di-
> vision (*Salierno* v. *Micro Stamping Co.*). The company argued that
> Salierno suffered his first heart attack while representing his union
> in contract negotiations, and not as an employee. Therefore, he
> should not have been awarded benefits from the company. Further-

---

[13]McCormack v. National City Bank of New York, 99 N.E.2d 887 (1951).

more, there was insufficient evidence that the first heart attack led to the second and disabling attack.

The court disagreed with the company. As a union steward, Salierno served the interest of the company as well as its employees, the court said. He had to deal with the company daily to solve employee problems and grievances, which could result in interruptions of production. Therefore, although he represented the union and employees, his union work also benefited the company because a mutually satisfactory contract would assure the company of labor peace and uninterrupted production and sales. Salierno's heart attack, then, was job-related.

As to the company's contention that Salierno's second heart attack was not related to his first attack, the court ruled that there was sufficient medical evidence to support a connection between the two.

Benefits granted.[14]

Occurrence Off the Premises but "On the Job"

The case just cited went, perhaps, to one extreme. This case goes to another. A production foreman asked one of his female employees to work four hours beyond her regular shift because of an emergency. Her answer was that she was a member of a car pool and unless she could be driven home she could not put in the overtime. (A company rule then in force required every foreman to stay on the job himself when any members of his work force were required or agreed to do overtime work.) Hence, on learning that the young lady in question lived only a few miles away from his own residence the foreman agreed to drive her home. As it happened, it was a stormy night and the roads were icy. The foreman's car skidded off the highway in an isolated area that was directly en route to the worker's home. As a result of the skid the young lady was propelled into the arms of her boss and one thing led to another. The foreman landed in the hospital the same night with a very personal injury.

The foreman promptly filed a compensation claim for lost time, hospital surgical expense, and permanent partial disability. His company contested the claim. It took the position that the grievous injury the foreman suffered at the roadside after hours in his own car was his own responsibility even though the company conceded that the foreman's injury was inflicted by his co-worker. The company lost. The state compensation authorities and the reviewing court decided that the foreman was still in the course of his employment and that his injury arose out of his job responsibilities. (The proceedings of this bizarre case are not available for

[14]*Right Off the Docket*, OCCUPATIONAL HAZARDS, Dec. 1975, 37(No. 12), 48-49.

examination by any researcher. Recognizing that truth may be stranger than fiction and that our highest courts might apply a different rule for truthful salacious material than they do for fiction, the state court deciding this case ordered the whole record to be permanently sealed and locked in the state archives in perpetuity.)

Loss of Consortium

A sequel to this compensation case was an out-of-court settlement of a lawsuit filed by the partially disabled foreman's wife for loss of consortium. In a much more recent case, the California Supreme Court reversed its former doctrine that recovery of this sort was obtainable only when the spouse had been killed but not when he had been negligently injured. The California high court ruled in 1974 that the wife of a man involved in an accident that left him totally paralyzed in both legs and much of his body was entitled to a loss of consortium award.[15]

With respect to the other and much more important gut issue in the case just summarized, the New York State Court of Appeals on deciding what was *not* compensable as a result of an off-the-premises accident proceeded lucidly to explain what *would be* compensable under different circumstances.

The case itself involved a plumber's helper who was fatally injured in an automobile accident one mile away from his employer's shop. He was on his way, after work, to call for his wife, who had spent the day visiting in another town. When his employer happened to hear that the helper was going to make this trip at the end of the day, he asked the workman to take his tools along to do a trifling repair job in a home in the town where the wife was to be called for. No more than 15 or 20 minutes would be needed to make the repairs. A special trip would have been unprofitable. The work could have been done at a later day in combination with some other assignment if the helper had not told his employer he was going to make the trip in any case.

The court concluded that the employee's death in the automobile accident after leaving his employer's shop did not arise out of and in the course of any service that he had been employed to render, for he had not started on the trip at the request of the employer or for the purpose of doing his employer's work.

But, the court declared:

---

[15]Rodriguez v. McDonnell Douglas Corp., et al., as summarized in ADJ DIGEST, Sept. 16, 1974. Copyright © Crawford and Co., P.O. Box 5047, Atlanta, Georgia.

Many cases there are in which the perils of travel on a highway are so related to the employment as to lay the basis for an award. The result at times has been that accidents the most bizarre have been held to be incidental to service in the line of duty.

The court further said:

Unquestionably injury through collision is a risk of travel on a highway. What concerns us here is whether the risks of travel are also the risks of the employment. In that view, the decisive test must be whether it is the employment or something else that has sent the traveler forth upon the journey or brought exposure to its perils. . . .

We do not say that service to the employer must be the sole cause of the journey, but at least must be a concurrent cause. To establish liability, the inference must be permissible that the trip would have been made though the private errand had been cancelled. . . . The test in brief is this: If the work of the employee creates the necessity for travel, he is in the course of his employment, though he is serving at the same time some purpose of his own. . . . If, however, the work has had no part in creating the necessity of travel, if the journey would have gone forward though the business errand had been dropped, and would have been cancelled upon failure of the private purpose, though the business errand was undone, the travel is then personal, and personal the risk."[16]

Sleeping On the Job

An Arizona court handed down a pontifical decision which held in effect that an employee was constructively at work while asleep in a motel room. This employee had been sent by his firm on an overnight trip. While asleep in his motel his head was caught between two metal slats and he suffocated.

Overruling the state industrial commission, the Arizona court held that sleeping was essential to the work of a travelling employee and that there was, accordingly, a compensable death claim.[17]

Preemployment Accidents

The reach of the workmen's compensation coverage can extend to unexpected lengths. It can extend and has extended to individuals involved in accidents occurring before they began work for the companies held responsible for their injuries.

[16]Marks' Dependents v. Gray, 167 N.E. 181 (1929).
[17]Peterson v. Industrial Commission, 16 Ariz. App. 41, 490 P.2d 870 (1971).

An extreme case, no doubt, but one that should be taken into account by personnel administrators responsible for setting the terms for hiring new employees, was one involving a fatal accident to an individual en route to a new position before he had actually reported for work.

The facts in this case were not in dispute, but the application of the law was contested because a novel issue was presented. As to the facts, a physicist teaching in California applied for a summer position in a research laboratory located in New Jersey. In doing so he indicated his intention ultimately to obtain permanent employment in the New York metropolitan area. The company to which he applied offered him temporary employment for at least 10 weeks, contingent on his meeting its prescribed physical standards. He was offered reimbursement of his travel expenses from California to New Jersey and return. He was permitted to have a physical examination by his own doctor and after the results of the examination were reported to his prospective employer and before he left California, he was notified that he had "passed."

While driving cross-country to New Jersey in his own car to report for work, his car skidded off the road and he suffered fatal injuries.

So much for the facts. With regard to the law, death benefits were claimed on behalf of the widow under the New Jersey statute. The ground was that the deceased physicist had already entered into an employment contract with the New Jersey establishment and that for all practical purposes he was already at work when he was travelling to his place of employment at company expense.

The prospective employer—or the actual employer as the court ultimately decided—challenged the claim, reasoning that no employment contract had been consummated, or, alternatively, if there was a binding contract, it had been completed in California.

The court found for the widow. It held that only the formalities of supplying routine personnel data had to be met upon the man's reporting for work, that the company's offer of employment had been accepted by the applicant, and that the contract had been made in fact in New Jersey. As the court pointed out on this issue: "It is well established that when a contract of employment is 'made' in this state our compensation act applies even if the accident occurs outside the state. Gotkin v. Weinberg, 1 N.J. 305 (1949)."

The question remained as to whether or not the fatal accident occurred while the man was, in effect, working for his new temporary employer. This question the court answered in the affirmative.[18] It declared that when transportation is provided by the employer under the contract of employment, injuries sustained by an employee while using transportation are compensable.

Post-Employment Accidents

Employer liability for workmen's compensation benefits can develop even when injuries are sustained by an ex-employee. It was a New Jersey court that decided a case presenting the reverse situation from the pre-employment case just reviewed.

A supervisor in a manufacturing company had been impelled to reprimand a subordinate several times. The latter retaliated with threats against his boss. Some days after the supervisor quit the company for a better position, he encountered the person who had previously threatened him and was attacked and injured by the latter. This incident occurred in a tavern where, presumably, neither of the individuals involved in the case had any occupational duties to perform.

As a result of the injuries sustained in the tavern, the victim filed a claim for disability benefits. When the claim was rejected the case went to a New Jersey appellate court that ruled that while the accident might have been connected with the man's prior employment, it was not compensable for it assuredly did not occur in the course of his current employment. The New Jersey Supreme Court reversed the lower court, however, and declared: "The sense of the concept is that an injury 'arises' in the course of employment whenever the work in fact envelops the victim with a danger which goes with him when he leaves the course of his employment."

Larson's Workmen's Compensation Law quoted the court and the court quoted *Larson's* in further explanation that may give qualms to personnel administrators as to how to control the activities of present and former employees unless they attempt to forbid them all to frequent taverns, even on their own time, and for self-declared nonbelligerent purposes.

Commenting on the post-employment case just cited, *Larson's Workmen's Compensation Law* stated:

> The court discussed with approval the "delayed action" injury approach in the text, and particularly stressed the contrast between "occurring" and "arising." The court said:
>> "*Larson* points out that the statute does not speak of an

---

[18]Filson v. Bell Telephone Laboratories, Inc., 77 N.J. Super. 320 (1962).

accident 'occurring' in the course of employment. Rather the word used is 'arising,' and that word, in one of its accepted usages, means 'originating.' Thus an accident may fairly be said to 'arise' in the course of employment if it had its origin there in the sense that it was the end-product of a force or cause set in motion in the course of employment."

Finally the court ruled that the most distinctive feature of the case, the fact that the employee had actually changed employers before the assault, should not change the fact that the burden of this injury should be borne "by the enterprise from which it so clearly emerged." The court could have added that there is no lack of precedent for placing liability on a previous employer, as in the silicosis, back strain, and other cases in which all or part of the liability is placed upon some earlier employer whose employment contributed to or caused the harm.[19]

Injuries During Recreational Activities

Management, as already indicated, can exert much control over situations that can lead to liability for workmen's compensation awards. It can certainly control the extent to which employees are permitted to engage in recreational activities outside of working hours when there is implied or express company sponsorship of such activities. There is much law on this subject and there are many shades of distinction between compensability and noncompensability.

A New York State appellate court denied any liability for workmen's compensation benefits arising out of membership in a bowling team that had been formed spontaneously by a group of employees of the same company. One of the members of the team was killed in an automobile accident on the way to a bowling match. The court's opinion indicated that the issue was not the travel, but, rather, it was the purpose of the bowling contest that was the determinative of compensability. This case reached the appellate court after the New York State Workmen's Compensation Board, upon finding that the company had encouraged participation in a bowling league and had derived advertising benefits from having its initials on its employee's bowling shirts, ruled that for these reasons, among others, participation in the bowling match constituted activity in the course of employment. In deciding otherwise the appellate court discounted the value to the company of having its initials on the bowling shirts, these having been put on them at the employee's initiative. Further reasons for the court's denial of compensation were that management did not

---

[19]Thornton v. Chamberlain Mfg. Co., 62 N.J. 235, 300 A.2d 146 (1973), in LARSON'S WORKMEN'S COMPENSATION LAW, Desk Edition, Supplement, pp. 5-106-107.

supervise the bowling activities, did not help pay for the use of the bowling alleys, did not control the off-hours schedule for the matches, and did not provide prizes or awards. The court observed, however, that where the circumstances were different, participation by employees in athletic activities with closer company relationships could be and had been properly recognized as giving rise to company liability for injuries considered to be occupationally connected.[20]

Indeed, where the factual situation indicated, a New York State Supreme Court judge ruled that employees who sustained injuries while playing softball in a company intermural league were entitled to workers' compensation benefits. The case in question, *Goldman* v. *Hazeltine Corp.*, has been summarized as follows:

> The court rejected the employer's plea [that the injuries had not occurred in the course of employment] and found the softball games incidental to and part of regular employment. The employer sponsored, supervised, and controlled softball teams in order to improve relations with employees. The employer helped finance the league, supported the activities by making the company bulletin board available for sports news, and sponsored a banquet for the players at the end of the year. Furthermore, the employer derived a substantial business advantage from the league.[21]

Another unusual situation where the ultimate finding in court was an occupationally connected injury arose out of developments occurring during a company's annual outing. The Appellate Division of the Supreme Court of New Jersey had to consider two separate sets of facts in reaching its decision. The first set is of special importance to personnel administrators having responsibility for company recreational activities. Essentially, the initial question centered about conditions under which the company decided to conduct an outing for its employees. On this question the company's position was in substance that its outing was not conducted for its own benefit and that, therefore, the accident that gave rise to the compensation claim was one that did not arise out of or in the course of the injured man's employment.

The appellate court gave short shrift to the company's contention as to the purpose of the outing and as to why the company had received no benefit therefrom. The court noted that for a number of years the company outing had been an annual affair and that when management decided to abandon it the year in

---

[20]Jablonski v. General Motors Acceptance Corp., 254 N.Y.S.2d 168 (1964).
[21]*Right Off the Docket*, OCCUPATIONAL HAZARDS, Oct. 1975, 37(No. 10), 56.

question there had been a protest by employees and a claim by union representatives that the outing was one of the benefits provided in the current labor agreement. While the court observed that there was no specific reference to the annual outing in the union agreement, some other stipulated benefits such as pensions were not spelled out in the agreement either. Without expatiating on its reasons the court concluded that in acceding to the employees' requests not to discontinue the annual outing, this affair became something of such a nature as to make the company liable for accidents suffered by employees while in attendance.

The second set of facts that had to be decided in this case had to do with the cause of the fatal injury sustained by the employee while at the outing. (He fell into a ravine and died as a result of his fall.) His employer contended that he was intoxicated at the time. If there had been persuasive evidence that this employee was in fact intoxicated when he fell into the ravine, this could have been a proper defense against the widow's claim for death benefits, the court indicated. So it is not necessarily imprudent for an employer to provide or permit the use of spiritous beverages at a company-sponsored affair. But if one of the employee participants incurs an injury and the preponderance of evidence does not lead to a conclusion of actual intoxication, then the company can he held responsible for injuries at such an affair — at least in the State of New Jersey.[22]

Horseplay and Fisticuffs

The desirability of stringent company rules prohibiting horseplay and fisticuffs on the job, and setting strong penalties for violations, is scarcely open to question. And yet the existance of such rules, no matter how well enforced, does not always relieve the employer of the consequences of employee injuries from wanton acts or employee brawls. There are landmark cases on these issues.

In one often-cited case Judge Benjamin Cardozo, then presiding over the New York State Court of Appeals, sustained an award to an employee for loss of most of the sight of one eye as a result of being struck by an apple thrown "in sport" at still another employee. The injured workman was not participating in the horseplay and had no awareness of it until hit by the apple. At the outset Judge Cardozo acknowledged that the decision he rendered in the support of the compensability of this injury was at variance with precedents established in some other states. He

---

[22]Kelly v. Hackensack Water Company, 23 N.J. Super. (1952).

therefore proceeded to explain his reasons for ruling as he did. Some of the judge's most cogent observations are quoted below:

> The question is whether the accident was one "arising out of and in the course of employment." . . . That it arose "out of" employment we now hold. The claimant's presence in a factory in association with other workmen involved exposure to the risk of injury from the careless acts of those about him. He was brought by the conditions of his work "within the zone of special danger." . . . Whatever men and boys do, when gathered together in such surroundings, at all events if it was something reasonably to be expected as one of the perils of his service. . . . The claimant was injured, not merely while he was in a factory, but because he was in a factory, in touch with associations and conditions inseparable from factory life. The risks of such associations and conditions were risks of employment. . . . The risks of injury incurred in the crowded contacts of the factory through the acts of fellow workmen are not measured by the tendency of such acts to serve the master's business. Many things that have no such tendency are done by workmen every day. The test of liability under the statute is not the master's dereliction, whether his own or that of his representatives acting within the scope of their authority. The test of liability is the relation of the service to the injury, or the employment to the risk.[23]

Possible Self-Inflicted Injuries

That "justice is blind" is an unwarranted conclusion insofar as workers' compensation law is concerned. It is true that in most cases of doubt administrative and court decisions may seem to be shaded in favor of the employee-claimant or his dependents if he has incurred fatal injuries. Most state statutes expressly provide that in case of doubt the employee shall be given the benefit thereof. Workers' compensation laws are by no means unique in this respect. There would be little point, therefore, in reviewing the multifarious decisions in which employers have successfully defended fraudulent claims or have successfully challenged dubious claims that may have been advanced in all honesty. One illustration of a judicious and, we think, eminently fair court decision should be sufficient to make the point that management does not have to go into court with its hands tied behind its back expecting an adverse verdict.

To be sure, it took an appeal to the highest court of the state of Colorado to obtain a final decision that despite the legal presumption against suicide in compensation, this presumption can

---

[23]Leonbruno v. Champlain Silk Mills, 128 N.E. 711 (1920).

be overcome by persuasive argument supported by credible testimony. As to the facts, a gasoline station attendant working alone on the graveyard shift was found by his station manager lying inside a car with its engine running behind the closed doors of the service station. He had obviously been overcome by carbon monoxide fumes. Nearby the engine of another car was running. The attendant's work orders gave no reason to presume that he had any need or occasion to run the engines of either car from which the lethal fumes came. Nor was there any plausible reason to motivate the lone attendant to lock all the doors to the outside of the station. Thus far the facts were purely circumstantial. As the high court of Colorado was diligent in noting:

> Testimony was offered by decedent's brother and by his sister-in-law who had visited him between the hours of 11 p.m. and 1:30 a.m. for the purpose of procuring a state inspection certificate for their vehicle. At that time he was in gay spirits and talked extensively of having his army medical examination within the next week. He ate two sandwiches which were procured by his brother and brewed a pot of coffee which they drank while cheerfully conversing. No hint of despondency was noted by either of these persons while they were with decedent.
>
> On the evening before he reported for work he had an extended conversation with his mother and discussed many impending plans which did not indicate he was in any wise despondent. Decedent had been separated from his wife and three small children for nearly one year but had talked to them from time to time and had visited his wife with apparent intention of striving to reconcile their marital difficulties, shortly before his death.

Now as to the applicable statute, the high court cited that the law provided, in part, as follows: "The right of compensation provided in this chapter . . . shall obtain . . . where the injury or death is proximately caused by accident arising out of and in the course of his employment, and is not intentionally self-inflicted."

In support of its conclusion that the employee had caused his own death and had done so deliberately, the court cited certain findings of the state referee who originally heard and decided the case. The evidence was sufficient to convince him that the attendant had deliberately committed suicide by so arranging the facilities inside the service station and running the engines of two cars in an enclosed area as to make his death from carbon monoxide poisoning inevitable. From this evidence the court supported the referee's decision that in spite of the legal presumption against a person taking his life the attendant had actually done so; and, accordingly, death benefits to his dependents were denied.

On hindsight this fatality conceivably could have been avoided, but only if the service station manager had been endowed with extraordinary prescience. The attendant had reported for work at 11 p.m. for a tour of duty ending at 7 a.m. One of the findings of the referee was that the attendant had telephoned his station manager at about 4 a.m. the morning of his death, asking him to come in a bit early and stating that he did not feel very well. The manager offered to come in to relieve the attendant immediately but was assured that would be unnecessary. This incident served apparently to clinch the court's finding of a suicidal intent for the court stated that "it may be inferred that this call was part of the attendant's plan and not merely notice of an unimportant illness. One does not normally disturb his employer at 4 a.m. unless he was doing it as part of a preconceived plan to accomplish some other purpose."[24]

It was unquestionably the statutory mandate that employees or their dependents should be given the benefit of the doubt in compensation cases that led to an award in New York State despite definite indications of suicide. A divided court upheld the findings of the state workmen's compensation board to the effect that an employee had gone to a railroad siding to check a car there and was struck and fatally injured by a passing train on the main line in the course of his employment. The deceased employee had been the office manager of a bakery. His plant manager testified that he had occasion to be at the railroad siding in order to check the car. The court majority considered this testimony sufficient to make operative the presumption of a compensable accident and the presumption against suicide.

A dissenting judge thought differently. He gave credence to the testimony of the locomotive engineer and fireman of the passenger train that struck the man. In his dissenting opinion he said:

> The engineer, seated on the right side of the cab, testified that at the time of the accident it was daylight and the weather was clear and bright and that as the train crossed a road just prior to the point of impact he blew the regular crossing warning. He further testified that as the train proceeded along at 40 miles per hour he suddenly saw a man leap from the east end of a boxcar, which was sitting on the siding at the rear of the employer's bakery, directly into the path of the oncoming train. At this point the train was about 50-60 feet from the point of impact and despite prompt application of the brakes impact could not be avoided. The engineer testified that the man's hands and arms were extended as if he were diving but he

---

[24]Industrial Commission of Colorado State Compensation Insurance Fund v. Peterson, 377 P.2d 542 (1963).

could not state with certainty if decedent fell, stumbled, tripped or jumped. [The siding, incidentally, was about 12 feet away from the main track.] The fireman, however, testified that decedent threw himself in front of the engine. He stated and maintained under cross examination that decedent did not stumble but looked at the train and made a headlong dive across the track with his entire body in the air as if diving into water.

Our purpose in quoting portions of the dissenting judge's opinion is neither to agree nor disagree with his conclusions. It is instead to provide an indication to personnel administrators and their compensation advisors of the types of evidence that may seem conclusive in litigated cases and to further indicate how the figurative laws of probability may operate in such cases.

Hence, a further portion of the dissenting opinion is quoted below:

The record also indicates that a physician whom decedent had been consulting for nervous tension during the six weeks prior to his death had recommended he take a leave of absence from his job and that decedent had been taking tranquilizers for a period of two years prior to consulting the physician. Decedent had resigned his position on May 17, 1959, just four days prior to his demise, effective June 13, 1959. The plant manager testified he did so because "the pressure was too great where he was," but his wife gave as a reason that since their children were no longer in school [his age was then 56], they were no longer financially dependent on decedent's job and his resignation would enable them to spend more time together and perhaps go into business together. . . . On motivation or suicidal tendency in this case we have the background of nervous tension, the taking of tranquilizers for a period of two years, and a resignation from his position ("because the pressure was too great") just four days before his demise. . . .[25]

Gross Negligence of Management

Penalties ranging from an additional 10 percent up to 100 percent of normal compensation awards to employees or their dependents can be assessed in some states upon findings of the administrative agencies or the reviewing courts that there has been gross negligence on the part of the employer. "Gross negligence" is a term not easily definable. Moreover, to select for citation particular cases out of the multitude that have reached the courts might be construed as pointing a finger at companies which have long since taken remedial action to prevent any recurrence of the incidents leading to the assessment of additional penalties against

---

[25]Matter of Phillips v. Spaulding Bakeries, Inc., 17 Ad.L.2d 684 (1962).

them. Hence, only two cases that might have reached the courts but actually never did will be summarized here.

A casualty insurance company safety inspector, after making a periodic inspection of one of his company's policyholder's plants, reported to the plant maintenance superintendent the existence of a defective conveyor and recommended immediate repairs. The superintendent agreed but the expenditure for the necessary repairs had to be approved by the works manager. Meanwhile the local union safety committee, being aware of the conveyor's condition, had been notified that the repairs "were in the works." In this instance "the 'works" happened to be the works manager's commodious briefcase where the written work order for repairs that needed his signature had languished until after a serious alleged accident had occurred. We say "alleged" accident because the circumstances were indeed questionable. An employee who customarily worked alone in a room where the conveyor was located was found one morning in a semiconscious stupor. Nothing about his physical condition or the condition of the work area gave any clue that he might have been involved in any sort of accident. He was carried to the works dispensary and upon being revived by the nurse was transported to the office of the company's part-time physician. He was subsequently hospitalized and after neurological tests, underwent a brain operation. While he was apparently recovering from the operation he suddenly "remembered" that on the day of his collapse at work a 50-pound bag had fallen off the conveyor onto his head. By the time this recollection was reported to the company and an attempt was made to find the bag and to ascertain whether it had ever been on or fallen off the conveyor, the workman had died. An autopsy indicated that the man had died of complications following the brain surgery with nothing to suggest that a traumatic incident had occasioned the need for the surgery or had contributed to the fatality.

Nevertheless, a claim for death benefits charging that the man had died as a result of an occupational accident was filed. An additional claim for double damages was also filed on account of management's alleged negligence in failing to repair the defective conveyor. The outcome of this tragedy of errors remained unpredictable until the very hour when the case was settled during the compensation hearing — out of court.

The out-of-court settlement presumably seemed desirable because there was a reasonable doubt that the deceased had ever been struck on the head by anything on the day of his collapse at work; there was similar doubt as to whether a blow on the head such as he belatedly recounted would have caused him to sustain any injury that might have contributed to the circumstances of his death. Moreover, there was doubt as to whether the conveyor had been operated at all on the day the supposed accident occurred. And there was still greater doubt as to whether the conveyor's condition was so defective that it could have spewed a bag of any substantial weight onto the head of an unsuspecting worker who had no job-connected reason to be in close proximity to it. The only question about which there was no doubt was that something had gone wrong with the conveyor.

The state in which this case arose — Massachusetts — permits recovery of double damages, or twice the amount awarded as regular compensation benefits, if and when employer negligence of any consequence can be established. It is thus a matter of conjecture whether double benefits would have been awarded if the case had not been settled out of court on the basis of full death benefits for the dependents, plus all hospital and surgical expenses but with no additional payments on account of alleged employer negligence — which was manifestly at least minimal if not gross.

A second case could have produced much greater expenses for the company responsible if it had occurred in a state authorizing by statute additional penalties for management negligence. In the second case the facts surrounding a fatal injury were not in dispute. A machine operator had carelessly left uncovered a container of highly flammable solvent used in the work process to which he was assigned. The container caught fire and enveloped the man in its flames. He quickly burned to death. Obviously this tragedy presented a clear-cut case of workmen's compensation liability. It was so treated and death benefits were paid without contest. And so the case seemingly ended.

But a subsequent company investigation disclosed that months before the fatal fire, an inspector employed by the casualty insurance company that covered the company's fire hazards had issued a written warning about the use of the solvent. If it had been heeded, the fatality could have been prevented. The insurance inspector's report had been submitted to the plant manager, the company insurance manager, and to other officials. None of them had taken any action. This was a situation that was readily correctible as far as future contingencies were concerned.

Now suppose a conflagration had erupted from the flaming container of solvent, burning and critically injuring a large number of employees. The consequences could well have extended far beyond the limits of workers' compensation liability. A diligent district attorney probably would have investigated. If his investigation revealed that management had knowledge of and had been warned of a hazard which was readily correctible, criminal prosecution probably would have ensued.

Criminal prosecution was, indeed, what developed from a catastrophe that brought about the death of more than 150 individuals. Not all of them were employees. Of course, the dependents of those victims who had been employees collected death benefits under the applicable state law. But the main significance of this catastrophe, for present purposes, relates not to compensation liability but rather to criminal proceedings involving management.

The catastrophe in point occurred in Hartford, Connecticut, in 1944, when a fire erupted during a circus matinee, ostensibly caused when the main tent, made of canvas that had not been adequately fireproofed, quickly burned out. Accounts in the *New York Times* of the aftermath of this disaster included the item that six circus officials were convicted on manslaughter charges and sentenced to prison. The *New York Times* also reported that the board of directors of the circus released a resolution saying that these men, including a general manager who was also a vice-president, had pleaded *nolo contendere* unselfishly for the benefit of the circus corporation despite their sincere belief in their innocence. If the defendants had not entered the pleas but had stood trial, the resolution of the board said, the result might have tied up the circus "and prevented its successful operation from which claimants would benefit."[26]

If there should be any unreasonable doubt in the minds of top management that elimination of hazardous conditions is no more than a casual responsibility, this one incident, coupled with the cost of resultant claims running to more than four million dollars, should be most persuasive.

Contributory Negligence of Management

Presently there seems to be no limit on the extent to which some courts will go in placing on management the responsibility for indemnifying the victims or the dependents of victims for casualties which the most foresighted employers could hardly take effective steps to prevent. Admittedly, what follows is a most extreme illustration. So be it. The case was summarized as follows in the trade journal *Occupational Hazards*.

---

[26]NEW YORK TIMES May 26, 1955.

Company and employee both negligent

Bach, a railroad fireman, was drinking on the job. He left his train to use a restroom at a station, and the conductor told him he'd better stay at the station and wait to be picked up on the train's return run. When Bach left the restroom he sat down on the track and drifted off to sleep. He was so drunk he didn't wake up when the returning train repeatedly sounded its whistle. No one on the train was watching out for him. Bach was struck and killed.

His wife brought suit against the railroad under the Federal Employer's Liability Act. The judge charged the jury to consider the State's laws against drinking on the job. The judge also instructed the jury to ignore inflation in making its award. The jury granted Mrs. Bach a minimal award.

She carried the case to the United States Court of Appeals, Sixth Circuit *(Bach v. Penn Central Transportation Co.)*. The appeals court stated that Bach's negligence was not the only factor to consider. The railroad was also guilty. The crew knew Bach was drunk, yet failed to take adequate precautions. No one bothered to learn where he was waiting, or even to look down the track. The court also ruled the judge erred in charging the jury to ignore inflation.

Judgment was vacated and the case was remanded for a new trial.[27]

Newspaper items are, of course, no substitute for full-text reporting services. Still, they can often provide clues to cases of precedential value. One such clue was provided by a brief story in the *New York Times* about the denial of a compensation claim made by an Episcopal priest. The clergyman had apparently become emotionally overwrought while delivering a sermon in which he denounced a retired Episcopal bishop for preaching on the "God Is Dead" theology. After finishing his denunciatory sermon, the priest-claimant was hospitalized and suffered complications that prevented him from performing the regular duties of his ministry. But the New York State Workmen's Compensation Board ruled that this rector, who could no longer fulfill his parish duties, was not entitled to any disability benefits. The state court's appellate division agreed.[28]

Contrast this tough stand on nebulous physical disability evolving from emotional stress with two more recent decisions of New York State appellate courts. The quotations below represent highly condensed digests of both cases:

The surviving wife of an assistant elementary school principal was entitled to death benefits for the death of her husband due to a

---

[27]*Right Off the Docket*, OCCUPATIONAL HAZARDS, Sept. 1975, 37(No. 9), 136-7.
[28]NEW YORK TIMES, Sept. 13, 1969, p. 13.

myocardial infarction where the evidence was sufficient to sustain the finding that the stress and strain of his employment contributed to his death. Although the decedent's activities, as evidenced by the record, may just as well have been found to have been routine and not precipitous of excessive strain, the board found that the decedent's work activities on the day in question involved undue stress and strain, beyond the ordinary wear and tear of life, which aggravated claimant's preexisting coronary condition and caused his death. There was substantial evidence in the record to support the finding by the board which should not be disturbed. The resolution of conflicting medical opinion as to the causal relationship also falls within the fact-finding power of the board and when supported by substantial evidence in the record, the board's determination must be sustained. Affirmed.[29]

The surviving wife of building manager was entitled to death benefits for the death of her husband due to an intercerebral hemorrhage. A portion of the cornice of the building which decedent managed, fell to the sidewalk. It was the contention of the widow that this incident, coupled with events that followed, brought about the emotional stress and strain which resulted in the decedent's cerebral stroke and death. There was testimony by business associates and employees as to the decedent's anxiety and physical appearance following the collapse of cornice. The decedent's doctor testified that, in his opinion, after reviewing the record, the decedent was under an unusual amount of emotional strain and that such strain, superimposed upon an existing illness, contributed to his fatal attack. The employer's medical expert testified that in his opinion the degree of so-called alleged emotional upset was not sufficient to even come close to causing the disease that he had and further felt that the decedent died of natural causes. On this record, the board could and did find that the emotional strain and tension upon the decedent was greater than the countless differences and irritations to which all workers are subjected and, thus, his death was compensable. Affirmed. (New York Supreme Court, Appellate Division, Third Judicial Department. No. 26,162. December 30, 1975.)[30]

The New York State Court of Appeals is notable, or notorious, for its liberal judgments as to facts that are deemed sufficient to sustain compensation awards in questionable cases. One such case as reported in the *Fordham Law Review* involved the question of whether mental injury precipitated by psychic trauma was compensable. The high court of New York State concluded that it was, indeed. The decision as summarized in the *Review* was as follows:

---

[29]Lagona v. Starpoint Central School, N.Y. Sup. Ct., App. Div., 3d Jud. Dept., No. 26,616, Dec. 30, 1975, in [1976] 13 WORKMEN'S COMP. L. REP. (CCH) 1368.

[30]Hannon v. Ellicot Square Associates, N.Y. Sup. Ct., App. Div., 3d Jud. Dept., No. 26,162, Dec. 30, 1975, in [1976] 13 WORKMEN'S COMP. L. REP. (CCH) 1369.

On June 9, 1971, John Forman, a department store security director, committed suicide. The claimant, his secretary, found him lying in a pool of blood. Forman had a history of becoming "agitated and nervous" due to the annual pressures of the Christmas season. Following the 1970 season the pressures did not abate and he became increasingly concerned about his job performance. The firing of a fellow security director at a neighboring store intensified his fears. Forman regularly confided these fears to the claimant, who, in an effort to ease his burden and boost his morale, increasingly assumed certain of his responsibilities.

After the suicide, the claimant alleged that she was beset by an obsessive feeling of guilt because of her failure to prevent Forman's death. There was no dispute that these guilt feelings developed into an "acute depressive reaction." Claimant lost twenty pounds and ultimately had to leave work for approximately six months. During these months she underwent two periods of hospitalization, receiving psychotherapy, medication and three weeks of shock treatment. The referee granted claimant's demand for compensation and the workmen's compensation board affirmed. On appeal, the Appellate Division reversed, holding that mental injury precipitated solely by psychic trauma was not compensable as a matter of law. The Court of Appeals in turn reversed, sustaining the recovery.[31]

It is special circumstances rather than a new interpretation of the law that cause divergence from what might seem to be well-established precedents. One unusual case where the issue of sufficiency of evidence was the main concern was decided in favor of a widow by the Appellate Division of the New York State Supreme Court in late 1975. It is summarized as follows by CCH:

The surviving wife of a milkman who died of a heart attack after rearranging milk cases on his truck was entitled to death benefits where the evidence was sufficient to sustain a finding that there was a causal connection between the accident and his employment. A medical witness testifying on behalf of claimant on the basis of this evidence related decedent's death to the work effort.[32]

Winnowing the Wheat From the Chaff

How can personnel administrators, their compensation staff men, and their attorneys determine which of the multitude of workers' compensation cases decided each year might be applicable to any given current claim? There is obviously no best answer to the question. It could easily be a full-time job for a knowledgeable young lawyer or safety expert to wade through the

---

[31]Wolfe v. Sibley, Lindsay & Curr Co., 36 N.Y.2d 505, 330 N.E.2d 603, 369 N.Y.S.2d 637 (1975), as summarized in 44 FORDHAM L. REV. 204 (1975).

[32]Leader v. Holland Farms, Inc., N.Y. Sup. Ct., App. Div., 3d Jud. Dept., No. 27,008, Dec. 30, 1975, in [1976] 13 WORKMEN'S COMP. L. Rep. (CCH) 1367.

published court decisions alone and try to ferret out the reasons why thousands of unpublished cases have been settled out of court. For present purposes the authors of this volume tried several methods with indifferent success. They have reviewed specialized publications such as *Occupational Hazards* for leads on decisions of considerable import. They have flipped through the current reports of management services such as BNA's *Occupational Safety and Health Reporter;* and they have utilized other sources such as the daily press, trade journals, and law reviews. The results are not at all conclusive or comprehensive. For practical guidance, the best that could be said about it is to repeat the adage of an anonymous contributor to *Punch* Magazine in 1846: "You pays your money and you takes your choice."

GOVERNMENT SAFETY AND HEALTH REGULATIONS

As indicated at the outset of this chapter, the Federal Government has moved in to take a large measure of control over the determination of what should constitute proper safety and health practices by private industry. This it did through the passage of the federal Occupational Safety and Health Act of 1970. To put that statute in proper perspective, as far as employers' obligations thereunder are concerned, a review of prior federal and state legislation is essential.

Walsh-Healey Safety Regulations

Up until 1971 by far the greatest degree of regulation of safety and health standards of private employers had come about through the enactment of state legislation. To be sure, the Walsh-Healey Act, which, as explained in Chapter 2, applies to thousands of companies that have supply contracts with federal agencies, has provided what has amounted to a negative incentive for employers to maintain safe and healthful working conditions. The Walsh-Healey Act authorizes the United States Secretary of Labor to blacklist for a three-year period any company having applicable government contracts when such company has been found by him to have permitted serious occupational hazards to prevail in any of its establishments producing goods or performing services for the government. With respect to each production or service contract covered by the Act, Walsh-Healey specifies:

> That no part of such contract will be performed nor will any of the materials, supplies, articles, or equipment to be manufactured or

furnished under said contract be manufactured or fabricated in any plants, factories, buildings, or surroundings or under working conditions which are unsanitary or hazardous or dangerous to the health or safety of employees engaged in the performance of said contract. *Compliance with the safety, sanitary, and factory inspection laws of the State in which the work or part thereof is to be performed shall be prima facie evidence of compliance with this subsection.* [Italics supplied]

Were it not for the proviso relating to compliance with state laws indicating prima facie compliance with the federal law, it might properly be assumed that for some 35 years the United States Secretary of Labor could have and should have exerted sweeping regulatory powers over the safety and health practices of a major segment of American industry and commerce. But successive Secretaries of Labor have proceeded with something less than "all deliberate speed," as the Supreme Court once phrased it in another context, in exercising their statutory mandate to enforce rigorous safety and health regulations upon government contractors. In fairness to these officials, it must be observed that Congress has never appropriated more than minimal amounts to finance the administration and enforcement of this part of the Walsh-Healey Act.

A foretaste of what lay ahead for government contractors, and presumably for nearly all industrial enterprises, appeared in a formidable document entitled "Safety and Health Standards for Federal Supply Contracts." This document was prepared in the fall of 1968, during the closing days of the Johnson Administration, and was proposed for adoption by then-Secretary of Labor, W. Willard Wirtz. The new incoming Secretary of Labor, George P. Shultz, temporarily stayed, pending further review, the effective date for promulgation of the new standards. They ultimately went into effect in May 1969.

How onerous or inconsequential some of the standards turned out to be may be gauged from textual comparisons between what was put out in 1969 and what ultimately was included in the *OSHA General Industry Safety and Health Standards Digest* (OSHA 2201, Revised June 1975). With a single trivial exception, both standards on machine guarding specified: "One or more methods of machine guarding shall be provided to protect the operator and other employees from hazards such as those created by point of operation, in going nip points, rotating parts, flying chips and sparks." (The single trivial difference was that the next to last word in the 1975 OSHA standard was changed to "or" instead of "and" as in the earlier version.)

State Regulation of Safety and Health Practices

Gradually, over a period of more than 50 years, the states have provided impetus for the adoption of adequate safety and health precautions in industrial commercial establishments. This had been done basically on a step-by-step basis. Thus, the catastrophic fire in 1911 in the New York City garment center in which nearly 150 young women lost their lives spurred the enactment of regulatory legislation not only in New York State but in several other states as well.

Successive disasters over the years in other states, disasters involving factory boiler explosions; mine cave-ins; the large-scale affliction of industrial workers as a result of such occupational diseases as silicosis, asbestosis, and radioactive poisoning brought about further state legislation aimed at specific preventable job hazards.

By 1976, 45 states had adopted laws providing general or specific regulation of industrial practices deemed by law or regulation to be unsafe or unhealthful. Among the industries singled out for special protective measures in many states are construction, mining, foundries, laundries, and electrical equipment installation. Typically, individual occupations singled out for safety controls are welding, spray painting, and the application of radioactive materials to consumer products. Equipment and facilities subject to similar controls include elevators, high pressure boilers, fire extinguishers, fire escapes and stairwells, derricks and cranes, drinking fountains, toilets, and washing facilities.

This is not to gloss over the real occupational hazards throughout many fields of business. One major deterrent to perpetuation of dubious working conditions is the trend to interpret the employer's liability under state workers' compensation laws to include payment of benefits to employees whose disabilities may seem to have only a borderline relationship to their job duties and working conditions. Another deterrent in unionized establishments is the inclusion in labor agreements of safety and health clauses that provide for eliminating job hazards through the grievance procedure.

THE OCCUPATIONAL SAFETY AND HEALTH ACT OF 1970

This statute, which became effective on April 28, 1971, and has been described by the National Association of Manufacturers' Law Department "as the most pervasive legislation of its kind ever enacted," vests in the Secretary of Labor the authority and obligation to promulgate mandatory federal safety and health standards applicable to every private employer in a business affecting commerce. For all practical purposes, the jurisdiction of the Secretary of Labor in the field of occupational hazards now extends to virtually all employers in the nation except the United States Government itself and state and local governments.

Findings and Policy

In Section 2 of the Act Congress declares it to be the policy of the Federal Government to assure as far as possible safe and healthful conditions for every working man and woman in the nation. To this end Congress declares that employers and employees have separate but dependent responsibilities and rights.

There are also other declarations of policy as to how the objectives of the law are to be accomplished, such as provisions "for research in the fields of occupational safety and health, including the psychological factors involved," and for "exploring ways to discover latent diseases, establishing causal connections between work in environmental conditions," etc.

Duties of an Employer

Section 5(a) of the Act provides that every employer must furnish each employee a place of employment which is free from recognized hazards causing or likely to cause death or serious physical harm; every employer must perforce comply with the occupational safety and health standards promulgated under the Act.

Duties of an Employee

Section 5(b) provides that each employee must comply with occupational safety and health standards and all rules and orders issued under the Act.

Multiplicity of Regulatory Agencies

Some seven years after the enactment of OSHA, controversy is still raging in and out of Congress about the shortcomings of the law, or conversely its unrealistic and perhaps unrealizable objectives. Then there is constant carping about the lethargy or overzealousness of the administrators. We say administrators advisedly, for their names could be legion. Whether justifiable or not, by 1976 there were said to be as many proposed amendments to OSHA in the U. S. Senate as there were senators.

At the outset it should be pointed out that the Washington legislators and bureaucrats have compounded confusion through the proliferative use of acronyms to identify specific laws and their enforcement agencies. In truth, there are two different OSHAs. OSHA No. 1 is the statute officially designated as the Occupational Safety and Health Act of 1970. No. 2 is an administrative branch of the United States Department of Labor known as the Occupational Safety and Health Administration. But OSHA No. 2 is only one of several federal agencies concerned with interpreting, administering and enforcing the law itself. The most formidable of the other agencies is referred to commonly by the acronym OSHRC, that is, the Occupational Safety and Health Review Commission, which operates in complete independence from the Labor Department. In an understatement of its own modus operandi, OSHA No. 2 likens its citations [of alleged violations by employers] and proposed penalties to *traffic violations.* By inference, OSHRC would be the equivalent of a police magistrate or traffic court where contested charges could be heard and decided by one of its staff members called an administrative law judge. That functionary can, after investigation, disallow an OSHA No. 2 citation against an employer if it is considered legally invalid. The judge can also schedule a hearing before reaching a decision. Any such decision may be appealed by the employer concerned to the Review Commission itself.

The Commission's decisions are in turn appealable to the federal circuit court of appeals for the circuit in which the case arose. To summarize, unless a complaint of employer violation gets accepted for review by a U.S. Circuit Court of Appeals, it is OSHA No. 2 that proposes but OSHRC that disposes.

But that's not all. Through OSHA, the statute, Congress created still another administrative and investigatory agency. This new bureaucracy—considerately christened NIOSH—is under the wing of HEW (the U.S. Department of Health, Education and Welfare). The National Institute for Occupational Safety and Health, the official title of the new agency, is authorized by the statute to:

> develop and establish recommended occupational safety and health standards and . . . conduct such research and experimental programs as . . . are necessary for the development of criteria for new and improved occupational safety and health standards, and . . . after consideration of the results of such research and experimental programs, make recommendations concerning new or improved occupational safety and health standards.

If what's just been quoted seems to be merely legislative gobbledygook, an explanatory comment in the House Labor Com-

mittee report recommending the adoption of OSHA may shed a bit
of light:

> The Secretary [of HEW or his deputy the director of NIOSH]
> shall also conduct special research, experiments and demonstrations
> relating to occupational safety and health as are necessary to explore
> new problems, including those created by new technology in occupa-
> tional safety and health, which may require ameliorative action
> beyond that which is otherwise provided for in the operating pro-
> visions of this Act. The Secretary . . . shall also conduct research
> into the motivational and behavioral factors relating to the field of
> occupational safety and health.

And OSHA gives official recognition to two other organizations of eminent repute, though they have always been privately
administered. One of these is popularly known as ANSI (American
National Standards Institute, Inc.), the other as NFPA (National
Fire Protection Association). Both of these organizations have engaged for many years in the development of what are now considered to be "consensus" standards for safe and effective operation
of machinery and equipment.

OSHA has required the Secretary of Labor to accept on an in-
terim basis those consensus standards already embodied by reference in safety and health standards promulgated under the Walsh-
Healey Act for required adherence by government contractors. As
explained in a BNA analysis of the legislative history of OSHA:

> ANSI is a voluntary non-profit organization with representation
> from scientific, technical, trade, professional and labor organ-
> izations. These groups numbered about 160 in 1970 and, according
> to ANSI, represent roughly 95 percent of the standards developing
> capability in private industry.
>
> Depending upon their primary interest organizations select
> membership in either ANSI's Member Body Council, which is
> responsible for standards development and administration, or, the
> Consumer Council which advises on consumer matters and reviews
> standards of interest to consumers. . . .
>
> The ANSI standards are promulgated for private use, but hun-
> dreds of them have found their way into local, state, and national
> law and regulation. . . .
>
> Standards proposed by a standards committee are submitted to
> ANSI's Board of Standards Review, whose members represent a
> cross-section of standards interest. Proposed standards also will be
> released for public review and comment to the trade and general
> press, ANSI members, and interested government agencies. This
> review procedure is new and was adopted in response to criticisms
> that ANSI committees in the past have been "closed shops" and have
> failed to consult fully with affected groups.

Once approved by the Board of Standards Review the proposed standard becomes an "American National Standard of ANSI."

ANSI has some 3,000 standards ranging from specifications for nuts and bolts and electrical wiring to safety requirements for power mowers and household appliances.

*   *   *   *   *

NFPA develops its standards in much the same manner as ANSI. It has produced National Fire Codes that are available in 10 volumes with individual codes, standards, and practices available in pamphlet form.

The titles of the codes are: flammable liquids; gases, combustible solids, dusts, and explosives; building construction and facilities; electrical; sprinklers, fire pumps and water tanks, alarm.[33]

"All About OSHA"

A decent respect for the opinions of mankind — a phrase coined by Thomas Jefferson 200 years ago — would suggest due deference be given to the views of the administrators of a law they are constantly called on to construe. Hence the following citations from an official publication of the Occupational Safety and Health Administration, United States Department of Labor. This publication bears the impressive title, *All About OSHA*[34] but is only 25 pages in length. Unquestionably, there's lots more that employers want and need to know beyond what this little booklet attempts to summarize. Thus, the booklet contains its own prefatory warning: "It is not intended as a legal interpretation of the provisions of the Act, and may not be relied upon as such."

Even so, the summary statements of employer responsibilities and rights provide a good jumping-off place for those responsible for compliance, in order to ascertain how onerous these responsibilities can be:

Employer Responsibilities

As an employer you should:

— be aware that you have a general duty/responsibility to provide a place of employment free from recognized hazards and to comply with occupational safety and health standards promulgated under the Act;

— familiarize yourself with mandatory occupational safety and health standards;

— make sure your employees know about OSHA;

---

[33]THE JOB SAFETY AND HEALTH ACT of 1970 (Washington: The Bureau of National Affairs, Inc., 1971), pp. 29-30.

[34]U.S. Department of Labor, Occupational Safety and Health Administration, ALL ABOUT OSHA, OSHA Pamphlet No. 2056 (1974).

— examine conditions in your workplace to make sure they conform to applicable safety and health standards;
— remove or guard hazards;
— make sure your employees have and use safe tools and equipment, including required personal protective gear and that they are properly maintained;
— use color codes, posters, labels, or signs to warn employees of potential hazards;
— establish or update operating procedures and communicate them so that employees follow safety and health requirements for their own protection;
— provide medical examinations when required by OSHA standards. . . .
— seek advice and consultation as needed by writing, calling, or visiting the nearest OSHA office (OSHA will not inspect you just because you call for assistance) . . .[35]

OSHA, the U.S. Labor Department administrative agency, functions on a decentralized basis. At last count it had more than 60 regional and area offices strategically situated in the nation's major industrial and commercial centers. It operates by adopting standards and checking work sites to see if standards are being met. Safety and health standards are "legally enforceable regulation[s] governing conditions, practices, or operations to assure safe and healthful workplaces."[36]

The States' Roles as OSHA Auxiliaries

Unlike most federal regulatory laws applicable to private-sector employers, the Job Safety and Health Act of 1970 has no general federal preemption provisions. That is to say, Washington does not retain complete control. There is instead a sharing of responsibility with the states, or rather through grants to those states which undertake on their own to promulgate and enforce safety and health regulations. *Any* state can take such action even in areas where the Federal Government has assured jurisdiction.

As summarized in one synopsis of the Act, for a state to assume major responsibility for protective safety and health programs, a state must submit a plan to the Secretary of Labor for that official's approval.

The Secretary's approval must be granted if in his (or her) judgment it meets the following requirements:

[35]*Ibid.*, pp. 4-5.
[36]*Ibid.*, p. 8.

• The plan designates a state agency or agencies as the agency or agencies responsible for administering the plan throughout the state.

• The plan provides for the development and enforcement of standards that are or will be at least as effective in providing safe and healthful employment as standards issued under the Federal Act and which when applicable to products used in interstate commerce, are required by compelling local conditions and do not unduly burden interstate commerce.

• The plan provides a right to enter and inspect work places that is at least as effective as that provided by Section 8 of the Federal Act. [This section stipulates, in part, that an authorized agent of the Secretary may (1) "enter without delay and at reasonable times any factory, plant, establishment, construction site," etc. and (2) inspect and investigate during regular working hours and at other reasonable times . . . all pertinent conditions, structures, machine apparatus, devices, equipment and materials therein, and privately question any employer, owner, operator, agent or employee.] Moreover, it [the plan] must include a prohibition on advance notice or inspections.[37]

No one can gainsay the obvious realities that delegation to some states of what could have been the primary responsibility of OSHA has been something a lot less than a howling success. As of the fall of 1975 only 22 of the 56 jurisdictions (states, territories, etc.) and the District of Columbia had OSHA-approved plans. Although approved plans had been operated in the states of Illinois, Montana, New Jersey, New York, and Wisconsin, these states became dropouts and returned full jurisdiction to the federal agencies; and this they did despite 50-percent funding of their programs.

Limitations on States' Autonomy

There could be many contradictory answers to the question as to why important industrial states such as Illinois, New Jersey, and New York abandoned their own safety and health programs and let OSHA take over again on its own. One speculative answer might materialize from scrutiny of OSHA's own official explanation as to how it has been monitoring state plans. The term *monitoring* in this context is euphemistic at least. Below are cited some of the methods OSHA itself asserts it has developed with the intent of assuring that state plans must be as effective as the federally administered programs.

---

[37]ABCs OF THE JOB SAFETY AND HEALTH ACT (Washington: The Bureau of National Affairs, Inc., 1971), p. 11.

OSHA compliance officers spot-check work sites recently inspected by the state as a means of assessing the effectiveness of state inspections. One measure of the effectiveness of the state program is the batement actions taken by employers found violating standards.

OSHA monitors check to make sure that the state has acquired the type, quality, and quantity of equipment necessary to meet its responsibilities.

The state standards are reviewed to assure (1) that they are "at least as effective as" federal standards and (2) that they include any recently promulgated OSHA standards or comparable ones.

OSHA monitors review the variances granted by the state to determine whether the variances are adequate and what their impact will be on individual workers.

Complaints Against State Program Administration (CASPA)

The Complaints Against State Program Administration (CASPA) procedure permits those interested to file a complaint about state program administration. Such complaints are investigated by OSHA, and if validated, must be corrected to assure continued approval of the state plan. Complaints must be as specific as possible and contain a statement of the reasons for criticism and a description of the aspect or aspects of the plan considered inadequate. For instance, among plan inadequacies one might find: "a pattern of delays in processing cases," "inadequate workplace inspections," "granting of variances without regard to state plan specifications."[38]

Aftermath of New York State's Withdrawal

Presumably without malice but apparently with tongue in cheek the New York State Department of Labor released in March 1977 some revealing statistics pertaining to federal vis-à-vis New York state inspections to determine compliance with safety and health standards. The last year in which New York State administered its own plan there were 230,200 inspections. Under the federal regime in 1976 there were only about 8000 inspections in the state. With no explanatory comment the N.Y. Labor Department published these figures:

---

[38]U.S. Department of Labor, Occupational Safety and Health Administration, How OSHA MONITORS STATE PLANS. OSHA Pamphlet No. 2221 (1975).

	Federal Inspections (1976)	State Inspections (1974)
Total safety and health inspections (excluding follow-up)	7,977	230,211
Inspections with violations (excluding "de minimis" violations)	6,723	92,856
Total violations (including "nonadministrative violations")	52,638	300,081

OSHA has interpreted its regulations that could result in finding of a "de minimis" violation as follows:

De minimis: A condition that has no direct or immediate relation to job safety and health. [Example: lack of toilet partitions.]

Nonserious violation: This has been explained by OSHA as a violation that have a direct relationship to job safety and health but probably would not cause death or serious physical harm. [Example: tripping hazard.] A proposed penalty of up to $1,000 is optional. A nonserious penalty may be adjusted downward by as much as 50 percent, depending on the severity of the hazard, employer's good faith, his history of previous violations, and size of business.[39]

Complying With OSHA Standards

The booklet from which some material used above has been extracted says nothing about what the qualifications of an OSHA compliance officer are or should be. Cynical critics of staff performance over the past few years have suggested that to become an acceptable compliance officer the person should be akin to "Jesus Christ with a union card."

The standards, published in the *Federal Register* (together ultimately with all amendments, corrections, insertions and deletions), are divided into three major categories — General Industry, Maritime, and Construction. As of July 1, 1975, the Labor Department's Occupational Safety and Health Administration had issued

---

[39]ALL ABOUT OSHA.

various series of regulations, interpretations, occupational standards, etc., that were published in a single volume of the *Federal
Register* (29 Labor Parts 1900 to 1919) that ran to more than 900
closely printed pages. Those whose concern or curiosity might be
whetted by a small sample should take a quick look at a 50-page
booklet entitled *General Industry—OSHA Safety and Health
Standards Digest*.[40] Among the items appearing in this digest are
the following:

> Safety-toe wear shall meet the requirements of ANSIZ 41.1-1967
> "Standard for Men's Safety Toe Footwear."
> Each hand-fed planer and jointer with a horizontal head shall
> be equipped with a cylindrical cutting head. The opening in the
> table shall be kept as small as possible.
> *Ladders, Fixed*
> . . . All rungs shall have a minimum diameter of 3/4 inch, of
> metal, or 1-1/8 inches if wood. They shall be a minimum of 16
> inches in clear length and be spaced uniformly no more than 12
> inches apart. . . .
> Metal ladders shall be painted or treated to resist corrosion or
> rusting when location demands.
> *Lunchrooms*
> Employees shall not consume food or beverages in toilet rooms
> or in any area exposed to a toxic material.
> *Machinery, Fixed*
> Machines designed for a fixed location shall be securely
> anchored to prevent walking or moving, or designed in such a
> manner that they will not move in normal operation.
> *Revolving Drums*
> Revolving drums, barrels, or containers shall be guarded by an
> interlocked enclosure that will prevent the drum, etc., from
> revolving unless the guard enclosure is in place.[41]

Special Emphasis Programs

OSHA has developed special emphasis programs in two areas
using the "worst first" principle—that is, singling out the most
hazardous industries or toxic substances for investigation first. In its
pamphlet, OSHA has described the program as follows:

> 1. *The Target Industry Program* is aimed at five industries with
> injury frequency rates more than double the national average of 15.2
> disabling injuries per million employee hours worked:
> • *Longshoring* (or Marine Cargo Handling, as it is called) - 69.9
> injuries per million employee hours
> • *Meat and Meat Products* - 48.1 per million employee hours
> • *Roofing and Sheet Metal* - 43.0 per million hours

---

[40]OSHA Pamphlet No. 2201, Rev. June 1975.
[41]*Ibid.*, pp. 22, 30.

- *Lumber and Wood Products* - 34.1 per million hours
- *Miscellaneous   Transportation   Equipment*   (primarily manufacturers of mobile homes, campers, and snowmobiles) - 33.3 per million employee hours.

   2. *The Target Health Hazards Program* is focused on five of the most commonly used and hazardous of the more than 15,000 toxic substances that have been identified by NIOSH;
- Asbestos
- Carbon Monoxide
- Cotton Dust
- Lead
- Silica[42]

"Worst-First" Delays in Action

   Note that asbestos was identified by NIOSH in 1974 or earlier as one of the most hazardous of toxic substances. There could be little cause for surprise about the thunder from the critical left in early 1976 when there was disclosure that the effective date of enforcement of exposure standards for asbestos had been postponed until after the November 1976 election. A news dispatch published in March 1976 gives a partial explanation for the tumult:

   The postponement of the promulgation of new standards setting industrial exposure levels for such cancer-causing agents as asbestos and beryllium and for more general health problems such as excessive noise was disclosed in a standards development schedule prepared by the Occupational Safety and Health Administration on Feb. 23. President Ford, business groups and businessmen all over the country have made the agency a favorite target in widespread criticism of all kinds of Federal regulations. In a speech early last month [Feb. 1976] in New Hampshire, for example, President Ford told his businessmen audience that he knew they would "like to throw OSHA into the ocean." He said he had instructed it to start dealing "with citizens as friends, not enemies."[43]

   The   present   authors'   purpose   in   reviewing   OSHA developments is not to castigate, condemn, or attempt to conciliate. There is more than one side to most of the crucial questions being raised in Congress and in the media. Here is a typical *pro* item:

   The Occupational Safety and Health Administration will be making an extra effort to help business avoid violations. Fully two thirds of its $10.4 million budget increase from this year's $117.6 million to $128 million in fiscal 1977 will be devoted to advice instead of enforcement.

---

[42]ALL ABOUT OSHA, p. 10.
[43]NEW YORK TIMES, March 4, 1976, p. 15.

OSHA intends to upgrade the educational and consultative services it provides to companies to help them comply with its
regulations.[44]

In contrast, here is a caustic editorial on the *con* side:

President Ford's admonition to the Occupational Safety and
Health Administration to treat businessmen as "friends, not
enemies," is apparently having its desired pre-election effect: a slow-
down in enforcement of safety rules that were underenforced to start
with.

The law creating OSHA was passed in 1970 as a belated recognition of the need for effective Federal action to halt the appalling
toll in deaths and injuries caused by industrial accidents and job-
related diseases. Unlike the parallel safety law in the coal mines,
OSHA never came close to achieving its objectives, principally
because of slack administration and industry foot-dragging.

Now the President is openly identifying with the law's critics as
part of his campaign determination to project a conservative image.
In the wake of his demand in a campaign speech to a business audience that the agency abandon "harassment" comes the disclosure
that it has deferred until after Election Day [1976] the effective date
for exposure standards covering such potentially noxious substances
as ammonia, arsenic, asbestos, beryllium, cotton dust and lead.

The safety of millions of workers must not be made a political
pawn. The Administration has been disgracefully negligent up to
now in enforcing the law; to worsen that miserable record in the
interest of winning corporate campaign support is an insupportable
sacrifice of employee health, as well as a breach of legal obligation.[45]

Another criticism was leveled by Ralph Nader's Health
Research Group. In an Oct. 1975 study prepared by the group it
was claimed that 98 percent of OSHA's "nonserious" violations resulted in low fines averaging slightly more than $19.00. Fines for
serious violations averaged $606.37 apiece.[46]

Guarded Optimism From a Veteran Safety Expert

Writing in January 1976, a veteran safety professional of
unquestioned stature stated:

Since the advent of OSHA, "Safety in the work place" has been
dramatically improved. More progress has been made in freeing the
workers' environment of unsafe conditions, since OSHA, than was
accomplished for the past twenty-five years. Federal legislation has
areas of weaknesses; however, in the case of OSHA the benefits far
outweigh the faults.[47]

---

[44]BUSINESS WEEK, Feb. 2, 1976, p. 73.
[45]NEW YORK TIMES, March 5, 1976, p. 30.
[46]*Ibid.*, March 4, 1976, p. 15.
[47]Confidential letter to authors from a senior staff safety executive of an insurance
brokerage firm operating on an international basis (Joseph G. Marcel, Chatham, N.J., Jan.
30, 1976).

What could possibly be regarded as a thoroughly unbiased and objective appraisal of OSHA, the law itself, its administration, and its compliance by management and labor is to be found in a study sponsored by the Ford Foundation, the results of which were published in late 1975.[48] The author, Nicholas A. Ashford, was the Senior Research Associate at the Center for Policy Alternatives, Massachusetts Institute of Technology. Ashford's study resulted in the conclusion that worker health and safety involved an area of conflicts. He noted with approval that OSHA has slowly served to raise the conciousness of both management and labor.

> The mandate to comply with health and safety standards is causing management to internalize costs, in much the same way that workers' compensation legislation did. The critical difference is that the emphasis is now on *prevention,* related to both health and safety, rather than treatment or compensation for injury, and management and labor now argue about the nature of safe and healthful work conditions. These new conflicts thus center on issues that, if resolved, are more likely to improve workers' health and safety (and productivity in the long run) than the resolution of conflicts over who will pay for the harm.

Ashford dwells at length on what he believes has been "the failure of society to recognize occupational health hazards." He notes for instance that safety professionals are more concerned "with the explosive nature of chemicals than with their toxicology and more with the effects of noise on hearing than with its role as a stressor and cocausitive factor of disease." He goes on to say,

> The very nature of the differences between health and safety hazards has resulted in a pervasive safety bias that has affected legislation, the setting of standards, enforcement, manpower development, employer and employee education, and technology development. . . .
> The safety bias that pervades this field is especially serious in the case of manpower and is manifested in a severe imbalance in the mix of safety versus health professionals and in the life of facilities available for their training. . . . The Occupational Safety and Health Act with its emphasis on safety has, if anything, worsened the manpower imbalance as firms demand additional *safety* personnel to comply with the Act and government demands additional *safety* personnel to enforce it.

But Ashford's findings include both good news and bad. On balance he predicts the good over the bad. In one of his final observations he states:

---

[48]Nicholas Ashford, *Worker Health and Safety,* Monthly Labor Review. U.S. Department of Labor, Bureau of Labor Statistics, Sept. 1975, *98* (No. 9), pp. 3-10.

In the short run the costs of complying with the Occupational Safety and Health Act will be high and unequal in different industries, and severe pressures to resist the enforcement of the legislation will arise. However, if enforcement persists and other activities to facilitate adjustment are pursued aggressively, the longer run should see an encouragement of new technology, substitute materials, and redesigned jobs that should result in higher total U.S. productivity, decreased worker absenteeism, and improved job health and safety.

What Ashford seems to conclude in reporting the results of his study is that the American people in general, the American work force, and American industry will ultimately be beneficiaries, if OSHA, the Act, is prudently and properly enforced.

"Bureaucrat Heal Thyself"

While the Carter Administration was struggling to select and support new administrators to achieve more equitable enforcement of such laws as OSHA, some of the press disclosed the need for drastic reform from within. One such disclosure was revealed in the April 1977 issue of *Fortune,* which noted: "The Occupational Safety and Health Administration inspected its own Washington, D.C., headquarters and cited itself for all sorts of violations: exits were blocked by furniture and trash, fire extinguishers were improperly maintained and safety notices were not properly posted. . . ."[49]

New Top Staff for OSHA

Late in 1975 then-Secretary of Labor John Dunlop effected a drastic shakeup in the management of the department's Occupational Safety and Health Commission. Dunlop's public explanation follows:

> During 1975 OSHA has been substantially transformed and the foundation has been laid for a positive approach to the Federal regulation of safety and health which will better protect the American Worker while obtaining greater cooperation and acceptance from those affected by the regulations.
>
> A new top management team has been installed . . .
>
> We have shifted attitudinally police-like enforcement to education, consultation and voluntary compliance.
>
> We are now selecting work places for inspections for specific reasons rather than on a random basis.
>
> We are concentrating on serious hazards and known dangers instead of seeing how many numbers of violations can be found in the work place.

---

[49]FORTUNE, April 1977, p. 69.

We are now working with business associations, companies—large and small—other governmental agencies and organized labor in advance consultation and problem solving.[50]

Whether or not the "new look" at OSHA appeased either the partisans of Ralph Nader or the liberal media editorialists clamoring for all-out action regardless of economic consequences remains highly doubtful. And organized business and industry have yet to stand up and be counted officially pro or con. Meanwhile, much can be learned by management from reflection on the often-asserted views of one of its own elder statesmen in promoting the cause of preventive occupational safety.

The individual to whom progressive administrators often look for guidance is Leo Teplow. A lawyer by profession, Teplow moved in the 1950s from directorship of industrial relations, Allis-Chalmers Corporation, to become head of the labor relations department of N.A.M. and then to the vice-presidency for labor relations of the American Iron and Steel Institute. Most recently, Teplow has been a special consultant, Organization Resources Counselors, Inc., Washington, D.C.

Teplow put management's problems with OSHA in clear perspective when he wrote in 1975:

> The rhetoric which ushered in the Occupational Safety and Health Act has served to becloud the fact that remarkable progress had actually been achieved in the 60 years which preceded the Act. Granted, there had been more emphasis on safety than on health, but an industrial history which saw the birth of formal voluntary company safety programs, which gave birth to the National Safety Council, which saw a dramatic decrease in the rate of occupational deaths and injuries, which gave rise to voluntary consensus standards organizations and their great contribution to safety, which saw safety committees and industrial medical committees and industrial hygiene committees being formed and playing active and constructive roles in industry after industry—this is not a history to be ashamed of. And if this sounds as though I would serve as an apologist for industry, or would cultivate smugness about occupational safety/health, I hasten to add that my purpose is only to place the subject in perspective. I am fully aware that not all businesses do as well as do the leaders; and for decades I have been urging that employers do more.[51]

Teplow has become well known over the years as a realist. He knows full well that to make every working place in the nation 100 percent safe and healthful for *all* employees or potential employees

[50]Occ. Safety & Health Rep. (BNA) 1003 (1975).

[51]Leo Teplow, *The Regulator and the Regulated*, Conference Board Record, April 1975, p. 26.

would be impossible. As Teplow queried, did Congress have in mind that "every place of employment [must] be so overregulated as to make it possible to assign persons with heart disease or limited respiratory capacity to the most hazardous operations?"

It takes little imagination to conjure up fantastic examples. Should it be mandatory for fine watchmaking machines to be so designed as to be run by aged, arthritic women? Should road sweeping equipment be developed to provide safe and healthy jobs for asthmatic men or women of any age?

But one of the present authors doesn't have to let his imagination run rampant to speculate how his business and personal life might have been affected any number of times had there been an equivalent of OSHA 50 or 60 years ago. Should, for example, two-ton grocery delivery trucks have been so safeguarded as to make it impossible for a clumsy, myopic youth to upset one over an embankment, destroying the truck and its contents and precipitating the hapless youth into the hospital with multiple contusions and abrasions? Or when that same youth several years later took a beginner's personnel position in a large manufacturing plant, should that plant's recreational facilities have been so safeguarded as to prevent this awkward young fellow from breaking his back the first and only time he tried to show his prowess at pole vaulting during his lunch period in the plant's miniature high-jumping and pole vaulting area?

And if the law ought to have made all equipment foolproof at the employee's workplace, how about equipment to be used at home? What safety experts of an earlier generation could conceivably have designed a power hedge trimmer so faultlessly as to preclude the chance that the same clumsy, myopic individual, now middle aged, could cut the electric cord while standing on top of a 10-foot step ladder and then fall on his back to the ground and be knocked out by the hedge trimmer *and* the ladder? And, finally, should any law have required the manufacturer of a gasoline-powered lawn mower to make it so foolproof that an aging, dimwitted or dim-visioned operator could not mow down a badminton net and simultaneously nearly sever several toes because his sneakers were not equipped with steel toe guards? Preposterous as they might seem these instances are *not* hypothetical.

"Ability to Pay" as a Criterion

Among the more consequential issues discussed by Teplow in his trenchant comments on OSHA is the degree that ability to pay should be the decisive factor in the imposition of a safety or health standard. He has cited an outstanding case and given his own forth-right opinion, as follows:

> In the *Goodrich* case (Docket No. 2038), the Occupational Safety and Health Review Commission administrative law judge held that it was feasible engineering control which Goodrich must under-take to build enclosures around the braiding machines employing a total of approximately 30 employees per shift, even when, in order to enclose the machines, Goodrich would have to relocate 50 of the 56 machines and enlarge the plant at a cost of $1,250,000, plus losing nearly a quarter of a million dollars' worth of production. The judge opined that "in relation to the size of Respondent corporation it cannot be held that the cost of abatement is prohibitively expensive."
>
> I submit that both regulators and regulated have reached a sor-ry pass when the question of feasibility is to be determined not on the seriousness of the hazard, not on the effectiveness of alternative modes of employee protection, but on the size of the employer cor-poration. No country, no matter how strong its economy, can afford to misallocate resources in this fashion. Obviously, the need for balance and judgment becomes even more essential in a period of rampant inflation and inadequate resources.
>
> If we hold to the basic premise that the purpose of the law is to protect employees, and if that purpose can be served by suitable ear protection, it is a shocking misuse of the regulatory authority to require so vast an allocation of resources to one minor hazard when many serious safety/health problems require management attention and fiscal and manpower support.[52]

Sage Advice for Management

From his vast experience in promoting proper safety measures for industry, Teplow has come up with a number of significant sug-gestions for continuing management action. Teplow urges that each company administrator

> 1. Review his corporate safety/health program to improve its effectiveness and set up priorities for improvement.
>
> 2. Directly or through his trade association, contribute to requests for information from NIOSH and OSHA in their preparation of cri-teria statements, proposed standards, and environmental and economic impact statements.
>
> 3. Set up a permanent system of record keeping of employee health records and employee exposures to toxic substances or physical agents.
>
> 4. Review each OSHA citation at a high level promptly enough to contest if the case calls for it on the basis of the significance of the issue rather than the amount of the proposed penalty. . . .[53]

---

[52]*Ibid.*, p. 31.
[53]*Ibid.*, p. 29.

Establishment of Federal Standards

The Occupational Safety and Health Act requires the Secretary of Labor to promulgate as soon as possible, and within two years from its effective date, April 28, 1971, existing "national consensus standards" and "established Federal standards," unless he determines that those standards will not improve employees' safety and health. The term "national consensus standards" means any standard that has been adopted and promulgated by a nationally recognized standards-setting organization under procedures indicating that employers interested and affected by it have reached substantial agreement upon its adoption and which was formulated in a manner affording an opportunity for consideration of diverse views. The term "established federal standards" means any operative occupational standards adopted by any agency of the Federal Government that are presently in effect or have been embodied in any Act of Congress.

But reaffirmation of presently accepted safety and health standards is only the beginning. At any time after April 28, 1971, the Secretary of Labor could promulgate new standards, or modify or revoke existing standards. He can also promulgate temporary emergency standards upon determining that affected employees are exposed to grave dangers from toxic or physically harmful agents or new hazards. Temporary standards are to remain in effect until superseded by permanent standards regularly adopted.

Any standard established by the Secretary must direct the use of labels or other appropriate forms of warning to assure that employees concerned are advised of the hazards to which they are exposed and to apprise them of relevant additional factors, such as symptoms, emergency treatment, etc.

The Secretary of Labor is not limited to action in developing standards on his own motion or on the advice of his staff. The Act authorizes him to consider information submitted in writing by any interested person or organization, *including a representative of any organization of employers or employees* and other federal agencies as well as state agencies, in determining whether or not a specific standard should be promulgated. Whenever any request is made for the adoption of a new or revised standard, the Secretary may appoint a special advisory committee and request its recommendations. Every such advisory committee must include among its members an equal number of persons qualified to present the viewpoint of the workers involved. Each committee must also include one or more representatives of the health and safety agencies of the states. Each committee so constituted is required to submit its recommendations regarding a proposed new standard and can take no longer than 270 days to do so.

Stays and Variances

An employer may apply for a stay or a variance with respect to a standard promulgated by the Secretary of Labor upon filing an application which establishes certain facts, such as his inability to comply with the standard by its effective date, the fact that the employer is taking all available steps to safeguard his employees and has an effective program for coming into compliance with the standard as quickly as possible.

In all such applications the employer must provide supporting representations from qualified outside persons having firsthand knowledge of the facts presented. The employer must also certify that he has informed his employees of his application so that they will have an opportunity to intervene in the matter.

Inspections, Investigations, and Record Keeping

The Secretary (also presumably any of his agents) is authorized to enter any employer's premises to inspect and investigate possible employee hazards at reasonable times, within reasonable limits, and in a reasonable manner. As stated in the Act's declaration of policy, such inspections have to be without advance notice. When an inspection is being made, a representative of the employer may accompany the agents as they perform their work. A representative authorized by the establishment's employees may also go along. Where there is no authorized representative an inspector must consult with "a reasonable number of employees concerning matters of health and safety in the workplace."

Federal inspectors are not restricted by the statute to investigating establishments that have been the subject of complaint by employees or anyone else. (Despite the fact that the law had not yet become operative and administrative staffs had not yet been appointed to enforce it, Labor Department officials were quoted as saying, in January 1971, that in selecting the initial group of establishments to look over, the inspectors would be instructed to inspect "the worst first.")

The Secretary may require the keeping of records and the compilation of reports on "work-related death, injuries and illness other than minor injuries requiring only first aid treatment and which do not involve medical treatment, loss of consciousness, restriction of work or motion, or transfer to another job."

Citations

The full scope of the Secretary of Labor's powers to require employers to comply with the law can be realized only by direct quotation of one of the applicable sections thereof. Specifically, Section 9 (a) reads:

> If, upon inspection or investigation, the Secretary or his authorized representative believes that an employer has violated a requirement of section 5 of this Act, of any standard, rule, or order promulgated pursuant to this Act, he shall with reasonable promptness issue a citation to the employer. Each citation shall be in writing and shall describe with particularity the nature of the violation, including a reference to the provision of the Act, standard, rule, regulation, or order alleged to have been violated. In addition, the citation shall fix a reasonable time for the abatement of the violation. The Secretary may prescribe procedures for the issuance of a notice in lieu of a citation with respect to de minimis violations which have no direct or immediate relation to safety or health.

Note that Section 9 empowers a Labor Department inspector to issue a citation to an employer *for apparent violation of any requirement of Section 5 of the Act.* To many knowledgeable employers this is perhaps the most ominous provision in the statute. Section 5 imposes on employers the general duty to prevent job hazards in their establishment. Thus, even though no safety or health standard applicable to a possible hazard may have been promulgated, a Labor Department inspector has the right and duty to cite an employer as violating the Act whenever the inspector discloses a working condition that he alone regards as constituting danger to employees' safety or health.

Possibly with some optimism, the Law Department of the National Association of Manufacturers has deprecated the significance of this catch-all authority of the Labor Department inspectors. It said in its bulletin of January 28, 1971,

> Inclusion of a general duty applicable to employers [in Section 5] is intended to cover the circumstance wherein there exists no specific standard applicable to a given situation. In view of the provision governing establishment of temporary standards [Section 6 (c) (1)], however, this general duty is intended to be relied upon infrequently.[54]

Imminent Danger

During the congressional debates on the Occupational Safety and Health Bill which has now been enacted into law, there was

---

[54]*Summary Analysis of Public Law 91-595 . . . ,* NAM Law Department Memo, Jan. 28, 1971, National Association of Manufacturers, Washington, D.C.

sharp dispute over the terms, if any, under which a plant could or should be shut down partially or completely on account of grave job hazards. The result of the debates in Congress was a compromise. Thus, it is now stipulated in Section 13 (a) of the Act that:

> The United States district courts shall have jurisdiction upon petition of the Secretary to restrain any conditions or practices in any place of employment which are such that a danger exists which could reasonably be expected to cause death or serious physical harm immediately or before the imminence of such danger can be eliminated through the enforcement procedures otherwise provided by this Act. Any order issued under this section may require such steps to be taken as may be necessary to avoid, correct, or remove such imminent danger and prohibit the employment or presence of any individual in locations under conditions where such imminent danger exists, except individuals whose presence is necessary to avoid, correct, or remove such imminent danger or to maintain the capacity of a continuous process operation to resume normal operations without a complete cessation of operations, or where a cessation of operations is necessary, to permit such to be accomplished in a safe and orderly manner.

Once again in layman's language, the foregoing apparently means that before an entire plant or an operation of a plant could be closed on account of seriously hazardous conditions, the Secretary of Labor would have to get a decree from a federal district court ordering the shutdown or cessation of operations.

The OSHA administrative staff has gone to some length to interpret the impact of the imminent-danger stipulation in the Act itself. Thus, OSHA has defined the term as referring to "any condition or practice where there is a reasonable certainty that a danger exists that can be expected to cause *death or serious physical harm immediately* or before the danger can be eliminated through normal enforcement procedures." "Serious physical harm" is defined not only as "any type of harm that would cause permanent or prolonged damage to the body. It is also the type of harm which, while not damaging the body on a prolonged basis, could cause such temporary disablement as to require in-patient hospital treatment."

Health hazards, OSHA has declared, are also included as involving imminent-danger situations. To be so included, "there must be a reasonable expectation that (1) toxic substances or dangerous fumes, dusts or gases are present, and (2) that exposure to them will cause irreversible harm so as to shorten life or cause reduction in physical or mental efficiency, even though the resulting harm is not immediately apparent."

Important Rights of Employees

OSHA has asserted its own concept as to the conditions under which employees unilaterally or at the instigation of union officials can cease work because of the apparent presence of seriously unsafe or unhealthful conditions. Its advice to employees is most certainly something not blithely to be ignored by management. Personnel administrators and safety staff persons should keep indelibly in their minds what OSHA has published about certain employees' rights. Thus, to quote OSHA precisely:

> Ordinarily you do not have the right to walk off the job because of potentially unsafe workplace conditions. If you do so, your employer may take disciplinary action.
>
> However, you do have the right to refuse in good faith to expose yourself to an imminent danger. . . . You are protected, under the Act, from discrimination if:
> * Where possible, you have asked your employer to eliminate the danger and he fails to do so
> * The danger is so imminent that there is not sufficient time to have the danger eliminated through normal enforcement procedures
> * The danger facing you is so grave that "a reasonable person" in the same situation would conclude there is real danger of death or serious physical injury, and
> * You have no reasonable alternatives.[55]

The brochure just summarized in part also indicates that the Secretary of Labor can bring action against an employer and seek relief for an employee with a complaint found valid if the employee has been discriminated against for exercising his statutory right to complain. The action could result, so OSHA insists, in rehiring or reinstatement of the aggrieved employee *with back pay*.

Here OSHA has emulated other recently established federal bureaucracies by asserting rights equal or superior to those possessed by the National Labor Relations Board. Suppose, by way of example, that an ambitious shop steward pulls out his department on the pretext that unduly hazardous conditions prevail, while actually he is seeking an extra-contractual rate increase for his constituents. Should this be a matter of meting out disciplinary action under the grievance procedure or the subject of a charge of Taft-Hartley violation to be investigated and processed by the NLRB? Management has to consider these alternative attacks when determining whether to take action against an individual employee or a

[55]U.S. Department of Labor, Occupational Safety and Health Administration, PROTECTION FOR WORKERS IN IMMINENT DANGER, OSHA Pamphlet No. 2205 (1975).

minor union official who instigates a work stoppage on the pretext of protesting serious job hazards.

If the discharged employee takes his case to arbitration charging dismissal without just cause and loses, he still has the apparent option to bring charges against the company to the NLRB. If he loses, then OSHA may entertain a suit on his behalf and seek federal court action to try to get a reinstatement order.

Multiple choices of allegedly aggrieved employees under different statutes were affirmed somewhat tangentially in one of the most controversial OSHA cases thus far decided by a federal appellate court. The basic issue heard by the Circuit Court of Appeals for the District of Columbia was whether an employee designated by fellow workers (presumably in a recognized bargaining unit) to go along with an OSHA official on a plant walk-around inspection has to be paid for the time so spent. The court had to determine whether either OSHA or the Wage-Hour Act had to be construed as requiring the employee to be present while on such an assignment. The court's verdict was that the walk-around time was *not* compensable per se under either statute. But the court did rule that an employee so involved would not have to pursue to finality his rights under the grievance procedure of the applicable union agreement before claiming pay on the grounds that there had been a violation of the Wage-Hour Act. On this rather murky set of circumstances, the National Manufacturers' Association had this to say in part:

> the court stated that although the OSHA legislative history contains evidence that Congress desired to permit employees to participate in the Act's safety inspections, the Act is silent on the issue of compensation for this inspection participation.
> The Court of Appeals stated that it is reticent to write a compensation provision into the statute as that is a function to be left to Congress. The opinion also notes that the employer and the employe's union can provide for the compensation in the collective bargaining agreement. . . .[56]

Reactions—One Company's Pro and Con

For more than two years the director of industrial hygiene of the Inspiration Consolidated Copper Company has been swamped by OSHA publications, directives, and mandatory standards. As reported by the *New York Times,* he now sits "almost surrounded by bookshelves lined with thick volumes and hundreds of smaller publications containing directives from the agency that dictates

---

[56]NAM REPORTS (Washington, D.C.), Jan. 12, 1976.

standards ranging from the dimensions of some restroom fixtures to the maximum amount of sulphur dioxide gas that can be emitted from Inspiration's copper smelter that turns the raw ore into copper through a heating process."[57] The hygiene director contends, the *New York Times* reported, that the agency's rules are often impracticable and unrealistic, a source of needless expense and bureaucratic overkill.

There are, unsurprisingly, two other angles to this picture. One point of view is that of the local business agent for an IBEW union representing some of the smelter's employees. He has been quoted by the *New York Times* as hailing OSHA standards as "a tremendously important thing for working people." He continued, "It means that we have someplace — OSHA — to go to if we have to when there is an unsafe situation; if you don't have somebody helping you, what can you do? You can't walk off every time."[58]

A second point of view was expressed by a senior OSHA industrial hygienist assigned to the Phoenix area where the Inspiration company has one of its smelter complexes. This official told the *New York Times* that

> while the copper industry generally has been more conscientious in dealing with health hazards in recent years, emissions of copper dust and sulphur dioxide gases in the smelting process remain a potentially very serious and little understood health problem. . . .
> No one has come up with a chronic disease resulting from the material we are talking about, but remember it took eight to ten years before the connection between work in asbestos plants and cancer was made.[59]

Inspiration's hygienist made this admission: "If it has any advantages, OSHA has awakened management to a lot of problems that maybe in the past were pushed under the rug. Now you can't push anything under the rug. . . . But I don't like their approach. It's like a bulldozer."[60]

A New Deal for OSHA

By the spring of 1977 OSHA had acquired its fourth chief administrator during its six-year span of existence. Its third administrator, Dr. Milton Corn, an industrial hygiene professor of high standing in scientific and academic circles, had announced early in

[57]NEW YORK TIMES, Dec. 21, 1976, p. L-22.
[58]*Ibid.*
[59]*Ibid.*
[60]*Ibid.*

1976 his plans and aspirations for his agency. His proposals, Corn insisted, would establish OSHA as an agency that, management, labor, and Congress could have confidence, was headed in the right direction. *Business Week* reported him as working to:

- Move vigorously into the area of health, without deemphasizing safety,
- Institute extensive training programs for his staff,
- Eliminate nitpicking standards and make those remaining more comprehensible,
- Change OSHA's enabling legislation so that the agency can move away from being an adversary to business and act as consultant to industry.[61]

But Dr. Corn did not have the enthusiastic backing of the Ford Administration. In Feb. 1976 in his primary reelection campaign, Ford told a New Hampshire audience of industrialists that he knew they would like to throw OSHA into the ocean. Moreover, OSHA's schedule for promulgation of preventive standards for use of potentially hazardous substances like asbestos and lead was deferred until after the Nov. 1976 election. The *New York Times* reported in March 1976 that a new exposure standard for ammonia, presumably affecting about one-half million employees, would not be issued until Feb. 1977, and, further, that a critical standard for lead usage affecting more than 120 occupations would not be promulgated until at least March 1977.

The principal reason advanced by OSHA for postponing promulgation of permanent standards for use of highly toxic substances was the necessity to comply with an executive order issued by President Ford in November 1974. That order required OSHA to produce an inflationary impact statement relating to estimated costs to companies and benefits to employees that might be obtainable.[62]

Corn was succeeded as the top OSHA Administrator by Professor Eula Bingham early in 1977. Then another set of plans and objectives was announced by her chief, President Carter's newly appointed Secretary of Labor, Ray Marshall. What Secretary Marshall and Professor Bingham will be up against in their efforts to revivify OSHA can perhaps be well illustrated by reference to some of that agency's problems, successes, and apparent failures up to and through 1976.

---

[61] *Why Nobody Wants to Listen to OSHA*, BUSINESS WEEK, June 14, 1976, p. 64.
[62] NEW YORK TIMES, March 4, 1976, p. 1-15.

All Is Not Gold That Glisters [sic] Or Blisters

A Jan. 1977 *Business Week* article criticizing OSHA bore the intriguing caption, "Making Lead as Costly as Gold." OSHA, said the article, "has partially succeeded where generations of alchemists have failed. If it has not actually turned lead into gold, it may be on the way to making it as costly." This comment pertained to a report released by a consulting firm, John Short & Associates, Inc., which estimated that OSHA had proposed a mandatory "maximum work place exposure standard for lead that would require the industry to put up nearly $1 billion for capital equipment and entail a cost of about $200 million a year for operation and maintenance."

It's not only the smelters of lead that are confronted with multi-million or billion dollars of costs by OSHA's proposed directive. Battery manufacturers, said *Business Week*, indicate that they would have to put out $115 million to comply and that "a vast majority of the independent producers would be eliminated, over time."[63]

Two of the most vigorous print media publications that have assigned key staff members as OSHA watchers have come out with recurrent criticisms of that agency's accomplishments and possible derelictions. *Must* reading for those personnel administrators who need to keep abreast of what has been going on in OSHA for the past few years is the special feature article in *Business Week* entitled "Why Nobody Wants to Listen to OSHA".[64] The article had this to say:

> Few companies are willing to discuss for the record their experiences with OSHA inspectors. "It would be like sassing the policeman," says one top executive. But those who will talk are almost unanimous in their frustration with OSHA's performance. John J. Ahern, director of security for General Motors, says: "There is no direct correlation between their regulations and the actual accidents that do occur. . . ."
>
> The company [GM] was inspected 614 times through last December [1975] and received 258 citations representing about 1,800 violations. Ahern claims that GM has invested $79 million and the equivalent of 1,100 man-years to satisfy OSHA requirements in 1974 alone but to no avail. "We had a good safety program going long before anybody ever heard of OSHA, and we haven't seen any effect from all the money that's been spent, so far as any reduction in our accident rate is concerned," he said.

DuPont is another company heard from in the *Business Week* special report. A verbatim quote follows.

> DuPont Co. for instance boasts that it had only one disabling injury for each 4 million man-hours worked—about one tenth the

---

[63]BUSINESS WEEK, Jan. 24, 1977, p. 20.
[64]*Why Nobody Wants to Listen to OSHA.*

rate for the chemical industry and about 1/20 that of all industry. DuPont executives point to their 60-year-old medical program and the work of their 41-year-old Haskell Laboratory for Toxicology & Industrial Medicine as signs that they are equally concerned about health. The lab is being expanded by 70% to handle carcinogenic studies. But even DuPont with its good record was slapped with $21,080 in fines in April [1976] and Ned K. Walters, the company's safety manager, complains that none of the citations was related to injuries. In fact 80% were for "improper placement" of guards on machines and lack of handrails on stairways.

The same article cited a McGraw-Hill survey indicating that American industry had planned to invest about $3.2 billion for employee safety and health in 1976, an increase of about 17 percent over 1975.

The *Business Week* feature article was not just negatively critical. To wit, it observed: "Despite the costs, few argue that OSHA — or something like it — was not needed. The statistics are too chilling. . . . Still, businessmen say that the agency's dubious methods have cost millions of dollars and have produced thousands of problems — without yielding much improvement." The following tabulation accompanied the *Business Week* article.[65] Compiled from data released by OSHA itself, it was entitled OSHA's Terrible 10 and tells its own story:

Area of violation	Violations in fiscal 75	Penalties levied Thousands of dollars
National Electrical Code requirements (from loose wires to ungrounded equipment)	37,273	$493.3
Safety of abrasive wheel machinery	6,662	37.1
Construction and placement of compressed gas containers	6,196	59.0
Marking of exits	6,121	14.1
Safety of pulleys in mechanical power-transmission gear	6,037	75.6
Maintaining portable fire extinguishers	5,965	29.6
Safety of drives in mechanical power-transmission gear	5,431	53.2
Guarding floor and wall openings, platforms, and runaways	5,321	140.2
General housekeeping requirements (from unmopped puddles to flammable rubbish piles)	5,204	74.8
Effectiveness of machinery guards	4,779	157.3

[65]*Ibid.*, p. 67. Reprinted from the June 14, 1976, issue of BUSINESS WEEK by permission. Copyright © 1976 by McGraw-Hill, Inc.

The New New Deal for OSHA

In May 1977, Ray Marshall, newly appointed Secretary of Labor in the Carter Administration, told a news conference that henceforth OSHA would concentrate on the most serious job hazards and try to eliminate "nitpicking regulations." Highlights from the press conference reflect changes in emphasis produced as a result of charges — by business groups, labor, and even another government agency, the General Accounting Office — that OSHA's activities had had little realistic impact on safety and health conditions of American workers. "Business groups," wrote a *New York Times* correspondent, "have concentrated their fire on what they called 'horror stories' about the arbitrary application of rules concerning such things as the number of coat hooks in rest rooms and the height of fire hydrants. Mr. Marshall said that after studying the agency and the criticisms of it he had come 'to the sad conclusion that both business and labor were right.' "[66]

It was disclosed by the *Times* that in fiscal 1976 OSHA made over 100,000 safety inspections but slightly fewer than 7,000 health inspections. Moreover, while over 5,000 safety standards were issued, there were only 15 new health standards.

The new chief administrator of OSHA, Dr. Eula Bingham, concluded at the May press conference, so the *Times* reported, that "95 percent of OSHA's inspection efforts will be devoted to the most serious health and safety hazards."[67] The other 5 percent will go to the lower risk sectors of the economy such as wholesale and retail trade, finance institutions, and service industries. According to Dr. Bingham, new rules issued by OSHA would cover broad areas, such as cancer-causing compounds, rather than individual compounds.

General Enforcement Procedure

Where no dire emergency is found to exist the regular enforcement procedure following the issuance of a citation against an employer gives the employer an opportunity to contest either the citation or the proposed penalty. If the employer does not notify the Secretary within 15 days of his challenge, and if no employee or representative of the employees files notice of challenge, the employer is deemed compelled to comply with the terms of the citation against him.

---

[66]NEW YORK TIMES, May 20, 1977, p. A-14.
[67]*Ibid.*

Occupational Safety and Health Review Commission

While the Secretary of Labor is empowered to propose remedies for occupational hazards and to propose assessment of penalties, it is the Occupational Safety and Health Commission that has exclusive authority to dispose of the penalties. This Commission is given powers that in most respects are analogous to the enforcement powers of the National Labor Relations Board. The three men on the Board are appointed by the President to serve staggered six-year terms.

Hearing officers, appointed by the Chairman of the Board, are responsible for taking evidence on contested cases resulting from a challenge by employers of either the citation of alleged violations of the Act or proposed penalties. Employees and their representatives also have the right to challenge proposed action by employers when cited by the Secretary and to participate in proceedings before hearing officers with full protection against reprisal.

Following a hearing and upon review of the findings and recommendations of the hearing officer the Commission is obligated to issue an order affirming, modifying, or vacating the citation and/or the proposed penalty. Each such order is to become final 30 days after its issuance, unless the employer can demonstrate that abatement of the violation could not have been completed because of factors beyond his reasonable control.

Judicial Review

Employers have the right of appeal from orders of the Occupational Safety and Health Commission. Judicial review of such orders is available much in the same manner as review is available with respect to orders of the National Labor Relations Board.

Penalties

An employer who wilfully or repeatedly violates the Act may be assessed a civil penalty of not more than $10,000 for each violation.

An employer who has received a citation for a serious violation of the Act may be assessed a civil penalty of up to $1,000 for each violation.

An employer receiving a citation for a violation specifically determined not to be of a serious nature may be assessed a civil penalty of up to $1,000 for each violation.

Failure to correct a violation for which a citation has been issued is punishable with a civil penalty of not more than $1,000 for each day that the failure continues.

An employer who willfully violates the Act and thereby causes death shall upon conviction be punished by a fine of not more than $10,000 or by imprisonment for not more than six months or both; for convictions other than the first the punishment may be a fine of $20,000 and imprisonment for not more than one year or both.

CHAPTER 6

Employees' Personal Rights

The long arm of the law can and often does reach deeply into employees' personal affairs. Here no pun is intended. But the U.S. Supreme Court held in March 1976 that certain types of affairs could validly be held to be a crime under state laws. To borrow from a lugubrious aphorism attributed to the biblical figure Job: "What the Law giveth, the Law can take away."

The Supreme Court case in point sustained the constitutionality of a Virginia statute forbidding "unnatural and lascivious acts such as sodomy and bestiality." Even though the unnatural act might be engaged in privately by consenting adults, the Virginia law makes consexual sodomy punishable to a maximum term of five years' imprisonment,[1] and the same day the Court upheld a North Carolina court's conviction of a man charged with sodomy.[2]

The Virginia court that had defended the validity of the state's ban on sodomy reached back into the Bible for justification. Henceforth, both Judean and Christian law may be essential reference sources for personnel administrators concerned with determining what sort of personal conduct by employees is tolerable as a condition of getting or retaining employment. The Book of Leviticus was expressly cited by the Virginia court in the passage which reads: "Thou shall not lie with mankind, as with womankind: it *is* abomination."[3]

What impact, if any, should the Supreme Court's latest posture on individual rights have on company personnel policies relating to hiring, discipline, and discharge? The short answer could well be, *"Plenty!"* A chief spokesman for the American Civil Liberties Union was quick to view the Court's position with alarm. ACLU Executive Director Aryeh Neier declared for publication, "The Supreme

---

[1]Doe et al. v. Commonwealth's Attorney for the City of Richmond, Va., et al., 425 U.S. 901 (1976).
[2]Enslin v. North Carolina, 425 U.S. 903 (1976).
[3]Leviticus, 18:22.

Court has demonstrated a great insensibility to claims for individual privacy. This is typical of the trend."[4]

The ACLU was not alone in its dismay about an apparent change in Supreme Court rulings affecting personal rights. The New York Times observed editorially:

> There was a time not so far distant when the United States Supreme Court was the staunch defender of civil rights and liberties; there was a time when the court alone, of the three great branches at the apex of power in Washington, systematically served as protector of the individual citizen against undue intrusion of government into private and personal affairs. . . . But . . . the court seems clearly to be beating a retreat from its once proud forward position in this delicate and difficult area of the relation between citizen and state. It may indeed be reflecting a gradual lessening of concern for such matters on the part of the American public.[5]

Whatever the trend of the Court might be, the courts continue to meet their obligation to grind out decisions where laws of relatively recent enactment necessitate seemingly preferential treatment of one group of citizens over others. To illustrate, the same week that the U.S. Supreme Court acted on the controversial sexual issue posed by the Virginia law, a federal district court in Massachusetts had a tough decision to make when it decided a job-rights case against veterans and for women. That court declared unconstitutional the Massachusetts law that gave veterans preference in civil service appointments. A female applicant had instituted the challenge to the law after she was rejected for a state mental health position even though she had scored better than eleven veterans in a pre-employment selection test.

The court stated in explaining its rationale that "the fact is that there are alternatives available to the state to achieve its purpose in aiding veterans, without doing so at the singular expense of another identifiable class, its women."[6]

The federal court in the case just cited faced the same inordinately difficult problem that federal courts may be plagued with for years to come—that is, determining how statutory employee rights for one group of citizens can be enforced without undue derogation of the statutory rights of other groups of citizens. (See the review of seniority rights versus rights of racial minorities and women in Chapter 3.) Not all of the problems of the judiciary in relation to personal rights originate from job-related legislation. Forced busing provides a not-too-extreme example. Whatever one's

---

[4]NEW YORK TIMES, March 30, 1976, p. 17.
[5]*Ibid.*, March 31, 1976, p. 40.
[6]*Ibid.*, April 4, 1976, p. 41.

views may be about school busing as a means of bettering educational opportunities of blacks, the fact remains that mandatory busing does in some measure encroach on the personal rights of one class of youthful citizens to the advantage of another class.

FEDERAL PRIVACY ACT

A federal law enacted in 1974 for the beneficent purpose of protecting individual citizens from undue intrusion into their private affairs has inevitably resulted in further intrusions. This particular law is the Federal Privacy Act of 1974. It had been in the making for six or seven years as a result of investigations by congressional committees into the activities of a number of federal agencies, most notably the FBI. Paradoxically, it not only *permits* but *requires* a number of government agencies to disclose to third parties much information they had amassed secretly or in the regular course of their statutory responsibilities to administer laws requiring them to elicit financial and other data from millions of citizens.

After signing the measure into law on Dec. 31, 1974, President Ford declared:

> The Privacy Act requires federal agencies to take steps to insure the accuracy and security of records that concern individuals and to limit record keeping to necessary and lawful purposes. In addition, individuals have a lawfully enforceable right to examine federal records containing such information and to challenge the accuracy of data with which they disagree.[7]

As soon as the Privacy Act became fully effective in 1975, the Social Security Administration was one of the federal agencies which made public a detailed account of terms under which personal information could be disclosed to third parties—public and/or private. Listed below are some of the "events" that have to be reported by social security claimants:

- Yearly earnings from employment or self-employment if higher than the applicable exempt amount
- Departure of a child from the care of a person entitled to benefits if benefits have been payable for the child's support
- Any change in the income, resources, household composition, living arrangements, or other circumstances affecting

---

[7]PROTECTING YOUR RIGHT TO PRIVACY: DIGEST OF SYSTEMS OF RECORDS, AGENCY RULES, RESEARCH AIDS (Federal Register; released to federal depository libraries, Feb. 1976). For a listing of publications in the FEDERAL REGISTER, see *Privacy Act Publications: Table of Dates and Pages*, 41 FED. REG. 4709 (1976).

eligibility of a person receiving supplemental security income.

Both civil and criminal penalties can be imposed on anyone improperly withholding information. Criminal penalties can be imposed for intent to defraud.

As stated in a lengthy document released to the public in 1976 by the Office of the Federal Register, among those to whom personal information held by the Social Security Administration can be disclosed are:

> Employees or former employees for correcting or reconstructing earnings records and for social security tax purposes. Unspecified third parties to establish or verify information provided by representative payee or payee applicants, or to obtain or to verify information regarding an individual's eligibility or entitlement to benefits under the social security programs, or the individual's capability to manage his/her affairs.
>
> The Treasury Department as pertinent to tax and benefit payments, including collection of social security taxes.
>
> Providers and suppliers of hospital and medical services for the purpose of administering the Medicare program.
>
> Private medical and vocational consultants for making medical examinations or vocational assessments requested by social security or a state agency.

It's not by any means enough for personnel administrators to familiarize themselves with public disclosure of personal data as mandated by the Privacy Act and as construed by the Social Security Administration. For the administrators' guidance and possibly for use by their legal counsel and a myriad of federal and state officials, there is the unique 700-plus-page document referred to in the previous paragraph. In its introduction, obviously addressed to private citizens, this advice is given:

> The Privacy Act was enacted in December 1974 to provide certain safeguards for individuals against invasion of privacy by Federal agencies. The Act, with few exceptions, applies to all information maintained by the Federal Government that can be retrieved by reference to your name or other identification such as your social security number, finger print, alien registration number, etc. Under the Act you have the right to —
> 1. Find out what, if any, information an agency has about you;
> 2. Find out who else has regular access to your records;
> 3. Get a copy of your record from the agency;
> 4. Have any errors in your record corrected, and
> 5. Approve certain disclosures of your records to people who would not otherwise see them.[8]

---

[8]U.S. Department of Health, Education, and Welfare, Social Security Administration, COLLECTION AND USE OF INFORMATION BY THE SOCIAL SECURITY ADMINISTRATION, Form SSA-5000 (9-75).

The foregoing is in essence a summary of what appears in Section 2(b) of the Privacy Act, which reads in full text as follows:

(b) The purpose of this Act is to provide certain safeguards for an individual against an invasion of personal privacy by requiring Federal agencies, except as otherwise provided by law, to—

(1) permit an individual to determine what records pertaining to him are collected, maintained, used, or disseminated by such agencies;

(2) permit an individual to prevent records pertaining to him obtained by such agencies for a particular purpose from being used or made available for another purpose without his consent;

(3) permit an individual to gain access to information pertaining to him in Federal agency records, to have a copy made of all or any portion thereof, and to correct or amend such records;

(4) collect, maintain, use or disseminate any record of identifiable personal information in a manner that assures that such action is for a necessary and lawful purpose, that the information is current and accurate for its intended use, and that adequate safeguards are provided to prevent misuse of such information;

(5) permit exemptions from the requirements with respect to records provided in this Act only in those cases where there is an important public policy need for such exemption as has been determined by specific statutory authority; and

(6) be subject to civil suit for any damages which occur as a result of willful or intentional action which violates any individual's rights under this Act.

In 1976 there appeared in the *Federal Register* a five-volume set of systems of records and agency rules—Privacy Act Issuances— setting out in bureaucratic gobbledegook how various federal cabinet departments and independent agencies have construed their own obligations to comply with the mandates of the basic statute. In volumes I and II of this set, the summarized rules that relate to various components of the Department of Defense extend to more than 1,100 pages.

Lay Persons' Overview of Privacy Act

Even the most erudite personnel administrators can become bewitched and bewildered if they deign to wade through the thousands of published pages comprising the "issuances" by various federal agencies as to how they construe their rights and obligations under the Privacy Act. So we suggest a shortcut. If in simple terms personnel administrators wish to explain to employees or prospective employees what the Privacy Act is all about, we suggest the use of a slight pamphlet written by lay persons for lay persons. Even though what is quoted below may be somewhat repetitious of what has been referred to above, we commend utilization of the brief pamphlet with the expressive title, *Opening Your File—A Citizen's Guide to—Fair Credit Reporting Act—Federal Privacy Act.* This was written by four undergraduates of Washington University, St. Louis, enrolled in a course in 1975 offered as an introduction to "MoPIRG," otherwise and officially known as the Missouri Public Interest Research Group Foundation.

Here are directly quoted some of the authors' interpretations of the least obscure provisions of the Privacy Act:

> The purpose of the Federal Privacy Act is, in the words of the Senate Committee on Government Operations, "to promote governmental respect for the privacy of citizens by requiring all departments and agencies of the Executive branch to observe certain constitutional rules in the computerization, collection, management, use and disclosure of personal information about individuals. . . .
>
> Under the law, all records that are maintained by federal agencies may contain only information that is either relevant to the individual on whom the record is maintained or necessary to accomplish a purpose of the agency as required by a presidential order or by statute.
>
> If the information gathered is adverse and may affect an individual's rights, benefits, or privileges under federal programs, the information should be collected directly from the individual involved. All other sources of information are to be informed of the principal purpose for which the information is to be used.
>
> Records that are maintained must be kept up to date, accurate, and complete in an effort to assure fairness to the individual. Before a federal agency can turn over your record to any authorized person, the agency must make a reasonable effort to assure the accuracy of the report.
>
> An agency may not maintain any records about how you express your 1st Amendment rights unless authorized by law or if you give your permission. As an exception, however, such records may be collected and maintained by authorized law enforcement agencies such as the FBI.
>
> The primary weakness of the above rule is in its wording. As in most acts, it is filled with words such as reasonable, fairness, completeness, principal purpose, relevant, necessary, and to the greatest extent. The narrowness or broadness with which these words are interpreted will determine the true meaning of the law. . . .
>
> Unless the agency has the permission of the individual to whom the record pertains, the record may only be disclosed to:
>
> 1. an officer or employees of an agency that is carrying out its duty,
> 2. the Bureau of Census for carrying out surveys,
> 3. someone who will use the record only for statistical research,

4. another U.S. agency if the record is to be used for civil or criminal law enforcement activity,
5. another U.S. agency when such transfer is authorized by law,
6. some person or agency with a court order.[9]

With all the loopholes in the Privacy Act, it's no wonder that professional civil libertarians continue to deplore progressively greater encroachment on personal rights by government agencies. Aryeh Neier has cited statistics compiled by the United States Senate Committee on Constitutional Rights showing that in 1974, 54 federal agencies had maintained 858 data banks on individual Americans and that 765 of the data banks had more than 1.2 billion records.[10]

Credit Checks

The Fair Credit Reporting Act of 1971 can affect, at least tangentially, management decisions relating to record keeping on employees. More likely a company executive is apt to be concerned about his own credit rating and who knows about how it stands. *Business Week* has propounded some pithy questions and provided answers obviously for the benefit of mature management folks. Following are excerpts from a "Personal Business" article about checking individual credit files:

> Have you ever tried to check your personal credit rating? Thanks to the 1971 Fair Credit Reporting Act, you now have the right to know the "nature and substance" of anything in your file. Unfortunately, the chances of your finding something amiss are high enough to warrant taking a look.
> The procedure for finding out what's in your file is simple. You can walk into most [credit] bureaus unannounced, fill out an interview request form, and see an interviewer within a matter of minutes. If you'd rather discuss your file over the phone, you will have to fill out and return the form, then wait for the agency to contact you. That could take a few days to three weeks.
> The interviewer will read your report to you, translating code numbers for banks and stores to their actual names. Most credit bureaus have little else on file about consumers. "We do no investigations," explains Ralph Godfrey, vice-president of the Credit Bureau of Greater New York. "We don't probe into a person's financial background, morals, or neighborhood."

[9]OPENING YOUR FILE: A CITIZENS' GUIDE TO—FAIR CREDIT REPORTING ACT, FEDERAL PRIVACY ACT, 1976 (St. Louis, Mo.: Public Interest Group Foundation, 1976). Those wishing a more detailed discussion of the Privacy Act, its strengths, and its weaknesses might want to look at THE RIGHT TO PRIVACY, edited by Grant S. McClellan (New York: H.W. Wilson Company, 1976).
[10]Aryeh Neier, DOSSIER (New York: Stein and Day, 1975), p. 14.

Because of a loophole in the Fair Credit Reporting Act, agencies do not actually have to let you see your credit report or give you a copy for your own use.

If you find a serious error in your file, the law requires the credit bureau to investigate "within a reasonable time." Inaccurate or unverifiable information must be corrected or deleted. And if certain discrepancies cannot be resolved, you are allowed to file a brief statement of your version of the dispute.[11]

The Fair Credit Reporting Act should not be confused with the Consumer Credit Protection Act that went into effect in 1970. That statute, as stated in its preamble, was meant to protect the consumer (1) "by requiring full disclosure of the terms and conditions of finance charges or in offers to extend credit" and (2) by restricting wage garnishment.

It is only the second objective of the law that is of direct concern to personnel administrators. Of special note are what the law asserted to be the "findings" of Congress. These were:

(1) The unrestricted garnishment of compensation due for personal services encourages the making of predatory extensions of credit. Such extensions of credit divert money into excessive credit channels and thereby hinder the production and flow of goods in interstate commerce.

(2) The application of garnishment as a creditors' remedy frequently results in loss of employment by the debtor, and the resulting disruption of employment, production, and consumption constitutes a substantive burden on interstate commerce.

(3) The great disparities among the laws of the several states relating to garnishment have, in effect, destroyed the uniformity of the bankruptcy laws and frustrated the purposes thereof in many areas of the country.

The sententious wording of these findings was no doubt intended to forestall any challenge to the constitutionality of the law based on assertions that it went beyond the regulatory powers of Congress with respect to routine decisions of private business establishments. Although the range of its applicability is not specifically set forth in the law, it is manifestly intended to apply to virtually all private employers and the people working for them.

GARNISHMENTS

In *Black's Law Dictionary* "garnishment," "assignment," and related terms are thus defined:

---

[11]BUSINESS WEEK. Dec. 7, 1975, p. 97.

Garnishment involves a writ warning a third party (garnishee) not to deliver money or property to the defendant but to appear and answer the plaintiff's suit. *Attachment* is the process of actually bringing the valuables under direct control of the legal authority until the suit is settled. Sometimes *garnishment* and *attachment* are used interchangeably. *Assignment* is the voluntary apportionment of pay to satisfy a claim. It is occasionally agreed to at the time of receiving credit as assurance that this credit will be repaid. *Execution* is generally considered the entire legal process from *garnishment* (warning) through *attachment* (seizure of the assets) to final settlement of the judgement. Often only that portion of the process following judgement of the suit is referred to as *execution*.[12]

To many, if not most, personnel administrators, garnishments present nothing but figurative headaches, unwanted payroll expense, and sometimes disruption of employee morale with attendant lowered efficiency. But all states have such laws, and now the Federal Government has entered the picture through new legislation and a landmark court decision, both of which place substantial limitations on management's obligations to honor garnishments or to discipline employees whose financial troubles induce their creditors to resort to garnishment proceedings.

The federal law restricts rather than prohibits utilization of garnishment proceedings. It prescribes the maximum portion of an employee's "disposable" earnings that can be attached for the payment of any debt to an outsider. The term "earnings" is defined to mean "compensation paid or payable for personal services, whether denominated as wages, salary, commission, bonus or otherwise and includes periodic payments pursuant to a pension or retirement program."

Inclusion in the law of the term "disposable earnings" is of particular significance. That term is declared to mean "that part of the earnings of any individual remaining after the deduction from those earnings of any amounts required by law to be withheld."

The maximum amount of an employee's disposable earnings in any work week that can be subject to garnishment is fixed by the federal statute. This amount cannot exceed either: 1) 25 percent of an employee's earnings for that week or 2) 30 times the current federal minimum wage, that is, in 1976, 30 times $2.30 or $69.

As is found in most federal laws, there are a few exceptions to the generally applicable requirements. Thus the restrictions on the portion of an employee's earnings subject to garnishment do not apply to: 1) any court order for the support of any person, 2) any

---

[12]BLACK'S LAW DICTIONARY (4th ed.; St. Paul, Minn.: West Publishing Co., 1975).

court order issued under the federal bankruptcy act, 3) any debt
due for any state or federal tax.

Restriction on Discharge

There is an explicit provision in the federal law prohibiting the
discharge of any employee because his earnings have been subjected
to garnishment for any one indebtedness. But the law also provides
for a limited kind of reverse preemption. In this regard it has two
separate stipulations as to its effect on state laws. These continue to
prevail to the extent that they may 1) prohibit garnishments entirely or provide more drastic limitations or 2) prohibit discharge
when an employee's earnings have been garnished for more than
one indebtedness.

In 1969 New York State enacted a law (A.3337) which went to
the extreme limit of placing an absolute prohibition against the discharge or layoff of any employee for "income execution" no matter
how many garnishments had been served against him on his employer. (The New York State Legislature has gone much further. In
a statute effective September 1, 1970, employers are prohibited
from honoring garnishments in cases where the earnings of the employee concerned are $85 a week or less.)

The federal court decision restricting management action with
respect to employee garnishments was handed down by the U.S.
Supreme Court on June 9, 1969 (*Sniadach* v. *Family Finance
Corporation*). In this case, the Court held that no longer can a garnishment be honored by an employer (in the sense that deductions
can be made from any employee's earnings) before the individual
has been given notice and an opportunity to be heard in court as to
the propriety of the garnishment. What the Court did, in substance, was to declare unconstitutional a Wisconsin state law
permitting so-called prejudgment garnishment. This law was ruled
by the Court to violate the Constitution's due-process clause. This
decision cast in doubt the constitutionality of the laws of some 20
other states having provisions comparable to the Wisconsin statute.

Pertinent passages from the Supreme Court decision invalidat-
ing the prejudgment provisions of the Wisconsin law are quoted below:

> What happens in Wisconsin is that the clerk of the court issues
> the summons at the request of the creditor's lawyer; and it is the
> latter who by serving the garnishee sets in motion the machinery
> whereby the wages are frozen. They may, it is true, be unfrozen if the
> trial of the main suit is ever had and the wage earner wins on the
> merits. But in the interim the wage earner is deprived of his enjoy-

ment of earned wages without any opportunity to be heard and to tender any defense he may have, whether it be fraud or otherwise.

Such summary procedure may well meet the requirements of due process in extraordinary situations. . . . But in the present case no situation requiring special protection to a state or creditor interest is presented by the facts; nor is the Wisconsin statute narrowly drawn to meet any such unusual condition. . . .

. . . We deal here with wages—a specialized type of property presenting distinct problems in our economic system. We turn then to the nature of the property and problems of procedural due process.

A prejudgment garnishment of the Wisconsin type is a taking which may impose tremendous hardship on wage earners with families to support. . . .

Recent investigations of the problem have disclosed the grave injustices made possible by prejudgment garnishment whereby the sole opportunity to be heard comes after the taking . . .

The leverage of the creditor on the wage earner is enormous. The creditor tenders not only the original debt but the "collection fees" incurred by its attorneys in the garnishment proceedings:

"The debtor whose wages are tied up by a writ of garnishment, and who is usually in need of money, is in no position to resist demands for collection fees. If the debt is small, the debtor will be under considerable pressure to pay the debt and collection charges in order to get his wages back. If a debt is large, he will often sign a new contract of payment schedule which incorporates these additional charges."

Apart from those collateral consequences, it appears that in Wisconsin the statutory exemption granted the wage earner is generally insufficient to support the debtor for any one week.

The result is that a prejudgment garnishment of the Wisconsin type may as a practical matter drive a wage-earning family to the wall. Where the taking of one's property is so obvious, it needs no extended argument to conclude that absent notice and a prior hearing . . . this prejudgment garnishment procedure violates the fundamental principles of due process.[13]

Arbitration of Garnishment Disputes

Robert W. Fisher of the U.S. Labor Department, in a published analysis of arbitration awards in garnishment cases, concluded that arbitrators are not free to assess such penalties as discharge or layoff under present laws but are free to impose lesser penalties than are permitted by law or to decide that no penalties are justifiable in individual cases. Fisher's analysis revealed arbi-

---

[13]Sniadach v. Family Finance Corporation, 19 WH Cases 5 (U.S. Sup. Ct., 1969).

trators have "split about equally over the issue of discharge, half ordering reinstatement and half affirming discharges."[14]

This is not at all surprising, for as Fisher notes, "discharging a worker for repeated garnishments is essentially punishment on the job for behavior off the job." In innumerable cases arbitrators have found justification for reversing discharges arising from non-job-connected offenses.

One of the leading arbitration decisions involving a discharge of an employee who had been subject to two garnishments resulted in an order for reinstatement. The essential facts were not in dispute. A female employee whose work performance was admittedly satisfactory had been warned by her employer that if she did not immediately settle with a creditor who had issued a writ of attachment of her pay, she would be discharged. She at once made the requisite settlement. Several months later, her creditor notified her employer of his intention to attach her pay again. She was warned again and her creditor took no action against her pay. But a month later when a writ attaching her pay was received by her employer, she was discharged forthwith.

The union representing this employee appealed to arbitration. The arbitrator who decided this case was Professor James J. Healy, one of the most respected practitioners in the field. Therefore, the basis for his finding that the employee whose wages had been garnished was improperly discharged merits more than casual attention.

Arbitrator Healy noted that there were two approaches to the analysis of this case. As he put it, "The first concerns the manner in which the rules formulated by the company are administered, with particular reference to the 'offense' of pay attachment action." He observed that the rule that led to the discharge had never been written and had never been posted on a bulletin board or conveyed to employees generally. Rather, the rule was made known to an employee only *when* the first offense occurred. He said:

> Such an *ex post facto* procedure leaves much to be desired when the nature of the employee-wrongdoing is pay attachment. By the time the first warning and the correlation instruction as to rule is given to the employee, it is not impossible that the employee's involvement has already gone so far as to make remedies difficult. In other words when one attachment is served, the seeds of the second or third

---

[14]Robert W. Fisher, *How Garnisheed Workers Fare Under Arbitration*, MONTHLY LABOR REVIEW. U.S. Department of Labor, Bureau of Labor Statistics, May 1967, *90*(No. 5), 1-6.

attachments have probably been sown. This is true, even though other employees in the company may have been ingenious enough to escape the second writ after a first writ warning. For still another reason, it is fair to expect the company to give advance, formal notice of a rule such as this before instituting any disciplinary measures, including warning. Unlike the more blatant offenses which have a direct bearing on the employer-employee relationship (e.g., poor quality work, absenteeism, tardiness, insubordination, etc.) this type of offense might not occur to one as affecting one's acceptability as an employee. If the company adjudges it to be a punishable offense (rightly or wrongly) it should at least make its policy known at the time of employment.

With regard to the second approach followed by Arbitrator Healy in his analysis of this case, he concerned himself with the question of the "basic justice" of the applicable state law (Rhode Island) permitting liberal use of discharge as a penalty for wage attachments. On this issue the arbitrator expressed the opinion that:

> the extreme penalty of discharge must be applied when the employee has indulged in behavior on one or more occasions which affects materially the employer-employee relationship. Pay attachments are definitely in the twilight zone; they only indirectly affect the relationship, either by becoming too burdensome on the employer or becoming so frequent that an employer has grave doubts as to an employee's character qualifications for the job. To illustrate, pay attachments on a person whose job calls for handling money could rightly result in dismissal. No such question was involved in this case and the company made no contention concerning character weakness necessitating discharge.
>
> Rather the company stressed the bookkeeping burden. This burden could become intolerable after a time, but the arbitrator doubts if two offenses are intolerable under the circumstances.[15]

PERSONAL RIGHTS AFFECTING EMPLOYMENT STATUS

Management's chief concern with personal-rights issues dealt with in law is quite properly concentrated on what applicable laws permit, respect, restrict, or prohibit. As was indicated in Chapter 5 in connection with workers' compensation, a diligent researcher can find in published court decisions precedents to support almost any position—pro or con—that may have previously been taken in personal-rights litigation.

---

[15]D.M. Watkins Co., Decision of Arbitrator James J. Healy, 14 LA 787 (1950).

Neier cites with evident approbation a 1974 New York State court decision that many personnel administrators might view with dismay. The case developed when a practical nurse had her license revoked on the grounds that she had been an habitual heroin user. The nurse had started using heroin while dating an addict. Indeed, she had undergone detoxification therapy in two treatment centers. Her troubles with the law began while she was getting therapy but after she had been employed by a New York City hospital.

Neier summarizes subsequent developments in the nurse's case as follows:

> The Committee on Professional Conduct of the State Board of Regents recommended that the [nurse's] license be revoked but because she was progressing well in the methadone maintenance program and had apparently not used heroin since enrolling in it, further recommended that the revocation be stayed and that she be placed on probation for five years. This did not satisfy the Board of Regents' Committee on Discipline, which decided to revoke [her] license unconditionally. The crucial factor for the Board of Regents was [her] 'lack of candor' in two employment interviews. She had told the people at the Flower Fifth Avenue Hospital that she was not using drugs.
>
> "In this case, it seems to us that the Board of Regents has placed altogether too much emphasis on two instances of concealing relevant information from an employer," the Appellate Court said.

Neier then quotes a portion of the court's decision which might raise the gorge of a lot of management people. The court asserted:

> While we certainly do not condone lying, we can understand how a young, divorced, addicted mother might think it is justifiable to withhold relevant information in order to obtain employment which one expert testified was "the next most important factor" aside from the use of methadone and counseling in the rehabilitation of a patient. There is nothing in this record to indicate that petitioner's . . . addiction affected the performance of her duties. To the contrary, her supervisors at the Flower Fifth Avenue Hospital testified that she was a competent nurse, that her performance evaluation contained ratings of "very good" or "satisfactory" in all categories, and that she had been given a merit raise in the course of her work.

Neier's concluding comment was that "All five judges on the Appellate Court concurred in reducing the nurse's penalty to five years' probation."[16]

Had this case come on appeal to the U.S. Supreme Court, it is anyone's guess what the outcome might have been. But a 1976 High

---

[16]Neier, p. 66.

Court decision may afford some sort of a clue. Even though the facts and the issues were not directly relevant, nevertheless it might be deemed a signal that the majority of the present Justices may be inclined henceforth to sustain the validity of a tremendous volume of state and local legislation previously stricken down as violating the personal constitutional rights of individuals.

The issue before the Supreme Court was not one that ordinarily would have resulted in a landmark decision. It was simply whether the police department of Suffolk County, New York, could regulate the hair length of police officers.[17]

It was a 6 to 2 decision reversing a N.Y. State Court of Appeals decision that had upheld the constitutional right of police officers to wear their hair in any style they thought becoming and to sport beards and mustaches too. Civil rights extremists may regard the Court's decision on limits to hirsuteness for employees having public contacts as opening the legislative doors to much tighter regulation of employees' appearance and conduct. They are probably right. In any event, 1976 became an opportune year for employers generally to take a hard look at personnel policies that went perhaps from tolerant permissiveness to allowing just about anything not specifically affecting employee job performance. In this connection, it is usually desirable for management periodically to review company manuals establishing work rules and the terms and conditions of employment. Such manuals usually serve invaluable purposes. They also can lead, unintentionally, to expensive litigation if not cautiously phrased and prudently administered.

Veteran personnel administrators will remember the years, not too distant, when the private sector set the pace for the public. That is to say, the compensation levels, bargaining rights, and fringe benefits of employees of private enterprises were usually much superior to those applicable to public servants. By the mid-1970s, the picture had markedly changed. Employees of the Federal Government and of many state and local governments have earnings, benefits, and job privileges that exceed in value those available to people working for private enterprises. There are, as usual, two sides to the picture. Conditions that government agencies can impose on terms of employment are probably translatable into equivalent conditions prescribable by business firms.

To allude to an absurd Aesopian metaphor, what's now sauce for the goose could be sauce for the gander, i.e., private employers. It could eventually be the aftermath of another 1976 Supreme

---

[17]Kelley v. Johnson, 425 U.S. 238 (1976).

Court decision, one that arose over a challenge by a Philadelphia city employee who had been fired for moving out of town. He did so in violation of a municipal ordinance requiring city employees to live within the city limits. In sustaining the validity of the Philadelphia ordinance, the Court inferentially endorsed the position of the city's Civil Service Commission. The object of the ordinance, the Commission had explained, was "to provide employment for those individuals who will demonstrate an interest in the City of Philadelphia, and to employ those citizens who will be most highly motivated to work for a better city and to enhance its overall environment."[18]

It could be a fair presumption that any challenge to a similar regulation by a private employer would not stand up in court, unless the demonstrable reason for it was unlawful discrimination. Thus a reactionary employer who moved his plant to a lily white suburb with high housing costs couldn't expect to get away with a local residence rule aimed to prevent disadvantaged minorities from taking jobs with his establishment.

A federal district court decision handed down in 1976 seemingly goes in the opposite direction. It struck down a provision in the New York labor law code requiring that in the construction of public works preference in employment must be given to citizens of New York State who have resided in the state at least 12 months. This court held that:

> The lawfully admitted resident alien who is denied employment because a citizen is preferred is almost as much the object of discrimination as the resident alien who is denied the right of employment at all. He has been classified as a person who need not receive the equal protection of the laws because of his status. Yet a resident alien is surely a 'person' within the meaning of the due process and protection clauses.

One dictum in this decision could be of vital concern to all managements. The court declared:

> The state has a duty to all its lawful residents, resident alien or citizen. It must try to see to it that they do not starve, that they have equal access to state public employment, as well as membership in the Bar and that they have equal access to private employment.[19]

Some 15 years ago Laurence Stessin, a distinguished commentator and consultant on employer-employee relations, listed in his book on employee discipline "a number of employee acts for which

---

[18]McCarthy v. Philadelphia Civil Service Commission, 424 U.S. 645 (1976).
[19]C.D.R. Enterprises, Ltd., et al. v. The Board of Education of the City of New York (U.S.D.C. E.N.Y., 1976), in [1976] 64 DAILY LAB. REP. (BNA) A-10, E-1.

discharge or some form of severe discipline is generally conceded."[20] Among the 40 acts listed were these: intoxication on the job, insubordination, absenteeism, disobedience, disorderly conduct, subversive activity, stealing, use of drugs, immoral conduct, improper language, political activity in the plant, carrying weapons.

More recently it has been more common practice for rule books to list only generally accepted major offenses accompanied by a catchall phrase such as, "for other just causes." There is a reason for this. An accepted principle of legal interpretation is that to define is to delimit. So failure to include a rule prohibiting taking home company tools or documents for personal use might foreclose a chance of making stick a discharge for that particular reason. Where there is a union contract with arbitration procedures, management's right to discipline employees for any reason may be subject to arbitral review and reversal. (See Chapter 8 for exposition of arbitrators' roles in disciplinary matters.)

Arrest and Conviction Records

Management inquiries about arrest and conviction records of job applicants have long been frowned on by some state and local civil rights agencies for fear such records will be used for discriminatory purposes. These agencies have usually acted on the presumption—rightly or wrongly—that a disproportionately large number of members of minority groups have run afoul of the law.

In 1973 the New York City Commission on Human Rights promulgated new guidelines. It took the unequivocal position that *any* inquiries by employers addressed to *any* prospective employees about arrest records are illegal *per se*. One of the new guidelines also declared it to be illegal for employers to reject job applicants because of prior convictions unless their crime was "job related." The Commission also announced that employers could not seek to obtain arrest records except from applicants themselves. Further, such records could not be made the basis for promotion or discharge. (Similar guidelines, the Commission noted, had previously been issued by Minneapolis and by the State of Michigan.[21])

The New York State Division of Human Rights has been much more explicit in issuance of guidelines than the City Commission has been. In 1976 the state agency, located in the World Trade Center in New York City, put out a 21-page booklet entitled *Rulings on Inquiries* that may be obtained free upon request. This booklet sets out examples of questions asked of prospective employ-

[20]Lawrence Stessin, EMPLOYEE DISCIPLINE (Washington: BNA, Inc. 1960), p. 25.
[21]NEW YORK TIMES, Jan. 5, 1973, p. 29.

ees that the agency now considers to be illegal by reason of the state's constitutional provisions against discrimination (Article I Section II). The rulings, so the N.Y. State Labor Department has announced, "are intended to be used by employers and others as guides in the interpretation of the Human Rights Law."

Among the questions sited in the booklet that may not be asked applicants for credit, jobs, and the sale or lease of property are the following: coloring, complexion, skin color; religion, religious holidays kept, religious affiliation, church attended, pastor of church; nationality, national origin, ancestry, mother tongue, lineage, parentage, descent; form of address preferred—i.e., Ms, Miss, Mr., Mrs.; marital status; spouse's place of work; childrens' ages; ability to have children; support for family planning or birth control; birth date (one may enquire if applicant is between 18 and 65); disabilities; arrest. In certain cases exceptions may be made for so-called bona fide occupational qualifications, approved affirmative action plans, court requirements, or other valid reasons.

Penalties for Character Disparagement

Some 15 years after he wrote his authoritative book on employee discipline, Stessin had occasion to comment in print on quite a different issue relating to employees' rights and employers' obligations to protect them. His subject was "What Your Ex-Boss Can't Tell Your Next Boss." The issue may seem to be a narrow one and its treatment superficial. It is referred to here merely as indicative of how federal and state courts are ruling on matters of personal rights without a restraining hand from the United States Supreme Court.

An Ominous Warning

When a manager makes public unkind remarks, even where references are not involved, trouble may beckon. In a case tried in 1972, General Motors paid out almost $30,000 to a former plant guard as balm for "hurt feelings." It seems that the security man was suspected of having "misappropriated company property." He was called into the chief's office and, as is standard operating procedure in many companies when minor thefts are involved, was offered the choice: "Be fired or resign." He chose the latter.

The man's departure unloosed a spate of rumors among the security staff. According to the grapevine the company was going to replace the private guards with a private protection agency. Management decided to act. Several plant guards were called in and told why their colleague had been let out.

Candor can be costly. How costly may be a monetary figure determined in court. The Wisconsin Supreme Court set a price tag of $56,000 on damages done to a rejected applicant for a position with the Internal Revenue Service. Certain facts leading to this 1975 decision were thus summarized by Stessin:

> At first the fates were kind to John Yates. He [was] a restless young man, proud possessor of an occupational halo—a master's degree in business administration from Harvard. He had become somewhat disenchanted with the job he took after graduation, feeling it was weighted down with the stamp 'dead end.' He gave appropriate notice and devoted all his time to finding a post with wider horizons. A lead came rather quickly for these times. Within three weeks he had a live prospect, the Internal Revenue Service. An invitation was extended, pending a routine reference check.
>
> Then came the bad news, a week of no news at all. Finally Mr. Yates bit the bullet and called his interviewer. The response was a quick freeze. Mr. Yates prodded the personnel man and was told in language bathed in caution, that the references from his previous job were far from effusive.
>
> 'In fact,' the voice at the other end said, relenting, 'I'll give it to you straight. Your ex-boss said, among other things, that you were something of a character.'
>
> Mr. Yates (not his real name) had no idea that his employment was under a cloud. He realized that without a favorable reference from his former boss—the controller of the company—the outlook for a job was worse than just bleak. And so Mr. Yates filed a suit in court to clear his good name.
>
> Mr. Yates won his case and $56,000. Judge Andrew Parnell of the Supreme Court of Wisconsin ruled [in May 1975] that labeling a person 'a character' was not an honest appraisal of his or her work and 'is the kind of humiliation and anguish that calls for financial damages.'[22]

Summarizing judicial attitudes that staunch supporters of the right of free speech might deem anathema, Stessin opined:

> An employer, say the courts, does not have an unfettered right to render unsolicited comments or opinions about former employees.
>
> When answering a reference by phone, letter or personal call management is obliged to confine its remarks to answers to specific questions.[23]

State laws designed to protect the employees from the machinations of unscrupulous employers who renege on commitments in money matters run a wide gambit. Typical statutes establish controls over such subjects as which fringe benefits constitute wages or salaries that are collectible by employees through legal proceedings,

---

[22]*Ibid.*, Dec. 7, 1975.
[23]*Ibid.*

how often employees shall be paid, how they shall be paid (e.g., in cash or by check, or in scrip), and what deductions can be made from their earnings, such as garnishments or wage assignments.

As to supplemental payments that may be considered as an integral part of wages or salaries, the New York State labor law is one of the most explicit. In the basic labor law code, the term "benefits or wage supplements" is defined to include, but not limited to, "reimbursement for expenses; health, welfare and retirement benefits; and vacation, separation, and or holiday pay." With respect to these types of supplemental compensation, the New York law provides that:

> Any employer who is party to an agreement to pay or provide benefits or wage supplements to an employee and who fails, neglects, or refuses to pay the amounts necessary to provide such benefits or furnish such supplements within thirty days after such payments are required to be made, shall be guilty of a misdemeanor, and upon conviction shall be punished for a first offense by a fine of five hundred dollars or by imprisonment for not more than one year, or by both such fine and imprisonment. *Where such employer is a corporation the president, secretary, treasurer or officers exercising corresponding functions shall each be guilty of a misdemeanor.* [Italics supplied.]

To be subject to penalties an employer doing business in New York must be a "party to an agreement." This does not mean only a union agreement. Of course, the terms of a collective bargaining contract covering specific types of supplemental compensation are enforceable under the state wage-collection laws. But other kinds of agreements such as oral or written understandings between management and individual employees are equally enforceable. In fact, when a new employee is hired and the employment interviewer or the prospective supervisor summarizes the salary terms and the other monetary benefits attached to his job and the employee accepts the position relying on that information, an agreement within the meaning of the law may well have been consummated. If, instead of detailing the benefits and economic perquisites pertaining to the position, the management interviewer gives the applicant a booklet which sets forth these benefits, the booklet itself may be deemed a part of an employment contract.

Hiring agreements are not the only ones that come within the purview of the laws regulating wage payment. *Termination* agreements may also be enforceable in the courts. Likewise, announcements in writing or oral explanations of the provisions of new or revised benefit plans may lead to litigation if implementation does not square with what the employees were led to believe.

Here is an actual case. Because of an impending reduction in force and prospective plant shutdown, a supervising accountant was told that his services in that capacity were no longer needed. Orally, he was given the option of accepting a lower-rated position or taking as much time off as he desired in the next month to look for a new position. If he elected the latter his job would come to an end; he would get an additional full month's salary and nothing more. He accepted the latter option, and was paid off at the end of one month, in June. His company had a vacation plan that fixed the annual vacation period from June 1 to December 31 in each year. The deposed accountant demanded two weeks' vacation pay, the amount to which his length of service would entitle him. The company refused to make any vacation payment. It took the position that by offering this employee a maximum of a month's time off to look for another position it had fully met all its obligations. But there was nothing in the company's published vacation plan that denied benefits to employees terminated for any reason after the vacation period had begun. So the accountant went into court, in New York, and collected.

As for company policies or practices — published or not, there is an inherent danger under most state wage-payment laws in retroactively reducing the benefits of employees currently on the payroll. The following, though hypothetical, parallels actual cases decided day after day in the state courts. A salaried employer is hired at a time when his company maintains a sick leave policy entitling all employees with two or more years of service to a maximum of four weeks of full pay for time lost due to illness. The maximum is payable even if there is nothing more than his own statement that he was ill. Subsequently the company enters into an agreement with a union representing salaried clerks in one of its establishments. This agreement provides that physicians' certificates must be produced by any employees claiming pay for lost time because of illness. To avoid the appearance or reality of discrimination between its union and nonunion groups of employees, the management applies the same rule for nonunion salaried employees as it negotiated with the office union.

A nonunion confidential secretary becomes ill. At least she considers herself incapacitated for work because of a recurrence of asthma. She had previously consulted her physician and at the outset of her new disability renewed the prescription he had given her, and feels it unnecessary to go back to her doctor for reexamination or treatment. She files the customary claim for full salary for the entire amount of time lost from work within the 30-day limit. The claim is rejected because of her inability to produce a certificate from any treating physician. She appeals to the state industrial commission which administers the relevant law in her state. It finds in her favor, which means that the rule requiring certification by a doctor is applicable only prospectively, i.e., only to employees hired after the date the new rule was promulgated.

MANNER OF PAYMENT OF WAGES

The authority of a state to require employers to pay their work force in lawful money rather than in scrip redeemable at a company store was asserted by the Tennessee Legislature in 1899. In the same year, the constitutionality of the law was tested and sustained by a state court decision which concluded:

> The legislature evidently deemed the laborer at some disadvantage under existing laws and customs, and by the act [one making it mandatory for an employer to redeem at face value wage payments made by so-called store order], undertook to ameliorate his condition in some measure by enabling him . . . to demand and receive his wages in money rather than in something less valuable. Its tendency, though slight it may be, is to place the employer and employee on equal ground in the matter of wages, and, so far as calculated to accomplish that end deserves commendation.[24]

The latest published compilations of the Department of Labor (which periodically analyzes developments in state "protective" labor legislation) indicate that:

1. In 34 states wages must be paid in lawful money and/or by check and not by scrip or orders on company stores.
2. In 33 states wage payments must be made at least as often as biweekly or semimonthly.
3. In 40 states "prompt" payment of wages has to be made to employees upon their discharge, promptness being variously defined as meaning immediately, within a few days, or, at most, on the next regular payday.[25]

TIME OFF FOR VOTING

An apparently simple issue involving employees' rights, that is, time off to vote with or without pay, has been dealt with by the

---

[24]Harbison v. Knoxville Iron Co., 103 Tenn. 421 (1899).
[25]U.S. Department of Labor, GROWTH OF LABOR LAW IN THE UNITED STATES (Washington: U.S. Government Printing Office, 1967), p. 110.

legislatures of some 30 states. All of them have affirmed employees' rights to leave their job to vote in some kinds of public elections when it would be impractical for them to vote outside of working hours. Some states' laws go much further. A common provision in state statutes is one prohibiting employers from deducting from an employee's wages any time lost from work when he has been authorized to leave his job to exercise his franchise. (Since the state laws are constantly subject to amendment, as well as to court review, it would be pointless to attempt to summarize here the current status of voting-rights legislation in all states.) Periodically, the Bureau of Labor Standards of the U.S. Department of Labor publishes a document, with up-to-date revisions, designated as Bulletin No. 138, *Time Off for Voting under State Laws*. This is a useful compendium to keep abreast of latest developments.

Complications frequently arise for employers in some states because of the conditions fixed by law both with respect to the amount of time off allowable for voting purposes and the times when it can be taken. Even more important are the terms under which employees are entitled to time off *with pay* in order to vote. Often the courts have been called upon to adjudicate these matters. Indeed, the U.S. Supreme Court has involved itself in questions of the validity or proper construction of state statutes. Thus, the Court refused to review an appeal from a decision by the Kentucky Court of Appeals in 1947, wherein that court struck down a provision of the state law requiring time off with pay for voting purposes under limited circumstances. In colorful language the high Kentucky court declared:

> Voting is the privilege of a few people. One of its primary purposes to to keep people free. There is no such thing as a popular election in some countries in the old world. Dictatorships will have none of them. This glorious country belongs to the farmers, to the working people, to the little people whose name is legion, to the middle-sized people who are the salt of the earth, to those of the big people who would yet remain big people because their God-fearing hearts make them humble. No group of people in America has a greater stake in its Government, in its rocks and rills, in its woods and templed hills, than ordinary working men. No group in America can be more interested in voting for a clean, righteous, free, statesmanlike Government than that group known as workers.
>
> The woman with the sunbonnet and the checkered apron who trudges off the mountainside in Leslie County and walks down the creek a mile to cast her vote — she is an American queen in calico, but her only pay for voting is the satisfaction of knowing that Columbia, by God's help and hers, shall continue as the gem of the mighty ocean. Let no man cease to thank his God as he looks in at the open

door of his voting place, as he realizes that here his quantity, though cast in overalls, is exactly the same as the quantity of the President of the United States. There is a satisfaction and privilege in voting in a free country that cannot be measured in dollars and cents.

But the Kentucky court then went on to say that "a statutory provision which has the effect of requiring an employer to pay an employee for four hours of unemployed time, whether or not he votes, whether or not he has the opportunity to vote before he starts to work, whether he spends just ten minutes in voting—this could not, we think, be constitutional." In support of its conclusion the court cited the passage of the Kentucky constitution that says, "Absolute and arbitrary power over the lives, liberty and property of freemen exists nowhere in a republic, not even in the largest majority."

The court construed the meaning of this provision in its state constitution as follows: "it inhibits the legislative power of this state from arbitrarily passing a law taking property from one person and giving it to another person without value received or without any contractual basis. And this inhibition still stands regardless of the merit or glory or value or need of the person on the receiving end of the transaction."

The Kentucky high court then declared in summary:

> The law will not countenance a public maintenance of a private enterprise. Neither should the law demand a private maintenance of a public enterprise. Voting is a public enterprise. But if its maintenance is required by the employer group rather than by the entire, broad, general public, then that amounts to a requirement of private maintenance of a public enterprise.[26]

As already noted, the U.S. Supreme Court upheld this court by refusing to consider its decision on appeal. But five years later the Supreme Court expressly sustained the constitutionality of two separate state laws requiring employers to give limited time off with pay in order to vote. (One of these was an affirmation of a California superior court decision upholding that state's law providing for "hours" of time off with pay for voting purposes.)[27]

A landmark Supreme Court decision on voting rights was handed down in 1953 when a divided court sustained the constitutionality of a Missouri law providing that an employee could absent himself from work for four hours between the opening and closing of the polls on election day. This law made it a misdemeanor for an

---

[26]Illinois Central Railroad Company v. Commonwealth of Kentucky, 7 WHCases 463 (Ky. Ct. App. 1947).
[27]Tidewater Associated Oil v. Robison, 344 U.S. 804 (1957).

employer to make any deduction from wages for such absence. The facts considered by the court were not contested. An employee working on the day shift from 8:00 A.M. to 4:30 P.M. with 30 minutes off for lunch had requested from his employer permission to be absent four hours to vote on election day. The polls were open from 6:00 A.M. to 7:00 P.M. His request was refused. He and the other employees on the day shift were permitted to leave work at 3:00 P.M., giving them four consecutive hours to vote before the polls closed, but no pay for time lost from work. The employer was found guilty and penalized for violation of the statute. The employer's appeal that reached the Supreme Court was grounded on the contention that the Missouri law violated the due process and equal protection clauses of the Fourteenth Amendment and the contract clause of Article I, Section 10.

We cite below pertinent passages from the majority and minority opinions of the Supreme Court decision in this case to illustrate a point that, we think, cannot be too strongly stressed. The point is that Newton's second law — "for every action there must be an equal and opposite reaction" — may be true in physics, but it is certainly not true in legislation or litigation. The reaction to an apparent abuse of management power may and often does lead to legislation that goes beyond prevention of abuses of the same sort. Through litigation, the courts may and do sometimes go still further.

To return to the voting rights decision of 1952, the majority opinion of the Supreme Court stated:

> Our recent decisions make it plain that we do not sit as a super-legislature to weigh the wisdom of legislation nor to decide whether the policy it expresses offends the public welfare. The legislative power has limits as Tot v. United States, 319 U.S. 463 holds. But the state legislatures have constitutional authority to experiment with new techniques; they are entitled to their own standard of the public welfare; they may within extremely broad limits control practices in the business-labor field, so long as specific constitutional prohibitions are not violated and so long as conflicts with valid and controlling federal laws are avoided.
>
> . . . Missouri by this legislation has sought to safeguard the right of suffrage by taking from employers the incentive and power to use their leverage over employees to influence the vote. . . . The protection of the right of suffrage under our scheme of things is basic and fundamental. The only semblance of substance in the constitutional objection to Missouri's law is that the employer must pay wages for a period in which the employee performs no services. Of course many forms of regulation reduce the net return of the enterprise; yet that gives rise to no constitutional infirmity. . . . Most regulations of

business necessarily impose financial burdens on the enterprise for which no compensation is paid. Those are part of the cost of our civilization. Extreme cases are conjured up where an employer is required to pay wages for a period that has no relation to the legitimate end. Those cases can await decision as and when they arise. The present law has no such infirmity. It is designed to eliminate any penalty for exercising the right of suffrage and to remove a practical obstacle to getting out the vote. The public welfare is a broad and inclusive concept. The moral, social, economic, and physical well-being of the community is one part of it; the political well-being, another. The judgment of the legislature that time out for voting should cost the employee nothing may be a debatable one. It is indeed conceded by the opposition to be such. But if our recent cases mean anything, they leave debatable issues as respects business, economic and social affairs to legislative decision. . . .

One might suppose from reading the full majority opinion, from which the foregoing has been excerpted, that a Missouri employer or a group of Missouri employers had gone out of their way to prevent their employees from exercising the right of franchise. The facts in the case did not so indicate. Actually, the employee who was denied pay for time off to vote lived about 200 feet from his polling place and it was stipulated that it took him about five minutes to vote. He had a full four hours after being let out from work one and a half hours early in which to cast his vote. As the minority opinion put it, for failure to pay the employee for the hour-and-a-half for which he did not work and for which his contract did not provide that he should be paid, his employer was convicted of crime under the statute.

MISCELLANEOUS EMPLOYEE RIGHTS

In the potpourri of state legislation establishing rights and privileges for individual employees, no state has achieved a monopoly in the development of ingenious protective measures. New York State seems, however, to be a leader in this field. A few of the singular provisions in the New York code of labor law are quoted below:

Article 7 Paragraph 201 a. *Fingerprinting of employees prohibited.* Except as otherwise provided by law, no person, as a condition of securing employment or of continuing employment shall be required to be fingerprinted. This provision shall not apply to the employees of the state or any municipal subdivisions or departments thereof, or to the employees of legally incorporated hospitals, supported in whole or in part by public funds or private endowment, or to the employees of medical colleges affiliated with such hospitals.

*   *   *   *   *

Paragraph 201 b. *Fees for medical examination.* 1. It shall be unlawful for any employer to require any applicant for employment to pay the cost of a medical examination required by the employer as a condition of original employment.

*   *   *   *   *

Paragraph 203 v. *Seats for female employees.* A sufficient number of seats, with backs where practicable, shall be provided and maintained in every factory, mercantile establishment, freight or passenger elevator, hotel and restaurant for female employees who shall be allowed to use the seats to such an extent as may be reasonable for the preservation of their health. In factories female employees shall be allowed to use such seats whenever they are engaged in work which can properly be performed in a sitting posture.

*   *   *   *   *

Paragraph 206 a. *Physical examination of females.* Whenever an employer shall require a physical examination of a female by a physician or surgeon she shall be entitled to have the examination made by one of her own sex or to have another female present if a male physician or surgeon makes the examination. The employer requiring the examination shall post a notice informing the party to be examined of her rights under this section.

The special rules for examining females were enacted by the New York legislature before the passage of all encompassing federal and state laws prohibiting discrimination on account of sex. Thus far, however, there have been no reported cases in New York State indicating a demand for "equal rights" either on the part of male applicants or male physicians and surgeons.

There are numerous other employee rights established by state statutes of which personnel administrators should be cognizant before the event, i.e., before becoming embroiled unnecessarily in litigation with dubious chances of success. Most seem too petty to warrant even casual mention. Nevertheless, it is frequently the trivial mistakes of management occasioned by lack of knowledge of the applicable state laws that generate friction in employer-employee relations that is easily avoidable. To cite a single example, so-called kickbacks are almost invariably proscribed by state labor codes. A generic definition of the term "kickback" appears in Article 6 of the New York consolidated statutes. The definition is:

Whenever any workman who is engaged to perform labor shall be promised an agreed rate of wages for his services, be such promise in writing or oral, it shall be unlawful for any person, either for himself or any other person to request, demand, or receive either before or after such workman is engaged, a return, donation or contribution of any part or all of workman's wages, salary, or other thing of value, upon the statement, representation, or understanding that failure to comply with such request or demand will prevent such workman from procuring or retaining employment.

Kickbacks of another sort are also commonly made illegal under state legislation. This other type relates to what might be better described as splitting of employment agency fees. Such fee splitting may involve an illicit relationship between a company employment interviewer or supervisor and a placement person connected with a private employment agency.

With further regard to private employment agencies, state laws usually apply to transactions between applicants and the agencies themselves. In nearly all states, private agencies are prohibited by statute from misrepresenting or falsely advertising positions that they have presumably been authorized by employers to try to fill. If anyone in management actually provided an agency engaging in such tactics with misinformation or gave advice or encouragement to agency staff people that might enable the latter to perpetrate fraud on guileless job-seekers, the management personnel could well be held guilty of conspiracy to commit either a state, statutory, or common-law offense.

DEFAMATION OF EMPLOYEES

When making charges of illegal conduct against employees presently on the payroll, management has to consider several dire possibilities: (1) an NLRB complaint on illegal interference with an employee's rights of self-organization, (2) a suit for false arrest, (3) an arbitration proceeding challenging the propriety of what a company representative said or did to an offending employee. A combination of the two latter developments has been summarized by a legal scholar and practicing attorney, Evan J. Spelfogel, as follows:

> The fear of false-arrest suits, for example, is a major obstacle to security enforcement; sometimes a company would rather overlook a theft than track it down. Recently two steelworkers employed by the American Bridge Division of U.S. Steel Corporation filed a false-arrest suit for $1.25 million against the company and a former agent of the William J. Burns International Detective Agency. The firm had suffered costly cable losses and had hired Burns to investigate. The plaintiffs were arrested and confessed, but a Gary, Indiana, judge threw the case out on technical grounds. The company subse-

quently fired the workers, who then took the case to arbitration and won reinstatement with back pay.[28]

Employees' rights in the employment relationship are not divorced from the general rules on slander or libel. By way of example, a case arose in a Rhode Island factory when a female production worker who was paid on a piecework basis was accused by her supervisor of "pencil pushing." That expression, as the court put it, "is the vernacular for padding production figures" and is a euphemism for cheating or misreporting individual output frequently used in establishments where workers are paid on an incentive basis.

The accused worker sued both her supervisor and her company for slander. (She also sued the company for libel; but having lost in the initial court proceeding, she waived her right of appeal when her cases came up for review by the Rhode Island Supreme Court.)

The day her supervisor accused her of "pushing a pencil," she was told to report the following day to the personnel manager. He discharged her. Meanwhile her supervisor had told several other co-workers on the production line that she had been discharged for "pencil pushing." The reason given by the supervisor to other employees laid the foundation for the slander suits.

At the trial of these cases, the then-discharged worker conceded that the totals shown on the work cards she had turned in exceeded her actual production. She explained the disparities by saying that the numbers she had reported had been altered without her knowledge.

The basic legal questions decided by the Rhode Island Supreme Court were: (1) whether her supervisor's statement to other employees about the reason for her discharge was "qualifiedly or conditionally privileged" and (2) whether in making this statement the supervisor was motivated by malice toward his subordinate. The court decided both questions in the negative. The significance of this decision to personnel administrators lies mainly in the court's dicta as to what would be considered illegal slander if the circumstances had been different.

With regard to what the court termed the "qualified privilege concept," the court said:

> It permits a person to escape liability for a false and defamatory statement made about another if the occasion for the publication [in this instance the oral statements to co-workers] is such that the pub-

---

[28]Evan J. Spelfogel, *Surveillance and Interrogation in Plant Theft and Discipline Cases,* in PROCEEDING OF THE NEW YORK UNIVERSITY ANNUAL CONFERENCE ON LABOR. Copyright © 1969, by New York University.

lisher [the supervisor] acting in good faith correctly or reasonably believes that he has a legal, moral or social duty to speak out, or that to speak out is necessary to protect either his own interests, or those of third persons, or certain interests of the public. The occasion, of course, must not be abused. Underlying the principle is the public policy consideration that unless such an occasion is privileged, persons would not speak, even though the interests of the community at large required that they do so, lest they be exposed to a suit for defamation for what they might say. Correlatively, of course, there must be a reciprocity of duty between the publisher and the person to whom the publication is addressed, and the circumstances should reasonably demonstrate that the recipients have an interest in receiving it corresponding to that of the publisher in making it.

Applying this legal principle to the factual situation surrounding the alleged slander, the court explained that the defendants, i.e., the company and the supervisor:

insist that the circumstances of this case are such that they shared with the recipients an interest in the communication of the defamatory matter. The common denominator, they say, was an acceptance of the principle that falsification of production records by an employee would result in the termination of his employment. Disclosure of plaintiff's [the discharged worker's] conduct was to defendants' interest because notice that the plaintiff had been padding her production figures would discourage the others from following suit and would assist in preventing future losses. And disclosure was also to the interest of co-employees because it made clear to them that they too would be discharged if they "pushed the pencil."

The court declared that it was satisfied that the supervisor had reasonably and in good faith concluded that the interest he had in protecting his employer from being defrauded required that he share the reason for the discharge of the worker in question with a limited group of her co-workers "who might thereby be discouraged from engaging in similar practices."

Regarding the second issue, the charge of *malice*, the court reviewed the application of the term to the instant case and then concluded the facts did not justify a finding that the discharged worker had been slandered with malicious intent.

On this point the court cited another Rhode Island Court decision as follows: "The word 'malice' as we used it . . . does not mean malice in law, or the absence of legal excuse, but malice in the popular sense, the motive of personal spite or ill will. This is sometimes called express or actual malice."[29]

---

[29]Tillinghast v. McLeod, 17 R.I 21 A. 345.

In applying this definition to the peculiar facts of the case before it, the court stated that where "the causative factor was the common interest, a publisher's resentment toward the person defamed is immaterial and any incidental gratification is without legal significance."

Malice was considered to be the second major issue to be decided by the court because the discharged worker had attempted to prove maliciousness in her supervisor's remarks about her discharge by citing an incident about two years prior to her dismissal. She had then been assigned to a job which she characterized as involving extremely dirty work and had worked under the same supervisor who had caused her discharge. When she requested a transfer to another department, her supervisor refused, and she went over his head to his superior, who granted her request. She also brought out testimony indicating that she was a remarkable producer whose output enabled her to make weekly earnings almost equal to those of her supervisor. But in dismissing the appeal from a lower court's decision that the discharged woman had not been illegally defamed, the court concluded that although a jury might have inferred that the supervisor had been resentful, the evidence in its totality did not reasonably yield to the conclusion that his primary motivation "was his ill will or spite toward her."[30]

DEFAMATION OF MANAGEMENT

A leading case decided by the U.S. Supreme Court set out what amounts to guidelines as to what may constitute defamatory statements either by employee or management spokesmen in union organizing campaigns. This case was considered of sufficient consequence to be reviewed at length in a book written primarily for the guidance of union officials, *Organizing and the Law*, by Stephen I. Schlossberg, General Counsel, UAW. In brief summary, Schlossberg pointed out that under this Supreme Court decision: "where false statements are made with malice—that is, with knowledge that they are false or with reckless disregard of whether they are true or false—and the person about whom the statements are made is injured by them, there can be a recovery of damages in the state courts." Schlossberg went on to say,

> injury is not often difficult to prove, so that, to all intents and purposes, the only requirement is that of "malice"—a loose standard indeed for potentially hostile juries.

---

[30]Ponticelli v. Mine Safety Appliance Company, 69 LRRM 2861 (R.I. Sup.Ct. 1968).

Among the injuries for which the Court holds that state courts may compensate the victims of labor-dispute libels are "general injury to reputation, consequent mental suffering, alienation of associates, specific items of pecuniary loss or whatever form of harm would be recognized by state court law." Punitive damages may also be recovered.

The government had urged the Court to confine liability to "grave defamations," such as accusations of criminal, homosexual, treasonable, or other infamous acts. But the Court refused to limit liability to these more flagrant kinds of defamation. Plainly, false accusations such as the above are actionable. So too, under some circumstances, might be the calling of names such as liar, cheat, thief, and the like.

Even "truthful" derogatory charges about an employer representative are hazardous, for the obvious reason that it is not always easy to prove that a statement is true. A good, safe rule for organizers would be to make their oral and written statements *positive* and *affirmative* rather than *negative* and *abusive*.[31]

Although this sage advice was addressed by Schlossberg to union organizers and related to tactics in campaigns to obtain union recognition, it manifestly should be heeded by management not only in similar situations but also in *all* relationships with employees and their representatives.

What the Supreme Court actually decided in the case cited by Schlossberg was not the merit of an alleged libel against a management official but rather the jurisdiction of state courts to accept and decide libel suits involving statements made when union organizers pursue their rights under the Taft-Hartley Act to obtain recognition for their union. The union argued unsuccessfully that judicial condemnation of the alleged libel would interfere with the jurisdiction of the National Labor Relations Board over the subject of a labor controversy essentially involving a question of union representation. The Court disagreed and ruled, in effect, that an overriding state interest in protecting its residents from malicious libels should be recognized.

As for the facts, an independent union seeking to organize one of the local Michigan offices of a national concern having an office in another Michigan city put out a leaflet that said, among other things, that certain of its members who had been voted into the union at the latter city had been *robbed* of pay increases. The leaflet also accused the company managers of *lying* to the union and stated that "somebody may go to jail."

---

[31]Stephen I. Schlossberg, ORGANIZING AND THE LAW (Washington: BNA Books, 1967), p. 43.

The libel suit that ultimately went to the Supreme Court was instituted on behalf of an assistant general manager of the company assailed in the union's literature, although his name was not mentioned in the leaflet. The company's complaint alleged that this official was one of the managers referred to and that the statements in the leaflet were wholly false, defamatory, and untrue. Recovery of $1,000,000 was sought on the grounds that the accusations were libelous *per se*. In remanding the case for adjudication by the Michigan state courts, the Supreme Court declared that

> the law in many states presumes damages from the publication of certain statements characterized as actionable *per se*. Labor disputes are ordinarily heated affairs; the language that is commonplace there might well be deemed actionable *per se* in some state jurisdictions. Indeed representation campaigns are frequently characterized by bitter and extreme charges, unfounded rumors, vituperations, personal accusations, misrepresentations and distortions. Both labor and management often speak bluntly and recklessly, embellishing their respective positions with imprecatory language.

In its final observation, the Court held that improper use of the known lie could be appropriately redressed "without curtailment of state libel remedies beyond the actual needs of national labor policy."[32]

EMPLOYEE RIGHTS AND MANAGEMENT OBLIGATIONS

It would be an encyclopedic task merely to catalogue all the rights of employees generally or of specific classes of employees as they have been spelled out by the laws of 50 states and by the administrative and judicial rulings. Many rights set forth in the statutes impose correlative obligations on employers, and it is these types of legislative control with which personnel administrators have to concern themselves in every state in which their companies operate.

It is, of course, much more important for personnel administrators, as we have repeatedly stressed, to have a good grasp of the interrelationships between federal, state, and municipal statutes that may impinge on their day-by-day dealings with employees. One perhaps extreme example should suffice. Suppose a sales clerk in a unionized store, who happens to be a Puerto Rican and a shop steward in his union, is caught redhanded walking out of the store

---

[32]Linn v. Plant Guards, Local 114, 383 U.S. 53, 61 LRRM 2345 (1966).

with merchandise worth, say, $40. Several of his fellow employees saw him stealing the merchandise and agreed to testify against him in court. He is discharged forthwith for stealing and promptly turned over to the police and charged with petty larceny. When his case comes to trial, no witnesses turn up to testify against him. In any event, he is acquitted and demands reinstatement to his former position. Meanwhile he applies for a job in another store. His prospective employer calls his former employer for a reference and verification of the cause of his termination. Can the former employer call him a petty crook with impunity? Probably not, for he has not been convicted of anything. And suppose while awaiting trial, he applies for state unemployment compensation, and the store manager contests the claim on the grounds that he has been fired for cause, thus disqualifying him from benefits. Can the unemployment office investigator or hearing officer be told orally or in writing that the man was discharged for stealing? Possibly not without the serious risk of a slander or libel suit.

And further suppose that after being discharged this employee ascertains that other nonminority sales clerks have been caught pilfering without being penalized or with a penalty short of discharge. Or suppose that as a union shop steward this man knows that minor management personnel not covered by the union agreement have been treated leniently when apprehended in making away with company merchandise.

Conceivably the employer could be confronted with several separate actions on behalf of the discharged employee before different tribunals. He might have to appear before a municipal, state, or federal antidiscrimination agency on racial discrimination charges. He might have to face unfair labor practice charges that he discriminated illegally against this shop steward because of allegedly overzealous union activity. Or he might have to defend in arbitration his action in dismissing an employee who had been exonerated of a criminal charge in court.

Obviously, there is no pat or patent solution for most of the horrendous hypothetical problems just outlined. But years ago the U.S. Supreme Court gave a trenchant clue as to how to minimize management's likelihood of running afoul of the law. "Motive," said the Court, "is a persuasive interpreter of equivocal conduct." Put in reverse, this plainly implies that a demonstrably nondiscriminatory and non-ulterior motive of management in a decision affecting an employee's status or statutory rights should go far to support the propriety of the management decision.

CHAPTER 7

Taft-Hartley and Related Statutes

Once hailed by its champions as the Magna Charta for organized labor and later, after substantial amendment, condemned by them as a "slave labor law," the federal Labor Management Relations Act, as it is now officially designated, has exercised a more profound influence on management's industrial relations policies than all other statutes — federal and state — combined. This law was originally known as the Wagner Act when it was passed by Congress in 1935. Since 1947 it generally has been designated as the Taft-Hartley Act because of the extensive overhauling of the statute by Congress in that year under the leadership of Senator Taft and Representative Hartley. In this book it will be referred to simply as Taft-Hartley.

Most of the original objectives and provisions of the Wagner Act have been retained in Taft-Hartley. In addition, however, Taft-Hartley has imposed upon labor organizations some of the same restrictions against interference with employees' rights that were embodied in the Wagner Act and still remain in the law.

Taft-Hartley was itself amended by the adoption in 1959 of the Labor-Management Reporting and Disclosure Act. Generally known as the Landrum-Griffin Act, that statute did not replace any of the basic provisions of Taft-Hartley but rather modified certain Taft-Hartley restrictions imposed upon management and also imposed additional limitations on unions' bargaining and strike tactics.

The Norris-LaGuardia Anti-Injunction Act of 1932 was in effect modified by both Taft-Hartley and Landrum-Griffin, as will be explained later in this chapter. The Norris-LaGuardia Act remains, however, an integral part of the structure of government regulation of management-labor relations.

No longer of vital concern to management, although still on the statute books, is the Byrnes Antistrikebreaking Act of 1938. This law forbids the utilization by management of interstate transportation to import persons for the purpose of interfering with peaceful picketing in labor disputes or with the processes of collective bargaining.

BASIC OBJECTIVES AND PROVISIONS OF TAFT-HARTLEY

The original Wagner Act declared that the policy of the U.S. Government was to encourage the practice and procedure of collective bargaining and to protect "the exercise by workers of full freedom of association, self-organization and designation of representatives of their own choosing for the purpose of negotiating the terms and conditions of their employment or other mutual aid or protection." This declaration of policy was retained in Taft-Hartley and is the law of the land today.

To effectuate this basic policy, Taft-Hartley makes it illegal for employers to engage in different types of unfair labor practices. In summary, employer unfair labor practices are declared to be:

1. Interference with, restraint, or coercion of employees in the exercise of their rights of self-organization
2. Domination or interference with the formation or administration of any labor organization
3. Discrimination in regard to hire or tenure of employment or any term or condition of employment to encourage or discourage membership in any labor organization
4. The discharge of or other discrimination against any employee because he has filed charges or given testimony in proceedings under the Act
5. Refusal to bargain collectively with a labor organization properly designated by a majority of the employees in an appropriate bargaining unit to represent them for bargaining purposes.

Many if not most of the problems of employers in avoiding illegal interference with their employees' rights of self-organization arise when labor organizations are first seeking recognition as bargaining agents. It is thus of paramount importance to management to have a good working understanding of the principles observed by the National Labor Relations Board as interpreted by court decisions in determining who has to bargain with whom, as well as what rights and obligations are imposed on employers when confronted with union organizing campaigns or demands for recognition.

APPROPRIATE BARGAINING UNITS

Taft-Hartley confers on the Board the authority to determine what are appropriate units for collective bargaining when disputes arise on representation issues. Such units may be held to embrace crafts, or production and maintenance employees, or office workers—within a given establishment or company-wide—or other combinations of occupational groups in multiplant situations. The Board's function is not spelled out with precision in the law. Its discretionary powers to determine appropriate bargaining units are subject to continuing controversy among management and union groups and to repeated challenges in the federal appellate courts. It might fairly be said that the usual posture of the Board is to decide upon whatever employee unit will give employees the most freedom of choice.

To be sure, the Board's authority in determination of bargaining units has some restrictions. For example, Taft-Hartley provides that the extent of union organization in a given enterprise shall not be controlling. That is, if a union has organized one department of a plant or part of a department, the Board may not direct an election among employees in that department or in part of it just because a union has not been able to organize employees elsewhere in the establishment.

Excluded Occupations

Professional employees may not be included in any unit with nonprofessionals unless the majority of the professional employees vote for inclusion in a separate self-determination election. Further, plant guards may not be included in a unit of production and maintenance workers; but if they seek union recognition, the unit must be limited exclusively to the guards themselves. Supervisors are automatically excluded from any appropriate bargaining unit by the terms of Taft-Hartley itself. Individuals employed as supervisors are not considered under the law to be employees at all. Hence, supervisors enjoy none of the protections guaranteed to employees against interference with their rights of self-organization.

As expressly defined in Taft-Hartley, the term "supervisor" means:

> any individual having authority, in the interest of the employer, to hire, transfer, suspend, lay off, recall, promote, discharge, assign, reward, or discipline other employees, or responsibly to direct them, or to adjust their grievances, or effectively to recommend such action, if in connection with the foregoing the exercise of such

authority is not of a merely routine or clerical nature, but requires the use of independent judgment.

The foregoing definition is similar to the definition of exempt supervisors embodied in the Wage-Hour Act (discussed in Chapter 2). Even so, a foreman held nonexempt under The Wage-Hour Act, by reason of expending a substantial amount of time doing nonexempt work, still might be considered an exempt supervisor for Taft-Hartley purposes and thus not entitled to any rights under that law.

Taft-Hartley does not prohibit recognition of separate units of supervisory employees. It simply does not *require* employers to recognize supervisory units. Their failure so to recognize would not constitute an unfair labor practice. But voluntary recognition would likewise involve no violation *per se.* In one leading Board decision, which incidentally involved unfair-labor-practice charges rather than a unit question, the Board held that a lead man who for all practical purposes was in charge of a plant department was a supervisor within the meaning of the Act. The Board found that this lead man assigned and directed the work to be done by the employees in the department and did not physically engage in the same sort of work except when the volume became heavy. While he had no authority to hire and to fire, he could recommend wage increases, and one of his responsibilities was to report to the "shop-wide supervisor" any employee who was not doing a good job.[1]

All management employees, regardless of function, were declared excluded from Taft-Hartley coverage in a U.S. Supreme Court decision handed down in 1974. In effect this reversed a long line of Board decisions limiting exclusions of supervisors to those management employees having some responsibilities in matters of labor relations. In a preliminary explanation of the basis for its decision, the Court stated:

> This case presents two questions: first whether the National Labor Relations Board properly determined that all management employees except those whose participation in a union would create a conflict of interest are covered . . . by the Act; and second, whether the Board must proceed by rule making procedure rather than by adjudicative proceedings in determining whether certain buyers are management employees. We answer both questions in the negative.[2]

---

[1]Redwing Carriers, Inc., 165 NLRB 60, 65 LRRM 1388 (1967).
[2]NLRB v. Textron, Inc., 416 U.S. 267, 85 LRRM 2945 (1974).

Typical Board Unit Rulings

There is not necessarily only one right answer when a union demands recognition for a bargaining unit of questionable propriety. If the management and the union agree on the unit the Board will not ordinarily intervene, unless a rival union enters a challenge. When either the employer or one or more labor organizations questions the appropriateness of a bargaining unit sought by a union in any given situation, the Board holds a hearing before deciding the issue, and at such a hearing management is entitled to present its own position pro or con.

In his handbook for union organizers, Stephen I. Schlossberg, general counsel of the United Auto Workers, has presented a shorthand summary of Taft-Hartley requirements on appropriate unit questions. He states:

> In order to determine whether a petitioning union has a sufficient showing of interest there must, at the very least, be a presumption that the unit in which the interest showing is tested is proper. If a union with an apparent majority seeks recognition in a plainly inappropriate unit, an employer may lawfully refuse to bargain. Finally, if there is to be an election, the Board will hold it only in an appropriate unit. Clearly, the issue of the scope of the unit is one of tremendous importance to the parties and to the employees involved.
>
> The Labor Board's power to define the bargaining unit comes from Section 9 of the Act which directs that the Board "shall decide . . . the unit appropriate for the purposes of collective bargaining." The Supreme Court has ruled that such determinations will not be overturned unless they are "lacking in a rational basis." [NLRB v. Hearst Publications, 322 US 111 (1944), 14 LRRM 614.] Very few unit determinations are so unreasonable as to be overturned by the courts. Although the Act has been amended since that time to include a number of minor considerations to be used by the Board when it acts, such as the special situations involving plant guards and professional employees, its unit-determination power and authority remain very broad. In most cases, NLRB representational decisions are not directly reviewable by the courts.
>
> The Board is not required to find the *most* appropriate unit. Often, employers try to enlarge the scope of the unit to the point where the organizing union cannot hope to win an election or, in some cases, even make the required showing of interest. But the Board has solidly established the proposition that a union need not seek an election in the *most comprehensive* unit possible but can, instead, have one in *any* appropriate unit. That is, one that constitutes a homogeneous, identifiable, and distinct grouping of employees.[3]

---

[3]Stephen I. Schlossberg, ORGANIZING AND THE LAW (Washington: BNA Books, 1967), p. 113.

Schlossberg, an unquestionably competent and successful attorney representing labor, has implied that employers sometimes seek to gerrymander proposed bargaining units to suit their own purposes, presumably to defeat a union's attempt to obtain certification of a unit in which they hope to obtain a majority, or in which they have already obtained it. Such tactics are not unknown to unions, either. Nor are they always reprehensible or illegal. Nor would many management attorneys—or, for that matter, impartial observers—necessarily agree that the Board's unit determinations have always served to protect the statutory rights of all workers to self-organization and self-determination of their bargaining agency.

It would appear from an examination of numerous Board representation decisions that in recent years the Board has placed less emphasis on unions' bargaining strength and greater emphasis on smaller units. This is especially the case in the retail field, where employees of the retail stores or restaurants that are part of chain operations have been held to constitute separate units. This has had the effect of facilitating union organization. In other words, there seems to have been a Board shift of emphasis from union bargaining strength to the immediate extent of organization of employees even when only in small groups.

Moreover, the Taft-Hartley changes in the law also curbed the Board's obvious prior preference for at least plant-wide units embracing all production and maintenance employees. (One of the Taft-Hartley amendments of 1947 expressly provided that the Board could not hold any craft unit inappropriate for bargaining purposes on the ground that a different unit had been established by a prior Board determination, unless a majority of the employees in the proposed unit voted against separate representation.)

On this issue and other unit questions, the observations of the respected law firm of Seyfarth, Shaw, Fairweather, and Geraldson, which primarily represents management, are significant. The firm declared in 1968:

> In general, the board purports to establish bargaining units on the basis of employee "community of interest"—that is, employees having the same or similar interests in wages, employee benefits, hours, and working conditions. The board also takes into account the history of collective bargaining at the establishment or establishments involved, and the desires of the union seeking recognition. In determining the appropriateness of a unit, the board may consider—but may not regard as controlling—the extent to which the union has organized the employees. The most commonly established bargaining unit is one encompassing all production and mainte-

nance employees of an employer at one plant. The board may also establish bargaining units encompassing two or more plants of an employer. Although there is no specific authorization in the act permitting the board to establish multiemployer (employer association) bargaining units, the board has done so, particularly where there was an established history of collective bargaining on a multi-employer basis.

The board may establish craft bargaining units confined to employees working in a traditionally recognized craft and their apprentices. However, before the National Labor Relations Act was amended by the Taft-Hartley Act of 1947, the board quite clearly favored large units of all production and maintenance employees and viewed with disfavor petitions of craft-based unions to establish craft units (units limited to employees of a particular skill). The board would often establish an all-inclusive production and maintenance unit and then reject subsequent petitions for craft units because there was an established history of bargaining on the broader basis. The craft unions reacted strongly to this board preference for all-inclusive units, and the Taft-Hartley Act specified that the board could not decide that a craft unit was inappropriate on the ground that a different unit had been established by a prior board determination. This made it considerably easier for craft unions to obtain a craft unit "carved out" of large, all-inclusive units. However, this provision did not change the trend to all-inclusive units, and craft units in manufacturing establishments in the United States continued to be the exception rather than the rule. . . .[4]

Inter-Union Representational Disputes

The AFL-CIO has its own rules for settling jurisdictional disputes among its affiliates, including disputes on representation issues that otherwise would be likely to come before the Board for adjudication. These rules are embodied in the AFL-CIO Constitution, Article XXI of which provides:

> Section 1. The principles set forth in this Article shall be applicable to all affiliates of this Federation, and to their local unions and other subordinate bodies.
> Section 2. Each affiliate shall respect the established collective bargaining relationship of every other affiliate. No affiliate shall organize or attempt to represent employees as to whom an established collective bargaining relationship exists with any other affiliate. For purposes of this article, the term "established collective bargaining relationship" means any situation in which an affiliate, or any local or other subordinate body thereof, has either (a) been recognized by the employer (including any governmental agency) as the collective bargaining representative for the employees involved

[4]Seyfarth, Shaw, Fairweather, and Geraldson, LABOR RELATIONS AND THE LAW IN THE UNITED KINGDOM AND THE UNITED STATES (Ann Arbor, Mich.: Bureau of Business Research, Graduate School of Business, University of Michigan, 1968), pp. 29-30.

for a period of one year or more, or (b) has been certified by the National Labor Relations Board or other federal or state agency as the collective bargaining representative for employees.

This constitution has further provisions for settlement of interunion disputes on representation questions, including mediation and arbitration as the terminal steps. In addition, the Industrial Union Department of the AFL-CIO has more elaborate procedures for assuring final adjudication of representation disputes among its constituent unions. Most of these unions are national or international labor organizations that previously constituted the CIO before its merger with the AFL.

The Board takes cognizance of no-raiding agreements among AFL-CIO unions when acting upon bargaining-unit petitions. As Schlossberg and Sherman have explained:

> Because of the AFL-CIO's constitutional prohibition of raiding and its internal procedures for dealing with interunion disputes, the NLRB always notifies the AFL-CIO when an affiliated union petitions it and another affiliated union is involved in the case. In these cases the Board will not act for two weeks, so as to give the Federation a chance to do something on its own. If a union not affiliated with the AFL-CIO is involved, the Board waits only one week. If one AFL-CIO union petitions where another is certified or has had a contract for more than a year, the Board notifies the AFL-CIO and withholds further action for a month. If the Federation has not resolved the problem during the waiting period, the petition is processed like any other.[5]

The inter-union arrangements for settling representation issues are not applicable to or binding on unaffiliated unions. Hence, the Board still has to wrestle with claims by rival unions to representation rights.

So-Called Self-Determination

The Board had an unusually intricate set of claims to adjudicate in a celebrated case decided in 1937. The result of its decision became known as the "Globe Doctrine." Though no longer bound by this doctrine, the Board can and often does follow the tenets prescribed in that case.

The Globe Doctrine declared that where conflicting demands between or among contesting unions resulted in almost evenly balanced considerations, the determining factor should be the desires of the employees themselves. So the Board ordered three

---

[5]Stephen I. Schlossberg and Frederick E. Sherman, ORGANIZING AND THE LAW (Washington: The Bureau of National Affairs, Inc., 1971), p. 111.

separate elections to be held simultaneously for the employees of a single plant. To state it this way is, however, an oversimplification of the actual situation.

Four different unions were contesting for recognition. Three of these were affiliated with AFL unions and the fourth with the United Auto Workers, then a part of the CIO. Of the three AFL unions, a local of the Metal Polishers Union claimed jurisdiction over the plant's polishers and buffers. A local of the International Association of Machinists limited its jurisdiction to punch press operators. A separately chartered Federal Labor Union claimed jurisdiction over all of the balance of the plant's production and maintenance workers. The UAW, on the other hand, had a local that admitted to membership and sought to represent all of the three groups claimed by the other petitioning unions. Upon reviewing the conflicting claims and desires of the four contestants, the Board observed that all of the plant production workers could appropriately be grouped in a single unit or alternatively in three different units, and the rather informal if not chaotic previous history of organizational and bargaining efforts at the plant lent support to both positions. It was for these reasons that the Board decided to let the employees decide for themselves. So the polishers and buffers could choose in their separate election between the Polishers Union (AFL) and the United Automobile Workers (CIO). The punch press operators could choose between the International Association of Machinists (AFL) and the UAW. All other production and maintenance workers had a chance to vote for either the Federal Labor Union (AFL) or the UAW. The result was a clear victory for the UAW, which the Board then duly certified as the bargaining agent for the entire production and maintenance work force.[6]

Unit "Clarification"

It took seven years of litigation before the Board made a final determination in what originated as a union petition to the Board for clarification of a pre-existing bargaining unit. The Board has unquestioned authority to decide clarification issues by ordering self-determination elections for employees of two or more plants of the same company. So ruled the U.S. Circuit Court of Appeals for the District of Columbia after a federal district court had enjoined the Board from conducting elections at two of the plants of the same company where the employees were represented by the same

---

[6]Globe Machine and Stamping Co., 3 NLRB 294, 1-A LRRM 122 (1937).

union but in separate bargaining units. By denying certiorari, the Supreme Court ratified the circuit court's decision.

To make heads or tails out of the tortuous developments in this case, it seems essential to review the basic facts in sequence. The case began in 1966 when the international union representing employees of Libbey-Owens-Ford Glass Company in a previously Board-certified multiplant unit filed a petition for unit clarification. The union's desire was to add to that unit coverage of employees in two other plants of the company where it represented the employees in two separate units.

To enlarge the scope of the unit necessitated either management acquiescence or Board sanction. The union had to go to the Board. There it successfully argued that the Board could conduct self-determination elections at the two plants concerned to let the employees themselves vote for or against being merged into what could have been a company-wide unit. By a split decision (3-2) the Board asserted its authority to conduct the elections sought by the union as an investigatory and factfinding tool that the Board majority thought it to possess. Consequently it ordered the elections to be held.

Meanwhile, a federal district court enjoined the conduct of the elections. That court supported the views of the two minority Board members who had contended that representation was not, in fact, a proper issue and that the Board was not empowered under the Act to order the elections. Before reversing the district court the appellate court granted a partial stay of the injunction. This stay permitted the Board to conduct the elections but not to issue any order based thereon. So the two plant elections were held. The union won both of them, i.e., to merge the separate units into a company-wide unit.

Subsequently, the company refused to bargain with the newly designated union representatives at one of the plants involved. The immediate result of its refusal was a filing by the union of an unfair labor practice charge against the company. To wit, it alleged illegal refusal to bargain.

At this juncture one of the Board members who had voted in the majority had left the Board and been replaced. A new majority of the Board rejected the union's unfair labor practice charge on the grounds that the Board never did have the requisite authority to order the elections in the first place.

In due course the whole complicated matter came before the

new majority of the Board, which held that the Board did have the authority to conduct the elections that had already been held. The final outcome was that the Board decided the expanded unit voted for by the employees of the plants concerned was appropriate under the law and that the company had indeed committed an unfair labor practice by refusing to bargain with the international union as the representative of the plant where its bargaining rights had been rejected.[7]

Inappropriate Single-Plant Unit

It is only logical to presume that when a union seeks determination by the Board of an appropriate bargaining unit and the employer objects, elements of opportunism color the respective positions of the parties. They will frequently try to stress the factors in a given situation that in their judgment come closest to meeting the Board criteria summarized by Schlossberg and Sherman above.

These tactics were obviously used when the Board in 1970 dismissed a petition by the IAM for an election among the employees of the Kendall Company in only one of two of its plants situated in Franklin, Ky. The two plants are on the same tract of land about 200 feet apart. As the Board observed: "The manufacturing process and the machinery and equipment utilized in the manufacturing process are substantially the same at both plants." It further found that 95 percent of the job classifications at the plant that the union sought to have designated as a bargaining unit also were utilized at the adjacent plant. There had been scores of interplant permanent transfers, as well as about 100 temporary transfers between the plants over a two-year period. While the plants had separate management staffs, wage and benefit increases had been the same at both plants and were implemented on the same dates. In the case of employees permanently transferred from one plant to another, there had been an arrangement for retention of seniority.

The foregoing circumstances, among others, were cited by the Board as reasons for its conclusion that a bargaining unit limited to the one plant was inappropriate and that the only appropriate unit would include the production and maintenance employees of both plants.[8]

---

[7]169 NLRB 126 (1968); 173 NLRB 187 (1968); 189 NLRB 869, 871 (1971), *remanded*, 463 F.2d 31 (3rd Cir. 1972); 202 NLRB 29 (1973); 495 F.2d 1195 (3rd Cir. 1974); 419 U.S. 998 (1974).

[8]Kendall Company, 184 NLRB 98, 74 LRRM 1623 (1970).

BOARD CERTIFICATION WITH OR WITHOUT ELECTIONS

Union Recognition Without Board Certification

The Taft-Hartley Act does not prohibit an employer from recognizing any labor organization which contends that it has been designated by a homogeneous group of his employees to represent them for bargaining purposes. (Of course, the labor organization must not have been or be "company dominated." Alleged or real company domination of labor organizations became in the 1930s a *cause célèbre* that has almost disappeared from NLRB litigation and will be given no further attention herein.) But a labor-management agreement resulting from recognition by management of a union without Board determination of the appropriateness of the unit or Board certification of the majority status of the union in the unit may be held to be illegal under some circumstances.

Illegality of Recognition *Sans* Election

In a notable decision handed down in 1961, the Supreme Court sustained Board findings that both the union and the employer had invaded the employees' statutory rights of self-organization and thus had violated Section 8 of the Taft-Hartley Act by making the union the exclusive bargaining agent at a plant where the union did not represent a majority of the employees. The good faith but mistaken belief of the parties that the union actually represented a majority was not an adequate defense, the Court ruled.

This case had its origin in a Texas textile mill in 1956. Late that year the International Ladies' Garment Workers' Union (AFL-CIO) undertook to organize the plant's employees. No rival union was contesting for the employees' support. Many months later, while the organizing campaign was still in progress, some of the employees struck to protest a wage reduction. As the Court expressly noted, however, that strike had no relation to the union's organizing efforts. The Court further stated: "Some of the striking employees had signed authorization cards solicited by the union during its drive, and while the strike was in progress, the union entered upon a course of negotiations with the employer. As a result of those negotiations, held in New York City where the home offices of both were located, on August 30, 1957, the employer and the union signed a 'memorandum of understanding.' In that memorandum the company recognized the union as exclusive bargaining representative 'of all production and shipping employees.' "

The crux of the Court's decision that held both the company and the union in violation of Taft-Hartley centered about the Board's findings as to the actual status of the union's organizational campaign at the time the memorandum agreement was executed.

The Court considered it of great significance that neither the employer nor the union had made any realistic effort to check the authorization cards in the union's possession against the company's roll of employees in the agreed-upon unit.[9]

Illegality of Nonrecognition Despite No Election

The inference might be drawn from the foregoing that to stay within the law an employer should always refuse to recognize a union unless it has been certified by the Board and then only after the Board has determined the appropriateness of the bargaining unit and after the union has won a Board-conducted election for the employees in that unit. But this is not always the case. Frequently management is confronted with what seems to be a Hobson's choice. Depending on the peculiar circumstances of its own situation, management may be found in violation of Taft-Hartley if it refuses to recognize a union despite the fact that the union has never invoked the Board's unit determination and representation election procedures.

There is still uncertainty on the broad question of what management can or cannot do when faced with a bald request for immediate recognition of a union asserting its majority status in a self-determined bargaining unit. One reason for this uncertainty stems from a landmark decision of the Board in 1950 which was sustained by the appellate courts. That is to say, the Circuit Court of Appeals for the District of Columbia directed enforcement of the Board's order and the Supreme Court denied certiorari. The case involved Joy Silk Mills, Inc. For some four years after its decision and before the partial reversal of its leading principle by the Board itself, the *Joy* decision brought intense joy to union organizers.

Very briefly, the Board's *Joy* decision held that the company had both interfered with its employees' rights of self-organization and had illegally refused to bargain with a union after refusing an offer of proof by the union of majority status. The Board ordered the company to bargain with the union even though the union had lost a Board-conducted election.

---

[9]International Ladies Garment Workers Union v. NLRB and Bernard-Altman Texas Corp., 366 U.S. 731, 48 LRRM 2251 (1961).

Although the Board's present policy with respect to the right of a union to gain recognition from an employer after losing an election has undergone considerable change since 1950, the basis for the Board's findings in the *Joy* case which the Circuit Court of Appeals considered valid is still of importance to management when confronted with a demand for union recognition. As related by the Court, the Board found that during a brief plant strike the United Textile Workers Union distributed authorization cards. These were signed by 38 out of 52 employees. The day before the strike was called off there was a meeting between the management and employees. At this meeting certain grievances were settled and paid vacations were promised. There was no discussion of the union. Several days later the company president received a telephone call from a union official concerning recognition. He also had a call from the Board's regional director in reference to a consent election. Within a week an agreement for a consent election to be held 20 days later was reached. At the conference which resulted in this agreement, a cross-check of membership cards was suggested but this was declined by the management representatives. The union lost the election and forthwith filed a protest with the regional director as to its conduct. He sustained the protest, ordered the election set aside, and directed that a new election be held.

Consent Elections

The Joy Silk Mills election was conducted under the type of arrangement that the Board terms an "Agreement for Consent Election." This is the kind of election Board agents usually recommend where there is no dispute as to the appropriate unit or other complications. If the parties agree to such an election, they authorize the Board's regional director to make a final determination of any objections to its conduct or any challenges of eligibility of employee voters. On the other hand, if the parties agree to a "Stipulation for Certification Upon Consent Elections," then subsequent disputes about the conduct or results of the election have to be decided by the Board itself.

After the union received notice that a second election had been ordered, it withdrew its petition for certification and filed unfair labor practice charges against the company. And it was nearly a year later that the Board found that the charges were sustainable and accordingly ordered the company to bargain with the union.

The really basic issue decided by the circuit court was whether or not certain statements by management personnel made shortly before the date of the consent election constituted unfair labor practices. One of these statements was prepared by the president but read to employees by the company's bookkeeper. It included the following: "As soon as equipment for the canteen which has been ordered arrives, you will be given a rest period at the company's expense so that you may eat your lunches and relax in comfort during the shift." Another prepared statement declared that the union was misleading the employees on the question of shift rotation and indicated that if the majority of the employees wanted rotation, the company would put it into effect. Then a day or two before the election the plant superintendent and the company bookkeeper had discussions with various employees in which they were said to have generally indicated their own dislike for the union. As the court summarized their remarks, they declared "that it was not a good idea to support the union, that job security might be threatened and that perhaps wage raises and other benefits might not be forthcoming if the union got in."

Taken in combination with other unfavorable remarks by management spokesmen about the union, the Board concluded that the company had interfered with its employees' freedom to organize, contrary to Section 8(a) (1). And the circuit court agreed.[10]

Refusal of Recognition for "Stalling Purposes"

In its landmark decision of 1964 in the *Bernel Foam* case, the Board found that the company had violated the Act both by refusing to bargain with a majority union and by demanding a Board-conducted election as proof of majority. The Board held that the company's insistence on the election was not motivated by a true doubt of the union's majority. It was rather apparently the desire of the management to gain time to undermine the majority support for the union.

According to the Board, the company attempted to dissipate the majority after its management had agreed to have the Board conduct an election but *before* the election was held. There was a meeting by the president with the employees on two shifts the last working day before the election, at which time he told them they were going to get a job classification system, would also "get Blue Cross, Blue Shield and other benefits, union or no union eventually," and that they could have a shop committee or shop union. The Board found also that on the day of the election the manage-

---

[10]Joy Silk Mills, Inc. v. NLRB, 185 F.2d 732, 27 LRRM 2012 (D.C. Cir. 1950).

ment circulated leaflets promising that job classification would be put into effect as soon as possible. The Board declared:

> . . . we find that the respondent's refusal to bargain with the union was motivated by a desire to create the opportunity to dissipate the union's majority. In reaching this conclusion we rely on the facts that (1) respondent refused to recognize the union without any reasonable basis for doubting the union's majority, rejecting its offer of proof and insisting on an election, and (2) shortly before the election respondent engaged in unlawful conduct consisting of promises of benefit to employees and a suggestion that they form a shop union or shop committee, which conduct, we find was designed to induce employees to repudiate the union.[11]

Refusal of Recognition Based on Doubt of Majority Status

In its highly significant 1966 decision involving Aaron Brothers Company, the Board ruled that the company had not violated the Act by insisting upon an election and rejecting union authorization cards or asserting unsupported doubt of the cards as proof of the union's majority. Such action, the Board declared, did not demonstrate lack of good-faith doubt about the union's status where (1) the company did not engage in substantial unfair labor practices calculated to dissipate the union's possible majority status; (2) it did not engage in any other conduct indicating a management objective of seeking delay and rejection of the collective bargaining concept as embodied in the Act; and (3) no affirmative evidence was offered from which the inference of bad faith might be drawn. True, in this case the company had laid off 13 of its employees shortly after receiving a letter from the union requesting recognition and bargaining. But the management was not shown to have knowledge of any union affinity of the employees selected for layoffs prior to receipt of the union's letter. Moreover, the layoff roster was decided upon prior to the union's request for recognition.

The Board promulgated a new rule respecting nonrecognition without an election in the following passage of its *Aaron* decision:

> While an employer's right to a Board election is not absolute, it has long been established Board policy that an employer may refuse to bargain and insist upon such an election as proof of a union's majority unless its refusal and insistence were not made in a good-faith doubt of the union's majority. An election by secret ballot is normally a more satisfactory means of determining employees' wishes, although authorization cards signed by a majority may also evidence their desires. Absent an affirmative showing of bad faith, an employer, presented with a majority card showing and a bargain-

---

[11]Bernel Foam Products Co., Inc., 146 NLRB 1277, 56 LRRM 1039 (1964).

ing request, will not be held to have violated his bargaining obligation under the law simply because he refuses to rely on cards, rather than an election, as the method for determining the union's majority.[12]

Somewhat new ground was broken by the Supreme Court in 1974 when it ruled that an employer does not violate Section 8(a) (5) of Taft-Hartley by its refusal to recognize authorization cards as evidence of a claimant's union majority status, *even though* the employer fails to petition the Board to conduct an election. In the absence of an agreement to permit the majority status to be determined by means other than a Board-conducted election, a union that has refused to seek an election because of its card account submissions has the burden of taking the next step by invoking the Board's election procedure.[13]

Employer's Obligation to Supply Employees' Roster to Unions

To enable labor organizations to propagandize effectively and to meet employers' preelection counterpropaganda, the Board now requires employers on request to furnish any union participating in a Board-conducted election with the names and addresses of employees eligible to vote. This rule was promulgated by the Board in its noteworthy decision in the case of *Excelsior Underwear, Inc.*, in 1966. The Supreme Court upheld the validity of the Board's rule.[14] In *Excelsior* the Board announced that:

> Accordingly we now establish a requirement that will be applied in all election cases. That is within 7 days after the Regional Director has approved a consent-election agreement . . . after the Regional Director or the Board has directed an election . . . the employer must file with the Regional Director an election eligibility list containing the names and addresses of all eligible voters. The Regional Director, in turn, shall make this information available to all parties in the case.[15]

Management's Preelection Rights and Obligations Summarized

The Supreme Court reviewed and decided major issues relating to preelection conduct of employers in 1969. In a sweeping decision applicable to four separate cases before it, the Court unanimously ruled in *Gissel Packing Co.* that an employer's duty to bargain collectively can arise without an NLRB election, and that union authorization cards, if obtained from a majority of the

---

[12]Aaron Bros. Co. of California, 158 NLRB 108, 62 LRRM 1160 (1966).
[13]Linden Lumber Co., 87 LRRM 3236 (1974).
[14]NLRB v. Wyman-Gordon Co., 394 U.S. 939, 70 LRRM 3345 (1969).
[15]Excelsior Underwear, Inc. 156 NLRB 111, 61 LRRM 1217 (1956).

employees without misrepresentation or coercion, are reliable enough generally to provide a valid alternative route to majority status. A pertinent passage from the Court's unanimous opinion is cited below:

> These cases involve the extent of an employer's duty under the National Labor Relations Act to recognize a union that bases its claim to representative status solely on the possession of union authorization cards, and the steps an employer may take, particularly with regard to the scope and content of statements he may make, in legitimately resisting such card-based recognition. The specific questions facing us here are whether the duty to bargain can arise without a Board election under the Act; whether union authorization cards, if obtained from a majority of employees without misrepresentation or coercion, are reliable enough generally to provide a valid, alternative route to majority status; whether a bargaining order is an appropriate and authorized remedy where an employer rejects a card majority while at the same time committing unfair labor practices that tend to undermine the union's majority and make a fair election an unlikely possibility; and whether certain specific statements made by an employer to his employees constituted such an election-voiding unfair labor practice and thus fell outside of the protection of the first amendment and Section 8 (c) of the Act.

The court gave affirmative answers to each of these questions.[16]

Contract Bar Rules

Relative stability in union-management relationships is one of the major objectives of Taft-Hartley as the Act has been construed by the Board. Such stability is obtainable, of course, through negotiation of contracts setting the terms and conditions of employment for fixed periods of considerable duration. To facilitate attainment of reasonable stability the Board has formulated a contract bar doctrine. Under this doctrine a valid contract currently in effect between an employer and a union constitutes a bar to an election sought by a rival union during the life of the contract.

Change From Two-Year to Three-Year Contract Bar

Up until 1962 there had been a long line of Board decisions culminating in a firm Board policy that a labor agreement of more than two years' duration could not constitute a bar to an attempt by another union to nullify such an agreement if the Board conducted a new election and the rival union won it. What was sacrosanct

---

[16]NLRB v. Gissel Packing Co., et al., 395 U.S. 575, 71 LRRM 2481 (1969).

about this doctrine of the Board? This was a question one of the present authors asked himself when it caused a predicament for the company with which he was affiliated. At first he had little expectation that to undertake any change in the Board doctrine would be other than an exercise in futility. It happened that early in 1962 he had participated in a conference of personnel executives at which a staunch advocate of the abolition of the Board and the establishment in its place of public labor courts had presented a long list of seemingly labor-biased Board rulings. These, the advocate argued, demonstrated the Board's propensity for "playing directly into the hands of organized labor." He further argued that the Board had repeatedly been changing its posture—and for the worse—from management's standpoint. Reflecting on these contentions, this author speculated: "With its vast powers to make and change the rules of the game involving labor-management negotiations, why couldn't the Board be persuaded to change its rules for the better?"

The Board could and did change its contract bar rule. To induce the Board to do so was not exactly a simple matter. First, the company concerned had to challenge the right of an intervening union to demand a new election just before the end of the second year of a valid three-year agreement. The company made this challenge in a formal hearing conducted by a representative of the Board's regional office on a petition by a union seeking to upset a three-year agreement. Its management sought and obtained the cooperation of the international union, which was a party to the agreement that the rival union sought to upset.

Evidence presented by the management at the hearing at the regional Board level was persuasive enough to convince the Board itself to review its current contract bar doctrine and to hold a formal hearing on the generic issue. The Board granted opportunity to participate to the company, to the unions directly involved, and to other management and labor representatives appearing as *amici curiae*. The final result was the promulgation of the new rule (still in effect) that three-year labor agreements constitute a bar to any change in representation during the entire life of such agreements and hence cannot be invalidated by new elections.[17]

MANAGEMENT INTERFERENCE WITH EMPLOYEE RIGHTS OF SELF-ORGANIZATION

When a union is seeking to organize groups of employees in a department, plant, office, or an entire enterprise, management

---

[17]General Cable Corp., 139 NLRB 1123, 51 LRRM 1444 (1962).

often has to walk a tightrope to avoid charges of illegal interference with the rights of employees guaranteed by Taft-Hartley. The prohibitions against interference, coercion, and discrimination also apply after the union is in the picture and, often, more drastically when two or more labor organizations are striving to replace the incumbent union.

The bare bones structure of the Wagner Act's enumeration of employer unfair labor practices involving unions was quickly fleshed out by the National Labor Relations Board within a few years after it began to function. Most of the Board's early decisions defining and delineating employers' obligations to refrain from interference, coercion, or discrimination were sustained by the courts and still are controlling. This is particularly true with respect to cases involving discrimination against union members.

Discharge for Union Activity

There is no longer any serious question about the illegality of discharging or otherwise discriminating against an employee for union activity. It matters little whether that activity occurred during an organizing campaign, after a union has won or lost an election, or when a rival union is seeking to displace the incumbent bargaining representative.

From the day the United States Supreme Court upheld the constitutionality of the Wagner Act in 1937, the Court has uniformly held, as it could hardly do otherwise, that employers cannot discharge employees on account of their union activities. In each case coming before the Board there must be, however, sufficient evidence to demonstrate that the discharges were *in fact* because of the employees' union activity. The Supreme Court so ruled in its first Wagner Act landmark decision. It sustained the Board's findings that Jones and Laughlin Steel Corporation had discharged a number of employees who were active leaders in a labor union. Having challenged the constitutional validity of the Act, the company did not take advantage of its opportunity to present evidence to refute the contentions of illegal discrimination and coercion. The Court found that the evidence supported the findings of the Board that the company had discharged the union leaders "because of their union activity and for the purpose of discouraging membership in the union." The Court in deciding the *Jones and Laughlin* case stated a fundamental principle regarding employers' rights that still is considered to bind the Board and the courts in ruling on discharge cases. The Court declared:

The Act does not interfere with the normal exercise of the right of the employer to select its employees or to discharge them. The employer may not, under cover of that right, intimidate or coerce its employees with respect to their self-organization and representation, and, on the other hand, the Board is not entitled to make its authority a pretext for interference with the right of discharge when that right is exercised for other reasons than such intimidation or coercion.[18]

As to the types of evidence other than illegal purpose considered persuasive in discharging or laying off active union employees, the Supreme Court gave a definitive answer in one of its initial decisions construing the Wagner Act. The Board had found Friedman-Harry Marks Clothing Co., Inc., in violation of the Act because it terminated some of its employees. After certain company employees had formed a local union affiliated with the Amalgamated Clothing Workers of America and were soliciting membership therein among their fellow workers, the management, as the Court observed, "at once indicated hostility to the organization of its employees." At one time the president of the company stated to a group of employees that he would discharge every one of them who attended a union meeting, so the Board stated. Additionally, the management had maintained surveillance over union meetings and activities and some employees who belonged to the union were laid off in slack periods, although previously the work had been shared, according to the testimony presented to the Board. Hence the Board concluded that by the discharge or laying off of employees because of their union activity the company had violated Sections 8(3) and 8(1) of the Wagner Act. This case, which was decided by the Supreme Court on the same day as the *Jones and Laughlin* decision, is still cited by legal authorities as establishing a significant precedent for adjudication of unionized employees' complaints of illegal discharge or other disciplinary action.[19]

Union Membership No Guarantee of Protected Employment

A third landmark case decided the same day as the two just cited was notable for the Court's explanation of what the law did not require. The Associated Press had discharged a nonsupervisory editorial employee. The Supreme Court accepted the Board's determination that this employee had not been discharged for unsatisfactory service but for his activities in connection with the union

---

[18]NLRB v. Jones & Laughlin Corporation, 301 U.S. 1, 1 LRRM 703 (1937).
[19]Friedman-Harry Marks Clothing Company v. NLRB, 301 U.S. 58, 1 LRRM 718 (1937).

known as the Newspaper Guild. As the Court put it: "The actual reason for his discharge, as shown by the unattacked finding of the Board, was his Guild activity and agitation for collective bargaining." In sustaining the Board's order to reinstate the editorial employee after rejecting the contention of his employer that constitutional protection of the freedom of the press was a valid defense for its action, the Court gave an exposition of its views as to the limitations of employees' rights as union members or advocates. It emphatically declared:

> The Act does not compel the petitioner [the employer] to employ anyone; it does not require that the petitioner retain in its employ an incompetent editor or one who fails faithfully to edit the news without bias or prejudice. The Act permits a discharge for any reason other than union activity or agitation for collective bargaining among employees. The restoration of Watson [the discharged editorial employee] to his former position in no sense guarantees his continuance in petitioner's employ. The petitioner is at liberty, whenever occasion may arise, to exercise his undoubted right to sever his relation for any cause that seems to it proper, save only as a punishment for, or discouragement of, such activities as the Act declares permissible.[20]

Illegal Employee Conduct Justification for Discharge

Two wrongs do not make a right. This was, in essence, the principle enunciated by the U.S. Supreme Court in the celebrated *Fansteel Metallurgical Corporation* case decision in 1939. As to the company's "wrongs," the Court sustained the Board's finding that by antiunion statements of a plant superintendent, by an attempt to introduce a company union, by the isolation of the local union president from his fellow employees, and by the use of a labor spy, the company had violated Section 8(1) of the Act. Further, by refusing to bargain with a union after it had obtained majority status the company had violated Section 8(5). (Its continued refusal to bargain with the union after the members began a sitdown was held by the Court not to have constituted an unfair labor practice.)

As to the union's wrongs, upon the refusal of the company to recognize and bargain with it the union decided on a sitdown strike. Nearly 100 employees took over and held two of the company's key buildings. Within a few hours after the strike began, the superintendent demanded that the strikers leave the buildings they were occupying. When they refused the superintendent announced that they were all fired. The next day the company obtained a state

---

[20]Associated Press v. NLRB, 301 U.S. 103, 1 LRRM 732 (1937).

court injunction requiring the sitdown strikers to surrender the premises. They refused and a pitched battle ensued in which the men successfully resisted an attempt by the local sheriff to evict and arrest them. Some 10 days after the sitdown strike began the men were ousted, after another battle, and placed under arrest. Most of the men were eventually fined and given jail sentences.

The Supreme Court took sharp issue with the Board's position that unfair labor practices of the company furnished ground for ordering the reinstatement of the sitdown strikers. The Court took note of the fact that Section 8(3) of the Act provides that nothing therein "shall be construed so as to interfere with or impede or diminish in any way the right to strike." Then the Court emphatically stated that recognition of the right to strike "plainly contemplates a lawful strike, — the exercise of the unquestioned right to quit work." It further declared:

> There is not a line in the statute to warrant the conclusion that it is any part of the policies of the Act to encourage employees to resort to force and violence in defiance of the law of the land. . . . We are of the opinion that to provide for the reinstatement or reemployment of employees guilty of the acts which the Board finds to have been committed in this instance would not only not effectuate any policy of the Act but would directly tend to make abortive its plan for peaceable procedure.[21]

Restated in layman's language the gist of the Court's *Fansteel* decision was that the company had the right to discharge sitdown strikers even though it had engaged in unfair labor practices prior to the strike. Because they were lawfully discharged, the Board had no authority to order their reinstatement, since after their discharge for unlawful conduct they no longer remained employees.

Illegal Refusal to Reinstate Strikers Because of Legitimate Union Activity

The *Fansteel* case did not afford carte blanche to an employer to reinstate strikers not found guilty themselves of illegal conduct. The Supreme Court had already decided this issue in reverse. That is to say, in an earlier decision *(Mackay Radio and Telegraph Company,* 1938) the Court determined that the company had illegally discriminated against a small number of strikers by refusing to reinstate them "for the sole reason that they had been active in the union." In the circumstances surrounding this case it must be noted that prior to the refusal to reinstate, neither the management nor

---

[21]NLRB v. Fansteel Metallurgical Corp., 306 U.S. 240, 4 LRRM 515 (1939).

the employees were considered by the Board to have engaged in illegal actions. But that was not the basis for the Board's findings and the Court's decision upholding the Board's order of reinstatement. The strike had been called by a local union in the San Francisco office of the company at a time when negotiations with the parent company and the national union had not produced an agreement. The strike was of short duration. A union spokesman soon asked a management representative if the men could return to work before their places were filled by new employees. The management agreed to reinstate the strikers on the condition that none of the group of employees reassigned from other locations to the San Francisco office who wanted to remain would have to be displaced. Only five of these men wished to remain. All but five of the strikers were thereupon put back to work, although in agreeing to the general callbacks the management had insisted that all named employees would have to file applications for reinstatement "to be passed upon in New York." This requirement was promptly waived with respect to six of the strikers. Five strikers who were "prominent in the activities of the union and in connection with the strike" as the Court noted, and whose names were on the list of 11, were told that the employment roll was complete and that they would have to file an application to be considered for future employment. When no job offers were made to any of them, unfair labor practice charges were filed in their behalf against the company.

The Supreme Court decision in this case was noteworthy from both a positive and negative standpoint. The Court held, in substance, that:

1. The striking employees remained employees within the meaning of the Act, for Section 2(3) provides that the term "employee" includes "any individual whose work has ceased as a consequence of, or in connection with, any current labor dispute . . . and who has not obtained any other regular and substantially equivalent employment." All the strikers hence remained employees and were protected against any management unfair labor practices including discrimination on account of their union activities.

2. The Board had adequate reason to conclude that the five employees denied reinstatement had been singled out for illegal discrimination because of their conspicuous union activities.

3. The statutory protection of employees' right to strike does not preclude an employer, guilty of no action denounced by

the statute, from protecting and continuing his business "by supplying places left vacant by strikers."

4. An employer "is not bound to discharge those hired to fill the places of strikers, upon the election of the latter to resume their employment, in order to create places for them."

5. *But,* since the company had discriminated against five of the strikers because they had been active in the union, they retained their status as employees and the discrimination that kept them from reinstatement was perforce illegal. Hence, they had to be reinstated with back pay.[22]

Absence of Convincing Reasons for Discharge

The employer's background attitude toward organization of his employees is considered of much significance when there is doubt as to the legitimacy of the reasons for discharging employees. This principle was clearly enunciated in a circuit court's review in 1942 of the Board decision in the case of *Condenser Corporation of America.* As the court explained, "the sole question with regard to them [three men who had been discharged] is whether they were discharged in violation of their rights under the statute. The Board does not dispute the contention that the employees may be discharged for a good reason, a poor reason or no reason at all, so long as the terms of the statute are not violated." Nevertheless, as the court stated, in an unfair labor practice proceeding wherein the employer is alleged to have discharged employees because of their union activity, failure of the employer to give a reason for their discharge or giving evasive or contradictory reasons may be considered by the Board in determining the real motive for their discharge.[23]

Timing of Punitive Action

The Board has always looked with suspicion upon the discharge, layoff, or other punitive action affecting an employee shortly after the management has learned of the employee's participation in union activities. In such circumstances it closely scrutinizes the reasons given by the employer for his action when illegal discrimination is charged against him.

A leading federal circuit court decision issued in 1952 upheld the Board's findings in the case of *Somerville Buick, Inc.,* to the

---

[22]NLRB v. Mckay Radio and Telegraph Company, 304 U.S. 333, 2 LRRM 610 (1938).
[23]NLRB v. Condenser Corp. of America, 128 F.2d 67, 10 LRRM 483 (3rd Cir. 1942).

effect that the company had discharged three employees because of their union activity, even though they were terminated because they were the least satisfactory of those in the work force at the time there was a reduction in employment due to lack of business. The Board and the court considered of significance evidence that a new employee had been hired the day after the discharge, and that the management had advertised for new employees soon thereafter. Even more significant was evidence to the effect that the three discharged employees were the leaders of a union organizing campaign in the shop and that they were discharged without notice two days after the union had written the management requesting a meeting to negotiate a contract.[24]

Lack of Substantial Business Justification Affecting Employees' Rights

The Supreme Court itself has reviewed cases where the management motive was the prime consideration in determining the legitimacy of a company's action affecting employees' organizational rights. Speaking for a majority of the Court, then Chief Justice Warren stated in 1967 in the case of *NLRB* v. *Great Dane Trailers, Inc.*, that several principles of controlling importance could be distilled from the matter before the Court. He said:

> First, if it reasonably can be concluded that the employer's discriminatory conduct was (1) "inherently destructive" of employees' rights, no proof of antiunion motivation is needed and the Board can find an unfair labor practice even if the employer introduces evidence that the conduct was motivated by business considerations. (2) If the adverse effect of the discriminatory conduct on employee rights is "comparatively slight," an anti-union motivation must be proved to sustain the charge *if* the employer had substantial business justification for the conduct. Thus in either situation, once that it has been proved that the employer engaged in discriminatory conduct that could have adversely affected employee rights to *some* extent, the burden is upon the employer to establish that it was motivated by legitimate objectives, since proof of motivation is most accessible to him.[25]

Employment or "Instatement" of Nonemployees

An employer may be found to have committed an unfair labor practice if he refuses to hire workers solely because of their known union affiliations. The Act does not require an employer, however,

---

[24]NLRB v. Somerville Buick, 194 F.2d 56, 29 LRRM 2379 (1st Cir. 1952).
[25]NLRB v. Great Dane Trailers, Inc., 388 U.S. 26, 65 LRRM 2465 (1967).

to favor union members in hiring employees. These generalized principles interpreting the scope of employer unfair labor practices forbidden by the law appeared in the Supreme Court's landmark decision of 1941 involving Phelps Dodge Corporation.

In the *Phelps Dodge* case the Board had found that after the termination of a strike at one of the company's mines 40 men had been refused employment because of their union affiliations. Thirty-eight of the men had been strikers. (All but one of the 38 workmen the Board ordered to be reinstated with back pay. The exception was a workman who had become unemployable, and the company was ordered to make this individual whole for the loss of pay until he could no longer work.) But it was the refusal to hire two men who were not employees at the mine when the strike occurred that gave rise to the basic issue decided by the Supreme Court. These two men had previously been employees before the strike but had left and were not strikers. According to the Board, they had union affiliations known to the company.

Section 8(3) of the Wagner Act prohibited discrimination in regard to *hire* as well as to tenure of employment for the purpose of encouraging or discouraging membership in any labor organization. Taft-Hartley contains the same prohibition. The Supreme Court in the case under review construed the reference to the term "hire" as enabling the Board to order the company to hire or to "instate" the two men who, the Board found, had been refused jobs on account of their union connections. In so deciding, the Supreme Court declared that the law "does not impose an obligation on the employer to favor union members in hiring employees. He is as free to hire as he is to discharge employees. The statute does not touch 'the normal exercise of the right of the employer to select its employees or to discharge them.' It is directed solely against the abuse of that right by interfering with the countervailing right of self-organization."[26] To paraphrase the Court's dictum in this case, an employer cannot refuse to hire an applicant with union affiliations for the purpose of discouraging unionization, but he is not obligated to hire anyone just because the applicant may have union affilations.

Questionable Restrictions on Intraplant Union Propaganda

Many of the leading court cases involving employees' rights as individuals tie in directly with the rights of unions to seek organization of a plant or other type of establishment. Thus, an employee

---

[26]Phelps Dodge Corporation v. NLRB, 313 U.S. 177, 3 LRRM 439 (1941).

might be held to have been illegally discharged for engaging in person in tactics inspired at the direction of outside union organizers. Two precedent-making cases of this sort were decided by the Supreme Court in 1945. In these cases the Court had to examine the Board's initial responsibility "in working out an adjustment between the undisputed right of self-organization assured to employees under the Wagner Act and the equally undisputed right of employers to maintain discipline in their establishments." The Court said in this connection:

> The Wagner Act did not undertake the impossible task of specifying in precise and unmistakable language each incident which would constitute an unfair labor practice. On the contrary, that Act left to the Board the work of applying the Act's general prohibitory language in the light of the infinite combinations of events which might be charged as violative of its terms.

After giving expression to this generality, the Court concluded that the Board was right in holding Republic Aviation Corporation and the Le Tourneau Company to have engaged in unfair labor practices by promulgating and enforcing plant rules prohibiting solicitation of union membership and distribution of union circulars on company premises during nonwork periods. The Court further sustained the Board's findings that the discharge of employees for disobeying "no solicitation" and "no distribution" rules during nonwork time constituted illegal discrimination against employees in violation of Section 8(3) of the Act. These two cases have often been cited in subsequent litigation as indicating the narrow margin between legality and illegality of comparable employer practices under somewhat dissimilar circumstances.[27]

Possible Legality of No-Solicitation and No-Distribution Rules

The narrow margin to which allusion has just been made was well demonstrated in another notable decision of the Supreme Court in 1958. Here in combined cases involving two different companies the Supreme Court decided that employer rules prohibiting organizational solicitation are not in and of themselves violative of the Act, "for they may duly serve production, order and discipline."[28]

The two companies that were the subject of this decision were Nutone Inc. and Avondale Mills. But the case itself was one that actually involved an issue between the Board and the Steelworkers

---

[27]Republic Aviation Corp. v. NLRB, 324 U.S. 793, 16 LRRM 620 (1945).

[28]NLRB v. United Steelworkers of America and Nutone, Inc., 357 U.S. 357, 42 LRRM 2324 (1958).

Union. Regarding this case, we must stress, as we have to stress in citing many other cases, that management must be chary about following the interpretations or dicta of any Board or court decision without close scrutiny of the entire text. Often, the footnotes or the footnotes to the footnotes contain data that may tend to distinguish specific rulings from the rulings in other cases that are not completely on all fours. There was such a footnote in the case referred to here, *Board v. Babcock and Wilcox.*[29] In this case the Supreme Court two years earlier found that the company had not illegally deprived employees of their right of self-organization by denying parking access to union organizers. Indeed, the Court held in the case that the Act "does not require that the employer permit the use of its facilities for organization when other means are readily available."

The facts in the *Babcock and Wilcox* case were undisputed. Some 90 percent of the employees of one of its plants drove to work and parked in a lot adjacent to the plant. Because of traffic conditions on the highway, the Board found it practically impossible for union organizers to distribute leaflets safely to employees on entering or leaving the lot. The company had maintained a consistent policy of prohibiting distribution of any type of leaflet on the grounds that such distribution would litter its property. The Board held the company guilty of an unfair labor practice because of its refusal to give union organizers limited access for the purpose of distributing their literature in the parking lot. In reversing the Board the Supreme Court stated: ". . . if the location of a plant and the living quarters of the employees place the employee beyond the reach of reasonable union efforts to communicate with them, the employer must allow the union to approach his employees on his property. No such conditions are shown in these records."[30]

But nearly 20 years later the Supreme Court took a somewhat different tack on the same generic matter. In 1974 the Court declared that the Board had properly found an employer in violation of Taft-Hartley because of attempting to enforce a rule forbidding distribution of union literature in nonworking areas during nonworking time, even though the union concerned had waived any objections to the employer's rule.

As summarized in the Court's majority opinion, it seemed that the union challenging the validity of the company rule had been hoisted by its own petard. And it took a Solomonic Court edict to get it off the hook. The Court obliged.

---

[29] 38 LRRM 2001.
[30] NLRB v. Babcock and Wilcox Co., 351 U.S. 105, 38 LRRM 2001 (1956).

From 1954 on, the IUE had been the bargaining agent for some employees at a Tennessee plant of Magnavox Company. When the union took over bargaining rights, the company had had in effect a rule prohibiting employees from distributing literature anywhere on its property, including parking lots and other nonwork areas. The union agreed in its initial contract and subsequent contracts to authorize the company to issue rules for its "maintenance of orderly conditions on plant property" provided the rules were "not unfair or discriminatory."

Ultimately the union challenged the validity of the company's rule. On denial the union charged the management with violation of Section 8(a)(1) of Taft-Hartley. The Board found for the union. One has figuratively to read between the lines of the Court's majority opinion to follow why the union belatedly sought annulment of a company rule to which it had previously not objected. The clue appeared in the passage referring to the employees' right "to have no bargaining representative, or to retain the present one, or to obtain a new one." As the Court stated, "When the right to such an issue is at substance, it is difficult to assume that the union has no self-interest of its own to serve by perpetuating itself as the bargaining representative. The Court concluded that it was the Board's function to strike a balance among "conflicting legitimate interests" — supporters as well as opposers of the union — which would "effectuate national labor policy."[31]

While the law of the land is whatever the U.S. Supreme Court declares it to be today, one can never be quite sure what the Court will declare it to be tomorrow. If the assertion seems to border on legal sacrilege, it is substantiated in part by what one Supreme Court Justice, noted for his candor as well as his wisdon, had to say in a 1976 decision of landmark proportions. Referring to the history of the litigation in the case at bar, Mr. Justice Stewart said,

> [It] has been a history of shifting positions on the part of the litigants, the Board and the Court of Appeals. It has been a history in short of considerable confusion, engendered at least in part by decisions of this Court that intervened during the course of the litigation. In the present posture of the case the most basic question is whether the respective rights and liabilities of the parties are to be decided under criteria of the National Labor Relations Act alone, under a First Amendment standard, or under some combination of the two. It is to that question, accordingly, that we now turn.
>
> It is, of course a commonplace that the constitutional guarantee of free speech, is a guarantee only against abridgement by government, federal or state. See *Columbia Broadcasting System, Inc. v.*

---

[31]NLRB v. Magnavox Company of Tennessee, 415 U.S. 322, 85 LRRM 2475 (1974).

Democratic National Committee, 412 U.S. 94. Thus while statutory or common law may in some studies extend protection or provide redress against a private corporation, or person who seeks to abridge the free expression of others, no such protection or redress is provided by the Constitution itself.

For these reasons, among others, the Supreme Court held in a 6 to 2 decision that the owner of a shopping center had not violated Taft-Hartley by threatening union pickets with criminal arrest if they did not depart forthwith from a private parking lot, for he had not by so doing abridged the pickets' right of free speech.

As for the relevant facts, it must be noted that the union pickets were not arrested. Instead they left the premises of the shopping center and proceeded to file unfair labor practice charges against the owner. The NLRB found the owner in violation of Section 7 of Taft-Hartley and issued a cease and desist order. This order was upheld and enforced by the Fifth Circuit Court of Appeals.

The pickets were members of a union representing warehouse employees of the Butler Shoe Company. They struck in protest over the company's unwillingness to accede to the union's demands for a new contract. (The company's warehouse, incidentally, was not located in the shopping center where the disputed picketing took place. But one of its retail stores was.)

The Board's cease and desist order was, as the Supreme Court stated, reasoned on the premise that "because the warehouse employees engaged in First Amendement right to picket on the shopping center, the owner's threat of arrest violated . . . the Act." After the Board's decision had come up for review in the federal circuit court and had been remanded for further findings, the Board still ruled that the owner had committed an unfair labor practice. Its conclusion was that the picketers were within the scope of the owners' invitation to members of the public to do business at the shopping center and that it was irrelevant whether there existed an alternative means of communicating with the customers of the store.

When the case came up again for review in the federal circuit court, the Board contended that its decision was controlled not by the *Babcock and Wilcox* case (referred to above), but by another case, i.e., *Republic Aviation Corp. v. NLRB.*[32] In that case an employer was held to have violated Taft-Hartley by enforcing on his premises a no solicitation rule against employees "who were union

---

[32]324 U.S. 793 (1945).

organizers," absent special extenuating circumstances. Whatever the precedents cited by the litigants in the case as ultimately reviewed by the Supreme Court, the Court handed down a decision de novo. The most pertinent passages are cited below:

> Under the [Taft-Hartley] Act the task of the Board, subject to review by the courts, is to resolve conflicts between Section 7 rights and private property rights, and to seek a proper accommodation between the two. . . . What is a proper accommodation in any situation may largely depend upon the content and context of the Section 7 rights being asserted. The task of the Board and the reviewing courts under the Act, therefore, stands in conspicuous contrast to the duty of a court in applying the standards of the First Amendment, which requires 'above all else' that expression must not be restricted by government 'because of its message, its ideas, its subject matter or its content.'

Hence the majority opinion concluded with the judgment that the Board should make a final decision as to violation or nonviolation of Taft-Hartley under the Board's statutory authority alone and without regard to First Amendment implications.[33]

Threats, Promises, and Other Discriminatory Management Tactics

Threats of Reprisal

In the 1967 case of the *Board* v. *Baltimore Luggage Company,* a federal circuit court held the Board warranted in finding the company in violation of Section 8(a)(1) for having made statements to employees that contained implicit threats of reprisal for their activities on behalf of a union. To grasp the import of the Board's findings and the court's support thereof, we quote a portion of the court's decision:

> The genesis of the present case is as follows: On April 12, 1965, the union disclosed to Vice-President Holtzman the names of the twelve employees who comprised its organizing committee. A week later, Holtzman toured the plant and singled out five employees, all committee members, for special comment. According to credited employe testimony, he remarked to a foreman, in the presence of two of the committee members, that "these are the two trouble makers in your department." Holtzman told a third employee that he could "be bounced out." Of a fourth he inquired "Is there something wrong? What is bothering you, boy? Something wrong with you?" and told the plant supervisor, Wissman, to "keep an eye" on the employee. Finally he informed the fifth committee member that "if I have any

---

[33]Hudgens v. NLRB, 424 U.S. 507 (1976).

more complaints, you will be putting power screws in [the type of work in which the employee was engaged] on someone else's job." Although Holtzman testified that during the tour he discussed the performance of numerous other employees, he was unable to recall either their names or specifically what he said.

The remarks were defended by the company as having been directed at and motivated solely by a salesman's complaints concerning defects in merchandise traceable to these and other employees. However, the trial examiner, and in turn the Board, relying in part upon the timing of the tour, the suspiciously vague recollection of Holtzman, and the fact that several of the comments rang false on the asserted purpose of merely informing the employees of defective workmanship, concluded that the remarks were in reality veiled threats in violation of Section 8(a)(1).[34]

Promises of Improved Benefits

The Exchange Parts Company violated Section 8(a)(1) by announcing and granting improved employee benefits prior to a representation election and so timed as hopefully to influence its outcome. So the U.S. Supreme Court decided in 1964, even though the benefit improvements were put into effect unconditionally and on a permanent basis, and even though no other interference with employee rights was found.

The promises were made to employees *as individuals*. But a union election was impending and the union lost it. The Board construed the promises as having been arranged by the company to induce the employees to vote against the union. The employer's conduct was held to infringe on the employees' right of self-organization. As for the company's promises, they related to the employees' option to take an extra day off, either on their birthdays or upon the vote of employees as a floating holiday, and a new system for computing overtime during holiday weeks with resultant increased wages, as well as an improved vacation schedule.

Referring to Section 8(a)(1) the Supreme Court declared:

We have no doubt that it prohibits not only intrusive threats and promises but also conduct immediately favorable to employees which is undertaken for the express purpose of impinging upon their freedom of choice for or against unionization and is reasonably calculated to have that effect. In Medo Photo Supply Corp. v. Labor Board, 321 US 678 [14 LRRM 581], this Court said: "The action of employees with respect to the choice of their bargaining agents may be induced by favors bestowed by the employer as well as by his threats or domination." Although in that case there was already a designated bargaining agent and the offer of "favors" was in response to a suggestion of the employees that they would leave the union if

[34]NLRB v. Baltimore Luggage Co., 382 F.2d 350, 66 LRRM 2086 (4th Cir. 1967).

favors were bestowed, the principles which dictated the result there are fully applicable here. The danger inherent in well-timed increases in benefits is the suggestion of a fist inside the velvet glove. Employees are not likely to miss the inference that the source of benefits now conferred is also the source from which future benefits must flow and which may dry up if it is not obliged. The danger may be diminished if, as in this case, the benefits are conferred permanently and unconditionally. But the absence of conditions or threats pertaining to the particular benefits conferred would be of controlling significance only if it could be presumed that no question of additional benefits or renegotiation of existing benefits would arise in the future; and, of course, no such presumption is tenable.[35]

Preferential Seniority for Strike Replacements

An employer violated Sections 8(a)(1) and (3) by offering 20-year seniority credit to strike replacements and to strikers who returned to work while a strike was still in progress. Under the particular circumstances of the case *(Erie Resistor Corporation)*, the company's offer necessarily had the effect, the Supreme Court decided, to discriminate illegally between the strikers and nonstrikers. The management's action was also held to have had a destructive impact upon a legal strike and upon legal activity of the strikers.

As related by the Court, these essential facts were, in sequence:

1. After three fruitless months of negotiations and upon expiration of an agreement, the union called a strike that was initially joined by all of the employees in the bargaining unit. Under intense competition and subject to customer demands to maintain deliveries, the company decided to continue production operations. (This it had, of course, the legal right to do.) For nearly a month, by utilizing management and other nonunit employees on production jobs, the company was able to produce at a rate of from 15 to 30 percent of normal.

2. The company then notified the union members that it intended to begin hiring replacements but that the strikers could retain their jobs until replaced. Replacements, i.e., newly hired employees, were told that they would not be laid off or discharged when the strike ended.

3. The company notified the union that it intended to accord the replacements some sort of superseniority. Over the union's protests, the company announced that it would award 20 years' additional seniority both to replacements

---

[35]NLRB v. Exchange Parts Company, 375 U.S. 405, 55 LRRM 2098 (1964).

and to strikers who returned to work. This superseniority was to be used only for credit against future layoffs and not for other benefits based on length of service.

4. When the number of new replacements and returning strikers approximated more than 25 percent of the regular work force, the union capitulated. It did so in the sense that it accepted a new economic agreement with the proviso that the company's replacement and superseniority policy would be resolved by the National Labor Relations Board and the federal courts. Meanwhile, the policy was to remain in effect.

The Board rejected the company's contention that its overriding purpose in granting superseniority was to keep its plant open and that business necessity justified its conduct. To excuse such conduct, the Board held, "would greatly diminish, if not destroy the right to strike guaranteed by the Act, and would run directly counter to the guarantees of Sections 8(a)(1) and (3) that employees shall not be discriminated against for engaging in protected concerted activities." Supporting the Board's conclusions, the Supreme Court declared that even though the company could claim that the adoption of its superseniority policy was made "in pursuit of legitimate business ends and that its dominant purpose was not to discriminate or to evade union rights but to accomplish business objectives acceptable under the Act," nevertheless the company's conduct spoke for itself. It was discriminatory, and it discouraged union membership. *Ergo,* it was illegal.[36]

Retroactive Seniority Rights

It is not usual for the United States Supreme Court to cite prior decisions construing one law as highly pertinent to its current decision construing another law. For this reason the Court's 1976 decision in a landmark case concerning the Civil Rights Act has tremendous significance because of its disclosure of the Court's present posture on crucial Taft-Hartley issues.

The case in question is the *Franks* v. *Bowman Transportation Co.* case (see Chapter 3, p. 89) in which the Court ordered retroactive seniority for persons illegally denied employment for reasons of racial discrimination. In support of its findings and judgment in this case the majority opinion of the Court went to some lengths to cite precepts established under its earlier Taft-Hartley decisions. Indeed, the Court reached further back into the early Wagner Act

---

[36]NLRB v. Erie Resistor Corp., 373 U.S. 221, 53 LRRM 2121 (1963).

days and in its 1976 decision cited its celebrated *Phelps Dodge* decision of 1941: In that case, a⁻ indicated above in this chapter (see page 311), the Wagner Act's proscription of discrimination with regard to hiring as well as tenure of employment (on account of union activity) justified the Board in ordering the *"instatement"* or hiring of individuals who had been refused jobs because of their union connections.

The central issue in the *Franks* v. *Bowman* case was whether or not an award of seniority retroactive to the dates when individual applicants had been rejected for employment was appropriate to effect the objective of Title VII of the Civil Rights Act—that is, make the applicants whole for injuries suffered because of unlawful employment discrimination. The Supreme Court decided that the federal courts could and should prescribe retroactive seniority, even though the result inevitably would be to diminish the benefits accruing to others because of their own contractually established tenure of employment. When it reexamined early decisions to consider those it deemed still viable and applicable to the issue before it, the Court referred, *inter alia,* to a number of pronouncements of academicians with special expertise in labor relations. One such, as summarized by the Court, was that:

> Seniority systems and the entitlements conferred by credits earned thereunder are of vast and increasing importance in the economic system of this Nation (S. Schlicter, J. Henly and E. Livernash, *The Impact of Collective Bargaining on Management,* 104-115 (1960.). [And] Seniority principles are increasingly used to allocate entitlements to scarce benefits among competing employment ('competitive status' seniority) and to compute noncompetitive benefits earned under the contract of employment ('benefit' seniority).[37]

The Supreme Court proceeded, in what amounted to a reaffirmation of previous decisions, to declare what the Taft-Hartley Act still requires in discrimination cases:

> Settled law dealing with the related 'twin' areas of discriminatory hiring and discharges violative of National Labor Relations Act . . . provides a persuasive analogy. It would indeed be surprising if Congress gave a remedy for one that it denied for the other. *Phelps Dodge Corp. v. NLRB,* 313 U.S. 177, 187 (1941). For courts to differentiate without justification between classes of discrimination 'would be a differentiation without substance but in defiance of that against which the prohibition of discrimination is directed.'
> Similarly, decisions construing the remedial section of the National Labor Relations Act, Section 10(c) . . . make clear that remedies constituting authorized 'affirmative action' include an

---

[37]Franks et al. v. Bowman Transportation Co., Inc., et al., 424 U.S. 747 (1976).

award of seniority status, for the thrust of 'affirmative action' redressing the wrong incurred by an unfair labor practice is to make 'the employees whole and thus restore the economic status quo that would have obtained but for the company's wrongful [act].' *NLRB* v. *J. H. Rutter-Rex Manufacturing Company*, 396 U.S. 258, 263 (1969). The task of the NLRB in applying Section 10(c) is 'to take measures designed to recreate the conditions and relationships that would have been had there been no unfair labor practice.'

Further to justify its conclusions, the Court in its majority opinion resorted to what some might term "highfalutin' " language. What follows is the majority criticism of the minority opinion for its criticism of the majority conclusion.

> The dissent criticizes the Court's result as not sufficiently cognizant that it will . . . directly implicate the rights and expectations of perfectly innocent employees. . . . We are of the view, however, that the result which we reach today—which, standing alone, establishes that a sharing of the burden of the past discrimination is presumptively necessary—is entirely consistent with any fair characterization of equity jurisdiction, —particularly when considered in light of our traditional view that attainment of a great national policy must not be confined within narrow canons for equitable relief deemed suitable by chancellors in ordinary private controversies. . . .
>
> Certainly there is no argument that the award of retroactive seniority to the victims of hiring discrimination in any way deprives other employees of indefeasibly vested rights conferred by the employment contract. This Court has long held that employee expectations arising from a seniority system may be modified by statutes furthering a strong public policy interest. . . . The Court has also held that a collective bargaining agreement may go further in enhancing the seniority status of certain employees for purposes of furthering public policy interests beyond what is required by statute, even though this will to some extent be detrimental to the expectations acquired by other employees under the previous seniority agreement. *Ford Motor Company v. Huffman*, 345 U.S. 330 (1953). And the ability of the union and employer voluntarily to modify the seniority system to the end of ameliorating the effects of past racial discrimination, a national policy objective of the 'highest priority,' is certainly no less than in other areas of public policy 'interests.'

The Supreme Court's decision in the case seemingly would set boundaries for awards of retroactive seniority not only under Taft-Hartley but also under the Civil Rights Act, the Age Discrimination Act, the Veterans Preference Act, and statutes having related purposes. The Court's final words were:

> Circumstances peculiar to the individual case may of course justify the modification or withholding of seniority relief for reasons that would not if applied generally undermine the purposes of Title

VII [of the Civil Rights Act]. In the instant case it appears that all new hirees establish seniority only upon completion of a 45-day probationary period, although upon completion seniority is retroactive to the date of hire. Certainly any seniority relief ultimately awarded by the district court could properly be cognizant of this fact. Amici and the respondent union point out that there may be circumstances where an award of full seniority should be deferred until completion of a training or apprentice program, or other preliminaries required of all new hirees. We do not undertake to delineate all such possible circumstances here. Any enumeration must await particular cases and be determined in the light of the trial courts' 'keen appreciation' of peculiar facts and circumstances.[38]

Employees' Job Rights Protected Despite a Strike Violating Contract

An explicit contract clause prohibiting strikes for the entire term of the contract does not enable an employer to discharge an employee for engaging in a strike while the contract is still in effect *if* the strike is caused by the employer's unfair labor practices. This briefly summarizes the conclusion that was reached by the Board and upheld by the Supreme Court in the celebrated *Mastro Plastics Corporation* case decided in 1956.

The Board found that the company had discriminatorily discharged an active union member because of his support for the union holding the current contract and his opposition to another union which was then seeking recognition with the ostensible support of the management. This man's discharge precipitated a strike in violation of the no-strike provisions of the contract. There was no escape clause in these provisions. The key words were: "The union further agrees to refrain from engaging in any strike or work stoppage during the term of this agreement." The strike lasted nearly three months. Then the union made an unconditional request to return to work. But the company refused to reinstate the one man it had discharged or any of the some 75 employees who had participated in the strike. The Board ordered the reinstatement of all concerned with back pay. Sustaining the Board's order, the Court tersely asserted, "Failure of the Board to enjoin the petitioners' illegal conduct or failure of the Board to sustain the right to strike against that conduct would seriously undermine the primary objectives of the Labor Act."[39]

"Two wrongs do not make a right" was the precept seemingly accepted by the Supreme Court in the *Fansteel* case referred to above. But courts are free to change their minds, and the Supreme

---

[38]*Ibid.*

[39]Mastro Plastics Corporation, et al. v. NLRB, 350 U.S. 270, 37 LRRM 2587 (1956).

Court is no exception. In *Mastro Plastics* the Court held that two wrongs do not justify a third wrong even though the perpetrators of the second wrong go scot free. At least, employers might well deem this remarkable decision as taking away from them some of the rights of punitive action against wildcat strikers. Prospective vendors of older homes, used cars, etc., often say in their advertisements: "This has to be seen to be appreciated." In this vein we urge any personnel administrator confronted with a situation appearing to justify action against legal or illegal strikers to make certain that his legal counsel closely scrutinizes all the fine print in the *Fansteel* and *Mastro Plastics* decisions, including especially in the latter case the vigorous dissent of Mr. Justice Frankfurter.

Other Types of Employer Interference

Quite obviously, the cases just cited are illustrative rather than inclusive. Many other leading Board and court decisions which have established, in effect, guidelines for management conduct in avoiding interference with the rights of self-organization are cited in a BNA manual, *Primer of Labor Relations*.[40] Some of the issues summarized in the manual relate to employer espionage or other surveillance, closing or moving a plant, withholding of employee privileges, unequal enforcement of plant rules, circulation of anti-union petitions, and questioning of employees about their union interests. Recent information regarding new or changed Board policies on employer unfair labor practices is summarized in each of the Board's annual reports.[41]

No generalized statement of the scope of the employer's rights and obligations relating to employee organizational activities could possibly even touch on all the management problems arising from Taft-Hartley's requirement of noninterference with employees. But Schlossberg's advice to union organizers in his book *Organizing and the Law* can well be heeded by management:

> Despite the claims of employer organizations and conservative critics, you must never forget that the public policy of the United States favors the right of union organization and the encouragement of collective bargaining. Many workers do not understand this simple truth. Organizers should deliver the message.[42]

---

[40]PRIMER OF LABOR RELATIONS (20th ed.; Washington: The Bureau of National Affairs, Inc., 1975), pp. 14-19.

[41]Annual reports of the National Labor Relations Board are issued usually a year or more after the close of the Board's fiscal year ending June 30. They are published by the U.S. Government Printing Office, Washington, D.C., and can be purchased from the Superintendent of Documents of that office.

[42]Schlossberg, p. 3.

UNION RIGHTS VERSUS INDIVIDUAL RIGHTS

There has been a trend in Taft-Hartley litigation for several years toward stress on collective rights of unions and away from emphasis on rights of individuals. Nowhere has this trend become more apparent than in the Supreme Court's 5-4 decision in the bitterly contested *Allis-Chalmers* case decided in 1967. It is true that the *Allis-Chalmers* case centered about an alleged violation of Taft-Hartley by the union and not by the company. The union had been charged with illegal interference with employees' rights and coercion against some employees. The employees affected were members of the union who had crossed its picket lines and gone to work during a strike authorized by the union. After being brought up on charges the recalcitrant union members were fined in amounts ranging from $20 to $100. The Supreme Court upheld the legality of this punishment.

It is far beyond the scope of this volume to summarize leading cases wherein labor unions have been held in violation of Taft-Hartley. Our purpose in citing this case is to call attention to the blunt fact that the majority of the U.S. Supreme Court held the view, only a decade ago, that majority rule by unions was *at the center of our federal labor policy.* The Court's majority opinion in the *Allis-Chalmers* case included the following dictum by Mr. Justice Brennan.

> National labor policy has been built on the premise that by pooling their strength and acting through a labor organization freely chosen by the majority, the employees of an appropriate unit have the most effective means of bargaining for improvements in wages, hours, and working conditions. The policy therefore extinguishes the individual employee's power to order his own relations with his employer and creates a power vested in the chosen representative to act in the interest of all employees. "Congress has seen fit to clothe the bargaining representative with powers comparable to those possessed by a legislative body both to create and restrict the rights of those whom he represents . . ." *Steele* v. *L. & N. R. Co.,* 323 U.S. 192, 202 [15 LRRM 708]. Thus only the union may contract the employee's terms and conditions of employment, and provisions for processing his grievances; the union may even bargain away his right to strike during the contract term, and his right to refuse to cross a lawful picket line. The employer may disagree with many of the union decisions but is bound by them. "The majority-rule concept is today unquestionably at the center of our federal labor policy."[43]

---

[43]NLRB v. Allis-Chalmers Manufacturing Company, 65 LRRM 2449, 388 U.S. 175 (1967).

Significantly, four Supreme Court Justices evidently thought that Mr. Justice Brennan had gone too far in his interpretation of the law. They joined in a strongly worded dissenting opinion which declared that the freedom of workers to go their own way in deciding what concerted labor activities they would engage in or decline to engage in, "completely unhampered by pressures of employers or unions, is and always has been a basic purpose of the legislation now under consideration."

MANAGEMENT'S BARGAINING OBLIGATIONS

One of the keystones of Taft-Hartley — and of the Wagner Act before it — was built into Section 8(a)(5). This section makes it an unfair labor practice, and hence illegal, for an employer: "To refuse to bargain collectively with the representatives of his employees, subject to the provisions of Section 9(a)." (As previously explained, Section 9(a) is the provision of the law relating to representation proceedings and proper bargaining units.) Under Section 8(b)(3), substantially the same bargaining obligations are imposed upon labor organizations.

To eliminate much of the uncertainty as to what the original Wagner Act required of employers in the way of bargaining obligations, Congress added in Taft-Hartley a concise definition of the term "to bargain collectively." This appears in Section 8(d) of the Act, which reads:

> For the purpose of this section to bargain collectively is the performance of the mutual obligation of the employer and the representative of the employees to meet at reasonable times and confer in good faith with respect to wages, hours, and other terms and conditions of employment, or the negotiation of an agreement, or any question arising thereunder, and the execution of a written contract incorporating any agreement reached if requested by either party, *but such obligation does not compel either party to agree to a proposal or require the making of a concession.* [Italics supplied.]

The last clause obviously is meaningful. So was the emphatic declaration of the then-Chairman of the Senate Committee on Education and Labor, Senator Walsh, that was made in the course of the Senate debate on the original Wagner Act in 1935. As one of the chief spokesmen for those urging the passage of the law, Senator Walsh asserted, "When the employees have chosen their organization, all the bill proposes to do is to escort them to the door of their employer and say, 'here they are, the legal representatives of your employees,' and the bill does not seek to inquire into it." Needless to say, with the passage of time Senator Walsh's assurances did not turn out to be 100-percent accurate.

Good-Faith Bargaining

To the Taft-Hartley requirement that management must bargain collectively, the Board and the courts have added the doctrine that there must be bargaining *in good faith*. What *"good-faith bargaining"* actually entails has led to interminable litigation that still plagues employers and labor unions. Final adjudication as to what constitutes good-faith bargaining is, of course, within the province of the U.S. Supreme Court. That Court has yet to come up with all-inclusive answers.

Legal scholars have found it much easier to glean from litigated cases the kinds of management actions that constitute lack of bargaining in good faith than they have to ascertain what the courts consider to be full compliance.

The list of subjects that have been judicially decided to be mandatory subjects of collective bargaining grows from year to year. It has expanded in the negative rather than the positive sense. That is to say, the subjects for mandatory bargaining enlarge with each valid Board or court edict holding the employer in violation of the Act by reason of his refusal to bargain at all on a given issue, or his refusal to bargain in good faith thereon.

Good-faith bargaining has been held to be lacking in such typical instances as when an employer:

1. Refuses to respond to the union's request for a bargaining conference
2. Refuses to send to the bargaining conference representatives who have the power to negotiate and bind the employer
3. Constantly shifts his position in regard to contract terms
4. Rejects union proposals without offering counterproposals
5. Refuses to sign a negotiated contract
6. Changes employment benefits unilaterally while concurrently negotiating with the union and prior to reaching an impasse
7. Refuses to comply with reasonable requests to furnish information
8. Refuses to produce reasonable proof to substantiate a claim of economic inability to raise wages or to provide benefits
9. Insists upon "patently" unreasonable terms

    10. Engages in a campaign to undermine the union and encourages employees to disavow their union affiliations

    11. Threatens employees with discharge if they go on strike.[44]

The foregoing list, like others produced in this book, is suggestive of the sweep of the statute rather than all-inclusive. It was compiled by a distinguished law firm, representing primarily management in labor relations cases, for the firm's objective appraisal of developments in labor relations law in the United States.[45]

Taft-Hartley cases, like cases involving other federal and state laws cited in this book, frequently hinge upon the application of skeletonized statutory provisions to specific situations. The cases reviewed below do not necessarily give a full picture of management's bargaining obligations. They have been selected instead to illustrate the complexities confronting management in discharging its obligations, as well as in asserting its rights under the law.

Good-Faith Bargaining in National Negotiations

The Board took many long and hard looks at what had gone on at the bargaining table when the General Electric Company negotiated for weeks with the IUE (AFL-CIO) over a multi-unit master contract in 1960. So it was not until December, 1964 — more than four years after the negotiations for the parties' three-year contract (finally ratified after a short strike in October 1960) were concluded — that the Board handed down its decision holding that the company had violated the Taft-Hartley Act by failing to bargain in good faith during the 1960 negotiations. And it was not until October 1969, after the negotiations for a new three-year contract for 1969-1972 had reached an impasse and a multiplant strike against General Electric had occurred, that a federal appellate court sustained the Board's findings that the company refused to bargain in good faith way back in the fall of 1960.

In summary, the U.S. Court of Appeals for the Second Circuit ruled in 1969 that the Board properly held in 1964 that the General Electric Company had violated Section 8(a)(5) of the Taft-Hartley Act during its negotiations with the IUE in the summer and fall of 1960. The Board was deemed warranted in its findings that the company had violated the law when in the course of national negotiations with the IUE it attempted to deal with the IUE locals on matters that properly were the subjects of national negotiation because (1) in the past the company had recognized the union as

---

[44]Seyfarth, et al., p. 107.
[45]*Ibid.*

representative of all locals acknowledged as bargaining agents for GE employees; (2) the company had a continuing obligation to respect the International IUE as the representative of all such locals; (3) additional terms that the company submitted to locals should have been submitted to the national negotiators beforehand or at the same time. The offers themselves constituted violations of the Act. (But the company's letter to one local setting forth the content of a management proposal previously made in the national negotiations did not violate the law because this letter was only for informational purposes and the public interest in free speech and informed choice must prevail over the slight possibility that the position of the IUE as the overall bargaining representative might have been undermined.)

The circuit court further held the Board justified in finding that the company had illegally refused to bargain by combining a method of "take it or leave it" bargaining—"Boulwarism'—with a widely publicized stance of unbending firmness precluding the company from altering its position once taken and announced to the union and to employees. This pattern of conduct became inconsistent with good-faith bargaining as demonstrated by the totality of relevant circumstances, including what the Court summarized and declared to be: (1) specific violations of the Act involving a unilateral take-it-or-leave-it group insurance offer and refusal to furnish cost information thereon; (2) insistence on doing no more at the bargaining table than the law absolutely required; (3) disregard of legitimacy and revelance of the union's position as to the employees' statutory representative; (4) display of a patronizing attitude toward the union even before general reopening of negotiations; (5) vague responses to the union's detailed proposals; (6) "prepared lecture series" instead of counteroffers when the union presented a plan; (7) persistent refusals after publicizing its proposals to estimate not only the cost of the components but the total size of the wage-benefit package the company would consider reasonable; (8) defense of unreasonable positions with no apparent purpose other than to avoid yielding to the union; (9) display of a "stiff and unbending patriarchal posture" even when it had become apparent that the union would have to concede to the management's terms; and (10) the company's publicity program, such as its refusal to withhold publicizing its offer until the union had the opportunity to propose suggested modifications. The court indicated that although absence of concessions does not prove bad faith, their presence would raise a strong inference of good faith.[46]

---

[46]NLRB v. General Electric Company, 418 F.2d 736, 72 LRRM 2530 (2d Cir. 1969).

Multi-Unit Collaboration

In the late 1960s these developed what might be considered almost a trend toward cooperation or collusion among separately designated bargaining units to force acceptance of identical terms, albeit without negotiating company-wide agreements. The union utilizing these tactics gained support from a federal circuit court decision in 1972. By rejecting certiorari, the Supreme Court in effect held the appellate court findings to constitute valid interpretations of Taft-Hartley.

It was a *Phelps-Dodge* case that brought about a decision in which the Board was reversed by a federal circuit court. The Board had declared that several local unions properly designated to represent some employees at Phelps-Dodge facilities had violated Section 8(b)(3) of Taft-Hartley by conditioning settlement of their current negotiations upon simultaneous satisfactory settlement of contracts in other bargaining units at different plant locations. By striking in support of their demands for a common settlement, the Board held, the local unions had attempted to engage in company-wide bargaining beyond the scope of established bargaining units. Separate negotiations had been conducted for each of the company's units, and no negotiations had gone on at any unit with regard to wages or other terms and conditions of employment. But the locals had insisted to the point of impasse on their demand for a "most favored nation clause" and a limited no-strike provision. These demands were finally withdrawn and a demand was then made for *simultaneous* settlement of all pending contracts. The circuit court decided that a demand of this nature was one of the mandatory subjects for bargaining under Taft-Hartley, and the fact of the union's insistence on acceptance did not constitute evidence of an illegal attempt to merge the bargaining of separate units.[47]

Unilateral Changes Prior to Impasse in Negotiations

Even though an employer may not be guilty of subjective bad faith in his negotiating tactics, he may nevertheless violate Section 8(a)(5) of Taft-Hartley by making unilateral changes in terms of employment. In the case designated as *NLRB* v. *Katz* the Supreme Court held that the Board was warranted in finding that the employer's unilateral changes in conditions of employment had been instituted before there was an actual impasse in negotiations.

---

[47]Phelps Dodge Corp. v. AFL-CIO Joint Negotiating Committee, 459 F.2d 374, 79 LRRM 2939 (3rd Cir. 1972).

The Supreme Court in deciding the *Katz* case in 1962 raised this question: "Is it a violation of the duty 'to bargain collectively' imposed by Section 8(a)(5) of the National Labor Relations Act for an employer, without first consulting a union with which it is carrying on bona fide contract negotiations, to institute changes regarding matters which are subjects of mandatory bargaining under Section 8(d), and which are in fact under discussion?" The Board had answered this question in the affirmative although expressly disclaiming any finding that the totality of the employer's conduct manifested bad faith in the pending negotiations. The Court upheld the Board's answer.

As to the facts, the Katz enterprise was a partnership engaged in steel fabricating. This partnership, designated in the Court decision as the employer, had instituted several unilateral changes in conditions of employment regarding which the law required it to negotiate. Specifically, the employer had modified its employees' sick leave plan unilaterally after changes in the plan had been proposed by the union. A new automatic wage increase system was introduced that was more generous than that previously offered to and rejected by the union. Additionally, merit increases were granted unilaterally to about 40 percent of the employees while negotiations were still in progress.

Taken in combination, the Supreme Court found the company had illegally refused to bargain collectively without necessarily acting in bad faith. The Court's conclusion was:

> A refusal to negotiate *in fact* as to any subject which is within §8(d), and about which the union seeks to negotiate, violates §8(a)(5) though the employer has every desire to reach agreement with the union upon an over-all collective agreement and earnestly and in all good faith bargains to that end. We hold that an employer's unilateral change in conditions of employment under negotiation is similarly a violation of §8(a)(5), for it is a circumvention of the duty to negotiate which frustrates the objectives of §8(a)(5) much as does a flat refusal.[48]

The Supreme Court in an especially important decision handed down in May 1970 had to construe the provision of Section 8(d) of the Act declaring that the employer's statutory obligations to bargain "do not compel either party to agree to a proposal or to request the making of a concession. . . . " The Court's decision was handed down in the case of *H. K. Porter Co.* v. *NLRB.* Having found bad-faith bargaining on the check-off issue, the Board had ordered the Porter Company to embody the check-off in its labor-

---

[48]NLRB v. Katz, et al., 369 U.S. 736, 50 LRRM 2177 (1962).

management agreement. For the Board to compel agreement on an issue when the parties themselves were able to reach an accord, the Supreme Court declared, would violate the fundamental premise under which the Act is based—private bargaining under governmental supervision of the procedure alone, without any official compulsion over the actual terms of the agreement. As the Court noted in the *Porter* decision,

> The object of this Act was not to allow governmental regulation of the terms and conditions of employment, but rather to ensure that employers and their employees could work together to establish mutually satisfactory conditions. The basic theme of the Act was that through collective bargaining the passions, arguments, and struggles of prior years would be channeled into constructive, open discussions leading, hopefully, to mutual agreement. But it was recognized from the beginning that agreement might in some cases be impossible, and it was never intended that the Government would in such cases step in, become a party to the negotiations and impose its own views of a desirable settlement.[49]

Management's Ability to Pay

When a company claims at the bargaining table that it cannot afford to meet the union's demands for higher wages, it may be found in violation of Section 8(a)(5) if it declines to produce information substantiating its claim. Each case of alleged refusal to bargain in good faith must, however, turn on its own facts.

One leading case that is still often considered as setting a firm precedent on this issue was decided by the Supreme Court in 1956. It concerned the Truitt Manufacturing Company, which had asserted inability to pay and had refused to give information to the union about its financial status. This dual position taken by the Truitt Company was considered by the Board and the Supreme Court to constitute illegal refusal to bargain in good faith. The Court stated the essential basis for its conclusion as follows:

> We think that in determining whether the obligation of good faith bargaining has been met the Board has a right to consider an employer's refusal to give information about its financial status. While Congress did not compel agreement between employers and bargaining representatives, it did require collective bargaining in the hope that agreements would result. Section 204(a)(1) of the Act admonishes both employers and employees "to exert every reasonable effort to make and maintain agreements concerning rates of pay, hours, and working conditions." . . . In their effort to reach an agreement here both the union and the company treated the com-

---

[49]H.K. Porter Company, Inc., etc. v. NLRB, et al., 397 U.S. 99, 73 LRRM 2561 (1970).

pany's ability to pay increased wages as highly relevant. The ability of an employer to increase wages without injury to his business is a commonly considered factor in wage negotiations. Claims for increased wages have sometimes been abandoned because of an employer's unsatisfactory business condition; employees have even voted to accept wage decreases because of such conditions.

Good faith bargaining necessarily requires that claims made by either bargainer should be honest claims. This is true about an asserted inability to pay an increase in wages. If such an argument is important enough to present in the give and take of bargaining, it is important enough to require some sort of proof of its accuracy. And it would certainly not be farfetched for a trier of fact to reach the conclusion that bargaining lacks good faith when an employer mechanically repeats a claim of inability to pay without making the slightest effort to substantiate the claim.

. . . The Board concluded that under the facts and circumstances of this case the respondent was guilty of an unfair labor practice in failing to bargain in good faith. We see no reason for disturbing the findings of the Board. We do not hold, however, that in every case in which economic inability to pay is raised as an argument against increased wages it automatically follows that the employees are entitled to substantiating evidence. *Each case must turn upon its particular facts.* [Italics supplied][50]

Lockout During Impasse

Should some employers still think that the cards are stacked against them in appealing from Board orders and that the *Porter* case cited previously in this chapter was a rare exception, they can take comfort from a 1965 decision of the Supreme Court wherein the Court reversed the Board and sustained the legality of a lockout after an impasse had been reached over the terms of a new contract. To be sure, it took four years of litigation before the management obtained a favorable decision.

The essential facts in this case, which involved the American Ship Building Company, were never in dispute. It was the consequences of the company's actions that gave rise to the protracted litigation.

As stated by the Supreme Court, American Ship Building was primarily engaged in the repairing of ships, "a highly seasonal business concentrated in the winter months when the freezing of the Great Lakes renders shipping impossible. What limited business is obtained during the shipping season is such that speed of execution is of utmost importance to minimize immobilization of the ships." The company had a contract with eight different unions with which it had negotiated for many years. This contract expired on August

---

[50]NLRB v. Truitt Manufacturing Company, 351 U.S. 149, 38 LRRM 2042 (1956).

1, 1961. By and after the expiration date there was an impasse on the economic issues for a new contract. On August 11, 1961, the company shut down one of its yards completely, laying off all of its workmen. And it laid off all but two employees of another yard. Some two months later after resumption of negotiations a new contract was entered into and the laid-off employees were recalled. As its management explained during the negotiations that led to the impasse, the company was fearful that the union would call a strike as soon as a ship entered one of its yards in the late summer or that it would delay negotiations into the winter "to increase strike leverage."

The partial cessation of operations by the company resulted in the filing of claims by the unions with which it had been negotiating charging the company with violation of Section 8(a)(1), (a)(3), and (a)(5) of the Act. In other words, the company was accused of interference with employees' rights of self-organization, discrimination to discourage union membership, and refusal to bargain in good faith. These accusations as here summarized were, of course, an oversimplication of the charges leveled against the company.

The Board by a 3 to 2 majority declared that the company, by curtailing its operations in one of its yards "with the consequent layoff of the employees, coerced employees in the exercise of their bargaining rights in violation of Section 8(a)(1) of the Act, and discriminated against its employees within the meaning of Section 8(a)(3) of the Act."

As the Supreme Court explained:

> The Board has held that, absent special circumstances, an employer may not during bargaining negotiations either threaten to lock out or lock out his employees in aid of his bargaining position. Such conduct the Board has held presumptively infringes upon collective-bargaining rights of employees in violation of Section 8(a)(1) and the lockout with its consequent layoff, amounts to a discrimination within the meaning of Section 8(a)(3). In addition the Board has held that such conduct subjects the Union and the employees it represents to unwarranted and illegal pressure and creates an atmosphere in which the free opportunity for negotiation contemplated by Section 8(a)(5) does not exist.

Before this case reached the Supreme Court, the U.S. Court of Appeals for the District of Columbia unanimously upheld the Board's decision.

The Supreme Court struck down the circuit court decision and in reversing the Board's findings unanimously supported the legality of the lockout by American Ship Building Company. Of

special note was the concurring opinion of Mr. Justice Arthur Goldberg who stated that "from the plain facts revealed by the record, it
is crystal clear that the employer lockout here was justifiable." He
wrote further that "this employer locked out his employees in the
face of a threatened strike under circumstances where, had the
choice of timing been left solely to the unions, the employer and his
customers would have been subject to economic injury over and
beyond the loss of business normally incident to a strike upon the
determination of the collective bargaining agreement."[51]

A Sidelight on the Role of the Courts

The seesaw developments in *American Ship Building* culminating in the exoneration of the management suggest the unreli-
ability of anyone's predictions as to the position any given appellate
court judge may take on a particular issue. To illustrate, when
Warren E. Burger was elevated from the circuit court bench to
become Chief Justice of the United States, close analysts of his
opinions over the years classified him as a conservative. Presumably
they thought that in considering labor-management cases he would
be inclined to seek to correct the seeming imbalance of federal law
in favor of unions over employers. And yet, as a member of the U.S.
Court of Appeals for the District of Columbia, Judge Burger was
one of the three judges of that court which unanimously decided the
American Ship Building case against the employer. And it was Mr.
Justice Goldberg, a former Secretary of Labor, and before that the
distinguished general counsel of the Steelworkers union, who
delivered the most perspicacious opinion of the Supreme Court in
its unanimous verdict that the Board was wrong and the employer
right on the particular lockout issue before the Court.

Management's Obligations to Furnish Fringe Benefit Data

In two different cases involving the same company and somewhat comparable issues, the same appellate court came out with
two diametrically opposite decisions barely five years apart. In 1961
the U.S. Court of Appeals for the First Circuit decided that Sylvania
Electric Products, Inc., had *not* illegally refused to bargain when
the company declined during contract negotiations to provide a
union with cost data relating to its noncontributory group insurance program. In 1966 the same court decided that Sylvania *had*

---

[51]American Ship Building Company v. NLRB, 380 U.S. 300, 58 LRRM 2672 (1965).

illegally refused to bargain by its unwillingness in contract negotiations to supply the union with information on the estimated cost of
proposed improvements in its fringe benefit plans. And by refusing
to grant certiorari in either case, the U.S. Supreme Court upheld
the validity of both of these circuit court decisions.

The 1961 decision stemmed from the company's refusal to give
cost information relating to its noncontributory group insurance
program on the grounds that it was bargaining, not on the basis of
costs, but benefits to be provided and, further, that it had no legal
obligation to provide cost data. The Board held that the premiums
paid for employee insurance benefits constituted in fact "wages"
and that therefore the company was obligated to furnish the union
with the data it demanded. The court disagreed, declaring that
such premiums "were neither wages nor conditions of employment
within any ordinarily accepted meaning of the words used." Hence
the court's reversal of the Board.[52]

The second case, decided in 1966, arose after the company had
offered the union during contract negotiations a package including
improvements in its noncontributory pension and group insurance
plans. The management acceded to the union's request for data
regarding the current cost of these but would not provide the union
with a breakdown of its costs. The union insisted it needed this
information in order to decide whether it might prefer to retain the
existing benefit program and opt for higher wage adjustments.
Again the management countered with the argument that it was
bargaining on the level of benefits, not costs, and had no legal obligation to give the union what it sought. The circuit court's conclusion, holding that in these circumstances the company was in
violation of Section 8(a)(5) of the Act, was expressed as follows:

> An employer is not required to disclose welfare plan cost information
> for the purpose of bargaining about whether he is receiving the best
> coverage for his money, because he is not obliged to discuss this
> matter with the union. . . . However, when the union makes the
> same demand in order better to evaluate the desirability of an
> increase in welfare benefits as against an equivalent increase in take-
> home pay, matters as to which the employer must bargain, the Board
> might properly conclude that the information, though collateral,
> was so necessary to effective negotiation that withholding it without
> good reason was inconsistent with the duty to "exert every reasonable
> effort to make and maintain agreements."[53]

---

[52]Sylvania Electric Products, Inc. v. NLRB, 291 F.2d 128, 48 LRRM 2313 (1st Cir.
1961).
[53]Sylvania Electric Products, Inc. v. NLRB, 358 F.2d 591, 61 LRRM 2657 (1st Cir.
1966).

Mandatory Bargaining on Pensions

The import of the *Sylvania* cases just summarized relates, of course, only to the data that an employer may or may not be obligated to present to a union when negotiating on fringe benefits generally. Nothing in these cases nullifies management's basic obligations to bargain on pensions or other fringe benefits upon demands of unions holding bargaining rights. These obligations were summarized in our review of the landmark *Inland Steel* case, accepted by the Supreme Court as the law of the land in 1949. (See Chapter 4.) As we there stated it is now well established by the courts that, however a pension plan was originally set up and regardless of the scope of its coverage, the terms of modification of an existing plan or the inauguration of a new plan must be negotiated with any union whose bargaining unit coverage of employees would be affected.

Exception for Retired Employees

The obligation to negotiate changes in pension plans for unionized employees does not extend to changes affecting persons already retired. This was made explicitly clear by the Supreme Court in a 1971 decision (briefly referred to in Chapter 4). The High Court's decision reversing an NLRB decision to the effect that retirees have to be deemed employees within the meaning of Taft-Hartley has been summarized as follows:

> The NLRB was not warranted in finding that employer violated Section 8(a)(5) of LMRA when it unilaterally modified benefits of retired employees since (1) retired employees are not "employees" within the meaning of the Act, (2) retired employees in present case could not be included within bargaining unit because they were not persons "working" or "who work" on hourly rates of pay, and in any event active and retired employees do not share community of interest broad enough to justify inclusion of retirees in bargaining unit, and (3) alleged industrial practice of bargaining over pensioners' rights cannot make retirees "employees" or bargaining unit members.[54]

Mandatory Bargaining on Subcontracting

If there be any one Supreme Court decision that attempts to delineate the often narrow line between compliance and violation of Section 8(a)(5) of Taft-Hartley, it is the celebrated *Fibreboard*

---

[54]Allied Chemical & Alkali Workers, Local 1 v. Pittsburgh Plate Glass, 78 LRRM 2974, 404 U.S. 157 (1971).

case decided by the Supreme Court in 1964. The primary issue before the Court was whether the contracting out of work previously performed by employees in the bargaining unit was a mandatory subject of collective bargaining under the particular circumstances involved. The Court decided that it was because terms and conditions of employment were involved.

The management of the Fibreboard Paper Products Corporation had made a unilateral decision to subcontract certain maintenance work currently being performed by members of the bargaining unit. Prior to doing so, being concerned about the high cost of its maintenance operations, it had undertaken a study of the possible savings to be effected in engaging an independent contractor to do the maintenance work. The management then notified the union representing its maintenance employees that upon the expiration of the then-current agreement, the maintenance work would be let out to an independent contractor and that consequently the negotiation of a new contract would be pointless. The services of the maintenance workers represented by the union were terminated on the contract expiration date with the result that the union filed unfair labor practice charges against the company.

After first holding the charges not supportable, the Board on reconsideration ordered the company to reinstitute the operation previously performed by union employees, and also to reinstate those employees to their former or substantially equivalent positions, and to fulfill its statutory obligation to bargain on the contracting-out issue. Both the U.S. Court of Appeals for the District of Columbia and the U.S. Supreme Court upheld the Board's decision.

Management Bargaining Rights and Obligations Summarized

Two separate opinions of the Supreme Court in the *Fibreboard* case go far to clarify the Court's views as to what employers may be compelled or not compelled to do to meet their Taft-Hartley obligations to bargain collectively. The majority opinion of the Court, delivered by Chief Justice Warren, pointed out that an employer's duty to bargain in good faith is limited to the subjects of "wages, hours and other terms and conditions of employment," and "within that area, neither party is obligated to yield . . . as to other matters, however, each party is free to bargain or not bargain." The Chief Justice declared that the contracting-out issue was "well within the literal meaning of the phrase, 'terms and conditions of employment.' " He further said that the Court's conclusion was reinforced by industrial practices in this country; and although not determinative, it was appropriate to look to industrial bargaining practices in appraising the propriety of including a particular subject within the scope of mandatory bargaining. Cynical critics of this passage in the Warren opinion have equated it to the infamous saying, "fifty million Frenchmen can't be wrong."

In explaining the Court's conclusion that the contracting-out issue had to be submitted to collective negotiation, the Chief Justice stated:

> The company's decision to contract out the maintenance work did not alter the company's basic operation. The maintenance work still had to be performed in the plant. No capital investment was contemplated; the company merely replaced existing employees with those of an independent contractor to do the same work under similar conditions of employment. Therefore, to require the employer to bargain about the matter would not significantly abridge his freedom to manage the business. . . .
>
> We are thus not expanding the scope of mandatory bargaining to hold, as we do now, that the type of "contracting out" involved in this case—the replacement of employees in the existing bargaining unit with those of an independent contractor to do the same work under similar conditions of employment—is a statutory subject of collective bargaining under § 8(d).[55]

The concurring opinion in *Fibreboard* of three Supreme Court Justices (Stewart, Douglas, and Harlan) provided tremendously important guidelines for management. These cannot be adequately and accurately understood without quotation.

Bargainable Conditions of Employment Defined

The phrase "conditions of employment," the concurring opinion stated, could be construed at the extreme to apply to any subject which is insisted upon as a requisite for continued employment, that is to say, any and all bargaining demands. Nevertheless, there is only a limited category of issues which are subject to the duty to bargain collectively. Thus, the concurring opinion declared as follows:

> In common parlance, the conditions of a person's employment are most obviously the various physical dimensions of his working environment. What one's hours are to be, what amount of work is expected during these hours, what periods of relief are available, what safety practices are observed, would all seem conditions of one's employment. There are other less tangible but no less important

---

[55]Fibreboard Paper Products Corporation v. NLRB, et al., 57 LRRM 2615, (U.S. Sup. Ct. 1964).

characteristics of a person's employment which might also be deemed "conditions" — most prominently the characteristic involved in this case, the security of one's employment. On one view of the matter, it can be argued that the question whether there is to be a job is not a condition of employment; the question is not one of imposing conditions on employment, but the more fundamental question whether there is to be employment at all. However, it is clear that the Board and the courts have on numerous occasions recognized that unions [sic] demands for provisions limiting an employer's power to discharge employees are mandatorily bargainable. Thus, freedom from discriminatory discharge, seniority rights, the imposition of a compulsory retirement age, have been recognized as subjects upon which an employer must bargain, although all of these concern the very existence of the employment itself. . . .

Managerial Decisions Not Necessarily Negotiable

The concurring opinion was emphatic in referring to typical management decisions on which negotiations are not necessary.

> While employment security has thus properly been recognized in various circumstances as a condition of employment, *it surely does not follow that every decision which may affect job security is a subject of compulsory collective bargaining.* Many decisions made by management affect the job security of employees. Decisions concerning the volume and kind of advertising expenditures, product design, the manner of financing, and of sales, all may bear upon the security of the workers' jobs. Yet it is hardly conceivable that decisions so involve "conditions of employment" that they must be negotiated with the employees' bargaining representative.
>
> In many of these areas the impact of a particular management decision upon job security may be extremely indirect and uncertain, and this alone may be sufficient reason to conclude that such decisions are not "with respect to . . . conditions of employment." Yet there are other areas where decisions by management may quite clearly imperil job security, or indeed terminate employment entirely. An enterprise may decide to invest in labor-saving machinery. Another may resolve to liquidate its assets and go out of business. Nothing the Court holds today should be understood as imposing a duty to bargain collectively regarding such managerial decisions, which lie at the core of entrepreneurial control. Decisions concerning the commitment of investment capital and the basic scope of the enterprise are not in themselves primarily about conditions of employment, though the effect of the decision may be necessarily to terminate employment. [italics supplied][56]

Other Optional Subjects for Collective Bargaining

While the *Fibreboard* decision gave many clues to issues not subject to mandatory bargaining, the Court's analysis of manage-

---

[56]*Ibid.*

ment's obligations and rights was not all-inclusive. There are many other issues on which the Board and the courts have firmly indicated that bargaining is permissive rather than mandatory, and the statute itself so implies on at least one issue. A partial list of such issues, compiled by the same law firm that summarized the mandatory bargaining matters quoted earlier in this chapter, includes:

1. A clause in the labor agreement requiring a prestrike vote accepting or rejecting the employer's last offer.
2. A change in the size or membership of the employer's bargaining team.
3. A bond to indemnify the employer from failure of the union to perform, or from the loss caused by an outside union's picketing, or from pressures from customers.
4. A provision that the contract would be nullified if the number of check-off authorizations fell below 50 percent of the number of employees in the unit.
5. A clause that the union will register under a state statute that makes it easier to sue the union.
6. The withdrawal of an unfair labor practice charge against the employer.
7. A clause providing that each grievance be signed by an aggrieved employee.
8. A requirement that an employer contribute to an industry-wide association to carry out research, marketing, public relations, and allied activities.
9. A requirement that supervisors be included in the bargaining unit.[57]

The last nonmandatory issue appearing in the foregoing list is one of those where the law itself is explicit. As has been pointed out previously in this chapter, it is not illegal *per se* to include supervisors in a bargaining unit consisting primarily of rank and file employees. But bona fide supervisors are expressly excluded from coverage of the Act. Consequently, an employer cannot be compelled through negotiation to give them recognition as members of any bargaining unit if he is disposed not to do so.

Lawful and Unlawful Union Security Clauses

Although union security clauses, like check-off clauses, have been held by the Board and the courts to be obligatory subjects for collective negotiation, some variations of union security are prohibited or restricted by Taft-Hartley. Furthermore, under no circumstances does management have to *agree* to embody in a contract any of the union security arrangements that have been prevalent in American industry, with or without sanction of law.

---

[57]Seyfarth, et al., p. 108.

The principal types of union security arrangements to be found in management-labor agreements have been defined as follows:

> *Closed shop*—Arrangement between an employer and a union under which only members of the union may be hired.
>
> *Union shop*—Arrangement with a union by which employer may hire any employee, union or non-union, but the new employee must join the union within a specified time and remain a member in good standing.
>
> *Maintenance of membership*—Union-security agreement under which employees who are members of a union on specified date, or thereafter become members, are required to remain members during the term of the contract as a condition of employment.
>
> *Agency shop*—A contract requiring nonmembers of the contracting union to pay to the union a sum equal to union dues.[58]

Except for special provisions applicable to the construction industry alone, the closed shop is clearly banned by Taft-Hartley. The law imposes this ban by making it an unfair labor practice for an employer to discriminate against an applicant on account of his membership or nonmembership in a union. It is also an unfair labor practice for a union to cause an employer so to discriminate.

The special Taft-Hartley provisions that permit something akin to a closed shop in the construction industry stipulate in substance that a contractor may enter into a pre-hire union security arrangement with a construction union under the following conditions:

- The contract may be executed before the majority status of the union has been established under the Act.
- The contract may require employees to join the union seven days after their employment or after the effective date of the contract, whichever is later.
- The contract may require the employer to notify the union of job opportunities and to give the union an opportunity to refer qualified applicants.
- The agreement may specify minimum training or experience qualifications for employment or provide for priority in opportunities for employment based upon length of service with the employer, in the industry, or in the geographical area.[59]

A union shop agreement is permissible under Taft-Hartley provided the following conditions, specified in Section (8)(a)(3), are met:

---

[58]See *Glossary of Labor Terms* in PRIMER OF LABOR RELATIONS, pp. 123-137.
[59]PRIMER OF LABOR RELATIONS, p. 54.

- Membership may be required only after 30 days following the effective date of the contract or the beginning of employment, whichever is later.
- The union must admit eligible employees to membership without discrimination, although the union retains the right to make its own rules of eligibility.
- When a union-shop contract has been made under these conditions, the union may seek an employee's discharge for non-membership only when membership has been withdrawn for failure to tender an initiation fee or the periodic dues.[60]

There is, however, one exception. As stated below, Taft-Hartley enables any state to enact a law making illegal union shop agreements in establishments operating within that state.

Maintenance-of-membership clauses, frequently regarded by management as less onerous than union shop clauses, are valid under Taft-Hartley. They are, however, subject to the same requirements as union shop clauses with respect to eligibility for union membership and discharge from union membership. Admission to and discharge from union membership must be based on payment or nonpayment of dues, not discrimination.

Taft-Hartley imposes no restrictions on conditions for the embodiment of agency shop clauses in labor-management agreements.

APPLICABLE STATE STATUTES

State "Right to Work" Laws

Section 14(b) of Taft-Hartley specifies that nothing in the Act "shall be construed as authorizing effect or application of agreements requiring membership in a labor organization as a condition of employment in any State or Territory in which effect or application is prohibited by State or Territorial law." The purpose of this section is to enable state legislatures to enact so-called right-to-work laws which take precedence over the permissive features of Taft-Hartley relating to the union shop, maintenance of membership, and the agency shop. Nineteen states now have such laws, with varying prohibitions on union security clauses. The Supreme Court in a 1949 decision upheld the constitutional validity of these laws in general.[61]

Labor unions have consistently opposed the enactment of right-to-work laws and in some states have been successful in

---

[60] *Ibid.*

[61] Lincoln Federal Union v. Northwestern Iron and Metal Company, et al., 335 U.S. 525, 23 LRRM 2199 (1949).

limiting their scope or in obtaining sanction for such modifications as agency shop agreements. For example, Indiana has a right-to-work law prohibiting labor contracts simply conditioning employment on union *membership*. A union proposal for an agency shop agreement in that state was challenged by management with the result that the issue came before the National Labor Relations Board. The Indiana courts construed the agency shop as being lawful under the state right-to-work law, despite the contention of the company raising the issue that such an arrangement could violate Taft-Hartley. The Board concluded that the agency shop clause would not violate Taft-Hartley and in so doing noted that non-members who would be required by the clause to pay the equivalent of membership dues or fees could become union members if they wanted to. The Board's conclusion was sustained by the U.S. Supreme Court in 1963. The Court observed that the type of union shop contract permitted under Taft-Hartley only allows the conditioning of employment upon payment of union dues and fees, and hence the agency shop is the practical equivalent of that kind of union shop and is thus lawful in a state that does not expressly prohibit such an arrangement.[62]

When Agency Shop Is Illegal

The Florida State Constitution includes an article prohibiting any type of union security clause in labor agreements. Presumably on the theory that the agency shop is not the equivalent of the union shop because it does not require actual union membership, a Florida employer entered into an agreement with a union which provided that employees who chose *not* to join the union had to pay "as a condition of employment, an initial service fee and monthly service fees" to the union. In a suit instituted by employees, the Florida courts struck down this contract as violating the terms of the state constitution. On appeal, the case reached the U.S. Supreme Court. The Supreme Court in 1963 sustained the verdict of the Florida court, holding that the particular union security agreement under review violated the "right-to-work" provision of the Florida Constitution and that the state courts had jurisdiction to afford a remedy.

The Supreme Court's conclusion was that:

> In the light of the wording of Section 14(b) and its legislative history, we conclude that Congress in 1947 did not deprive the States of any and all power to enforce their laws restricting the execution and enforcement of union-security agreements. Since it is plain that

---

[62]NLRB v. General Motors, 373 U.S. 734, 53 LRRM 2313 (1963).

Congress left the States free to legislate in that field, we can only assume that it intended to leave unaffected the power to enforce those laws.[63]

State Labor Relations Acts

At least passing notice must be given to what have become known as "Little Wagner Acts." Immediately after the U.S. Supreme Court sustained the constitutional validity of the Wagner Act in 1937, five states enacted similar laws applicable to enterprises that their legislatures thought were not engaged in activities affecting interstate commerce and, therefore, were not covered by the federal statute.

Thirteen states, as well as Puerto Rico, now have laws of the same sort as the Taft-Hartley Act or Wagner Act on their statute books. These laws rarely concern business enterprises of any consequence, at least if such enterprises are engaged in other than purely intrastate activities. Among the enterprises considered intrastate activities are laundries, beauty parlors, places of amusement, and some restaurants. The employees of a company restaurant or cafeteria are, however, covered by the Taft-Hartley Act if the nature of the company's business is such that it is engaged in or affects interstate commerce.

There is, of course, the customary exception. If, by chance, the functioning of an establishment that might be subject to the Taft-Hartley Act is so inconsequential in relation to its effects on interstate commerce that the National Labor Relations Board declines to take jurisdiction, then the applicable state law may be invoked. It is so provided in the Landrum-Griffin Act of 1959 (summarized below). Previously, the U.S. Supreme Court had ruled in the celebrated case of *Guss* v. *Utah Labor Relations Board*[64] that no state could take jurisdiction over a matter where the federal law applied even when the Board refused to act because of such matter's inconsequentiality.

The Landrum-Griffin Act

First a word about the interrelationship between Taft-Hartley and the Landrum-Griffin Act. There is now one single, comprehensive federal statute officially designated as the Labor Management Relations Act. This is the law more commonly referred to, as it is in this book, as Taft-Hartley. The Act embraces the terms of the

---

[63]Retail Clerks International Association, Local 1625, et al. v. Schemerhorn, et al., 375 U.S. 96, 54 LRRM 2612 (1963).

[64]39 LRRM 2567 (1957).

original Wagner Act of 1935, as substantially revised by the Taft-Hartley Act of 1947 and amended—with relatively inconsequential amendments—by Public Law No. 189 (82nd Congress, October 22, 1951) and the Judicial Review Act (Public Law 85-791, 85th Congress, August 28, 1958). Second only to the Taft-Hartley amendment in importance were the amendments included in "The Labor-Management Reporting and Disclosure Act of 1959." This statute, commonly designated as the Landrum-Griffin Act, incorporated features designed to give special protection to individual members in the internal affairs of their labor organizations. Some of its provisions, however, became an integral part of Taft-Hartley and are therefore administered by the National Labor Relations Board. These provisions have been characterized by Professor Charles O. Gregory as follows:

> Title VII (of the Landrum-Griffin Act) included a miscellaneous collection of unrelated and somewhat ill-thought-out amendments to the 1947 NLRA. Some of these seem to have been included to placate elements in Congress who wished to eliminate certain union self-help techniques involving economic coercion. Others were probably included to secure the support of some of the unions not found guilty of the offensive practices revealed in the McClellan committee hearings.

Gregory previously noted in the same analysis of federal labor legislation that "The revelations following the investigations of the McClellan committee of the United States Senate during the late 1950s indicated serious maladministration of various kinds within unions." Referring to what he designated as "the 1947 statute's strictures against secondary boycotts," Gregory said:

> Actually, Section 8(b)(4) in the 1947 Act was difficult for both lawyers and laymen to comprehend. The changes introduced in Section 704 of the 1959 Act greatly increased the complexities always associated with secondary boycotts. The basic stricture against secondary boycott pressures remained much the same; but in the new Act it was unfair for a union to force an employer to make a "hot cargo" agreement in which he agreed in advance to cease doing business with, or using the goods of, another employer if the union should have a labor dispute in the future with such other employer. Also, under the new act a violation might occur regardless of what secondary employer was involved (a substantial change from the 1947 statute) and even if the secondary pressure was achieved through appeal to the secondary employer's employees singly and not in concert—apparently except where that result was achieved indirectly through lawful picketing of the primary employer.[65]

---

[65]Charles O. Gregory, *Labour Law*, ENCYCLOPAEDIA BRITANNICA, Vol. 13 (Chicago: Encyclopaedia Britannica, Inc., 1969), p. 543.

Rights of Employees as Union Members

Employers are only tangentially affected by most of the other provisions of the Landrum-Griffin Act that are administered, not by the National Labor Relations Board, but by the Office of Labor-Management and Welfare-Pension Reports (LMWP) of the U.S. Department of Labor.

In some crucial situations it may be vital for management at least to know how the law can be applied to labor organizations in their dealings with a company's own employees and in the bargaining relationships with management. The U.S. Labor Department has published a brochure entitled "Rights and Responsibilities Under the LMRDA."[66] It includes, among other data, a summary of the "Bill of Rights" established by Landrum-Griffin for employees subject to union agreements whether or not they actually belong to a union. Thus summarized, the principal rights of employees now specifically set forth in the law are:

1. Equal rights of all union members to participate in membership meetings and to vote in union elections and referenda.
2. Freedom of speech and assembly with other union members.
3. Opportunity to vote on changes in union dues and assessments either directly or through delegates to conventions at which they are so represented.
4. The right to sue a labor organization of which an employee is a member, or the officers of such organization.
5. Protection against disciplinary action by a union without advance notice and opportunity for a fair hearing.
6. The right to obtain a copy of any union agreement directly affecting the employee's own terms and conditions of employment.

Authority of International Union Over Its Locals

Personnel executives who negotiate and administer union agreements have much reason to be concerned about what authority, if any, an international union has over its locals. Reference to one leading case may perhaps suffice to indicate to management how its operations could be affected by internal disputes culminating in Landrum-Griffin litigation.

Unsanctioned Strike Resulting in Expulsion of Local Union

The case in point is *Parks et al.* v. *International Brotherhood of Electrical Workers*, decided by the U.S. Court of Appeals for the

[66]U.S. Department of Labor, Labor-Management Services Administration, RIGHTS AND RESPONSIBILITIES UNDER THE LMRDA (1967).

Fourth Circuit in 1963. The nature of the *Parks* case, as the court explained in preliminary comment, required "not only close examination of the proximately objective facts, but also of the context in which the dispute developed." In the light of the fact that the court itself considered lengthy exposition essential for an understanding of its conclusions, it might be misleading merely to summarize the decision without first citing underlying circumstances the court deemed highly relevant. (The court's decision, incidentally, ran to some 30 closely printed pages replete with more than 80 footnotes with ancillary facts, citations from academic and legal authorities, and references to other court decisions that might well provide a bibliography for a doctoral dissertation on Landrum-Griffin and federal labor legislation in general.)

A local union of the International Brotherhood of Electrical Workers and five of its members brought suits in federal court seeking to nullify the revocation of the local union's charter for defiance of the international president's orders, first, to refrain from engaging in a strike and, then, to terminate it forthwith. They charged violation of two sections of Landrum-Griffin. One was Section 101(a) of that Act, which states:

> No member of any labor organization may be fined, suspended, expelled, or otherwise disciplined except for nonpayment of dues by such organization or by any officer thereof unless such member has been (A) served with written specific charges; (B) given a reasonable time to prepare his defense; (C) afforded a full and fair hearing.

The other, Section 609, states:

> It shall be unlawful for any labor organization or any officer, agent, shop steward, or other representative of a labor organization, or any employee thereof to fine, suspend, expel, or otherwise discipline any of its members for exercising any right to which he is entitled under the provisions of this chapter.

The members of Local 28, IBEW, were primarily employed in electrical construction in the Baltimore, Md., area. The local had an agreement with the Maryland chapter of the National Electrical Contractors Association which provided for the functioning of a bipartite body called the Council of Industrial Relations. The function of the Council was to render final and binding decisions on collective bargaining issues when local negotiations reached an impasse and thus to make strikes unnecessary.

The constitution of the International Brotherhood of Electrical Workers vested extraordinary powers in its international president. (In the court decision that officer is referred to as the IP and hereafter will be designated as such.) Every local agreement of any kind must be approved by the IP. No work stoppage can be undertaken without his consent. No agreement can be abrogated without his approval. To assure enforcement of his decrees, the IP is empowered by the constitution to suspend or revoke the charter of any local union for violation thereof. Locals may appeal the IP's decisions to the executive council, which meets quarterly, and to the international convention, which meets every four years.

In the face of the foregoing controls on strike action, members of Local 28 engaged in an apparent wildcat strike during an impasse over the terms of a new wage structure. It was of short duration. After direct negotiations were resumed a new impasse was reached and the local voted to strike. It did so, according to the court's findings, after its business manager had "falsely" told the members that the IP had "given the green light." The IP was promptly notified of the strike vote by telegram. He advised the local that a strike without his consent would violate the IBEW constitution and refused his consent to a strike or other work stoppage. Following direct consultation with officers of the local, the IP again refused strike authorization and indicated that he wanted the unresolved issues to be submitted to the Council. He insisted that the strike then in progress be called off. It was not.

After consultations and hearings with a futile attempt by Local 28 to obtain an injunction to prevent the IP from requiring the local to surrender its autonomy, the IP ordered the local's charter revoked and its jurisdiction transferred to a new local union. Local 28 then made a timely appeal to the IBEW's International Executive Council. That body affirmed the revocation decision of the IP in every particular. Thereupon the two suits against the international were brought in an attempt to obtain court orders restoring the local to good standing.

The ultimate result of these suits was the complete vindication of the IP and the Executive Council of IBEW. As to the "gut issue" relating to Landrum-Griffin, the court held that revocation of the local's charter for striking in defiance of the international's hierarchy could not be set aside as unreasonable or unjust, even though the result of the revocation might constitute "discipline" of union members within the meaning of Landrum-Griffin by reason of the effects on their employment opportunities and their rights in union pension and welfare funds. In so deciding the court observed that there was no indication that rank and file members of the outcast local would be unable to preserve their memberships in the IBEW because, after the revocation of Local 28's charter, its members were offered chances to transfer to another local.[67]

ENFORCEMENT OF LABOR-MANAGEMENT AGREEMENTS

On its face Section 301(a) of the Taft-Hartley Act is clear and unambiguous. It reads:

> Suits for violation of contracts between an employer and a labor organization representing employees in an industry affecting commerce as defined by this Act, or between any such labor organizations, may be brought in any district court of the United States having jurisdiction of the parties, without respect to the amount in controversy or without regard to the citizenship of the parties.

Nevertheless, the U.S. Supreme Court has deemed it necessary to construe this section of the law in numerous cases, and in doing so it has sometimes reached diametrically opposite conclusions.

Statutory rules for enforcement of labor-management agreements, it might be presumed, are of direct concern only to legal counsel for employers. This is just not so. All management personnel having responsibility for formulating basic labor relations policy and for negotiating agreements need to keep abreast of developments relating to remedies for contract violations by their unions. Equally important are developments relating to employers' defenses in suits by individual employees or unions for alleged violation by management of contract terms. Why? Because the acceptability to management of specific kinds of no-strike and no-lockout clauses, as well as procedures for arbitration or other means of settling disputes arising over interpretation or violation of an agreement, may hinge directly on how the courts currently interpret Taft-Hartley's enforcement provisions.

To cite a truism, a contract is hardly worth the paper it's written on if it does not contain enforceable provisions against work stoppages for its entire duration. In this period of continuing inflation, employers are usually willing to agree to substantial increases in wage and fringe benefits to insure stability in labor costs and freedom from interruption of production or service operations. But how is this freedom to be attained? Of what value is a no-strike clause if union members can cripple operations by engaging in job action for higher wages or other concessions while a contract has months or years to run? What deterrents are there to such action in

---

[67]Parks, et al. v. International Brotherhood of Electrical Workers, 314 F.2d 886, 52 LRRM 2281 (4th Cir. 1963).

the way of penalties that may be imposed either on individuals or on unions for breach of contract obligations? How long a period usually elapses where there is recourse to the courts to enforce no-strike clauses before remedial action is attained? These and other questions are of vital consideration to employers in determining how to formulate contract provisions providing preventive and remedial measures.

The Supreme Court's *Boys Markets* decision, referred to below, provides partial answers to some of the questions just raised. The Court's *Vaca-Sipes* decision, also summarized below, raises, perhaps, more questions than it answers.

For personnel administrators who have confidence in the capacity of international officers of labor unions with which they negotiate to police and enforce no-strike clauses, the *Parks* case may also provide a partial answer. The Supreme Court has yet to rule on one of the tangential issues that arose in that case. The circuit court did, however, rule explicitly that Section 301 of Taft-Hartley permits federal courts to adjudicate disputes between a parent labor organization and one of its locals. In other words, that court decided it had jurisdiction to decide whether the action of IBEW International in revoking the charter of Local 28 was an interunion dispute involving violation of contractual obligations that could be resolved in a federal court.

It should be noted additionally that the landmark Supreme Court decision in the *Drake* case summarized in Chapter 8 also can have a vital bearing on management's decisions as to what contract provisions they should seek to obtain to assure compliance with antistrike clauses in their agreements.

Relationship of Norris-LaGuardia Act to Taft-Hartley

From June 1962 until June 1970, the Supreme Court had interpreted Section 301 as being subordinate to the prohibitions of Norris-LaGuardia against using the injunctive process in federal courts as a remedy for breaches of collective bargaining agreements. The Court's firm mandate on this issue was handed down in the tremendously important case of *Sinclair Refining Company* v. *Atkinson et al.*, decided in 1962. But the Court expressly reversed its decision in that case by its landmark decision in *Boys Markets, Inc.* v. *Retail Clerks*, issued June 1, 1970.

The 1962 *Sinclair* decision held that when Congress, through Section 301 of Taft-Hartley, gave the federal courts jurisdiction of suits alleging violation of labor agreements, it did not implicitly repeal Section 4 of the pre-existing Norris-LaGuardia Act of 1932. With certain limited exceptions regarded by the Supreme Court as immaterial, the Court ruled that Norris-LaGuardia barred federal courts from issuing injunctions "in any case involving or growing out of *any labor dispute.*" (Italics supplied.) Thus, the Sinclair Company could not get immediate relief through the courts to put an end to the extra-contractual strikes that had developed into a critical labor situation.

Even though the Supreme Court has now decided that the injunctive relief of the sort that the Sinclair Company was denied in 1962 henceforth could be available in like situations, the developments that led to its futile appeal to the courts are still of much significance.

The company and the union had negotiated and ratified a contract which provided for final and binding arbitration of "any difference regarding wages, hours or working conditions between the parties hereto or between the employer and an employee covered by this working agreement which might arise within any plant or any region of operations." The contract also contained a provision by which the union agreed that "There should be no slow-downs for any reason whatsoever" and "no strikes or work stoppages . . . for any cause which is or may be the subject of a grievance." Notwithstanding these promises, the Supreme Court noted in its decision, the company charged that members of the union over a period of some 19 months had engaged in work stoppages and strikes on nine separate occasions, each of which grew out of a grievance "which could have been submitted to arbitration under the contract and therefore fell squarely within the union's promises not to strike." The company contended in seeking injunctive relief both preliminarily and permanently that the pattern of repeated violations of the contract indicated disregard by the union for its obligations under the contract and the probability of the union's continued subversion of the contract clauses forbidding strikes over grievances.

The company lost its case for an injunction in a federal district court, a federal court of appeals, and finally in the Supreme Court. Holding that the case did indeed involve "a labor dispute" within the meaning of the Norris-LaGuardia Act, the Supreme Court stated that the company's own complaint showed "quite plainly that each of the alleged nine work stoppages and strikes arose out of a controversy which was well within this definition." Hence, no injunction could be obtained as a remedy for the breaches of the collective agreement. The only remedy under Taft-Hartley was the right of the company as a private party to sue the union in federal district court for damages, or to seek a court order requiring the union to proceed to arbitration, or, in such a suit, to seek to persuade the court to invoke any of the rest of the arsenal of weapons at the court's disposal in private litigation.[68]

Right to Seek Injunction for Breach of Contract

In the light of the Supreme Court's 1970 *Boys Markets* decision reversing the conclusion it had reached in the *Sinclair* case, employers now have the opportunity to seek an injunction against a union *or* to sue a union in federal court for breach of contract. But the option to seek an injunction is available, the Court ruled, only *if* the grievance precipitating the strike was subject to arbitration under the contract, *and if* the employer was ready to proceed with arbitration, *and if* the employer suffered irreparable injury by reason of the union's violation of its no-strike commitment.

The material facts in the *Boys Markets* situation closely paralleled those in the *Sinclair* case. The company had obtained a restraining order in a California state court against a union that pulled a strike when the company did not accede to the union's demand that certain work done by non-unit employees be redone by unit personnel. Upon petition of the union, a federal court, following the *Sinclair* doctrine, reversed the grant of the state court. To upset the federal court action the Supreme Court had in effect to reverse itself. That was exactly what it did. Mr. Justice Black in a dissenting opinion pointed out that nothing in Norris-LaGuardia or in Taft-Hartley had been changed since the *Sinclair* decision. He made a further acerbic comment, "Nothing has changed, in fact, except the membership of the Court and the personal views of one Justice."[69]

Boys Markets Aftermath

At least three federal appellate court decisions that have been handed down after *Boys Markets* and that relate to somewhat parallel issues seem to have continuing significance. One of these, *Buffalo Forge Co.* v. *United Steelworkers*,[70] originated in the company's suit in a federal district court as a result of a work stoppage instigated by two of the union's locals representing production and

---

[68]Sinclair Refining Company v. Atkinson, et al., 370 U.S. 195, 50 LRRM 2420 (1962).
[69]Boys Markets, Inc. v. Retail Clerks, 398 U.S. 235, 74 LRRM 2257 (1970).
[70]Buffalo Forge Co. v. Steelworkers, 517 F.2d 1207, 89 LRRM 2303 (2d Cir. 1975), 428 U.S. 397 (1976).

maintenance (P&M) employees in support of a strike called by another local union (and two others not affiliated with the Steelworkers) during an impasse in negotiations for their first collective bargaining agreement. These locals had just been certified to represent office and clerical-technical (O&T) employees at the same three plant locations where two Steelworkers' locals were parties to contracts applicable to production and maintenance employees.

In addition to seeking damages, the company petitioned the district court to issue a temporary restraining order and a preliminary injunction against the P&M locals' work stoppage and an order "compelling the parties to submit any 'underlying dispute' to the contractual grievance and arbitration procedures." As summarized in the syllabus of the ultimate U.S. Supreme Court decision issued nearly a year and a half later in July 1976, the district court denied the temporary restraining order and found that the P&M work stoppage was not the result of the specific refusal to cross the O&T picket line:

> the District Court concluded that the P&M employees were engaged in a sympathy action in support of the striking O&T employees. The District Court then held itself forbidden to issue an injunction by §4 of the Norris-LaGuardia Act because the P&M employees' strike was not over an "arbitrable grievance" and hence was not within the "narrow" exception to the Norris-LaGuardia Act established in *Boys Markets, Inc.* . . .

After granting the company's petition for a writ of certiorari — granted because the federal appellate courts were divided on the question of enjoining a sympathy strike of the same nature — the Supreme Court affirmed the judgment of the Second Circuit Court. The Court stated:

> (a) The strike was not over any dispute between respondents and petitioner that was even remotely subject to the arbitration provisions of the collective-bargaining contract, but was a sympathy strike in support of sister unions negotiating with petitioner with neither the purpose nor the effect of denying or evading an obligation to arbitrate or depriving petitioner of its bargain. *Boys Market supra*, distinguished.
>
> (b) Nor was an injunction authorized solely because it was alleged that the sympathy strike violated the no-strike clause, since although a §301 suit may be brought against strikes that breach collective-bargaining contracts, this does not mean that federal courts may enjoin contract violations despite the Norris-LaGuardia Act.
>
> (c) While the issue whether the sympathy strike violated the no-strike clause was arbitrable, it does not follow that the District Court was empowered not only to order arbitration but also to enjoin the strike pending the arbitrator's decision, since if an injunction could

so issue a court could enjoin any alleged breach of a collective-bargaining contract pending the exhaustion of the applicable grievance and arbitration procedures, thus cutting deeply into the Norris-LaGuardia Act's policy and making courts potential participants in a wide range of arbitrable disputes under many collective-bargaining contracts, not just for the purpose of enforcing promises to arbitrate, but for the purpose of preliminarily dealing with the factual and interpretative issues that are subjects for the arbitrator.

A second case, involving the scope of the *Boys Markets* high court decision, has been characterized as an expansion and clarification of that decision. The members of a local of the United Mine Workers union with which Inland Steel Company had an agreement had refused to cross picket lines set up by another union at one of the company's facilities. The applicable agreement contained provisions requiring submission to arbitration of issues arising out of "any local trouble of any kind." The appellate court ruled that the question of whether the union's agreement allowed its members to honor the picket line of another union was arbitrable. Hence, a federal district court had jurisdiction to enjoin the work stoppage.[71]

The third case went to much greater lengths in its interpretation of the Supreme Court's "teachings" through *Boys Markets*. A summary of this 1976 case follows:

> After Local 13,744 of the Allied and Technical Workers Union struck in violation of a no-strike provision in its contract with the Dow Chemical Company at Allyn's Point, Conn., the company cancelled its collective bargaining contract, discharged the striking employees, and withdrew its recognition of the union. A divided three-member panel of NLRB upheld the employer's post-strike actions on the grounds that the strike was not a protest of a 'serious' unfair labor practice.
>
> The appeals court refuse[d] to sanction the employer's post-strike conduct and remand[ed] the case to the Board to be considered in light of 'recent trends in labor policy.' The court [found] that even though a Boys Markets injunction was not available to the employer to compel arbitration, the company had both legal and contractual remedies available to it short of contract termination.

This decision was rendered by the Third Circuit Court of Appeals. Among other things, the court declared that a strike in breach of a contract does not automatically give management the right to terminate the contract and that employers should be warned by its decision that they must take certain precautions before resorting to self-help when faced with a no-strike clause.[72]

---

[71]Inland Steel v. Local 1545, UMW, 505 F.2d 293 (7th Cir. 1974).
[72]DAILY LAB. REP. (BNA), No. 29, Feb. 3, 1976, pp. 1-2.

Only the basic facts rather than the meaning of applicable law were in dispute when this case reached the circuit court. These facts were briefly summarized by the court as follows:

> Prior to May 1971, 16 of the 19 latex department employees worked on a '7 and 2' shift — seven days on the job, then two days off; three others worked a regular five-day week. After the company lost a large customer, with a resulting sales drop, it decided to institute a five-day work week for all latex department employees. The company estimated that as a consequence, the 16 affected employees would earn approximately $570 less annually due to the reduction in hours worked, the elimination of overtime and the loss of weekend and holiday premiums. (The union estimated that each affected employee would lose about $1,500 – $2,000 annually.) The union protested the company's proposed action, contending that the company could not implement the change without first bargaining.
>
> The company answered that under the labor contract's management-rights clause, it could make the change without bargaining.
>
> The collective bargaining agreement in effect at the time contained a no-strike, no-lockout provision which reserved to the union a limited right to strike. The union could not strike, however, unless and until three pre-conditions had been satisfied: first a five-step grievance procedure had to be exhausted; second a written request to proceed to arbitration had to be filed within 30 days of the completion of the five steps; third, the arbitration process had to be completed or refused by the company. . . . The parties agree that they had completed the first four steps of the grievance procedure.

Before the end of the prescribed limit in which the company could accept or reject arbitration, what began as a seemingly spontaneous walkout soon turned into a plantwide strike. Further development followed in short order, including:

1. Letters by the company beseeching the employees to discontinue the "unlawful strike"
2. Notice to the employees that the company would begin to hire replacements
3. Rescission of the current agreement by the company
4. Termination of the striking employees
5. Petition by a majority of the employees notifying the company that they no longer wished representation by the union.
6. Notice by the company to the union that it would no longer be recognized as the bargaining agent
7. Filing by the union of unfair labor practice charges against the company.

The resultant Board proceedings produced a split decision with these findings by the Board's majority members:

1. By unilaterally scheduling and announcing shift changes that started the controversy, the company had violated Section 8(a)(1) and 8(a)(5) of Taft-Hartley.[73]

2. Since the union had prior to this time violated the no-strike clause, the company had not broken the law by rescinding the agreement.

3. Firing the striking employees was not unlawful, and they had lost their right to reinstatement because they had taken part in an unprotected strike.

4. By withdrawing recognition from the union the company would not violate the law since the employee terminations were legal.

Perhaps in the expectation that its review and partial reversal of the Board's decision would become regarded as a landmark decision, the circuit court went to great pains to present the facts and the law. With respect to the facts the court dramatically declared:

> Here first the union and then the company resorted to the tooth and claw of industrial warfare, rather than availing themselves of procedures provided in their collective bargaining agreement and encouraged by the congressionally mandated national labor policy. The union failed to complete the grievance procedure and to invoke arbitration; instead it struck to protest what it considered to be an unfair labor practice. The company disdained the available arbitral forum and ultimately resorted to rescission of the contract, to discharge of the employees and to termination of the collective bargaining relationship. A more primitive, abrasive and disrupting example of labor-management relations is difficult to imagine. Indeed the avoidance of such traumatic ruptures in industrial relations is the precise aim of the national labor policy. Yet the Board and the intervenor company would have us hold that the national labor policy will sanction the company's ultimate actions.

Not so, said the circuit court. Rather, not entirely so. In summarizing the decision the court declared that "the Board had erred in reasoning that the strike was an unprotected, material breach of the contract because the company's initial unfair labor practice was 'non-serious.' "

The court, therefore, did not disturb the Board's finding of a Taft-Hartley action in unilaterally changing work schedules, but remanded for reconsideration by the Board all the other aspects of the proceedings. Some of the dicta in this possibly landmark decision might serve as future guidelines to companies and unions faced with the sort of problems that confronted Dow's management and

---

[73]Section 8(a)(1) prohibits employer interference with employees' bargaining rights. Section 8(a)(5) prohibits employers from refusing to bargain (with some specified exceptions).

the union whose contract it rescinded. Certainly informative and possibly useful passages are quoted below.

> The *Boys Markets* Court characterized its opinion as "a narrow one"; the Court dealt "only with the situation in which a collective-bargaining contract contains a mandatory grievance adjustment or arbitration procedure," 398 U.S. at 253, and an explicit no-strike clause. The more recent *Gateway Coal Co. v. UMW* . . . indicates that, although the *Boys Markets* holding may have been narrow, its impact is to be far greater. Specifically, the *Gateway* Court held that "injunctive relief also may be granted on the basis of an implied undertaking not to strike", as well as a specific no-strike clause, 414 U.S. at 381. Second, the Court held that this court had erred in limiting the presumption of arbitrability to disputes over economic matters; strikes precipitated by safety disputes also could be enjoined. . . .
>
> As we understand these recent Supreme Court teachings, the basic tenets of contemporary labor policy may be summarized as follows:
>
> > (a) Today's interdependent and technologically advanced economy dictates that labor-management relations be as peaceful as possible. . . .
> >
> > (b) Where labor and management agree on a forum for the peaceful resolution of disputes, that agreement should be honored and may be enforced by an injunction, mandating resort to that forum. . . .
> >
> > (c) Arbitration is a favored alternative forum for dispute resolution . . . *Gateway, Sinclair Refining Co. v. Atkinson* . . . (Brennan, J., dissenting) ("a kingpin of federal labor policy"). . . .
> >
> > (d) Congressional emphasis in labor legislation has shifted "from protection of the nascent labor movement to the encouragement of collective bargaining and to administrative techniques for the peaceful resolution of industrial disputes."[74]

Personnel administrators who are laymen may find difficulty in fully fathoming the peregrinations of the NLRB and the courts in the aftermath of *Boys Markets*. They might enlarge their knowledge of the law and its recent implications by close reading of a learned article with the improbable title, "Wildcat Strikes and Minority Concerted Activity—Discipline, Damage Suits and Injunctions." This article, written by a practicing attorney with unquestioned expertise in labor relations, points to the need for further legislation rather than judicial clarification of the present law. In any event, the cases cited therein should be of particular concern to management's labor relations counsel. The article concludes as follows:

---

[74]DAILY LAB. REP., pp. D-4–D-5.

The decisions of the Supreme Court in *Sinclair v. Atkinson* left in their wake a continuing conflict — the conflict between the encouragement of the collective bargaining and arbitration processes and the desirability of a uniform national labor policy. Although this conflict has to some extent been resolved by *Boys Markets,* providing some measure of accommodation between Taft-Hartley and Norris-LaGuardia, the accommodation is incomplete and other problems have been created. The immediate establishment of some method of accountability with respect both to irresponsible union leadership and real dissident minorities is essential to the continuing efficacy of our free collective bargaining system.

Either unions must be held strictly to, and perhaps as guarantors of, the no-strike contract commitment, or those individuals actually engaged in a wildcat strike in breach of contract must be held accountable. Perhaps some combination of these alternatives may be the solution.[75]

Management Options for Curbing Wildcat Strikes

The Supreme Court decisions in *Sinclair* and *Boys Markets* did not affect management's rights to utilize methods other than federal injunctions or law suits as deterrents to wildcat strikes.

Discipline of Strike Leaders

One weapon, always available to management, is the right to discipline or discharge union leaders or even rank and file employees who have instigated and/or participated in a walkout in violation of the terms of a current agreement. To be sure, when management imposes a penalty on employees for such tactics, it may have to defend its action in arbitration proceedings and try to convince the arbitrator not only that the employee's conduct was impermissible but that the penalty imposed was justifiable. Disciplinary penalties against union leaders, moreover, are in many instances subject to review and modification by the National Labor Relations Board if the dismissal results from retaliation against a "claimed" unfair labor practice. (See *Mastro Plastics* case above.)

Restraining Order Through Arbitration

It may even be possible to persuade an arbitrator to issue a restraining order against a union holding a contract that bans work stoppages while it is still in effect. (See *Kheel* decision in brewery case summarized in Chapter 8.)

---

[75]Evan J. Spelfogel, LABOR LAW JOURNAL, Sept. 1973. Copyright © 1973, Commerce Clearing House, Inc., Chicago, Ill.

Restraining Order Against Individual Employees

Another option is available to management in many states. This can involve seeking an injunction in a state court against individual employees covered by a contract with a no-strike clause who nonetheless participate in a walkout and by picketing or other means induce fellow employees to join with them. Such an injunction was sought in the State of Michigan in 1968 by a company confronted with a wildcat work stoppage that brought about complete cessation of its plant operations. While no permanent injunction was issued, a Michigan county circuit court granted a preliminary restraining order. The initiation of contempt proceedings against the employees violating it quickly brought the stoppage to an end.

Since the case in point was decided only by the first court of record in Michigan and did not reach an appellate court, no reference to the proceedings appears in any law reporting service or legal periodical.[76] Among the states where similar proceedings have been sanctioned by state courts are Connecticut, Kentucky, Missouri, New York, Ohio, Oregon, Washington, and Wisconsin.

Individual Employee's Right to Sue Employer
Under Taft-Hartley

An employee charging wrongful discharge or other disciplinary action in violation of a union agreement applicable to him can sue his employer for damages or other remedies. If, however, the union contract allegedly violated by the employer provides for grievance arbitration and the union arbitrarily and without just cause refuses to take the employee's case to arbitration, the employer can successfully defend the lawsuit if he can demonstrate the union's refusal to arbitrate prevented the employee from exhausting his other statutory remedies before proceeding against the employer.

The foregoing is a greatly oversimplified statement of the complex issues decided by the Supreme Court in its landmark decision in *Vaca* v. *Sipes* in 1967. In addition to an exhaustive majority opinion, there was an equally extensive concurring opinion subscribed to by three Justices and a caustic minority opinion by Mr. Justice Black.

---

[76]Information regarding the legal techniques used, the precedents cited, and the results obtained is available only by communicating with the law firms representing the company in this matter (Electric Products Company, Niles, Mich.). The law firms are Seyfarth, Shaw, Fairweather, and Geraldson, Chicago, Ill., and White, Klute, and White, Niles, Mich.

The germinal legal issue centered on a discharged employee's right to sue his union in a Missouri State Court for damages due to his discharge on the grounds that the union had arbitrarily and without just cause refused to process under arbitration a grievance challenging the propriety of his discharge. His services had been terminated by the company on the basis of physical unfitness to perform the heavy work duties of the job he had held in a packing plant. Following a period of hospitalization and treatment for high blood pressure, he was rejected for reinstatement by a company doctor. He obtained from his personal physician a statement of fitness, and armed with this statement he filed a grievance, seeking return to his former job. The union diligently pursued the grievance up to the last step before arbitration. The union went so far as to send the man to a new doctor at union expense, hoping to obtain better medical evidence to justify resort to arbitration. When the union's executive board determined that such medical evidence did not support the grievant's claim of physical fitness, it voted not to arbitrate the matter. It was then that the employee sued the union in a state court and after a jury trial was awarded $7,000 compensatory and $3,300 punitive damages. Upon appeal the Missouri Supreme Court affirmed the jury's verdict.

The U.S. Supreme Court reversed the Missouri court's decision, not on the grounds of lack of jurisdiction but rather improper interpretation of Taft-Hartley. Among the most significant findings and conclusions of the Court were the following:

(1) Sections 301 and 303 of Taft-Hartley permit anyone injured by a violation of that law by an employer or a union to recover damages in a federal court or in a state court, provided any such court adheres to the provisions of the federal statute.

(2) An aggrieved employee, thinking he has been wrongfully discharged in violation of the agreement by which he is covered, may sue his employer in a state court and get a jury to assess damages if his discharge is determined to be in violation of the applicable labor agreement.

(3) The aggrieved employee may sue either his employer or his union or both. By implication, employees alleging wrong action affecting their job status on such a matter as promotion, wage rates, benefits, overtime rates, etc., can get a jury trial to determine the remedy awardable if and when the ground for such a lawsuit is alleged to be for breach of contract.

(4) On the record of the trial in the Missouri Supreme Court there was not sufficient evidence to justify the holding as a matter of federal law that the union had breached its duty of fair representation of the employee through the applicable grievance procedure. "A breach of the statutory duty of fair representation occurs only when a union's conduct toward a member of a collective bargaining unit is arbitrary, discriminatory, or in bad faith."

(5) A union does not breach its duty of fair representation merely by dropping, short of arbitration, an employee's grievance alleging discharge in violation of the contract. When a union decides that the evidence to support a grievance is insufficient to sustain it in arbitration, the union can legally do so, for an employee has no absolute right to have his grievance arbitrated under a collective bargaining contract. A breach of the union's duty of fair representation is not established even though there might be subsequent proof that the employee's grievance is meritorious.

(6) Therefore, unless an employer can prove in court that a union's refusal to arbitrate constituted a breach of its duty of fair representation, and thus involved an unfair labor practice, an employer's defense in an employee's suit for unlawful discharge must involve proof that he had contractual justification for the discharge. That is to say, the employer has to prove that the discharge was on the merits and not in violation of any terms of the applicable labor agreement.[77]

Employers and unions are still baffled by the implications expressed in all three opinions in *Vaca* v. *Sipes*. Some personnel administrators and their legal counsel foresee the necessity for drastic changes in company policies relating to discharge and discipline, and for recasting the grievance machinery under union contracts unless the Supreme Court modifies or at least further clarifies its *Vaca-Sipes* dicta. In any event, that decision has pointed to the need for serious consideration of the legal implications and complications arising under arbitration proceedings that are the subject of Chapter 8.

Current Styles in Law Suits

To keep abreast of current clothing fashions, the daily newspapers provide the only practicable guidance. Much the same could

---

[77]Vaca v. Sipes, 385 U.S. 895, 64 LRRM 2369 (1967).

be said about what goes on in the courts, in the NLRB, in the arbitrating profession, and in Congress. The judgments of unions as well as those of management are subject to critical review in all four quarters.

How unsure management and labor can be in striving for full compliance with their rights and obligations under Taft-Hartley can be well illustrated by reading some of the implications of a 1976 Supreme Court decision. The case in point is officially known as *Hines et al.* v. *Anchor Motor Freight, Inc., et al.* The "et als" on both sides could conceivably include almost every corporate management and almost every major union hierarchy.

The case began in 1967 when several truck drivers were discharged by their firm, Anchor Motor Freight, Inc. It presumably ended in March 1976 when in a 6-2 decision the Supreme Court held that three of the litigants who were still alive were entitled to "an appropriate remedy against the employer as well as the union."

The truck drivers, designated by the court as the petitioners, were discharged without just cause, so their case is of considerable interest. The contract of the Teamsters' Union under which the drivers worked forbade discharges without just cause. The management believed them to have been dishonest—specifically, to have chiselled on their company expense accounts. When the drivers were on the road overnight they were entitled to reimbursement for the cost of lodging. The motel bills they presented for overnight stays, the company contended, were for amounts in excess of the actual charges. At a pre-arbitration grievance meeting with union representatives the management presented documentary evidence purporting to show that inflated receipts for bills due had been furnished by a motel to its overnight guests. The union representatives asserted the drivers' innocence and opposed the discharges. No solution was reached other than an agreement to have the drivers' grievance presented to a joint area arbitration committee. Meanwhile they were temporarily reinstated.

In due course there was a hearing before the joint area arbitration committee. While the drivers denied any dishonesty, neither they nor their union presented any evidence contradicting documents produced by the company that indicated overcharging for motel accomodations. The discharges were sustained by the arbitration committee. A request for a rehearing based on a statement by the motel owner as to possible culpability of a registration clerk was unanimously denied by the committee.

As the Supreme Court noted, there were later indications that a motel clerk was in fact the culprit. These indications were the basis of a suit filed against the company and the union charged breach of contract for improper causes of discharge.

What the Supreme Court considered of material significance was the allegation by the claimants that the motel clerk was the culprit and that the falsity of the charges against the dischargees could have been discovered with a minimum of investigation: Further, that the union had made no effort to ascertain the truth. The union was accused of having thereby violated its duty of fair representation "by arbitrarily and in bad faith depriving petitioners of their employment and permitting their discharge without sufficient proof." In pretrial discovery proceedings a deposition of the motel clerk was produced revealing that it was he who had falsified the records and had pocketed the difference between the sums shown on the receipts and the registration cards.

When the case came to the federal district court for trial, motions for summary judgment filed by the company and the union were granted on the ground that the decision of the arbitration committee was final and binding on the employees and for failure to show facts comprising bad faith, "arbitrariness or perfunctoriness" on the part of the union. The circuit court of appeals thought differently. It concluded that there had been sufficient facts from which bad faith or arbitrary conduct could be inferred by the trier of fact and that petitioners should have been afforded an opportunity to prove their charges. Nevertheless, the court of appeals affirmed the judgment in favor of the company and the union.

Earlier the observation was made that footnotes to a court's decision may be more revelatory of basic issues than the body of the text. The rationale underlying the dischargees' claims of inadequate representation in the arbitration proceedings was disclosed in a footnote to the Supreme Court's decision. This footnote is reproduced in full below.

As summarized by the court of appeals, the allegations in the case

> consist of the motel clerk's admission, made a year after the discharge was upheld in arbitration, that he, not plaintiffs, pocketed the money; the claim of the union's failure to investigate the motel clerk's original story implicating plaintiffs despite their requests; the account of the union officials' assurances to plaintiffs that 'they had nothing to worry about' and 'that there was no need for them to investigate'; the contention that no exculpatory evidence was presented at the hearing; and the assertion that there existed political antagonism between local union officials and plaintiffs because of a wildcat strike led by some of the plaintiffs and a dispute over the appointment of a steward, resulting in denunciation of plaintiffs as 'hillbillies' by Angelo, the union president.

The Supreme Court's own findings were summarized succinctly in the "syllabus" accompanying its decision. These findings and conclusions of law were:

(a) A union's breach of duty relieves the employee of an express or implied requirement that disputes be settled through contractual procedures and, if it seriously undermines the integrity of the arbitral process, also removes the bar of the finality provision of the contract.

(b) Respondent employer, if the charges of dishonesty were in error, played its part in precipitating the dispute, and though the employer may not have knowingly or negligently relied on false evidence in discharging petitioners and may have prevailed before the arbitration committee after presenting its case by fair procedures, petitioners should not be foreclosed from the Section 301 remedy otherwise available against the employer if the contractual processes have been seriously flawed by the union's breach of its duty.

(c) While the grievance processes cannot be expected to be error-free, enforcement of the finality provision where the arbitrator has erred is conditioned upon the union's having satisfied its statutory duty fairly to represent the employees in connection with arbitration proceedings; otherwise, a wrongfully discharged employee would be left without a job and a fair opportunity to secure an adequate remedy.

Consequently, the Court ruled:

Petitioners, if they prove an erroneous discharge and the union's breach of duty tainting the decision of the joint committee, are entitled to an appropriate remedy against the employer as well as the union. It was error to affirm the District Court's final disposition of petitioners' action against Anchor.[78]

Sympathetic Suggestions for Management

Some NLRB rulings and the appellate court decisions upholding, modifying, or reversing them have gone in entirely opposite directions in recent years. Employers' experiences in seeking full compliance with Taft-Hartley and related statutes are somewhat analogous to their experiences in complying with workers' compensation laws. To repeat Professor Arthur Larson's pungent comment about that aggregation of state statutes: "Compensation law is so prolific that sooner or later it provides an actual case to fill any gap."

Hence, instead of giving advice we shall offer sympathetic suggestions to employers currently wrestling with problems of union-management relations that ultimately may have to be resolved through litigation.

---

[78]Hines, et al. v. Anchor Motor Freight, Inc., et al., 424 U.S. 554 (1976).

True, the United States Supreme Court has handed down many landmark decisions construing what is now officially designated as the Labor Management Relations Act of 1947. That statute has been amended several times, most importantly by inclusion of the Labor-Management Reporting and Disclosure Act of 1959 (Landrum-Griffin). Many crucial decisions have been consistently sustained in the 40-year period since the constitutional validity of the original Wagner Act was upheld. But a lot have been struck down.

The late Justice Black made this point perfectly clear with an acerbic comment in his dissenting opinion in the noteworthy *Boys Markets* case of 1970. That case necessitated judicial interpretation of provisions in both Taft-Hartley and Norris-LaGuardia. And the Supreme Court, as explained earlier in this chapter, partially reversed its prior interpretations of both these statutes. Justice Black observed that nothing in these two statutes had been changed by congressional action since the *Sinclair* decision of 1962, except, as he noted caustically, the Court membership and the opinion of one Justice, Mr. Justice Stewart.

It is true that one Justice had changed his mind. In his concurring opinion in *Boys Markets,* Mr. Justice Stewart explained why with remarkable candor:

> When *Sinclair* v. *Atkinson* was decided in 1962, I subscribed to the opinion of the Court. Before six years had passed I had reached the conclusion that the *Sinclair* holding should be reconsidered and said so in *Avco* v. *Aero Lodge* [67 LRRM 2881]. Today I join the Court in concluding that *Sinclair* was erroneously decided and that subsequent events have undermined its continuing validity. . . .
>
> In these circumstances the temptation is strong to embark upon a lengthy personal *apologia*. But . . . [a]n aphorism of Mr. Justice Frankfurter provides me refuge: "Wisdom too often never comes, and so one ought not to reject it merely because it comes late."

Given the shifting views of the courts and agencies, personnel administrators and their legal counsel should examine in depth early and recent decisions of appellate court judges and members of the National Labor Relations Board and of all federal public servants in the judicial system and independent agencies. Those appointed for limited five-year terms to membership on the NLRB are probably least likely to reverse themselves in their official rulings. More than a cursory examination of Board decisions over the past 15 years supports this conclusion. Special insight is obtainable from scrutinizing the Board's frequent split decisions. These may provide some sort of guideline for employers uncertain as to what the NLRB might do next in case they engage in tactics that border on the illegal.

If this suggestion seems cynical or worse, it must be noted that in the thousands of cases decided by the Board in the more than 40 years of its operations, countless numbers of complaints of unfair labor practices by both unions and management have been dismissed, even though in many cases there were factual bases for the complaints.

Beleaguered Management and Union

No review of management's problems in endeavoring to comply with NLRB and court decisions interpreting Taft-Hartley could be considered to be authoritative without reference to the monumental case history of the J. P. Stevens Company. It is the second largest textile manufacturing company in the U.S. It has more than 45,000 employees in more than 80 plants, nearly all of them in southern states. The Stevens Company and the principal union that vainly thus far has attempted to negotiate collective bargaining agreements in any of its plants, i.e., the Amalgamated Clothing and Textile Workers Union (AFL-CIO), have been embroiled in litigation for more than the last decade. As of 1978 it appeared to some observers that Stevens might still be winning its war against unionization, even though it had lost most of its battles before the NLRB and the appellate courts.

At the outset of this discussion, the authors disclaim any intent to present value judgments of their view. Instead they are disposed here to cite authoritative journalistic commentators on the labor scene, whether or not any of them have special axes to grind, pro or con.

Beyond doubt one of the most authoritative and disinterested commentators is A.H. Raskin of the *New York Times*, who had covered labor relations issues for that newspaper during the past 36 years. Commenting on developments in the Stevens-Union-NLRB conflict in early 1977, Raskin wrote that since 1963 Stevens had been battling unionization and had been the subject of 15 Labor Board citations for violation of the Taft-Hartley Act for refusal to bargain or intimidating or dismissing employees. Up to early 1977 the company had lost 11 appeals in federal courts and had paid out over a million and a quarter dollars in back wages to workers whose union rights had, it was asserted, been violated. For its part, management contended that union loss of 14 elections in Stevens' southern plants was " 'irrefutable evidence' " that most of the company's

44,000 employees rejected the union. Stevens' chairman admitted to " 'occasional' " misjudgments and honest misinterpretations of labor law, but averred that the company never condoned law violations by employees.[79]

In a paid advertisement in the *New York Times* Albert Shanker, president of the United Federation of Teachers, attacked Stevens' labor relations policies and practices, citing examples of alleged violations of labor law, and vowed to continue the boycott of Stevens' products.[80] In connection with this boycott, it may be stated that there is patently nothing illegal per se about the 1977 campaign to boycott Stevens' products. By the same token, it seems essential to point out that nothing in the National Labor Relations Act or any other statute compels a company to do more than bargain at arm's length with a union properly certified as an exclusive bargaining agent for an appropriate group of employees. The law doesn't compel an employer to welcome a union into negotiation proceedings. The law doesn't prevent an employer from exercising the inherent right of free speech to inform his employees why he thinks it is in their best interest not to become affiliated with a union. There is of course the limitation that "free speech" cannot be reduced to the level of coercive statements or promises of rewards to those employees failing to exercise their rights of self-organization.

Incomplete as the case study of the Stevens-union entanglements must necessarily be, managements seeking to avoid the pitfalls into which the company apparently has fallen can profit by exploration with their legal counsel of some of the step-by-step Board and court decisions that have plagued Stevens management for more than a decade.

One set of cases involved such intricate issues that even an elementary understanding of the outcome can be reached only by a rather legalistic summary such as that presented below. The following summary is quoted from a survey of certain cases declared by the NLRB to constitute flagrant violations.

> In five cases involving [J. P. Stevens and Company] and what the NLRB called "massive and deliberate" unfair labor practices, the Board devised remedies that went beyond the usual reinstatement, back-pay and notice-posting order. In the first case, the Board ordered the company to take this additional action: (1) mail to each of its employees in each of its North and South Carolina plants, not just those involved in the case, a copy of the cease and desist order,

[79]NEW YORK TIMES, March 2, 1977, pp. D-1, D-5.
[80]*Ibid.*, Feb. 27, 1977, p. E-9.

which was to be signed by a company official; (2) convene working time meetings of employees in the various departments of all the plants and have a company official read the notice to the assembled employees; (3) give the union reasonable access to plant bulletin boards for a period of one year. In its second decision, the Board added the requirement that the company supply the union with the names and addresses of all employees in the two states. In its orders in Stevens III and IV the Board modified the public reading requirement to permit the company to have the order read by a Board rather than a company official. The names-and-addresses requirement was not in the Stevens III order but it was in the Stevens IV order. The Stevens V order was the same as in Stevens IV.

In a split decision a majority of a three-judge panel of the U.S. Court of Appeals at Richmond enforced parts of the orders in Stevens III and IV and modified other parts. The parts enforced in full were those requiring the posting of appropriate notices in all the company's North and South Carolina plants for sixty days, mailing a copy of the notice to each employee, giving the union reasonable access to the company's bulletin boards for a period of one year, and having a company official or Board agent read the notice to employees during working time in the plants in which the violations were found. The names-and-addresses requirement was modified to limit it to employees in the three plants involved in Stevens IV. . . . The Board's order in J.P. Stevens V, which was the same as the order in Stevens IV, was enforced by the U.S. Court of Appeals at New Orleans.[81]

As for the orders I and II, the union was successful in having the management's appeals reviewed by the Second Circuit Court of Appeals in New York where the company had its principal headquarters. Again to quote from the Stevens survey:

In reviewing the Board's decision on the first case the New York Court went along with the notice-posting and notice-mailing requirement of the order. But because of the "element of humiliation" involved in the public-reading provision, the court modified the order to require reading of the order only in the plants in which unfair labor practices were found to have been committed and to give the company the alternative of having the notice read by a representative of the Board rather than a company official. The court also refused to enforce the part of the order in the first case that required the company to give the union "reasonable access to the plant bulletin boards," stating that the Board did not establish need for such a provision. The order as thus modified was denied review by the Supreme Court. In reviewing the order in the second case, the court approved the provision requiring the company to give the

[81]MAJOR LABOR LAW PRINCIPLES ESTABLISHED BY THE NLRB AND THE COURTS, DECEMBER 1964—DECEMBER 1975 (Washington: The Bureau of National Affairs, Inc., 1976), pp. 138-139.

union "reasonable" access to the bulletin boards, but it would not approve the names-and-addresses requirement.[82]

At this point an appropriate query from our readers would be, "Why the cart before the horse?" Why dwell on the penalties rather than the management actions that brought about unusually severe penalties? One need only look to the text of several Board decisions that were sustained totally or in the main by federal circuit courts to get an apt answer. This answer is that over and over again, the Board and the courts found—rightly or wrongly—such a massive and deliberate management program to avoid unionization that much more severe penalties seem warranted than would be imposed on run-of-the-mill or unintentional management committers of unfair labor practices.

Viewed separately and in retrospect, few of the violations could be regarded as horrendous. Moreover, in a considerable number of instances complaints of unfair labor practices arising from discharge of known union partisans were dismissed by the Board as unproved or without a solid factual basis. Still, there was a lot of fire as well as smoke in Board decisions of the 1960's that led to the description of the Stevens Company as perhaps the nation's No. 1 corporate union hater and/or buster.

With NLRB cases and appellate court decisions affecting the Stevens Company continuing through 1975-1976, a somewhat fragmentary picture of developments is obtainable by examining the latest published court decisions—not necessarily in order of importance.

One series of Board decisions was subject to review by the Fourth Circuit Court of Appeals in 1976. These Board cases originated from company actions three and four years earlier. The company both partially won and lost in the circuit court decision summarized below.

An employee at the company's Turnersburg, N.C., plant was fired because she had disrupted a pre-election representation meeting at which the plant manager had given "a lawful speech" opposing the union's organizational activities. She twice interrupted the manager with questions. He told her to remain silent or return to her shift. When she refused, the manager adjourned the meeting and then proceeded to discharge her. The Board found this discharge to be in violation of Section 8(a)(3) on the grounds that her behavior had been spontaneous rather than premeditated. The circuit court upheld the Board's decision, explaining that there may

---

[82]*Ibid.*

be some leeway for impulsive behavior so that not every impropriety committed during an organizing campaign, although excessive, necessarily places the employee beyond the protection of the statute.

But in the same decision the circuit court upheld the Board in its findings that the Stevens Company had *lawfully* discharged 22 employees at two of its South Carolina plants. These employees had followed the advice set out in a magazine article which stated that an employee could *not* be discharged for insisting on the right to ask questions during an employer's lawful pre-election speech.

When a series of such speeches were conducted by the management of the two plants involved, employees interrupted the speakers and after they had refused to sit down when asked, were summarily dismissed. The circuit court supported the Board's finding that the acts of the 22 dischargees were premeditated and intended to disrupt meetings "lawfully" called by the company to express its views. Hence these employees were properly subject to discharge.

In the same decision, the circuit court ruled against the company and sustained the Board in another issue only tangentially related to the two just mentioned. Here is a summary. About two months before a 1973 Board-ordered representation election at Stevens' Wallace, S.C., plant, a company supervisor approached one of his workmen. As related by the court, the supervisor asked this employee "if he believed 'this stuff the union people are telling you.' " The workman walked away but was again approached by his boss. This time, so the court declared, the supervisor said that "if unions move in, plants will close and new industry will by-pass the area and that 'you have got the welfare of your kids to think about.' " The supervisor denied having said any plants would close or move. But as the court pointed out, "the determination of credibility of witnesses, however, is within the province of the Board, not the reviewing court. The court's conclusion was that the supervisor's conversations with his subordinate were "coercive interrogations and threats."[83]

Another federal circuit court decision handed down in September 1976 upheld in part management's tactics in union relations but also held the Stevens Company in civil contempt for failing to comply with certain portions of prior Board orders that the circuit court had deemed valid. Rather extensive review of the court decision seems imperative to demonstrate its significance to

---

[83]Stevens v. NLRB; Textile Workers Union of America v. Same, Nos. 75-1830, 75-2058, 4th Cir., Sept. 17, 1976, 93 LRRM 2262 (1976).

employers facing issues such as those that were originally held by the Board to be nonviolative of the law or patently illegal.

Twice in 1971, the U.S. Court of Appeals (Fifth Circuit, New Orleans) directed the Stevens Company to bargain in good faith with the Textile Workers Union. This union had been duly certified as the proper bargaining agent for production and maintenance employees at one of its plants located in Statesboro, Georgia. In the shortest of short strokes, the court declared: "The Board asserts it has contemptuously failed to bargain in good faith. In three respects we agree."

Before acting upon the Board's petition to have the company held in civil contempt for illegally disobeying two prior court decisions ordering the company to bargain with the union, the court referred the petition to a Special Master for findings of fact and recommendations. As stated by the court:

> The Master found that the Company had failed to meet its good faith bargaining duty in three broad categories. First, the Company had undertaken unilateral changes in workload, work organization, and wages without first affording the Union a chance to negotiate the changes. Second, Stevens had unreasonably delayed furnishing, or had failed altogether to furnish, information needed and requested by the Union to negotiate an employees' contract. Third, the Company had not bargained in good faith concerning the subject of union dues checkoff, an arrangement whereby employees could choose to have their union dues automatically withheld from their paychecks. The Master recommended that Stevens be held in contempt. The Master did determine that Stevens had not breached its duties when it refused to enter into tentative agreement on identical contract proposals.[84]

With respect to the company's proposed changes in workload and its intent to put certain curtailed operations on a four-day week basis, the court concluded that "the employer's power to alter working conditions in his plant is not contingent upon union agreement with his proposed change. The company has only to notify the union before effecting the change so as to give the union a meaningful chance to offer counter-proposals and counter-arguments."[85]

The court observed that the union had been duly notified of its intent to institute a partial layoff. The Board and the Special Master contended that the result would be to cause increases in work assignments for holdover employees and layoff effects which the union did not foresee. But the court concluded that the Stevens action relative to plant layoffs did not constitute anything like con-

[84]NLRB v. Stevens, No. 73-3175, 5th Cir., Sept. 20, 1976, 93 LRRM 2265 (1976).
[85]Ibid., at 2272.

tempt for the Board "bargaining in good faith" directive. Instead the court stated:

> Stevens' duty was merely to present the Union with a meaningful chance to offer input into the decisional process. Given that opportunity the Union could negotiate the change so as to get the best possible deal for the employees. The Union was notified of the layoffs. Common sense would tell the Union that the unit could not operate as had theretofore been the case. We are of the opinion that the facts surrounding the dye house layoff do not establish a clear and convincing case of contempt.[86]

Merit Increases Violative of Law

The Board and the appellate court bore down hard on the company's contentions that unilateral merit increases given maintenance employees in the bargaining unit after it was subject to the Board's and the court's orders to bargain in good faith involved a matter of management discretion rather than well-established rules. The court found no merit in the management's argument that the increases, granted without notification to the union when bargaining sessions were under way, were *de minimis*.

The circuit court cited a U.S. Supreme Court decision to support its conclusion as to the illegality of the merit increases for maintenance employees. To quote:

> In *NLRB* v. *Katz*. . . . merit wage increases were granted 20 of the 50 employees in the bargaining unit. The Supreme Court held such increases to be violations of the duty to bargain unless the company granted them as part of a long-standing, non-discretionary pattern of pay raises. If not "a mere continuation of the status quo," Katz (supra) 369 U.S. at 746, 82 S.Ct. at 1113, the employer had failed to bargain.
>
> The Union received no prior notice of the merit increases involved here. Moreover, the Master found that employer discretion primarily influenced the Company decision, and the record clearly supports that conclusion. Stevens had no tangible guidelines to determine which employees received an increase, when they should receive it, nor how much increase should be granted. Management discretion, rather than well-established rules, decided each variable. Consequently, Stevens' action was not a "mere continuation of the status quo."
>
> Moreover, apparently insignificant unilateral action that may constitute *de minimis* activity when undertaken by a company with a clean slate in labor law, must be viewed more warily when committed by one who enjoys a record for intransigence like that of J.P. Stevens Company. When a company has historically evinced disdain for em-

---

[86]*Ibid.*, at 2273.

ployees' rights and the Congressional mandate, its prior history is relevant to the question of a *de minimis* failure to bargain.[87]

When Proposed General Increases Are Illegal

The circuit court also found the Stevens Company in civil contempt for refusal to bargain in good faith by reason of its announcement at a bargaining session in Oct. 1972 that its management had filed with the then existing temporary federal pay board an application for approval of a general wage increase for all of its hourly employees. The company did in fact seek pay board approval of general wage increases higher than an offer made to the union at Statesboro, then engaged in contract negotiations. A summary of the circuit court's ruling on the illegality of the general wage increases offered by Stevens in 1972 had this to say:

> Employer that unilaterally granted general wage increases to employees is in civil contempt of court decree requiring it to bargain in good faith with union, even though employer informed union before actually implementing increases, since employer's prior unilateral application, without notice to union, to pay board for permission to grant higher than any offer made to union was tantamount to granting raise without prior union consultation.[88]

The circuit court gave a lucid explanation as to why it had agreed with the Board's finding and to the illegality of the general wage increase announced by Stevens in late 1972. The court declared it to be "rudimentary that a company cannot legally institute a general wage increase without first consulting its employees' bargaining representative. . . . Agreement by the union is not a prerequisite to implementation of the raise, but the union must be allowed to air its views beforehand. . . . Even when the parties cannot agree to the amount of an increase, a company cannot unilaterally implement any raise higher than offers made to and rejected by the union. . . ."

There was in the Stevens case here under review what the circuit court referred to as "a slightly different wrinkle." This developed because the current negotiations took place during Phase II of the government's wage and price controls then in effect and hence the pay board's involvement. The "different wrinkle," so the court observed, was that "unilateral application to the pay board for permission to grant a raise higher than any offered to the Union must, in all logic, be viewed as tantamount to granting the raise without

---

[87]*Ibid.*
[88]*Ibid.*, at 2265.

prior Union consultation." The court observed that the results of its dealings with the pay board were that "by unilaterally asking the Pay Board to permit a wage increase higher than any previously offered the union, Stevens refused to bargain. . . . It matters not that Stevens may have intended the Pay Board amount as a base for higher bargaining." Ergo, the court decided, Stevens by its pay board propositions had violated the applicable orders respecting good-faith bargaining.

Union Dues Checkoff

The Stevens Company did something right, or at least entirely legal, when it rejected a union demand for inclusion in a proposed agreement of a provision relating to the checkoff of union dues. Federal appellate courts have held that the checkoff is a mandatory subject for collective bargaining.[89] The court noted in the cases here under review that while the union and company must bargain about dues checkoff, they do *not* have to agree on the subject. In addition, the court stated:

> Every position on mandatory issues, like dues checkoff, must reflect a legitimate business purpose, otherwise the company has not bargained in good faith. . . . Disagreement on the mandatory subject of dues checkoff is present here, thus we analyze Stevens' bargaining posture for evidence of legitimacy.
> Although it deducts numerous items from paychecks, including some deductions not required by law, Stevens defends its negative posture on the ground that more deductions create pressure for wage increases. The Union countered by proposing optional substitution of dues checkoff for an elective deduction already offered by Stevens. Stevens did not budge, and it was not required to sacrifice a program already in successful operation.
> Stevens' desire to minimize pressure for wage increases, although somewhat emasculated by the optional substitution proposal, is a legitimate business purpose. The Master believed the company had failed to bargain in good faith. However, under all the circumstances we cannot say the Board has met its burden of proof on the issue. Consequently, Stevens may not be found in contempt relative to dues checkoff.[90]

Man Bites Dog—Figuratively and Futilely

The war between the Stevens Company and the Amalgamated Clothing Workers' Union was continuing apace in early 1977. But the company lost another small battle in late January of that year.

---

[89]Sweeney and Co. v. NLRB, 76 LRRM 2321, 437 F.2d 1127 (5th Cir. 1971).
[90]93 LRRM 2275 (1976).

The company had taken the initiative in accusing the union of not having bargained in good faith during contract negotiations at its Statesboro, Ga., plant. That plant was closed in 1975, ostensibly for legitimate economic reasons, although the union thought otherwise. What useful purpose would currently be served by finding that the union had become a lawbreaker too is not certain. Anyhow, the company's charge against the union was considered insubstantial by the Georgia regional office of the NLRB. On appeal to Washington the Board declined to process the complaint against the union.[91]

The Stevens Company suffered what may be a crucial setback in its Taft-Hartley litigation in Aug. 1977. On Aug. 31 the U.S. Court of Appeals, Second Circuit, held the company to be in civil contempt by failing to take appropriate action pursuant to a court decree enforcing prior NLRB orders. *Inter alia,* as attorneys might say, the management was ordered (1) to instruct all management personnel in all of its plants fully to comply with prior NLRB orders; (2) to require such personnel to acknowledge receipt of these instructions; (3) in collaboration with the Board staff to institute programs for management (including supervisors) to "educate them about the rights of union organizers and the rights of plant employees to organize and/or become members of a union"; (4) to arrange meetings for plant employees *during working time* to have notice of applicable Board orders read to attendees; (5) to develop in writing nondiscriminatory rules relating to solicitation of prospective union members and distribution of union literature on company property, providing union representatives with reasonable access to plant bulletin boards for one full year.[92]

The Board decided on Nov. 30, 1977, to take the preliminary steps to try to get a nationwide court injunction to restrain the company from engaging in unlawful tactics to prevent unionization in any of its plants. Such an injunction, the Board indicated, was necessary because: "Given the employer's past history and given the evidence that its unfair labor practices will continue after all these years, the Board fears that without judicial protection union campaign efforts will continue to be met by unlawful conduct that will effectively stifle the statutory rights of the employees involved."

The Stevens management promptly issued a press release from Washington. This release included the statement that: "No suit has been filed and to our knowledge it was not even drafted. We believe

---

[91]10CB 2626 NLRB, Ga. Regional Office (no published decision).

[92]For the implications of the circuit court's order, and for guidance as to its application to personnel and line managers, the authors suggest consultation with legal counsel. For a summary and commentary on the decision, see 96 LRRM 2748 (1977).

that any decision to file such a suit would be inappropriate and not warranted and we are confident that any court would view it in the same manner."

Proposed Remedies for "Bad Faith Bargaining"

Given the history of the Stevens case there most likely will be much more litigation before the Stevens Company settles its differences with the NLRB, the federal courts, and the labor organizations desperately trying to bring it to terms by consumer boycotts and direct unionization efforts. At 1977's end an NLRB administrative judge reported to the Board that he had found the company in violation of Taft-Hartley by reason of bargaining with the union in bad faith and without any "intention of concluding a collective bargaining agreement." Under the Board's investigative and enforcement set-up, administrative judges on its staff can hold hearings, take testimony to consider briefs previously submitted, and in general act as factfinders as well as advisors to the Board itself.

The administrative judge assigned to the Stevens cases was Bernard Ries, Esq. He minced no words in his caustic report to the Board. He said, for example: "I know of no instance in the past 14 years in which [the company] has evidenced good faith by voluntarily impressing on employees any sense of renewed commitment to honor and respect their exercise of statutory rights. . . ." One of Ries' main findings was that the company had not bargained in good faith with the clothing and textile workers' union (for nearly two years) at its seven plants in Roanoke Rapids, N.C. Ries recommended, in the light of the Aug. 1977 contempt edict of the Second Circuit Court of Appeals, that the court-ordered remedies applicable only to some Stevens plants in North and South Carolina be extended to apply to all of the company's plants in the United States. He further recommended that remedies for what he deemed to have been illegal company actions include reimbursement to the union of all costs it incurred in negotiations with the company and in Board hearings. Ries further proposed that the company be required to reimburse the Board for all costs incurred by the NLRB in its hearings leading to the contempt decree of Aug. 1977.

Twenty days were allowed the company to appeal to the full Board. The management promptly announced that it would appeal. The company spokesman declared that, "It appears that he [Ries] has completely misunderstood the facts involved in the Roanoke Rapids negotiations. It also appears that he has recommended a number of unusual remedies which have been repeatedly rejected by the courts."[93]

The Board itself lost little time in deciding to take drastic action in line with Judge Ries' recommendations. In late January 1978 the Board applied to a New York district federal court for a sweeping injunction intended to prevent the Stevens company from further interference with its employees' Taft-Hartley rights. The injunction would extend to all of the company's plants in the United States that had not previously been subject to court order and adverse Board decisions.

NLRB-Stevens Settlement Agreement

The National Labor Relations Board announced on April 27, 1978, that it had approved a settlement agreement with the J.P. Stevens Company and that the Board would no longer seek a national injunction under Taft-Hartley. Under this settlement the company agreed to reinstate 11 of 15 employees alleged to have been unlawfully discharged for union activities.

The Board's General Counsel Irving declared that the company had further agreed to take nearly all of the remedial and preventive actions sought by the Board in the injunction proceedings. He further stated that these issues and full remedies for any violations found committed are subject to further Board proceedings, subject to review by the appropriate federal appeal courts.[94]

Not the Union's Last Word

"NLRB-Stevens settlement settles nothing for workers." So declared the union in question (ACTWU) in May 1978 in an extra edition of its publication, Social Justice. The union also put out another statement saying that the so-called settlement "emphasizes that a lawless company can escape punishment by making an empty promise to a powerless NLRB which is charged with enforcing a toothless law." Manifestly, while the Board and the company have come to the truce stage, the union does not consider its war with the company to be anywhere near over.

---

[93]For a summary of Judge Ries' findings and recommendations, see DAILY LAB. REP. (BNA), No. 252, Dec. 30, 1977, p. A-1 and Section D.
[94]DAILY LAB. REP., No. 83, April 28, 1978, p. 1.

CHAPTER 8

Arbitration and the Law

No law places compulsion on employers in private enterprise to agree to a contractual provision to arbitrate any labor dispute. This conclusion was stated emphatically by Mr. Justice Brennan of the U.S. Supreme Court in his concurring opinion in the Court's celebrated "Trilogy" decisions of 1960.[1] The labor disputes that gave rise to the Trilogy came about as a result of uncertainty regarding the proper scope and limitations of arbitration clauses embodied in labor agreements voluntarily entered into by employers and unions. The Supreme Court considered it necessary to construe the application of existing law to what had been agreed to by the parties.

More than 15 years after the Trilogy decisions, the courts have yet to come up with fully conclusive answers as to how Taft-Hartley and other federal statutes impinge on the grievance arbitration provisions of current labor agreements. Indeed the staunchest Supreme Court advocate of the virtual impregnability of arbitral awards, Mr. Justice Douglas, backtracked in one of the final cases in which he participated before his retirement in 1975. (The case in point, *Gateway* v. *United Mine Workers,* is referred to briefly later in this chapter.)

What has just been mentioned about the lack of statutory compulsion for utilization of arbitration procedures by private enterprises is still the law of the land. Few employers save those engaged in interstate transportation and subject to special federal regulatory legislation have had any inclination to have the terms of new agreements dictated by an arbitrator. And yet there has been a tremendously important exception to the prevailing management view. It was in 1973 that major steel companies broke the ice in concert with the United Steel Workers Union by entering into agreements substituting for the right to strike the authority of arbitrators to prescribe contract terms over which impasses had developed.

---

[1]Concurring opinion of Mr. Justice Brennan in United Steelworkers of America v. American Manufacturing Company and United Steelworkers of America v. Warrior Navigation Co., 46 LRRM 2427 (U.S. Sup. Ct. 1960).

THE BIG STEEL EXPERIMENT

Significant labor-management history was undoubtedly made in 1974 by the first Big Steel Experimental Agreement. The objective of the experimental agreement was set forth in an introductory section as follows:

It is highly desirable to provide stability of steel operations, production and employment for the benefit of the employees, customers, suppliers and stockholders of the Steel Companies, and the public.

To attain this objective requires that the Union and the Steel Companies settle issues which arise in collective bargaining in such a way as to avoid industry-wide strikes or government intervention.

The parties are confident that they possess the requisite ability and skills to resolve whatever differences may exist between them in future negotiations through the process of free collective bargaining.

The parties believe that the success of the 1974 negotiations to replace the current basic labor agreements dated Aug. 1, 1971, will be enhanced by use of this Experimental Negotiating Agreement. [This passage referred to what amounted to a modification of the three-year agreement due to expire in 1974 and the equivalent of a pledge to embody in the 1974 agreement the substantive clauses of the "experimental" plan.] * * *

In view of the foregoing it is agreed by the Union and the Steel Companies that they will make every effort to resolve through negotiations any differences which may arise in bargaining. After thorough bargaining in good faith the parties may submit any unresolved issue (which is not excluded from arbitration by this agreement or any subsequent agreement between the parties) to final and binding arbitration by an impartial arbitration panel in accordance with the procedures hereinafter set forth. It is expressly understood, however, that the submission of any issue to final and binding arbitration shall not preclude the parties from continuing to bargain on such issue prior to the issuance of a decision by the impartial arbitration panel.

Except as otherwise provided in D-5 of this agreement, the Union on behalf of its members employed by the Steel Companies agrees not to engage in strikes, work stoppages or concerted refusals to work in support of its bargaining demands, and the Steel Companies agree not to resort to lockouts of employees represented by the Union to support their bargaining positions.[2]

The exceptions to the basic no-strike, no-lockout guarantees were relatively minor. The three-year contracts generally applicable had provided mechanisms for separate plant negotiations on

---

[2]*Steel Industry Arbitration Agreement,* 14 COLLECTIVE BARGAINING NEGOTIATIONS & CONTRACTS (BNA) 341 (1973).

local issues. These mechanisms were slated to continue. A local bargaining issue was defined as being:

> a proposed change in a condition of employment at a particular plant which:
> (1) would not, if adopted, be inconsistent with any provision of a company agreement . . . or involve any addition to or modification of any such provision or agreement;
> (2) would not be an arbitrable grievance as defined in the applicable basic labor agreement; and
> (3) does not relate to a grievance settlement or an arbitration award. . . .[3]

The foregoing provisions were supplemented by a requirement that unsolved local issues properly subject to negotiation shall either be withdrawn or be subject to a secret ballot vote available for actively employed persons potentially affected. If the vote favors insistence on inclusion of a disputed clause in a local supplement, and authorizes a strike if necessary to try to force management acceptance, no such strike can be pulled without prior approval of the Union's International President.

How the Big Steel Experiment Has Worked

The Big Steel Experimental Agreement in collective bargaining has continued to receive the support of steel company managements and the Steel Workers' Union. It has also gained a tribute from the somewhat iconoclastic president of the AFL-CIO, George Meany. In a 1976 advertisement, paid for, incidentally, by U.S. Steel Corporation, Meany stated:

> Labor and management do agree that responsible and free collective bargaining is the way to settle disputes.
> Of course, collective bargaining is not perfect. Labor and management are constantly striving to improve it. For example, in the steel industry, labor and management have agreed on an alternative to the strike—binding arbitration.
> It has been successful but only because both sides *agreed*. Nobody forced either the union or the companies to agree.

The Steel Corporation put in a few pregnant words of endorsement of Meany's declaration. In its ad there was the following comment:

> U.S. Steel joins Mr. Meany in noting the land-mark agreements between the nation's major steel companies and the United Steel Workers of America. In this agreement both sides agreed voluntarily

---
[3]*Ibid.*

to resolve future differences by binding arbitration, thus providing uninterrupted production of steel through July 1980, without the threat of an industry-wide strike. This agreement ended boom-and-bust swings in production and employment that occurred regularly at every contract expiration.

That is why U.S. Steel thinks this agreement is collective bargaining at its best — the parties were free to work out their own problems, and the results are good for employees, customers, and stockholders and the entire country.[4]

In April 1977 the major steel companies that were parties to the 1974 experimental agreement entered into a new long-term contract extending from May 1, 1977, to July 31, 1980. With one minor modification relating to the timing of guaranteed annual wage increases, the terms of the first experimental agreement were readopted and will govern all aspects of the 1980 big steel negotiations. The new contract was ratified by the companies and the union without necessitating submission of any unsettled issues to final and binding arbitration.

As explained by a spokesman for the management team that negotiated the new 1977-1980 agreement, the readoption of the Experimental Negotiating Agreement means that there cannot be an industry-wide strike until at least Aug. 1, 1983. Such a strike would be banned by the continuation of the provisions requiring submission of issues unsettled at the bargaining table (except purely local issues) to final determination by a panel of impartial arbitrators.

USE OF ARBITRATION IN LABOR DISPUTES

Astute arbitrators, union and management representatives in arbitration proceedings, and academic authorities on labor relations recognized long ago that arbitration cases are frequently won (or lost) at the time the parties present to the arbitrator the precise issues they authorize him to adjudicate. In actual practice, the arbitrator's award is often controlled by what the parties agree he should hear and decide and what limitations, if any, they stipulate as to the range of his discretion in resolving the dispute. To state that the outcome of a grievance arbitration case may be decided just as an arbitration hearing is beginning is only half true, just as the Duke of Wellington was only partially right when he said, "The Battle of Waterloo was won on the playing fields of Eton." Labor relations pundits would be more accurate to point out that victories in labor disputes culminating in arbitration proceedings are often

---

[4]BUSINESS WEEK, May 3, 1976, pp. 82-83.

achieved long before the actual disputes develop. It is what is negotiated and agreed to in advance at the bargaining table in the way of grievance and arbitration machinery that often controls the ultimate result.

Crucial decisions have to be made by personnel administrators during the course of negotiating arbitration arrangements. In their judgments they and their legal counsel have to give substantial weight to precedent-making court decisions interpreting existing statutes that more than peripherally affect management prerogatives in determining what to agree to arbitrate and when resorting to the courts or to other measures may be more effective.

Applicable Federal Statutes

Taft-Hartley Provisions

There is in Taft-Hartley a provision declaring a government policy which obviously encourages utilization of arbitration for settlement of contract grievances. This is Section 203(d), which states, "Final adjustment by a method agreed upon by the parties is hereby declared to be the desirable method for settlement of grievance disputes arising over the application or interpretation of an existing collective-bargaining agreement."

Section 203(d) is one of the provisions of Taft-Hartley's Title II, which had the main purpose of reestablishing the Federal Mediation and Conciliation Service. In the same subsection it is stated that "[t]he Service is directed to make its conciliation and mediation services available in the settlement of such grievance disputes only as a last resort and in exceptional cases." The declared policy is not implemented anywhere in Taft-Hartley; it is permissive rather than mandatory. Nevertheless, Mr. Justice Douglas in one of his Trilogy opinions implied that the policy *should be* virtually a "must" for employers and unions when he declared, "That policy can be effectuated only if the means chosen by the parties for settlement of their differences under a collective bargaining agreement is given full play."[5]

Section 9(a) of Taft-Hartley has been invoked in litigation wherein the right of individual employees to process grievances to arbitration has been challenged. After the declaration that majority representatives shall have exclusive negotiating authority, there are the following provisos:

---

[5]United Steelworkers of America v. American Manufacturing Company, No. 360, 46 LRRM 2414 (U.S. Sup. Ct. 1960).

Provided. That any individual employee or a group of employees shall have the right to present grievances to their employer and to have their grievances adjusted, without the intervention of the bargaining representative, as long as the adjustment is not inconsistent with the terms of a collective-bargaining contract or agreement then in effect. *Provided further,* That the bargaining representative has been given opportunity to be present at such adjustment.

Sections 8(a)(1) and (3) of Taft-Hartley often have been construed by the courts in connection with arbitration cases involving management decisions that might be considered as unfair labor practices proscribed in this section. As will later be explained, the National Labor Relations Board insists upon its authority to review and in its discretion to modify or reverse arbitrators' decisions in cases of alleged breaches of agreements that also involve alleged violations of Taft-Hartley.

The section of Taft-Hartley which was the main concern of the Supreme Court's Trilogy decisions is Section 301(a), which enables employers, labor organizations, and individual employees to institute suits for violation of contracts. It reads as follows:

Suits for violation of contracts between an employer and a labor organization representing employees in an industry affecting commerce as defined in this Act, or between any such labor organizations may be brought in any district court of the United States having jurisdiction of the parties, without respect to the amount in controversy or without regard to the citizenship of the parties.

The grievance arbitration provisions of labor agreements quite obviously have been considered by the courts to be within the purview of judicial review under this section.

The United States Arbitration Act

The prime purpose of the United States Arbitration Act, enacted in 1925, is to make agreements to arbitrate enforceable in the federal courts. Section 3 of this Act states:

If any suit or proceeding be brought in any of the courts of the United States upon any issue referable to arbitration under an agreement in writing for such arbitration, the court in which such suit is pending, upon being satisfied that the issue involved in such suit or proceeding is referable to arbitration under such agreement, shall on application of one of the parties stay the trial of the action until such arbitration has been had in accordance with the terms of the agreement, provided the applicant for the stay is not in default in proceeding with such arbitration.

Federal courts have had to construe this law in its relationship to Section 301(a) of Taft-Hartley. The leading decisions (summarized later in this chapter) hold that violations of no-strike clauses can be held arbitrable if arbitration is the final step in the grievance procedure and that therefore suits instituted as a result of alleged violation of a no-strike clause can be stayed pending arbitration.

Norris-LaGuardia Act

That hardy perennial, Norris-LaGuardia, has often been brought to bear in litigation invoking arbitration questions. The severe restrictions on the issuance of injunctions to restrain alleged breaches of labor agreements that Norris-LaGuardia imposed prior to the Supreme Court's *Boys Markets* decision in 1970 have been delineated in Chapter 7. And as will be later referred to in this chapter, "failure to arbitrate was not a part and parcel of the abuses against which the Act was aimed."

State Arbitration Laws

Some state legislation relating to labor-management arbitration has become of negligible consequence. There are still on the statute books in several states laws providing for compulsory arbitration of labor disputes affecting public utilities. But in 1951 the U.S. Supreme Court declared unconstitutional the Wisconsin law that required arbitration of public utility labor disputes because of its conflict with Taft-Hartley. The validity of other state laws of the same general purpose is so doubtful that we have pointed out with complete assurance early in this chapter that no private enterprise is obligated by law to agree by contract to arbitrate any type of labor dispute.

In the absence of specific state legislation some state courts prior to 1960 had accepted jurisdiction over disputes based on voluntary agreements to arbitrate. The Supreme Court has decided, in effect, that common law when applied by state courts is no longer applicable to enterprises subject to Taft-Hartley.[6]

Likewise, the Supreme Court has all but nullified the provisions of state laws that seemingly had authorized their courts to determine whether or not a labor dispute issue was arbitrable. The Supreme Court struck down in one of its Trilogy decisions *(American)* the validity of provisions in a New York state statute under which the New York appellate courts had held: "If the meaning of

---

[6]United Steelworkers of America v. Warrior and Gulf Navigation Company, No. 443, 46 LRRM 2414 (U.S. Sup. Ct. 1960).

the provision of the contract sought to be arbitrated is beyond dispute, there cannot be anything to arbitrate and the contract cannot be said to provide for arbitration."[7]

In 1963 the New York State Civil Practice Act was amended to conform to the standard set out by the Supreme Court in its *American* decision. The pertinent provision of that Act now reads: "In determining any matter arising under this article [Section 7501] the court shall not consider whether the claim with respect to which arbitration is sought is tenable, or otherwise pass on the merits of the dispute."

The Uniform Arbitration Act

More than half the states now have in effect laws patterned after a uniform arbitration law as drafted by the National Conference of the Commissioners on Uniform State Laws in 1955 and 1956 and approved by the American Bar Association. This model statute applies to commercial disputes as well as labor-management disputes.

The key provision of the Uniform Arbitration Act is Section I *(Validity of Arbitration Agreement)*. It reads:

> A written agreement to submit any existing controversy to arbitration or a provision in a written contract to submit to arbitration any controversy thereafter arising between the parties is valid, enforceable and irrevocable, save upon such grounds as exist at law or in equity for the revocation of any contract. This act also applies to arbitration agreements between employers and employees or between their respective representatives (unless otherwise provided in the agreement).

Although under Section 301 of Taft-Hartley most suits to compel arbitration or enforce arbitration awards are filed in federal courts, state courts have concurrent jurisdiction. But the state courts must apply federal law in case of conflict. Taft-Hartley is silent, however, as to particular grounds for setting aside arbitrators' awards by the courts. Hence, the terms of the Uniform Arbitration Act have much significance. Section 12 *(Vacating an Award)* of the model law states:

> (a) Upon application of a party, the court shall vacate an award where:
>   (1) The award was procured by corruption, fraud or other undue means;

---

[7]United Steelworkers of America v. American Manufacturing Company, in reference to International Assn. of Machinists and Cutler Hammer, Inc., 19 LRRM 2232, 20 LRRM 2445 (1947).

(2) There was evident partiality by an arbitrator appointed as a neutral or corruption in any of the arbitrators or misconduct prejudicing the rights of any party;

(3) The arbitrators exceeded their powers;

(4) The arbitrators refused to postpone the hearing upon sufficient cause being shown therefor or refused to hear evidence material to the controversy or otherwise so conducted the hearing, contrary to the provisions of Section 5 [Hearings procedures] as to prejudice substantially the rights of a party; or

(5) There was no arbitration agreement and the issue was not adversely determined in proceedings under Section 2 [Proceedings to compel or stay arbitration] and the party did not participate in the arbitration hearing without raising the objection; . . .[8]

MANAGEMENT OPTIONS IN GRIEVANCE ARBITRATION

Some arbitrators, rightly or wrongly perhaps, have asserted the authority to construe and apply the law as it may affect a grievance dispute that they have been designated to adjudicate. The plethora of court and arbitral rulings coming in the wake of the 1960 Trilogy decisions of the U.S. Supreme Court has given much pause to personnel administrators and their legal advisors in attempting to reach conclusions as to the proper place of arbitration proceedings in a company's contractual relationships with unions. The presently applicable laws and landmark court decisions have generated for management such questions as the following:

• Should the grievance procedure in a labor agreement grant an arbitrator what amounts to legislative authority as well as judicial authority? In other words, should he be authorized to add to or rewrite a contract clause in order to reach a satisfactory solution to a major grievance which, if decided within the terms of the contract, could produce a solution unsatisfactory to both parties?

• Should an arbitrator be expressly authorized to determine on his own whether a complaint is an arbitrable grievance, thus obviating the possible necessity for court determination of arbitrability?

• Should management strive at the bargaining table to get an agreement for exclusion from the grievance procedure of all issues not specifically covered by the substantive provisions of the agreement? Or would it be more desirable for management to insist on

---

[8]American Arbitration Association, THE UNIFORM ARBITRATION ACT (New York: American Arbitration Association, 1968).

specific exclusions such as its right to close a plant, to sub-contract, or to transfer operations from one plant to another?

• Should the grievance procedure bind both parties to use arbitration as the final step for resolution of all disputes involving contract interpretation or violation and to agree not to resort to the courts or government agencies for preventive or remedial action when alleged contract violations might also constitute violation of applicable laws? Conversely, should management attempt to ex-clude from the arbitration process any issues on which government agencies such as the National Labor Relations Board or the Equal Employment Opportunity Commission might assert jurisdiction?

• Should the grievance procedure permit nonunion employees or dissident union members to process their own grievances to arbi-tration?

A more complex series of questions relates to appropriate means for assuring compliance with clauses in labor agreements banning wildcat strikes, work stoppages, or other job action. Is a bilateral grievance procedure a sound solution? Under a bilateral grievance procedure, there could be provisions authorizing an arbi-trator to assess monetary penalties against the union, its officers, or individual members when held in violation of a work-stoppage clause, or to impose other remedial measures. (Up to now most management authorities have not favored the inclusion of such pro-visions in grievance procedures. Most prefer to take unilateral action against employees participating in extracontractual work stoppages, or to seek restraining orders or to sue for damages in fed-eral or state courts. A growing minority believes, however, that arbitration of management grievances may be a much faster and more effective means for minimizing work stoppages banned by the terms of their labor agreements.)

When employers agree to provide for arbitration of disputes arising under labor agreements, they are free to attempt to nego-tiate conditions as broad or as narrow as they wish. This, in sub-stance, was what Mr. Justice Brennan concluded in one of the three Trilogy decisions (Enterprise). Employers accordingly have many options. How realistic some of these options are depends in part upon management's strength and persistence at the bargaining table. Is management, for instance, willing to take a protracted strike to accomplish the objective of assuring freedom from work stoppages throughout the life of a labor agreement?

If the right to close a plant might seem of paramount impor-tance to management, there would be good reason for seeking to exclude such potential action from arbitratable issues. One of the leading court cases cited in the 1976 annual report of the American Arbitration Association's General Counsel, Gerald Aksen, would so indicate. Aksen noted that in *Bressette* v. *International Talc Co., Inc.*, 527 F.2d 211, 91 LRRM 2077 (2d Cir. 1975), "Where an agreement contained a broad arbitration clause and the union claimed that the company had violated various provisions of the agreement when it terminated operations, the court held this issue was arbitrable."

The Supreme Court's noteworthy 1976 decision in the case of *Buffalo Forge Co.* v. *United Steelworkers* suggests to some personnel administrators and their legal counsel the desirability of trying to get a broad definition of prohibited work stoppages that would include a ban on sympathetic strikes—more specifically, a clause that would preclude a union and its members from honoring another union's lawful picket line. (See an extended discussion of this case in Chapter 7.)

Three other highly significant recent federal court decisions on closely related issues were summarized by Aksen in his 1976 report, as follows:

> A no-strike clause in a collective bargaining agreement did not preclude its members from engaging in work stoppages which resulted from refusal to cross a stranger [sic] union's picket line. [*Hyster Co.* v. *International Towing and Lifting Machine Assoc. et al.*, 519 F.2d 89, 90 LRRM 1544 (7th Cir. 1975)].

> In an agreement containing both a no-strike clause and a provision allowing the union to honor lawful picket lines, a determination of the applicability of these conflicting provisions was for the arbitrator. [*Valmac Industries* v. *Food Handlers Local 425*, 579 F.2d 263 (8th Cir. 1975), *vacated*, 44 U.S.L.W. 3757 (1976)].

Aksen also singled out for mention in his 1976 report the case of *Local No. 358, Bakery and Confectionery Workers' Union* v. *Nolde Brothers*, 530 F.2d 548 (4th Cir. 1975), 54 U.S.L.W. 4251, 94 LRRM 2753 (1977), a case in which he said, "the issue of whether a company's obligation for severance pay survived the contract was an arbitrable issue."

There are no sure-fire answers to any of the questions just propounded. The courts, the administrative agencies such as NLRB, and the arbitration profession have expressed highly diversified and often conflicting opinions. Not to provide solutions but rather to indicate guidelines for, and obstacles to, the various management options afforded under the law, we present below summaries of typical leading cases.

LEADING CASES INFLUENCING
MANAGEMENT OPTIONS

The three cases that make up the U.S. Supreme Court's note-worthy Trilogy decisions of 1960 are usually referred to in short as *American,* *Warrior,* and *Enterprise.* In all three the Court had to construe the meaning and application of Title III, Section 301(a), of Taft-Hartley in suits originating in controversies about arbitration proceedings.

Merits of Dispute Beyond Court Jurisdiction

In *American* the Court ruled that when a party to an agreement to arbitrate all questions of contract interpretation sues under Section 301 to obtain specific performance of the arbitration promise, the function of the courts is limited to ascertaining whether the claim is on its face governed by the terms of the contract. The courts may not undertake to determine the merits of a grievance under the guise of interpreting the arbitration clause of the contract. Arbitration therefore must be ordered if the dispute involves a claim that a substantive provision of the contract has been violated.

As to the underlying facts, the union had brought suit against the company because it had refused to arbitrate the grievance of an employee who had been denied reinstatement to his job after accepting a monetary settlement for permanent partial disability as a result of a compensable injury. This settlement, the company contended, foreclosed the employee from any opportunity to claim seniority or other rights.

The Court declared, in summary, that the courts "have no business weighing the merits of the grievance, considering whether there is equity in a particular claim, or determining whether there is particular language in the written instrument which will support the claim. The agreement is to submit all grievances to arbitration, not merely those the court will deem meritorious." Then the Court pronounced a dictum that has generated continuing distress in some management circles. It said, "The processing of even frivolous claims may have *therapeutic values* [italics supplied] of which those who are not a part of the plant environment may be quite unaware."[9]

---

[9]United Steelworkers of America v. American Manufacturing Company.

Exclusive Management Functions Delineated

The Court's *Warrior* decision caused much greater consternation among many industrial relations executives and their counsels. In that case the Court ruled that in suits under Section 301 for specific performance of collectively bargained arbitration agreements, arbitration should be ordered unless it may be said with positive assurance that the arbitration clause is not susceptible to an interpretation that covers the asserted dispute. *Doubts should be resolved in favor of coverage.*

On the specific issue before it the Court decided that the union was entitled to an order requiring the company to arbitrate a grievance alleging that its contracting-out of work violated its labor agreement, notwithstanding the provision in that agreement excluding from arbitration the matters which are "strictly a function of management." The Court undertook to interpret the meaning of the contract clause in dispute, despite the fact that in its *American* decision, announced on the same day, it had asserted that the courts have no business determining "whether there is particular language in the written instrument which will support the claim." The Court expressly declared that the phrase " 'strictly a function of management' must be interpreted as referring only to that over which the contract gives management complete control and unfettered discretion." Rejecting the company's contention that its contracting-out of work fell within this category, the Court ruled that there had been no "showing that the parties designed the phrase 'strictly a function of management' to encompass any and all forms of contracting-out." Hence the union's grievance was deemed arbitrable.

A further observation of the Court relates directly to management options as to what to include in a grievance procedure. This was the dictum:

> A specific collective bargaining agreement may exclude contracting-out from the grievance procedure. Or a written collateral agreement may make clear that contracting-out was not a matter for arbitration. *In such a case a grievance based solely on contracting-out would not be arbitrable.* [Italics supplied][10]

(Had Fibreboard Company sought and obtained a clause in its labor agreement either specifying contracting-out as a nonarbitrable issue or affirmatively establishing its right to contract out, the *Fibreboard* case summarized in Chapter 7 might never have required litigation.)

---

[10]United Steelworkers of America v. Warrior and Gulf Navigation Company.

The *Warrior* decison has its pluses such as the dicta just noted, but there are drastic minuses from the standpoint of employers who hopefully negotiate agreements fixing all bargainable terms and conditions of employment for a definite period.

One of the most disturbing passages, to management at least, in the Court decision was the following:

> Arbitration is the means of solving the unforeseeable by molding a system of private law for all the problems which may arise and to provide for their solution in a way which will generally accord with the variant needs and desires of the parties. The processing of disputes through the grievance machinery is actually a vehicle by which meaning and content is [sic] given to the collective bargaining agreement.
>
> Apart from matters that the parties specifically exclude, all of the questions on which the parties disagree must therefore come within the scope of the grievance and arbitration provisions of the collective agreement. The grievance procedure is, in other words, a part of the continuous collective bargaining process.[11]

Once again, employers who wish completely to stabilize their labor relations situations for the entire duration of an agreement can well heed the Court's dictum that unless specific matters are excluded, any issues in dispute are arbitrable if the agreement provides for grievance arbitration.

Broad Role of Arbitrator

One passage in the *Warrior* decision caused great surprise and some consternation among labor relations lawyers and also in the arbitration profession. Its full import can be understood only through direct quotation. After pointing out that arbitrators perform functions that are not normal to the courts, the Supreme Court declared:

> The labor arbitrator's source of law is not confined to the express provisions of the contract, as the industrial common law — the practices of the industry and the shop — is equally a part of the collective bargaining agreement although not expressed in it. The labor arbitrator is usually chosen because of the parties' confidence in his knowledge of the common law of the shop and their trust in his personal judgment to bring to bear considerations which are not expressed in the contract as criteria for judgment. *The parties expect that his judgment of a particular grievance will reflect not only what the contract says, but insofar as the collective bargaining agreement permits, such factors as the effect upon productivity of a particular result, its consequence to the morale of the shop, his judgment whether tensions will be heightened or diminished.* For the parties'

---
[11]*Ibid.*

objective is primarily to further their common goal of uninterrupted production under the agreement, to make the agreement serve their specialized needs. [Italics supplied][12]

It might be inferred from the forceful phraseology of the italicized sentence that the Court suggests that arbitrators go beyond the contract to make an award acceptable to the grievant if such would be conducive to avoidance of industrial strife. If that kind of award is what the parties want and expect, they are certainly not barred by law from writing into a grievance procedure clauses that authorize the arbitrator to use his own judgment and any criteria he wishes to assure a Solomonic award. On the other hand, either management or union is free to insist on the formulating of provisions in the grievance procedure that contain explicit language that limits the arbitrator's authority only to interpretation of the applicable contract provisions. If, as some authorities believe, the Supreme Court opened a Pandora's box in its *Warrior* decision, there are thoroughly appropriate legal ways to close it. Law professor Sam Kagel of the University of California, a veteran practicing arbitrator, has suggested explicit contract phraseology, to wit:

> Assume an arbitration clause that reads: "It is hereby agreed that all matters relating to the interpretation and application of this agreement shall be submitted to arbitration." This narrow and restricted language grants to the arbitrator only the right to apply the agreement as written. If the parties wish to limit the arbitrator's powers to this extent, it is also advisable to add the following clause: "The arbitrator has no power to add to, detract from, or change in any way the provisions of this agreement." To be certain that a narrowly drafted arbitration clause will restrict the arbitrator to an interpretation and application of the collective bargaining agreement, as written, it may be necessary to incorporate in the agreement another clause which states, "This written agreement represents the entire agreement on all subject matters covered herein. Neither party has the right to request arbitration on any subject matter not specifically covered herein."[13]

Controlling Force of Arbitrator's Contract Interpretation

In the third Trilogy decision *(Enterprise)* the Court buttressed its dicta about the discretionary powers of an arbitrator and did so without equivocation. The Court ruled that insofar as an arbitrator's decision concerns the construction of a contract, a court may

---

[12]*Ibid.*

[13]Sam Kagel, ANATOMY OF A LABOR ARBITRATION (Washington: BNA Books, 1961), p. 135.

refuse enforcement if it appears that the decision was not based on the terms of the agreement. *But* the court should not overrule the arbitrator merely because its interpretation differs from his. The Court concluded, "It is the arbitrator's construction which was bargained for, and so far as the arbitrator's decision concerns construction of the contract the courts have no business overruling him because their interpretation of the contract is different from his."[14]

Trilogy Aftermaths

It was primarily the opening of Pandora's box in the *Warrior* decision that impelled management negotiators to reconsider the scope of the grievance procedures they would be willing to embody in labor agreements.

In 1963 two distinguished professors who were both practicing arbitrators sought and reported on the reaction of management spokesmen to the Trilogy and ancillary cases. Professors Russell A. Smith and Dallas L. Jones addressed 750 letters of inquiry to industrial relations staff men and to attorneys representing management. The more than 300 responses varied widely. By way of example, Professors Smith and Jones made the following comments of their own:

> A few believed these decisions have little importance. One respondent stated: "We have not felt that the world came to an end when Justice Douglas [who wrote the majority opinions in all three cases] took off from mountain climbing to say what he said in the 'Trilogy.' " Some of our respondents, on the other hand, would fully concur in the remark that arbitration has become so offensive by reason of these court decisions and the unsuitability of certain arbitrators that we are reluctant to continue arbitration in old contracts or to add it to new contracts."
>
> These views represented the extremes. Only 13 of our employer respondents were concerned to the point of achieving or contemplating the elimination of arbitration, and, on the other hand, only five indicated little or no concern with the decisions. The typical attitude of our management respondents is exemplified in the following comment:
>
>> "There is no question that from management's point of view the 'Trilogy' and related decisions have added appreciable difficulty in labor arbitration. Arbitrators so inclined can find in these decisions ample authority for assuming a legislative as opposed to a judicial function and for virtually abolishing the reserved rights theory. . . . This, in our judgment does not

---

[14]United Steelworkers of America v. Enterprise Wheel and Car Corporation, No. 538, 46 LRRM 2423 (U.S. Sup. Ct. 1960).

mean that management should seek, at least for this time, to eliminate arbitration provisions in labor contracts."[15]

The Gardner-Denver Decision—A Brand New Ball Game?

Another perplexing and controversial U.S. Supreme Court decision, handed down in 1974, has given rise to much pontification by legal scholars as to its implications for use of labor arbitration procedures by private enterprises. What has the celebrated *Gardner-Denver* decision done to the doctrines established under Trilogy? Some authorities say not much. Others are inclined to believe that *Gardner-Denver* has generated an entirely new ball game on labor-management playing fields. Minimally, as an American Bar Association committee has pointed out (see pages 6-7), arbitration as a forum for settling disputes in the equal opportunity field was set back by the *Gardner-Denver* decision. Still, as the committee also noted, "an opinion and award of an arbitrator selected to hear a dispute involving the charging party may be received into the record as evidence for trial court consideration."[16]

Furthermore, as quoted in Chapter 3, the Supreme Court has ruled that:

> An employee's statutory right to trial *de novo* under Title VII of the Civil Rights Act of 1964 is not foreclosed by prior submission of his claim to final arbitration under the nondiscrimination clause of a collective bargaining agreement.[17]

After the confusion instigated by the *Gardner-Denver* decision had had time to subside and the dust of implications had settled, there was good reason to believe that the Supreme Court had not sounded the death knell of arbitration as a primary means for settling disputes over matters of contract interpretation and application. This was the well-reasoned conclusion of Gerald Aksen, General Counsel, American Arbitration Association. In a 1975 address at the National Academy of Arbitrators' annual meeting, Aksen said, " 'To Arbitrate or Not to Arbitrate,' that is the question that now perplexes unions, employers, and labor arbitrators." He

---

[15]Russell A. Smith and Dallas L. Jones, *The Impact of the Emerging Federal Law of Grievance Arbitration on Judges, Arbitrators and Parties*, 52 VA. L. REV. (University of Virginia, Charlottesville) 888 (1966).

[16]American Bar Association, Section of Labor Relations Law, *Report of the Committee on Equal Employment Opportunity Law—Development of the Law, Practice and Procedures as It Affects Labor Relations*, 1975 COMMITTEE REPORTS, Part 1 (Chicago: ABA Press, 1975), p. 38.

[17]Alexander v. Gardner-Denver, 346 F. Supp. 1012 (1971), *aff'd per curiam*, 466 F.2d 1209 (10th Cir. 1972), *rev'd*, 415 U.S. 36, 7 FEP 81 (1974).

answered his own question with a vigorous go-ahead sign, supported by learned references to Supreme Court dicta.

Aksen's basic conclusion was that although "the Supreme Court had surely gone too far [in the Trilogy cases of 1960] in permitting frivolous grievances to be arbitrated," *Gardner-Denver* would not signal the demise of arbitration as a most successful method of private dispute settlement. In support of his conclusion Aksen delineated seven clear signs that "labor arbitrators have not lost favor with the nine final arbiters of all U.S. law."

Aksen's reasoning on the matter is presented in part below:

1. The Court [in the *Gardner-Denver* case] acknowledged its awareness of labor arbitration law. It cited and took the trouble to summarize its major prior decisions, indicating its reaffirmation of "the federal policy favoring arbitration of labor disputes."

2. Title VII legislative history was cited to accentuate a lack of congressional intent to affect any "rights or obligations under the NLRA or the Railway Labor Act."

3. Realizing that its decision might carve an exception into the doctrine of finality of arbitral awards, the Court reminded us of the "therapy that labor arbitrators can bring to 'a complicated and troubled area.'" Thus, while on the one hand the Court departed from traditional labor arbitration dogma, on the other it encouraged discriminatees to utilize the "arbitrator's couch."

4. The Court left open, in my opinion, the question of whether employees could voluntarily consent to *submit* an existing Title VII discrimination case to final arbitration when they freely and knowingly relinquished this legal right. Only prospective waiver was involved in Mr. Alexander's case.

5. The opinion states squarely that discriminatees have "a strong incentive" to arbitrate (Title VII) grievances because the arbitration "may often eliminate those misunderstandings or discriminatory practices that might otherwise precipitate resort to the judicial forum."

6. The decision does not prevent or even discourage discriminatees from arbitrating pursuant to the collective agreement. Indeed, the Court balanced the two federal policies by holding that discriminatees be permitted "to pursue fully" both labor arbitration and Title VII cause of action."

7. Finally, after carefully explaining why a "Spielberg-type" deferral rule was inappropriate, and after indicating that the "more demanding 5-point deferral standard" formulated by the Fifth Circuit in *Rios* v. *Reynolds Metals* was an unconvincing solution, the Court nevertheless ended its opinion with the following sentence: "The arbitral decision may be admitted as evidence and accorded such weight as the court deems appropriate."[18]

---

[18]Gerald Aksen, *Post-Gardner-Denver Developments in Arbitration Law*, ANNUAL PROCEEDINGS OF THE NATIONAL ACADEMY OF ARBITRATORS (Washington: The Bureau of National Affairs, Inc., 1975), pp. 26-27.

Those labor relations attorneys representing management who had believed or hoped that the Supreme Court would redefine its Trilogy doctrine with clear guidelines for determination of the authority of arbitrators could get little comfort from Mr. Justice Douglas' dissent in the *Gateway* case alluded to earlier in this chapter. Although having convinced the majority of his brethren in the Trilogy decisions that almost any labor dispute could or should be arbitrable, Douglas reversed his field in *Gateway*. In his dissent he argued that the majority erred in ruling as arbitrable a dispute originating in a work stoppage instigated by a local union mine safety committee.

The stoppage was in protest against continuance of work assignments in an allegedly unsafe mine area. The arbitration clause in the applicable agreement encompassed "any local trouble of any kind arising at the mine." But Douglas contended that this clause was not controlling and that the agreement authorized the safety committee to make a binding recommendation for removal of all waters from an unsafe area. On the other hand, the Supreme Court majority concluded that the arbitration clause could properly be invoked by management. Hence, the company was justified in suing under Section 301 of Taft-Hartley to compel arbitration of the safety dispute and to enjoin the work stoppage. In so ruling, the Supreme Court reversed the appellate circuit court's judgment which theorized that when workers leave their jobs in good faith because of abnormally dangerous conditions their action should not be deemed an unlawful strike.[19]

It is not inconceivable that one or more of the present Supreme Court Justices might follow Douglas' example and hold that arbitration is not the be-all and end-all for labor controversies, no matter what the explicit contract language prescribes. After all, perhaps Mr. Justice Douglas was doing precisely what Mr. Justice Stewart did in 1970 when he admitted seeking refuge in an aphorism of the late Justice Frankfurter, to the effect that wisdom ought not to be rejected simply because it arrives late. (See Chapter 7, p. 365.)

At least two Supreme Court decisions relating to the feasibility of arbitration seem unlikely to be reversed or modified by what the Court held in *Gardner-Denver*. In one of these, referred to as *Iowa Beef Packers*, Mr. Justice Douglas was also a dissenter.

The following summary appeared in American Arbitration Association's *Review of Court Decisions:*

---

[19]Gateway Coal Co. v. Mine Workers, UMW, District 4, Local 6330, 85 LRRM 2049, 414 U.S. 368 (1974).

FAIR LABOR STANDARDS ACT—RIGHT TO SUE WITHOUT FIRST ARBITRATING—CERTIORARI DISMISSED AS IMPROVIDENTLY GRANTED

A suit was brought under §(b) of the Fair Labor Standards Act and the District Court refused to dismiss for failure to first exhaust the grievance arbitration procedures in the collective bargaining agreement. The Iowa Supreme Court affirmed. Certiorari was granted to determine whether an alleged statutory violation regarding the failure to pay overtime wages for a lunch period which may also be a violation of the agreement in that the employer may have required employees to be on call, was subject to the grievance arbitration clause. The court determined at oral argument that the arbitration clause was too narrow to encompass the FLSA claim and dismissed certiorari as improvidently granted. Douglas, J. dissented contending that the claim was arbitrable and the important question of access to the courts should be decided on the merits.[20]

The outcome of a more recent federal court decision relating to the finality of arbitration is much more readily understandable to laymen. It's quite likely to remain the law of the land unless and until Congress acts to amend the Wage-Hour Act to permit what the court said could not be done. This case appears on the record books as *Satterwhite* v. *United Parcel Service*. The U.S. Supreme Court in 1974 denied certiorari, thus upholding the decision of the Second Circuit Court of Appeals summarized below in the American Arbitration Association Review of Court Decisions:

LABOR—FINALITY OF ARBITRATION AWARD PRECLUDES SUIT UNDER FAIR LABOR STANDARDS ACT—TITLE VII DIFFERENTIATED

An employee's right to sue under §16 (b) of the Fair Labor Standards Act, 29 U.S.C. §216 (b), for overtime compensation claimed under §7 (a) (1), 29 U.S.C. §207 (a)(1) is foreclosed by prior submission of the claim to final arbitration under the grievance procedure of a collective-bargaining agreement. The court distinguished FLSA from Title VII. Under the recently decided Alexander v. Gardner-Denver decision, 94 S.Ct. 1011, an arbitration award based upon a collective bargaining agreement dispute was held not to bar the individual from judicial review of his Title VII rights arising from the same facts. The anti-discrimination provisions of Title VII do not equate with the wages and hours provisions of the FLSA. The right of the private individual to enforce his rights is a factor under Title VII but not under FLSA. Further, Title VII provides for overlapping relief. The court found that "the absence of such procedures in FLSA suggests a greater reliance on contact remedies and a lesser emphasis on individual enforcement."[21]

---

[20]Iowa Beef Packers, Inc. v. Edward D. Thompson, 405 U.S. 228 (1972).
[21]*Review of Court Decisions*, THE ARBITRATION JOURNAL, June 1974, *29*(No. 2), 139.

If the principles of judicial construction of federal laws relating to labor relations that were enunciated in the case just cited do not stand the tests of changing times, no one without access to a crystal ball could accurately predict what the federal courts might end up by doing to or for the binding settlements of labor disputes through arbitration proceedings.

Contract Interpretation Without Arbitration

When a labor agreement contains no arbitration clause, either party charging a breach by the other party has the right to seek adjustment of its dispute by the National Labor Relations Board if the alleged breach might be construed by the Board to involve an unfair labor practice. This was the main thrust of the U.S. Supreme Court's judgment in the important case of *NLRB* v. *C & C Plywood Corporation,* decided in 1967. For all practical purposes the Court held that the Board could perform the function of construing an article of an agreement, which function might have been performed much more expeditiously by an arbitrator.

The factual situation in *C & C Plywood* presented a curious anomaly. Shortly after the ratification of a labor agreement, the company unilaterally instituted a premium pay plan for certain crews of employees which would have enabled them to get higher earnings than the wage scales just negotiated. The potentially higher earnings were conditioned on meeting specified production standards.

Three provisions of the contract were considered relevant by the Court in deciding this case. These in substance were:

1. "Wages" were closed for the term of the agreement.
2. Neither party would be obligated to bargain collectively with respect to any matter not specifically referred to in the contract.
3. Grievance machinery was established but no ultimate arbitration of grievances or other disputes was provided.

When the union requested a conference with the company to discuss the new premium pay plan, the company assented but refused to rescind the plan pending these discussions. It was this refusal that caused the union to file unfair labor practice charges against the company in violation of Section 8(a) (1) (5) of Taft-Hartley. The Board directed the company to bargain with the union about the disputed plan and to rescind it pending negotiation. On consideration of the history of negotiations between the parties and the express provisions of their agreement, the Board ruled that the union had not ceded power to the employer unilaterally to change the wage system the way it had done.

The Supreme Court upheld the Board's directive order against the company. In this case, the Court stated, "The Board has not construed a labor agreement to determine the extent of the contractual rights which were given the union by the employer." The Court went on to say:

> It [the Board] has not imposed its own view of what the terms and conditions of the labor agreement should be. It has done no more than merely to enforce a statutory right which Congress considered necessary to allow labor and management to get on with the process of reaching fair terms and conditions of employment, "to provide a means by which agreement may be reached." The Board's interpretation went only so far as it was necessary to determine that the union did not agree to give up these statutory safeguards.[22]

We imply no moral from citation of this case. Had the issue been subject to arbitration, conceivably the arbitrator might have reached the same conclusion as did the Board and the Supreme Court. At least he would have been obligated to render his decision much faster. It took some four years from the time the union filed its charges with the Board to the date when the Court handed down its decision. In all fairness it must be pointed out that an arbitrator's decision against the union on an issue of this sort might have led to challenge of its legality in unfair labor practice proceedings before the Board and ultimate review by the Supreme Court. Perhaps in that event five years or more would have elapsed from the filing of a grievance to the Supreme Court's judgment.

Work-Stoppage Arbitration

From management's standpoint the chief objective of grievance arbitration is to provide a fair and effective means for preventing or terminating work stoppages occurring during the life of a labor agreement. *"Arbitration is the means for solving the unforeseeable by molding a system of private law for all the problems which may arise and to provide for their solution and in a way which will generally accord with the variant needs and desires of the parties."* This passage, quoted above from the text of the *Warrior* decision, may be overly idealistic, and unrealistic too. Nevertheless, as will appear from the review of typical cases cited herein, the courts are earnestly striving to implement the declared policy of the

---

[22]NLRB v. C&C Plywood Corporation, No. 53, 64 LRRM 2065 (U.S. Sup. Ct. 1967).

Federal Government honoring arbitration but making its usage wholly voluntary.

Breach of Agreement—Absent No-Strike Clause

Notwithstanding the absence of a no-strike clause, a union may be found in violation of its agreement by striking over a grievance if the agreement imposes on both parties the duty of submitting grievances to final and binding arbitration. It is not necessary that an agreement contain an express no-strike pledge if the parties have accepted arbitration as the terminal point in the grievance procedure. The U.S. Supreme Court handed down in 1962 a decision to this effect in the case of Local 174, *Teamsters* v. *Lucas Flour Company.* The precepts in this decision would seemingly apply to management were it to engage in a lockout as a result of a grievance dispute required by the agreement to be adjudicated through the arbitration process.

The facts in this celebrated case can be simply stated. The company had discharged an employee after he had damaged a new fork-lift truck. A union business agent protested the discharge but failed to get the employee reinstated. The union then called a strike hoping to force the management to rehire the discharged employee. The strike lasted eight days. After it was over the issue of the discharge was submitted to arbitration. The discharge was sustained by an arbitration board.

Meanwhile the company brought suit in a state court asking damages for business losses caused by the strike. The court entered judgment in favor of the company in the amount of some six thousand dollars. The court in making the award against the union reasoned that the strike was in violation of the collective bargaining agreement, it having been an attempt to coerce the company to forego its contractual right to discharge an employee for unsatisfactory work. Sustaining the state court's judgment against the union, the Supreme Court said in summary:

> The collective bargaining contract expressly imposed upon both parties the duty of submitting the dispute in question to final and binding arbitration. In a consistent course of decisions the Courts of Appeals of at least five Federal Circuits have held that a strike to settle a dispute which a collective bargaining agreement provides shall be settled exclusively and finally by compulsory arbitration constitutes a violation of the agreement. The National Labor Relations Board has reached the same conclusion. . . . We approve that doctrine. To hold otherwise would obviously do violence to accepted principles of traditional contract law. Even more in point, a contrary view would be completely at odds with the basic policy of national

legislation to promote the arbitral process as a substitute for economic warfare.[23]

Breach of No-Strike Clause Not Waiver of Arbitration

The Supreme Court's 1962 decision in the landmark *Drake* case reemphasized the importance of management's determining during negotiations whether to insist on an all-inclusive grievance-arbitration clause or to attempt to reserve the right to sue for damages when a union breaches the no-strike clause in an agreement. The main question decided by the Court was whether a union's alleged breach of the no-strike clause in its contract constituted a repudiation or waiver of arbitration of the company's damage claim and thus prompted the company to take damage action against the union under Section 301 of Taft-Hartley. The Supreme Court said the issue of contract violation had to be arbitrated and that therefore the company's damage suit was, as a layman might put it, out of order.

Once again, the significance of the Supreme Court's decision to employers concerned with the recurring problems of what types of grievance-arbitration clauses are desirable can be appreciated only if the underlying facts are reviewed. Consequently, we present the facts as summarized in the Supreme Court's decision:

1. Before the year-end holidays in 1959, the company notified the union representing its employees in a bakery plant that because Christmas and New Year's Day would fall on Friday the employees would not be scheduled to work the Thursday before each holiday. They would be required instead to work both following Saturdays in order to have fresh bakery products to sell on each following Monday.

2. At meetings with management, upon receipt of this notice and before the holidays, the union argued that the temporary change in the work schedule violated its contract. The company's position was that it merely exercised one of its management prerogatives. Despite the differences of position a compromise was worked out for December 26 and some 40 percent of those scheduled worked that day. Further discussions were not fruitful, however, and on January

---

[23]Local 174, Teamsters, Chauffeurs, Warehousemen & Helpers of America v. Lucas Flower Company, No. 50, 40 LRRM 2717 (U.S. Sup. Ct. 1962). Not mentioned in the text of this chapter was a jurisdictional ruling, primarily of concern to labor relations attorneys. The Court indicated that the state courts had concurrent jurisdiction with federal courts over suits for violation of collective bargaining contracts but that they had to apply federal labor law as set forth in Section 301 of Taft-Hartley.

2, no production was possible because fewer than 15 percent of the scheduled crew reported for duty.

3. The company promptly filed a damage suit in federal district court seeking damages pursuant to Section 301 of Taft-Hartley and alleging that the union had instigated and encouraged its members to strike or not report for work on January 2.

4. Thereafter the union filed a motion for a stay of the suit in the district court. In an affidavit in support of its motion for a stay, the union specifically denied that it had instigated a strike or had encouraged its members not to work on January 2. But the ground for its motion was that the dispute between it and the company was a subject for arbitration and not a suit for damages.

5. The company disagreed entirely with the union's contention. In opposing the motion for a stay the company argued that it and the union could not have intended to arbitrate so fundamental a matter as a union strike in breach of contract. As the Court put it, "central to the company's position [was] its assertion that the union was bound to arbitrate, rather than strike over, its claim that the company breached the contract by scheduling Saturday work."

It was quite obviously the precise language of the grievance procedure in the contract that had to be construed by the Supreme Court, and it was this language which impelled the Court to decide against the company's contention that it could go to court instead of arbitration for redress. The key provision was in Article V(a) of the grievance procedure, which said, "The parties agree that they will promptly attempt to adjust all complaints, disputes or grievances arising between them involving questions of interpretation or application of any clause or matter covered by this contract or any act or conduct or relation between the parties hereto, directly or indirectly."[24]

Arbitration Agreement Not Sanctioning Employer Grievances

If a labor agreement limits arbitration to employee grievances, employer's damage suit under Section 301 may be dismissed or stayed on the contention that all issues related to the suit are referable to arbitration. The Supreme Court reached this conclusion in

---

[24]Drake Bakeries, Inc. v. Local 50, American Bakery and Confectionary Workers International Union, No. 598, 50 LRRM 2440 (U.S. Sup. Ct. 1962).

the case of *Atkinson* v. *Sinclair Refining Company*, decided the same day in 1962 as the *Drake* decision. There was no inconsistency in the Court's rulings on these two cases, for the Sinclair labor agreement contained no provisions that could be construed either to require or permit the company to invoke arbitration as a means for obtaining redress against the union for allegedly instigating wildcat strikes.[25]

(The case just referred to is now generally designated as *Sinclair II* because a different but related *Sinclair* decision was delivered simultaneously by the Court. *Sinclair I*, which primarily invoked the application of Norris-LaGuardia to damage suits for breach of no-strike agreements, was reviewed in Chapter 7.)

The implications of the two *Sinclair* cases in their relation to *Drake* were succinctly summarized by Professors Russell A. Smith and Dallas L. Jones in a paper published in 1966. Their summary comments were:

> In *Sinclair Refining Company* v. *Atkinson (Sinclair I)* it was held that a federal injunction against a peaceful strike over arbitrable grievances was barred by the Norris-LaGuardia Act, even though the strike was in breach of a contractual no-strike pledge. The other two cases posed the question, pertinent for present purposes, whether the employer's claim for damages for alleged violation of the union's no-strike pledge could be decided in a Section 301 suit without resort to arbitration. In *Atkinson* v. *Sinclair Refining Company (Sinclair II)* it was held that such a suit was not barred where the arbitration clause did not provide for the submission of employer grievances against the union. However, in *Drake* . . . , the decision went the other way where the arbitration clause was "bilateral."
>
> *Sinclair I* made no contribution to the federal substantive law concerning the arbitration process. But *Sinclair II* and *Drake* represented important developments of that law in three respects. First, they established the principle that, with respect to arbitrable issues, a party to the arbitration agreement has the right to insist upon arbitration in the first instance, rather than litigation. Second, they seemed to imply that there is no arbitral jurisdiction of an employer's contractual grievance unless the arbitration clause provides for the submission of employer grievances to arbitration, but that a court should order arbitration of such a grievance, including a claim of breach of a no-strike agreement, if the arbitration process is available to the employer and there is a broad arbitration clause. In addition, *Drake* rejected the employer's claim that it was excused from any duty to arbitrate because of the union's breach of its no-strike pledge.
>
> It is interesting that in *Sinclair II* the Court assumed the task of determining whether the particular arbitration clause was intended

---

[25] Atkinson et al. v. Sinclair Refining Company, No. 430, 50 LRRM 2433 (U.S. Sup. Ct. 1962).

to provide for the submission of employer grievances. The Court did not rule that the issue should be determined by an arbitrator, and its decision kept the issue away from arbitration. In *Drake*, on the other hand, the Court, while making a determination of the availability of the arbitration procedure to the employer, in effect sent the entire matter to arbitration (if the employer should persist in its attempt to obtain legal redress). Left to the arbitration process were all the issues presented by the claim of the employer, including questions of arbitral authority.[26]

Court Enforcement of Arbitration

No longer of much concern except to legal scholars and academicians is the question of the applicability of the Norris-LaGuardia Act to suits to compel arbitration of grievance disputes. Prior to 1957, there had been federal court decisions holding that the anti-injunction strictures of Norris-LaGuardia prevented the courts from compelling compliance with collectively bargained agreements to arbitrate grievances. The Supreme Court's decision in *Textile Workers* v. *Lincoln Mills* (1957) was explicit in its holding that federal courts had the power to decree specific performance of the arbitration provisions of labor agreements and that Norris-LaGuardia did not deprive the courts of jurisdiction.[27]

Arbitrator's Authority to Enjoin Slowdowns

When evaluating the pros and cons of grievance arbitration limited to employee grievances and not enabling an employer to process a grievance against a union, management may wish to consider whether time is of the essence in putting an end to a wildcat work stoppage. At least one company found it to have been advantageous to have in its agreement provisions permitting it not only to enter grievances against the union but also to have expedited arbitration proceedings to adjudicate claims of contract violation by the union. In fact, by reason of the provisions in its agreement for expediting arbitration proceedings, a New York company (Ruppert) quickly obtained an arbitration award containing an injunction. The injunction enjoined two union locals from continuing slowdowns. Even though the company's contract with the locals did not directly affirm or deny the power of an arbitrator to order an injunction, New York State's highest appellate court upheld the

---

[26]Smith and Jones, p. 836.
[27]Textile Workers Union of America v. The Lincoln Mills, No. 211, 40 LRRM 2 (U.S. Sup. Ct. 1957).

tinued for nearly two weeks, however, but collapsed the day after a state court judge issued an injunction against the picketing.

Meanwhile the company had suspended the 42 employees whom its management considered to be the strike leaders. The picketing, the company contended, was "the sole manifestation of their leadership of the wildcat strike." They were notified that they had been suspended for engaging in an unauthorized work stoppage and picketing in violation of the no-strike provisions of the applicable agreement. Pursuant to other terms of the agreement, hearings were promptly held by the management for the suspended employees, except for one who resigned, with the result that eight employees were reinstated without loss of pay or seniority and that the suspension of the remaining 32 was converted to discharge.

These discharges were directly appealed to arbitration. As the arbitrator stated in his award, all employees who picketed, induced other employees not to work, or who were scheduled but remained away from work during the work stoppage were "guilty of engaging in a prohibited strike, work stoppage, or interruption of work. Such violations constituted proper cause for suspension and ultimate discharge." It was therefore the management's selection for discharge of 32 employees out of a total of more than 1,000 participating in the wildcat strike that was the main issue to be adjudicated by the arbitrator. He formulated this issue as follows:

> In the instant case the principal point of contention involves whether or not the company is guilty of having discriminated against the thirty-two grievants in question by imposing upon them selective discipline, that is, by imposing upon them the penalty of discharge while not invoking any dicipline upon other employees who wrongfully walked off their jobs and/or remained away from work during the term of the wildcat strike.

The arbitrator found for the company. He pointed out that the discharged employees had actively encouraged the continuance of the work stoppage and by their presence on the picket lines induced other employees not to return to work. "It is not necessary," the arbitrator observed, "that physical activity be exercised or threats be voiced to constitute picketing. It is a matter of common knowledge that there is great antipathy on the part of working men, especially Union members, to cross a picket line." In sustaining the discharges and thereby upholding the company's basis for singling out the pickets as strike leaders, the arbitrator concluded:

> Selective discipline in and of itself does not constitute discrimination. It is an academic principle of Labor/Management relations, followed by the majority of Arbitrators, that an employer may select

certain employees for discipline, including discharge, provided the selection is made on reasonable standards. There is reasonable basis for such doctrine. Otherwise, employers would, in many instances, be forced to close down their businesses or forego discharging those actually responsible for contractually prohibited wildcat strikes and work stoppages. In the instant case it was neither practical nor just to discharge 1200 or 1300 employees who participated in the strike by merely staying home from work. Furthermore, to have done so would have unjustly penalized the Company, the victim, rather than the culprits.[35]

The decision of the arbitrator in this case has not yet been published. Hence, we quote from his own citation from his 1969 award in a case concerning American Hoist and Derrick Company:

An employer who is the victim of an illegal wildcat strike is not required to deprive itself of the services of all its employees participating in a prohibited strike. It may select those for punishment for the offense as it deems fit, provided such selection is not capricious. Employees who elect to participate in illegal walkouts and strikes run the risk that they may be more severely diciplined than others who engage in like activity.[36]

Termination of Work Stoppage Conditioned on Arbitration

Amnesty for illegal strike leaders is often demanded by union officials as a condition of an agreement for terminating a walkout. But amnesty provides no deterrent for future contract breaches. In fact it may encourage subsequent wildcat strikes, particularly if the terms of the strike settlement include concessions to the union that might not have otherwise been obtained through the orderly processes of the grievance procedure.

Knotty questions of law may develop in some situations when both the management and top representatives of the union have a common interest in terminating wildcat strikes without setting vicious precedents. Such questions are likely to arise in situations where the strike leaders are dissident local union officials or when they are in fact acting as agents for a rival union seeking to win adherence in a forthcoming representation election or decertification proceedings before the Board. Even though the work stoppage may have been demonstrably illegal, the instigators are entitled to nondiscriminatory representation in negotiations for its settlement and in arbitration proceedings that may follow.

---

[35]American Car and Foundry Division, ACF Industries, Inc., Huntington, and U.S. Steelworkers of America, Local 1652, Vernon L. Stouffer, Esq., Arbitrator; decision Jan. 11, 1971.

[36]American Hoist and Derrick Company, 53 LA 45, 58 (1969).

Any semblance of Taft-Hartley unfair labor practices either by the company or by the international union was adroitly avoided in the settlement of a protracted work stoppage where a demand for amnesty for the local's chief steward was a major stumbling block. He had been suspended from employment during the strike and was given notice that the final disciplinary penalty to be imposed upon him by management would be determined only after full production was resumed. His suspension, however, was to continue indefinitely. For weeks the strikers refused to return to work unless the chief steward was allowed to go back on the job too. Finally the international representative persuaded the management to lift the suspension and permit the chief steward to go back on the job and to resolve the question of disciplinary action against him through the grievance procedure. This management concession ended the work stoppage.

At a high-level grievance meeting convened when the strike ended, the management, being more concerned with prevention of illegal work stoppages rather than drastic punitive action, proposed a one-month disciplinary layoff for the chief steward. The management served notice at the grievance meeting that should its proposal be rejected and should the union insist on arbitrating the penalty, it would urge the arbitrator to find that outright discharge was in order. The union representatives vigorously protested but decided to let the chief steward make his own determination as to whether to take the one-month suspension or take his chances on perhaps complete exoneration, a lesser penalty, or, conversely, outright discharge. He decided to take the risk. Even though he may have had genuine doubts about the loyalty of the chief steward to the incumbent union, the international representative arguing the case in arbitration tenaciously defended the chief steward's conduct during the work stoppage—but to no avail. The arbitrator's award was discharge, period.[37]

Individuals' Rights in Grievance Arbitration

As was pointed out in Chapter 7 in the review of the Supreme Court's *Allis-Chalmers* decision in 1967, the emphasis of Taft-Hartley litigation has been in the direction of collective rights of unions and away from the rights of individual employees. In re-

---

[37]This decision was never published. It had certain murky aspects, including a lapse on the part of the arbitrator who in his award stated that the company's discharge of the steward was justified. Actually, the arbitrator had to decide what the penalty should be and parties concluded that what he meant to say was that he ordered the discharge.

ferring to national labor policy in one of the passages of that decision, the Court declared:

> The policy therefore extinguishes the individual's power to order his own relations with his employer and creates a power vested in the chosen representative to act in the interest of all employees. "Congress has seen fit to clothe the bargaining representative with powers comparable to those possessed by a legislative body both to create and restrict the rights of those whom he represents . . ."

The Supreme Court and other federal appellate courts have indicated by some of their decisions endorsement of one of Emerson's aphorisms. He said, "A foolish consistency is the hobgoblin of little minds, adored by little statesmen and philosophers and divines. With consistency a great soul has simply nothing to do." Despite its recent stress on collective rights, the Supreme Court has not in recent years repudiated the dictum in one of its 1962 decisions which vindicated individual employees' rights arising from labor agreements. The Court then said:

> The rights of individual employees concerning rates of pay and conditions of employment are a major focus of the negotiation and administration of collective bargaining contracts. Individual claims lie at the heart of the grievance and arbitration machinery, are to a large degree inevitably intertwined with union interests and many times precipitate grave questions concerning the interpretation and enforceability of the collective bargaining contract on which they are based. To exclude these claims from the ambit of Section 301 would stultify the congressional policy of having the administration of collective bargaining contracts accomplished under a uniform body of federal substantive law. This we are unwilling to do.

To be sure, the matter before the Court involved the right of an individual employee to sue in federal court rather than to go to arbitration when he thought he had grounds to collect compensation from his employer for time lost due to a strike by another union. As to the specific issue, the employee complained in court that he and other fellow employees were ready and available to work on their regular jobs on the staff of a newspaper but were not permitted to work during a strike of employees belonging to another union, even though other employees of the publisher not covered by bargaining agreements were permitted to report for work and given full pay, although there was no work available for them to do. The employee who sued charged that the company had violated a clause in the contract applicable to him which provided that there should be no discrimination against any employee because of his membership or activity in the union.

It would not necessarily follow that since the Supreme Court sustained the right of the individual employee to sue his company for violation of the terms of the union contract under which he was covered, he could have sought a remedy through the grievance procedure unless that procedure expressly provided arbitration was available only to a union, not to an individual.[38]

The rights of individuals to assist on arbitration of their own grievances over the opposition of the union that has negotiated and administered the contract by which they are covered have been challenged in the courts, and with some success. Thus, in 1962 a federal appellate court construed a rather ambiguously phrased grievance procedure as letting an individual employee only file his own grievance and have it answered by his foreman. Thereafter it was exclusively for the union to decide whether to proceed through any of the next steps of the grievance procedure, or finally to arbitrate. The court declared:

> The Union represents the employees for the purpose of negotiating and enforcing the terms of the collective bargaining agreement. This is the modern means of bringing about industrial peace and channeling the resolution of intraplant disputes. Chaos would result if every disenchanted employee, every disturbed employee and every employee who harbored a dislike for his employer, could harass both the union and the employer by processing grievances through the various steps of the grievance procedure and ultimately bringing an action to compel arbitration in the face of clear contractual provisions intended to channel the enforcement remedy through the union.

This appellate court did not, however, deny the right of an individual to utilize a grievance-arbitration procedure if the applicable contract gave him such right. The final words of the court were:

> If employer and union deem it consonant with the efficient handling of labor disputes to repose power in the individual employee to compel the employer to arbitrate grievances, then they may do so, by incorporating such a provision in clear language in the collective bargaining agreement. They have not done so here.[39]

The U.S. Supreme Court declared in its somewhat ambiguous decision in the case of *Republic Steel* v. *Maddox* (1965) that an individual employee is not entitled to take his own grievance to arbitration *unless the applicable contract so permits*. But the Court implied, without so stating explicitly, that grievance procedures

---

[38]Smith v. Evening News Association, No. 13, 51 LRRM 2646 (U.S. Sup. Ct. 1962).

[39]Black-Clawson Company v. International Association of Machinists, 313 F.2d 179, 52 LRRM 2038 (1962).

culminating in arbitration should be available only to the incumbent union and not to individuals. Moreover, the Court left in limbo the question as to whether an employer who sought but failed to gain acceptance by the union of contract provisions permitting individuals to utilize the arbitration machinery on their own is thereby estopped from voluntarily agreeing with any employee or group of employees to arbitrate grievances over the objections by the union.

In the case of *Republic* v. *Maddox,* the Court indicated that the general federal rule requires that individual employees wishing to assert contract grievances must "attempt" full use of the grievance procedure as the mode of redress before the individual employees may seek judicial relief. The Court went on to say that:

> If the union refuses to press or only perfunctorily presses the individual's claim, differences may arise as to the forms of redress then available. . . . But unless the contract provides otherwise, there can be no doubt that the employee must afford the union the opportunity to act on his behalf. Congress has expressly approved contract grievance procedures as a preferred method for settling disputes and stabilizing the "common law" of the plant. . . . And it cannot be said, in the normal situation, that contract grievance procedures are inadequate to protect the interests of an aggrieved employee until the employee has attempted to implement the procedure and found them so.

Unfortunately the Supreme Court in its *Republic* v. *Maddox* decision did not address itself to an essential question relating to construction of the proviso of Taft-Hartley which states that:

> . . . any individual employee or a group of employees shall have the right at any time to present grievances to their employer and to have such grievances adjusted, without the intervention of the bargaining representative, as long as the adjustment is not inconsistent with the terms of a collective-bargaining contract or agreement then in effect: *Provided further,* that the bargaining representative has been given opportunity to be present at such adjustment.[40]

The proviso in Section 9(a) was put to the test of an actual arbitration proceeding in 1953 with the result that the arbitrator ruled he had the right and duty to decide individual employees' grievances despite the vigorous objections of the incumbent union. The arbitrator who heard this case was Paul R. Hays, Esq., then professor of law, Columbia University, and subsequently a judge of the Federal Court of Appeals, Second Circuit. The contract he was called upon to interpret simply provided for a grievance procedure

---

[40]Republic Steel Corporation v. Maddox, No. 43, 58 LRRM 2193 (U.S. Sup. Ct. 1965).

for the settlement of "differences, disputes and grievances" that might arise between the union and the company. The arbitrator found no language in the agreement which could be taken "as an indication of the employer's intention to surrender its privilege of adjusting individual grievances. The union cited no express provision of the agreement to support its contention that grievances could be presented exclusively by the union. And the arbitrator concluded that the proviso of Section 9(a) was insufficient to prevent the adjustment of individual grievances if the employer desired to make such adjustment. Accordingly, the arbitrator ruled that the agreement between the parties did not prevent the company and the individual employee from entering into an agreement "to submit to arbitration a dispute which the action permits the employee to present and the employer to hear and adjust."[41]

Arbitrator Hays' ruling as to the application of the law and the contract was announced tentatively before he proceeded to hear the grievance on its merits. At the same hearing the union was represented, but only to enter an added objection to the proceeding. Its representative then withdrew. The final outcome, incidentally, was an award that the specific grievance of the individual employee was unsupportable under the contract and it was therefore denied.

Why should management even consider negotiating or attempting to negotiate a grievance clause permitting individuals to process their own grievance up to and including the final step of arbitration? Here are some of the reasons advanced by those favoring such provisions in the grievance machinery. It is not true that arbitration invariably is the result of hostile relations between the management and the union. Nor are all cases presented to arbitrators necessarily of an adversary nature. There may be sincere differences among local union officers and stewards, for example, as to which one of two or more employees who bid for a better job should get it. The same sort of disagreement may exist when it becomes necessary to bump employees on curtailment of the work force. Such differences often arise when absolute seniority is not spelled out as the decisive factor in promotions or layoffs. The union grievance committee in situations of these sorts well might be agreeable to having an aggrieved employee take his own grievance to arbitration, particularly if he would be willing to defray the portion of the expense normally charged to the union.

There are other aspects to the issue from management's standpoint. Some industrial relations executives, albeit a small minority, consider that granting individuals the right to process their com-

---
[41]Vaccaro and General Cable Corp., Hays, Arbitrator, 20 LRRM 443 (1953).

plaints all the way through the grievance procedure would keep management off the figurative spot of seeming to show either favoritism or prejudice in responding to grievances concerning members of rival factions contesting for control of the local grievance committee. Even in situations where there are union shop contracts, such contests often occur. They sometimes occur when one or more unions are striving to displace the recognized bargaining agent despite its holding a union shop contract.

More important in the eyes of some industrial relations administrators, permissive utilization of the grievance procedure in its totality by individual employees provides a strong deterrent to the filing of individual complaints with state labor commissions or other state or federal agencies such as those involved with civil rights, or initial resort to the courts for redress of alleged contract violations. The same matter, it is argued, could be settled much more quickly and decisively on the home grounds through arbitration.

Once again, there may be an advantage both to management and the union in granting the right of every employee to have an arbitrator decide his grievance since such grant would tend to lessen markedly the chance of protracted court proceedings of the sort that developed in the *Vaca-Sipes* case, i.e., litigation arising from charges that the union had breached its duty of fair representation.

By raising these controversial issues we do not imply our own advocacy of either position. In any event the final word on the validity of contract clauses permitting individuals to process grievances in arbitration has yet to be spoken by the U.S. Supreme Court.

NLRB JURISDICTION IN ARBITRATION MATTERS

The U.S. Supreme Court has ruled that the National Labor Relations Board has authority to intervene in labor disputes where unfair labor practice complaints or representation questions develop, even though arbitration has been agreed to as a means for settling such disputes. The Board can intervene prior to arbitration proceedings. It also has the power to upset the arbitrator's award if in the Board's judgment the award would constitute a violation of Taft-Hartley. The Court has held in diverse situations that the Board may exercise independent jurisdiction, concurrent jurisdiction, or final jurisdiction depending upon the nature of the issue presented for its resolution.

Information Essential for Arbitration

Employers have an obligation to furnish unions information enabling the unions to proceed to process grievances. And the Board has jurisdiction to order employers to furnish such data when the union contends a labor agreement has been violated and if the alleged violation might also continue illegal refusal to bargain under Taft-Hartley.

The Supreme Court so decided in one of its landmark decisions (*Acme Industrial Company*, 1967). This case originated in the refusal of the company to respond to union questions about the removal of machinery from its plant to a new location. After this refusal, the union filed a number of grievances asserting violation of a contract clause relating to rights of employees to transfer to a new location. It also filed unfair labor practice charges with the Board. The Board ruled that the company had refused to bargain in good faith by denying the union information necessary to enable it to evaluate intelligently the grievances it had filed. A federal circuit court refused to enforce the Board's decision, holding that the existence of an agreement for binding arbitration foreclosed the Board from taking any action.

The Supreme Court sustained the Board's authority to insist that the employer supply prior to arbitration the information sought by the union. In so doing the Court observed that the Board was not making a binding construction of the labor contract. Rather, as the Court said, the Board "was only acting upon the probability that the desired information was relevant, and that it would be of use to the union in carrying out its statutory duties and responsibilities." The Court further stated,

> Far from intruding upon the preserve of the arbitrator, the Board's action was in aid of the arbitrable process. Arbitration can function properly only if the grievance procedure leading to it can sift out unmeritorious claims. For if all claims originally initiated as grievances had to be processed through arbitration, the system would be woefully overburdened.[42]

Board Criteria in Reviewing Arbitration Awards

There are no legal barriers to prevent management from including in the grievance procedure machinery of a labor agreement provisions for arbitrating the kinds of disputes that might also be subject to the jurisdiction of the Board. Nor are there legal barriers preventing an employer and a union from making agreements out-

---

[42]NLRB v. Acme Industrial Company, No. 52, 64 LRRM 2069 (U.S. Sup. Ct. 1967).

side of the terms of their labor contract to arbitrate the conditions for settling work stoppages. The Board intimated as much in the leading case now referred to as *Spielberg*, decided in 1955. The gist of the Board's decision was that it would not upset an arbitrator's award holding that the Spielberg company was not obliged to reinstate four strikers who had allegedly engaged in misconduct on a picket line.

The company's refusal to reinstate four strikers was the bone of contention that prevented a strike settlement until the parties agreed to submit the issue to final and binding arbitration by a three-man arbitration panel. As the Board noted, the four employees accused of picket-line misconduct actively participated in and acquiesced in the arbitration procedure, and so did the union representing them.

The majority of the arbitration panel made an award stating that the company had justification for not reinstating the four strikers. Despite this decision, to which the management, the union, and the employees concerned had agreed to be bound, unfair labor practice charges were filed against the company for its refusal to reinstate these particular strikers. After pointing out explicitly that it did not consider itself to be bound, as a matter of law, by an arbitration award, the Board nonetheless concluded:

> In summary, the proceedings appear to have been fair and regular, all parties had agreed to be bound, and the decision of the arbitration panel is not clearly repugnant to the purposes and policies of the Act. In these circumstances we believe that the desirable objective of encouraging the voluntary settlement of labor disputes will best be served by our recognition of the arbitrators' award. Accordingly, we find that the Respondent did not violate the Act when, in accordance with the award, it refused to reinstate the four strikers.[43]

The Spielberg Doctrine as Currently Construed

The NLRB decisions and pronouncements by Board officials have been varied and sometimes seemingly contradictory in interpreting what has now become known as the *Spielberg* doctrine. This doctrine has never been expressly renounced by the Board. It has not been regarded as controlling where the factual situation in a given case was not precisely on all fours with that presented in the original *Spielberg* case.

To illustrate changing interpretations of the doctrine, there are quoted below official declarations (1) by the Board's General

---

[43]Spielberg Manufacturing Company, 112 NLRB 1080, 36 LRRM 1152 (1955).

Counsel, Arnold Ordman, in 1967, and (2) by the Board's then newly appointed chairman, Edward B. Miller, in 1970.

Ordman stated at a session of the National Academy of Arbitrators in 1967 that:

> The Spielberg safeguards were required to foreclose the possibility that encouragement of private adjudication of disputes might be undertaken at the expense of public rights the National Labor Relations Act is designed to guarantee.
>
> There are differences between the private grievance-arbitration rights and duties and the statutory administrative processes of the Board established to protect and enforce. . . . the rights of the public in connection with labor disputes affecting commerce.[44]

In his resort to vague legalistic phraseology characteristic of federal bureaucrats, Ordman never attempted to outline what "public rights" the Board had so zealously to protect.

The *Spielberg* doctrine and its limitations pose continuing problems for industrial relations executives attempting to negotiate equitable terms for ending either wildcat strikes or legitimate economic strikes in which employee-strikers may have been guilty of violence or other illegal tactics. To agree to arbitrate the question of reinstatement or discharge of such strikers amounts to giving them "two bites at the apple." When management agrees to be bound by the arbitrator's decision and the decision is adverse to its position, it has no practical legal recourse. On the other hand, when the union agrees to be bound by arbitration, the *Spielberg* doctrine still permits it to appeal to the Board on the allegation of unfair labor practices. Should this seemingly pose a dilemma for employers, a pronouncement of the Board's chairman, Edward B. Miller, who took office in 1970, did little to solve it. Shortly after taking office he delivered an address in which he said:

> We have struggled, for example, in recent years to arrive at a rational accommodation between our decision making processes and the decision making processes of labor arbitration. I do not think that any of the members of the Board believe that we have yet reached the end point of the evolution of the details of that accommodation. . . . Now that voluntary arbitration of contractual disputes has become so widespread and so much an integral part of the collective bargaining process, we cannot help but be aware of the potential confusion which may arise if we cannot satisfactorily accommodate the two sometimes overlapping jurisdictions.[45]

---

[44]Arnold Ordman, *Arbitration and the NLRB, A Second Look,* in THE ARBITRATOR, THE NLRB, AND THE COURTS (Washington: The Bureau of National Affairs, Inc., 1967), p. 481.

[45]Edward B. Miller, *The NLRB—Hero or Villain?,* LABOR RELATIONS YEARBOOK (Washington: BNA Books, 1970), p. 216.

It would be less than kind to describe as gyrations the shifting attitude of the Board's majority on how to apply or to deviate from its own *Spielberg* doctrine. In 1975, however, the Board's current standard was declared by the American Bar Association Committee on Labor Arbitration and Collective Bargaining to be as follows:

> [W]e believe the better application of the underlying principles of *Collyer* and *Spielberg* to be that we should give full effect to arbitration awards dealing with discipline or discharge cases under *Spielberg*, except when unusual circumstances are shown which demonstrate that there were bona fide reasons, other than a mere desire on the part of one party to try the same set of facts before two forums, which caused the failure to introduce such evidence at the arbitration proceedings.[46]

The Board's reference above to *Collyer* requires some explanation. In its 1971 *Collyer* decision the Board ruled that it would defer to a contractual grievance arbitration procedure where there was an unfair labor practice charge in addition to a contractual issue *if* such a charge had been filed with the Board prior to arbitration. This Board ruling was qualified by a reservation that the Board would retain jurisdiction for a limited purpose. As it explained in its *Collyer* decision:

> In order to eliminate the risk of prejudice to any party, we shall retain jurisdiction over this dispute solely for the purpose of entertaining an appropriate and timely motion for further consideration upon a proper showing that either (a) the dispute has not, with reasonable promptness after the issuance of this decision, either been resolved by amicable settlement in the grievance procedure or submitted promptly to arbitration, or (b) the grievance or arbitration procedures have not been fair and regular or have reached a result which is repugnant to the Act.[47]

It should be noted that the Collyer decision applied to Board proceedings commencing before arbitration proceedings had a chance to run their course. Conversely, the *Spielberg* case and the doctrine ensuing from it related to challenges to arbitral awards already issued.

Post-Collyer "Ping-Ponging"

The various gyrations of the NLRB following its celebrated *Collyer* decision cannot always be disclosed by examination of published Board orders. One unpublished edict of the Board in 1976 has been aptly described as "Ping-Ponging." This somewhat sa-

---

[46]American Bar Association, *Report of the Committee on Labor Arbitration and the Law of Collective Bargaining Agreements,* 1975 COMMITTEE REPORTS, p. 178.
[47]Collyer Insulated Wire, 192 NLRB 837, 77 LRRM 1931 (1971).

tirical reference appears in a quarterly publication, "Study Time," put out by the American Arbitration Association. In a preliminary observation the editor, Morris Stone, said that "whether the Collyer Doctrine is beneficial depends on how wisely it is applied by the NLRB and how parties react to it." This point was illustrated last year in the experience of a company and union in Massachusetts that found themselves shuttling back and forth between arbitration and the Board, finally getting a decision that might have been obtained more expeditiously by resorting to one forum alone.

As reported by Stone the basic facts were not in dispute. A Massachusetts public utility company that had previously granted its employees the privilege of getting discount prices on appliances terminated this concession. The union challenged the company's right to do this on the ground that it represented a change in working conditions without prior negotiation. It had done so by entering a grievance and demanding arbitration, if necessary.

While the management insisted that this was not an arbitrable issue, it agreed with the union to let an arbitrator decide this threshold question. The parties then agreed on an arbitrator. Meanwhile the union went to the NLRB with an unfair labor practice charge about the unilateral change in working conditions. Pursuant to then prevailing *Collyer* dicta, the Board delayed action on the charge pending the arbitrator's decision on the preliminary question of arbitrability. That dignitary ruled that the abandonment of the employee discount plan was *not* arbitrable. He wrote that the union's claim was "not rooted in any mutual understanding of the parties but in the NLRA," thereby being "still a statutory issue, dressed in contractual clothing."

After the union had filed its unfair labor practice charge with the Board and before the arbitrator reached his conclusion, the union joined the company in its stance that the entire issue should be adjudicated by NLRB. Stone opined:

> An arbitrator, sensitive to his role, should be reluctant to proceed when both parties believe that the dispute should be decided in another forum. . . . It is difficult to understand how the Board can add to it [the arbitrator's authority], whether it be done in the guise of "deferring," "delegating," or "refusing to proceed," for there is no visible statutory support for the Board deciding whether the arbitrator has such authority.

The dénouement, as explained by Stone—for there never was any recorded NLRB decision—was that "the merits were finally heard by an Administrative Law Judge of the NLRB, who found that the company had violated its obligations under the Taft-

Hartley Act by not negotiating the proposed end of the discount plan with the union."[48]

In the past few years the federal appellate courts and the Board have often cited both cases as a precedential basis for either defferal or nondeferral to the arbitration processes. As pointed out by the ABA committee, the Supreme Court has cited *Collyer* with favor, stating in *Arnold Co.* v. *Carpenters District Council*, 417 U.S.12 (1974), that the Board's policy is to refrain from exercising jurisdiction where conduct is arguably an unfair labor practice and a contract violation and where the parties have voluntarily contracted to establish grievance-arbitration procedures." *Arnold* was one of the important circuit court cases in which the Board's deferral decision was sustained after the Board had heard on its merits a complaint of an alleged violation by a union of Section 8(b) (2) of Taft-Hartley. (Section 8(b) (2) of the Act proscribes a union attempt to cause an employer to discriminate against an employee who has fallen out of favor with the union.) To quote from the Committee report:

> The Board did not misuse its discretion where it found that the arbitration procedure could fairly determine the issue which boiled down to factual determinations and questions of contract law and interpretation fully cognizable by an arbitrator. (*Enterprise Publishing Co.* v. *N.L.R.B.*, 493 F2d 1024, 1st Cir. 1974.)[49]

As for the other side of the picture, the Bar Association Committee has cited several recent cases of more than passing importance. As the ABA report noted:

> In a number of cases the Board has refused to defer to available arbitration procedures where an employer has indicated it will not willingly participate in the grievance procedure. See *Bunker Hill Co.*, 208 N.L.R.B. No. 17, 85 L.R.R.M. 1264 (1973) and *Southwestern Bell Telephone Co.*, 212 N.L.R.B., No. 10, 87 L.R.R.M. 1446 (1974) where the employer would not waive timeliness provisions for arbitration; *Diversified Industries*, 208 N.L.R.B. No. 7, 85 L.R.R.M. 1394 (1974) employer unlawfully sought to inhibit or preclude access to grievance procedure and breached voluntary settlement agreement. . . .[50]

Deferral to Arbitration Awards (Per Spielberg)

The cases involving appellate court and/or Board interpretation of the *Spielberg* doctrine have become too numerous to permit

---

[48]STUDY TIME, American Arbitration Association, April 1977.

[49]American Bar Association, *Report of the Committee on Labor Arbitration and the Law of Collective Bargaining Agreements*, p. 175.

[50]*Ibid.*, p. 178.

ready selection of those of most significance. To cite just one—at random—on the *pro* side, by a 3-2 decision in *Malrite of Wisconsin, Inc.*, the Board favored an arbitration award and dismissed a complaint alleging that an employer had violated Taft-Hartley's collective bargaining requirements by unilaterally changing certain terms and conditions of employment.[51]

In its 1975 report the Bar Association Committee singled out several significant cases of nondeferral on the basis of the *Speilberg* doctrine:

> The Board will not defer to a prior award where the issue before it is accretion. *Hershey Foods Corporation*, 208 N.L.R.B. No. 70, 85 LRRM 1312 (1974.) Where the arbitrator did not consider questions of (1) employer intent to be bound by the contract and (2) whether the employer and a security agency should be considered joint employers under the Act and where the security agency was not a party to the arbitration, the Board will not defer to a prior award in a case alleging violations of Sections 8(a)(2) and 8(b)(1)(A) of the Act, *Waterfront Guards Ass'n Local 1852*, 209 N.L.R.B. No. 87, 86 LRRM 1238 (1974.) Neither will the Board defer solely on a stipulation that a grievance of some kind was presented and some board decided the question adversely to the charging party. A burden of specificity as [to] the prior arbitration proceeding and the issues decided therein must be met by the party wishing to rely on a Spielberg defense. John Sexton and Co., 213 N.L.R.B. No. 111, 87 L.R.R.M. 124 (1974.)[52]

Arbitration of Representation Issues

Management may have a long road to travel (or of travail) when it agrees to or is committed by a labor contract to arbitrate a dispute about the coverage of particular occupations in a given bargaining unit. The Board has declared it would apply the *Spielberg* doctrine to this type of issue. Its application in one celebrated case led to a reversal of the arbitrator's decision. That case or series of cases (generally designated as *Carey* or *Carey* and *Westinghouse*) went from a state court, to the U.S. Supreme Court, to an arbitrator, and finally to the Board.

The litigation commenced after the IUE had filed with the company a grievance alleging that members of another union were performing work of the same sort that under the terms of its contract would have been done by its members. The company refused to arbitrate on the ground that the issue was one of representation which was within the exclusive jurisdiction of the NLRB. The

---

[51]Malrite of Wisconsin, Inc., 198 NLRB 241, 80 LRRM 1593 (1972).

[52]American Bar Association, *Report of the Committee on Labor Arbitration and the Law of Collective Bargaining Agreements*, p. 178.

company's position was sustained by a state court (Maryland) when the union sought a court order to arbitrate. As for further developments, we quote Board General Counsel Ordman's summary.

> . . . the Supreme Court reversed the state court's decision and held that "whether the dispute was regarded as a jurisdictional dispute or as a representation dispute," arbitration was not precluded between the contracting parties even though only one of the two unions would be a participant and be bound by the result. Arbitration might, said the Court, have some therapeutic value or, if the award should run against the participating union, end the controversy. The Court found, therefore, that arbitration could be ordered, stating, however, that: "The superior authority" of the Board might "be invoked at any time."
>
> Subsequent to the decision in *Carey* v. *Westinghouse* 375 U.S. 261 (1964) [55 LRRM 2042] the arbitration was held. . . . The arbitrator found that the issue before him was a representation issue. He split the unit in the sense that he divided the employees whom the IUE claimed to represent into two groups based on the wage level of the individual employees.
>
> The Board also found that it was a representation issue because the IUE disputed the unit placement of the employees doing the work and complained of the failure to apply the IUE agreement to those employees. The IUE did not seek to replace the employees represented by the SEA, the rival union, with its own members.

The final result was a Board order superseding the arbitrator's decision. As Ordman explained it, "the ultimate issue of representation could not be decided by the arbitrator's interpretation of the contract under which he was authorized to act but could be resolved only by Board criteria for making unit determinations. In such cases the arbitrator's award must 'clearly reflect the use of and be consonant with Board standards.' Accordingly, the Board, while giving 'some consideration to the award,' applied its own criteria and made a different unit allocation."[53]

An Epochal Decision Affecting Management's Rights and Obligations in re Arbitration

A truly momentous decision of the U.S. Supreme Court handed down in 1975 was the *Emporium Capwell Co.* case. This case should be *must* study for every personnel administrator who is concerned with formulating or administering company policies where the industrial relations administrator has any responsibility for

---

[53]Ordman, p. 55.

negotiating or administering union agreements. Management's labor relations counsel would be well advised to study and restudy this decision, including its copious footnotes.

Paradoxically, the case originated in certain employees' efforts to bypass the grievance mechanisms in the applicable union-management agreement, so no arbitration proceedings took place. Instead, there was resort to the Board, a federal appellate court, and, finally, the Supreme Court. In the tortuous process of deciding if the Court (with Mr. Justice Douglas dissenting) considered it essential to review and reaffirm prior decisions relating to employees' rights and management rights and obligations under Taft-Hartley and the Civil Rights Act, the place of arbitration in the highly complicated picture had to be given most serious consideration in the Court's findings and conclusion.

Emporium was not a case that can be readily summarized without risk of distortion or omission of vital factors. Hence, the syllabus prepared by the Court's reporter of decisions is reproduced below in full:

> A union, after investigating complaints that the company with which it had a collective-bargaining agreement was racially discriminating against employees, invoked the contract grievance procedure by demanding that the joint union-management Adjustment Board be convened "to hear the entire case." Certain employees who felt that procedure inadequate refused to participate and against the union's advice, picketed the company's store. The company, after warning the employees, fired them on their resumption of picketing, whereupon a local civil rights association to which the fired employees belonged (hereinafter respondent) filed charges against the company with the National Labor Relations Board (NLRB) under §8(a)(1) of the National Labor Relations Act (NLRA), which makes it an unfair labor practice for an employer to interfere with an employee's right under §7 to engage in concerted action "for the purpose of collective bargaining or other mutual aid or protection." The NLRB found that the employees were discharged for attempting to bargain with the company over the terms and conditions of employment as they affected racial minorities and held that they could not circumvent their elected representative's efforts to engage in such bargaining. On respondent's petition for review the Court of Appeals reversed and remanded, concluding that concerted activity against racial discrimination enjoys a "unique status" under the NLRA and Title VII of the Civil Rights Act of 1964; that the NLRB "should inquire, in cases such as this, whether the union was actually remedying the discrimination to the *fullest extent possible by the most expeditious and efficacious means*"; and that "[w]here the union's efforts fall short of this high standard, the minority group's

concerted activity cannot lose its section 7 protection." *Held:* Though national labor policy accords the highest priority to non-discriminatory employment practices, the NLRA does not protect concerted activity by minority employees to bargain with their employer over issues of employment discrimination, thus bypassing their exclusive bargaining representative.

(a) The NLRA in §9(a) recognizes the principle of exclusive representation, which is tempered by safeguards for the protection of minority interests, and in establishing this regime of majority rule, Congress sought to secure to all members of the collective-bargaining unit the benefits of their collective strength in full awareness that the superior strength of some individuals or groups might be subordinated to the majority interest.

(b) Separate bargaining is not essential to eliminate discriminatory employment practices, and may well have the opposite effect. Here the grievance procedure of the collective-bargaining agreement was directed precisely at determining whether such practices had occurred.

(c) If the discharges here involved violate Title VII, its remedial provisions are available to the discharged employees, but it does not follow that the discharges also violated §8(a)(1) of the NLRA.[54]

Some of the relevant questions that the Court felt impelled to consider can no doubt be better understood by personnel administrators if translated into layman's language. Accordingly, without any pretext of presenting a legal opinion (that would be wholly out of place in a book of this kind), we are formulating questions of continuing concern to management and answers that seem justified on close examination of the *Emporium* decision itself and other related decisions that the Court has construed as constituting settled law.

Q. 1. Is the majority rule concept of Taft-Hartley utterly sacrosanct?

A. Almost. Citing earlier landmark cases, the Court noted that

Central to the policy of fostering collective bargaining, where the employees elect that course is the principle of majority rule (1937). . . . In establishing a regime of majority rule, Congress sought to secure to all members of the unit the benefits of their collective strength and bargaining power, in all awareness that the superior strength of some individuals or groups might be subordinated to the interest of the majority: Vaca Sipes (1957). . . . The Court most recently had occasion to examine the underpinnings of the majoritarian principle in NLRB v. Allis Chalmers . . . (1961). . . . Thus only the union may contract the employee's terms

---
[54]Emporium Capwell Co. v. Western Addition Community Organization, 88 LRRM 2660, 420 U.S. 50 (1975).

and conditions of employment, *and provisions for processing his grievances.* [Emphasis supplied.][55]

Q. 2. Do individuals or minority groups have independent statutory recourse to contractually established grievance procedures, including binding arbitration?

A. We qualified our answer to Question 1 by using the word "almost" because the Court has not yet come out with a completely definitive interpretation of the scope of Section 9(a) of Taft-Hartley. This section expressly assures any individual employee the right to present a grievance to his employer and seek adjustment of it subject to some qualifications and limitations as referred to above (see page 383). But the Court has never gone so far as to rule that Taft-Hartley bans recourse to arbitration procedures by dissident union members, when and if an employer is willing to allow them such recourse. Significantly, as the *Emporium* case developed the union was willing and eager to proceed to arbitration on the minority group's behalf, but the claimants would not agree to participate in the attempt to go to arbitration on their own.

Q. 3. Does Taft-Hartley give employees allegedly discriminated against under the Civil Rights Act special rights to negotiate with their employer directly and in so doing bypass the designated exclusive bargaining representatives in an NLRB-accepted appropriate bargaining unit?

A. Positively *not,* as is clear from the following statement from *Emporium:*

> Plainly, national labor policy embodies the principles of nondiscrimination: Alexander v. Gardner-Denver Co. (1974) and it is commonplace that we must construe the NLRA in light of the broad national labor policy of which it is a part. See Textile Workers v. Lincoln Mills (1957.) The collective-bargaining agreement involved here prohibited without qualification all manner of invidious discrimination and made any claimed violation a grievable issue. The grievance procedure is directed precisely at determining whether discrimination has occurred.
>
> That orderly determination, if affirmative, could lead to an arbitral award enforceable in court.

The two footnotes to the *Emporium* decision quoted below have special pertinence:

> (a) The union in this case had been prepared to go into arbitration "to enforce its position [supporting the claimants' allegations of discrimination] but was advised by its attorney that it would be difficult to do so without the dissident members' testimony.

---

[55]420 U.S. at 62.

(b) Even if the arbitral decision denies the putative discriminatee's complaint his access to the processes of Title VII and to the federal courts is not foreclosed. Alexander v. Gardner-Denver Co.

Q. 4. If the union had not attempted to remedy the employer's alleged racial discriminatory practices by leading to arbitration, should the complainants' subsequent actions in picketing, boycott,etc., in *Emporium* have protected them from discharge on the grounds that their course of conduct was protected by Section 7 of Taft-Hartley?

A. Not under the particular circumstances. The Board ruled that even if the discharged employees had believed in good faith that there had been illegal discrimination against minority employees, their post-discharge activities fell nothing short of a demand that the company bargain with them for all minority employees. The Board concluded, and the Supreme Court so declared, that protection of an attempt by picketers to bargain for the entire group of minority employees "would undermine the statutory system of bargaining through an exclusive, elected representative. . . ."

Q. 5. For whatever relevancy it might have to the final disposition of this case, had the claimants proved or attempted to prove through the means available to them under the Civil Rights Act, any actual instances of illegal employment discrimination on the part of their employer?

A. Categorically *no*. A footnote in the *Emporium* decisions reveals that although the claimants had been in contact with the California Fair Employment Practices Commission and the EEOC, they had filed no charges with either agency.

Q. 6. Has any employee, a group of employees, or an ex-employee the statutory right to ignore established contractual grievance and arbitration procedures and by demanding direct negotiations with a company's top management thereby assure that Taft-Hartley's guarantee of self-organization rights will protect against discharge or other disciplinary action?

A. Again, the answer is a categorical no: Any appeal to obtain such access, the Supreme Court ruled, should be properly addressed to Congress and not to this Court or the NLRB. To quote the Court's last words in *Emporium:* "In order to hold that employer conduct violates Section 8 of Title VII, we would have to override a host of consciously made decisions well within the exclusive competence of the legislature. This obviously we cannot do."

New Guidelines for Management in Presenting Arbitration Cases

Recent federal appellate court decisions that necessitated the review of arbitral awards have given rise to a need for reconsideration of management methods for preparing and presenting management positions in arbitration hearings. There was a time when informality, simplicity, and the absence of formal legalistic tactics were commonly considered pluses favoring arbitration over resort to lawsuits. Now there may be a patent reversal in procedural tactics. Judges, accustomed as they are to insistence on sworn testimony, affidavits, strict rules of evidence, detailed stenographic records of proceedings, etc., are inclined to place much weight on the completeness of the record and the legalistic formality of arbitration proceedings when they have to determine the propriety and validity of arbitral awards. It thus may be prudent for management to abandon the informal give and take atmosphere of an arbitration hearing and to retain counsel to present the company position in such a way as to build up an impressive record for court examination. In this connection, the Supreme Court's final passage in its *Gardner-Denver* decision is noteworthy. The Court declared in remanding the case to a federal district court that the controversial arbitral decision "may be admitted as evidence and accorded such weight as the court deems appropriate." There was appended a footnote that is perhaps of greater import than this passage. The footnote read:

> We adopt no standards as to the weight to be accorded an arbitral decision, since this must be determined in the court's discretion with regard to the facts and circumstances of each case. Relevant facts include the existence of provisions in the collective-bargaining agreement that conform substantially with Title VII, the degree of procedural fairness in the arbitral forum, adequacy of record with respect to the issue of discrimination, and the special competence of particular arbitrators. Where an arbitral determination gives full consideration to an employee's Title VII rights, a court may properly accord it great weight. This is especially true where the issue is solely one of fact, specifically addressed by the parties and decided by the arbitrator on the basis of an adequate record. But courts should be ever mindful that Congress, in enacting Title VII, thought it necessary to provide a judicial forum for the ultimate resolution of discriminatory employment claims. It is the duty of the courts to assure the full availability of this forum.[56]

---

[56]Alexander v. Gardner-Denver, 415 U.S. at 60.

Arbitration Considered Mandatory

In two other comparatively recent cases the Supreme Court went four-square for arbitration as required by contract or by law. These involved dissimilar issues, i.e., (1) the legal imputations of "laches" and (2) the kinds of disputes arising under the federal Railway Labor Act that required compulsory arbitration of disputes unsettled through prior grievance procedure steps.

The term "laches" has a clear meaning when invoked in lawsuits. As the *Random House Unabridged Dictionary* defines it in simple phraseology: "Law: failure to do a thing at the proper time, esp. such delay as will bar a party from bringing legal proceedings."

The United States Supreme Court (in the case of *Flair Builders, Inc.*) affirmed decisions of lower federal courts on the grounds that while the employer was bound to arbitrate any labor dispute within the limits of the applicable arbitration clause, the union was guilty of laches in seeking enforcement:

> The master agreement contemplates initiation of arbitration proceedings if any dispute is not settled within 48 hours of its occurrence, and further provides that the Board of Arbitrators shall meet 'within six (6) days.' Yet demand for arbitration was not made in this case until April, 1969, almost five years from Flair's first alleged failure to comply with the contract and nearly three years from the inception of the alleged breach sought to be arbitrated. . . .

The Supreme Court construed the long-ignored contract to which the company was alleged to be a party as including among the class of disputes subject to arbitration the issue of "laches" itself. The question of the union's alleged offense of laches should therefore have gone to arbitration. In conclusion, the Supreme Court stated:

> Of course, nothing we say here diminishes the responsibility of a court to determine whether a union and employer have agreed to arbitration. That issue, as well as the scope of the arbitration clause, remains a matter for judicial decision. See Atkinson v. Sinclair Refining Co. . . . (1962). But once a court finds that, as here, the parties are subject to an agreement to arbitrate, and that agreement extends to "any difference" between them, then a claim that particular grievances are barred by laches is an arbitrable question under the agreement. . . . Having agreed to the broad clause, the company is obliged to submit its laches defense, even if "extrinsic," to the arbitral process.[57]

---

[57]International Union of Operating Engineers, Local 150, AFL-CIO v. Flair Builders, Inc., 406 U.S. 487 (1972).

The second recent Supreme Court decision upholding the primacy of arbitration, albeit in entirely dissimilar circumstances, is designated as *Andrews* v. *Louisville & Nashville Railroad Company*. In this case (decided in 1972), the Court sustained the rulings of a federal district court and a circuit court of appeals on the grounds that an individual claiming wrongful discharge had failed, before going to court, to exhaust the arbitrational remedy available to him under the federal Railway Labor Act.

The underlying facts were not in dispute. Andrews while an employee of the railroad suffered a nonoccupational automobile accident. He contended that when he had fully recovered and was able to return to work the carrier refused to reinstate him. He considered the management's decision to be the equivalent of wrongful discharge. Instead of grieving his case and invoking the arbitration procedures of the Railway Labor Act, Andrews filed a suit in a Georgia state court charging breach of contract. On the initiative of the respondent railroad company the case was removed to a federal district court. That court, and later the Fifth Circuit Court of Appeals, dismissed the complaint. They did so on the grounds that the only proper forum for determining whether or not Andrews had actually and improperly been discharged was the National Railroad Adjustment Board. In order to sustain the lower courts' findings, the Supreme Court had to do an about-face, in the sense of renouncing some of its own prior decisions. The basic decision overruled in the instant case was one handed down in 1941 in which the Court held that procedures for adjustment of "minor disputes" under the Railway Labor Act were intended by Congress to be optional, not compulsory, and that therefore a state was free to accord an alternative remedy to a discharged railroad employee under its law of contracts (*Moore* v. *Illinois Central R.R. Co.*, 1941). After some twistings and turnings in subsequent cases, the Supreme Court declared:

> When the issue was again before the Court in *Walker* v. *Southern R.R. Co.* . . . (1966) it was observed:
> > "Provision for arbitration of a discharge grievance, a minor dispute, is not a matter of voluntary agreement under the Railway Labor Act; the Act compels the parties to arbitrate minor disputes before the National Railroad Adjustment Board established under the Act. . . ."
> Thus the notion that the grievance and arbitration procedures provided for minor disputes are optional, to be availed of as the employee or the carrier chooses, was never good history and is no longer good law.[58]

---

[58]Andrews v. Louisville & Nashville Railroad Co., 406 U.S. 320 (1972).

A Douglas Dissent and Its Implications

Personnel administrators concerned about determining what arbitration procedures they are willing to embody in collective agreements may learn as much by scrutinizing closely minority opinions as well as majority decisions in landmark Supreme Court decisions. Hence, the surprising defense of individual civil rights set out in Mr. Justice Douglas's dissent in the *Andrews* case merits close consideration. Douglas said in part:

> Everyone who joins a union does not give up his civil rights. If he wants to leave the commune and assert his common-law rights, I had supposed that no one could stop him. I think it important under our constitutional regime to leave as much initiative as possible to the individual. What the Court does today is ruthlessly to regiment a worker and force him to sacrifice his constitutional rights in favor of a union. I would give him a choice to pursue such rights as he has under the collective agreement and stay with the union, or to quit it and the railroad and free himself from a regime which he finds oppressive. I would construe the federal law as giving the employee that choice. The choice imposed by the Court today raises serious constitutional questions on which we have not had the benefit of any argument.
>
> This is a plain, ordinary common-law suit not dependent on any term or provision of a collective-bargaining agreement. I cannot, therefore, join those who would close the courthouse door to him. Under the First Amendment, as applied to the State by the Fourteenth, he is petitioning the Government "for a redress of grievances" in the traditional manner of suitors at common law; and by the Seventh Amendment is entitled to a jury trial.[59]

Arbitrators' Authority to Construe Contract and Conflicting Statutes

Not infrequently management may be faced with the problem of answering a grievance charging contract violation because of the company's insistence on compliance with a law which in its management judgment overrides the language of the contract. Sometimes two or more laws may bear on the problem. When such a situation develops, the choice of the arbitrator to decide the question of contract violation versus noncompliance with an applicable statute may go far towards determining the outcome. To put it differently, will the arbitrator decline to consider arguments as to the applicability of a particular law? Will he merely apply the facts of the grievance to the contract clauses invoked by the grievant? Or

---

[59]*Ibid.*

will he undertake to determine whether a specific statute super-seded the language of the contract?

One outstanding arbitration proceeding in which the fore-going questions arose was the case decided in 1969 by Robert G. Howlett, Esq. It involved the Simoniz Company.[60] In the process of making his award Howlett had to pass judgment on an explicit contract provision specifying how job openings would be posted, bid on, and filled. He also had to determine whether the manage-ment's rejection of a female employee for a posted opening was made mandatory by a state law regulating working hours for women, or was prohibited by the Civil Rights Act.

Divergent Views on Arbitrator's Jurisdiction

Howlett concluded in the Simoniz case that he had the right and duty to construe not only the applicable contract clause giving rise to the grievance but also the federal law and the state law that considered separately would have warranted different management action in filling the job that became the grievance issue. For em-ployers who might be caught in the same bind that confronted the Simoniz management, Howlett's views on the jurisdiction of an arbitrator in situations such as he faced are of continuing signif-icance.

Recognizing the divergence of views in the arbitration profes-sion and among legal scholars, Howlett said:

> [The] decision depends on the proper role of the arbitrator. There are arbitrators who confine themselves strictly to the contract language and leave employers and unions to the courts or admin-istrative tribunals for interpretation or enforcement of statutes and governmental regulations.
>
> There are arbitrators, *including the arbitrator in this case, who are of the opinion that contracts include all law applicable thereto* [italics supplied], hence the arbitrator should apply the law (constitutional, statute and common) to each collective bargaining agreement.
>
> Other arbitrators take a middle ground, expressing the view that no arbitrator should render an opinion which, if followed, would require an employer (or union) to breach a statute, and that the arbitrator may apply the law if it is clear and not ambiguous.[61]

Federal Law Superseding State Law

Arbitrator Howlett decided the *Simoniz* case in accordance with his declared duty to apply two applicable laws to the facts of

---

[60]Simoniz Company and International Chemical Workers Union, Local 559, Robert G. Howlett, Arbitrator, Sept. 10, 1969.

[61]*Ibid.*

the case and the controlling contract language. There was no dispute as to the essential facts. A female employee was not accepted by the company for a job for which she had bid and for which she admittedly had the requisite skill, ability, and seniority. There were the factors spelled out in the contract for the filling of job vacancies. In addition, the contract contained a clause against discrimination on account of sex. The grievance that went to arbitration charged the company with breach of the nondiscrimination clause by reason of sex, and also violation of the section of the Civil Rights Act prohibiting discrimination against women.

The company had rejected the female employee's otherwise acceptable bid for the open job because the inherent nature of the job necessitated regular overtime in excess of the limits for women imposed by the Illinois law. That law prohibited the employment of women for more than one nine-hour workday during a workweek with a maximum of 48 hours in any workweek. With obvious good faith, the company had sought to persuade the Illinois Department of Labor to exclude the job in question from the limitation imposed by law on the maximum hours for women. It failed in this attempt despite the dilemma posed by the apparent conflict between the federal and state laws. The answer the company received from the state authorities included the following statement: "The Illinois Eight-Hour Day for Women Law is still being enforced since its terms are mutually exclusive of the discrimination program under the federal Civil Rights Act." So the company considered itself bound not to put the woman on the job for which she had qualified.

Arbitrator Howlett forthrightly asserted:

> The only basis for the exercise of state jurisdiction under the Illinois law is that the statute is reasonably necessary for the safety and health of female employees. A blanket limitation that women may not work overtime more than one day each week is not, in the world of 1969, a reasonable regulation. . . . Management's refusal, relying on the Illinois statute, to recognize grievant's bid deprives grievant of an employment opportunity in direct contravention of the Civil Rights Act of 1964.

Howlett's decision directed the company to offer the female grievant an immediate opportunity to take the job on which she had bid. Had he ruled otherwise, he explained, "the union could have sought a declaratory judgment in either the United States District Court or Illinois Circuit Court but final judgment might have been prevented on the ground that the contract provides for arbitration of grievances."[62] In other words, under the Supreme Court's *Drake*

---
[62]*Ibid.*

doctrine, referred to earlier in this chapter, and cited by Howlett in a footnote, a court might have ordered an arbitral decision instead of rendering the court's own judgment as to which statute had to be observed.

It is quite obvious that the celebrated *Gardner-Denver* decision of the United States Supreme Court has done a lot to complicate the problems of arbitrators in private disputes where the applicability of some federal or state law is called into question. Nevertheless the plethora of federal court cases upholding the preemption doctrine has greatly lessened the burden of arbitrators to construe state laws giving special protection to women as against the federal law prohibiting sex discrimination in employment practices. In the light of the latest Supreme Court decisions, Arbitrator Howlett would have had of necessity to uphold the federal statute's requirements as against the Illinois law in construing the application of the Civil Rights Act to the above-mentioned case, which he had to decide in 1969.

Ambiguous Advice From Olympus

Many practicing arbitrators are also distinguished scholars preeminent in their specialized fields of labor economics or labor law. The arbitration profession, incidentally, is not notorious for hiding its lights under the proverbial bushel and failing to come out in public with forthright statements on controversial issues. Even so, the president of the American Arbitration Association, Robert Coulson, was unable to glean anything like a consensus when he sought to obtain the views of hundreds of seasoned arbitrators as to how they would deal with discrimination issues in the wake of *Gardner-Denver*.

The results of the replies received by Coulson from some 250 practicing arbitrators have been summarized as follows:

1. In general, labor arbitrators are informing themselves about job discrimination legislation, government agency policies and court cases.
2. Most arbitrators express a reluctance to extend their authority beyond the terms of the collective bargaining contract or relationship.
3. At the same time, most arbitrators recognize that job discrimination laws can have an effect upon the parties' contractual rights.
4. Significant differences exist as to how arbitrators will respond to some of the questions being raised by job discrimination cases. For example, there is substantial disagreement about whether an arbitrator should:

a) give "more sympathetic consideration" to minority grievants;
b) permit independent counsel over the objection of one or both parties;
c) make an effort to bring out evidence as to a "pattern of discrimination";
d) make recommendations to the parties on how to eliminate discrimination;
e) attempt to mediate a solution to the problem posed by such a pattern. . . .

Most arbitrators felt that contractual remedy powers are *usually*, but not *always*, adequate. Significant numbers felt that arbitrators also needed the power to enjoin, to create a monitoring device, to change contract language, to adjust seniority systems or to expand the class of grievants.

One arbitrator advocated providing the arbitrator "with the authority to act as a Federal District Court," particularly in view of *Gardner-Denver*. Others believe that arbitrators should not "attempt to perform a function properly that of a judge with continuing power" and should not "assume the role of a Federal and state judge."

In conclusion, both the returns and the cases illustrate a lack of consensus among labor arbitrators as to their appropriate role in job discrimination issues. Where such uncertainty exists, parties would be well advised to clarify such matters with their arbitrator, in an effort to avoid misunderstandings about their expectations before the arbitrator begins to fashion the final award.[63]

In retrospect it would appear the *Gardner-Denver* decision raised no serious questions that had not been considered by the arbitration profession many years ago. Perhaps the most penetrating analysis of these questions was presented in a 1970 address before his peers in the National Academy of Arbitrators by Michael Sovern, Dean of the Columbia Law School. Sovern's speech was entitled "When Should Arbitrators Follow Federal Law?" His conclusions were as follows:

In answering the question before us, we seek to have the best possible forum or forums resolve any particular dispute with the minimum of litigation possible under our trifurcated system. That has led me to ask, first, whether the arbitrator is qualified to decide the noncontractual issue. If he is not, he is obviously not the best possible forum and he ought not to decide the question.

If he is qualified, I ask next: What is the alternative to his deciding the legal issue? Unless the case also involves a contract question, the alternative is simply a proceeding in whatever tribunal normally would have heard the legal issue. A grievant with a Title VII, FLSA, or any other claim that does not require an inter-

---

[63]STUDY TIME, American Arbitration Association, Jan. 1976, pp 4-5.

pretation of the contract has no reason to be in arbitration and his being there unnecessarily complicates his litigation. Hence my second condition: The arbitrator should not decide a question of law unless it is implicated in a contract dispute that is also before him.

But even when that condition is satisfied, we still need to ask: What are the consequences of a decision by the arbitrator? What is the probability that his award will effectively terminate the dispute? If he doesn't decide the legal question, who will? When? My third and fourth conditions are an attempt to be responsive to these concerns. When the courts are competent to deal with the matter, let them. The arbitrator's refusal to decide then permits a relatively swift answer from a competent tribunal likely to dispose of the matter.

Even when the courts are not competent, I have suggested that arbitrators should decide only those questions of law tendered by claims that the law immunizes or requires a contract violation. This limitation would have the arbitrator decide only when his decision seems likely to advance the interests we pursue—to diminish the chances of a decision by an incompetent tribunal and avoid increasing confusion and complexity.[64]

Continuing Dilemmas for Management

Management problems in trying to reconcile current contractual commitments with unions and the persistent demands of the EEOC and other federal agencies to assure full compliance with the Civil Rights Act have been intensified rather than abated by the progressively tougher stances taken, particularly by the EEOC. If there is anything like a new deal resulting from shifts in the top personnel in early 1977 it most certainly will be a tougher deal for management. The latest appointee as Chairman of the Commission is Eleanor Holmes Norton, previously for several years New York City's Commissioner of Human Rights. Long a crusader for aggressive action in supporting more equitable treatment for women and minority groups, Mrs. Norton, herself a black, can be expected to go all out to insist that various contract provisions giving preferential seniority or other job rights to nonminorities will not stand up in arbitral decisions, NLRB rulings, and edicts by federal appellate courts. It is most unlikely that Chairman Norton will repudiate the stark positions taken in an official EEOC publication entitled *Affirmative Action and Equal Employment, A Guidebook for Employers,* published in 1974. Cynics could logically assert that through its guidebook the EEOC has in effect urged that the em-

---

[64]Michael Sovern, ARBITRATION AND THE EXPANDING ROLE OF NEUTRALS (Washington: The Bureau of National Affairs, 1970), pp. 45-46. On direct inquiry to Dean Sovern, he informed one of the authors that he had written nothing new on this subject since his 1970 paper and had no special reason to revise the views expressed therein.

ployers subject to its jurisdiction flout much existing law as construed by appellate courts on certain vital issues and also perhaps violate express terms of applicable union agreements as construed by arbitrators. Note, for example, the following passage from the guidebook:

> Discrimination on the basis of race, religion, or national origin may violate rights arising under these laws. It may be unlawful for employers to participate with unions in the commission of any discriminatory practices unlawful under these Acts, or to practice discrimination in a manner which gives rise to racial or other divisions among employees, to the detriment of organized union activity; or for unions to exclude individuals discriminatorily from union membership, thereby causing them to lose job opportunities, to discriminate in the representation of union members or non-members in collective bargaining, in processing of grievances, or in other respects, or to cause or attempt to cause employers to enter into discriminatory agreements or otherwise discriminate against union members or non-members.

>   *   *   *   *   *

> Trade unions are specifically subject to Title VII requirements; their failure to cooperate in removing discriminatory practices has resulted in legal action against many unions. Union cooperation should be sought to remove discriminatory factors revealed in the analysis of your employment practices. However, union refusal to cooperate in such action does not eliminate the employer's obligation to eliminate identified discriminatory practices.

>   *   *   *   *   *

> —*Identify jobs* held by minorities and females in terms of job progression and opportunities for upward mobility compared to other employees.
> — Be sure your analysis includes both union and non-union (exempt) jobs. Under Title VII, there is no meaningful distinction between jobs covered or not covered by a bargaining agreement, in terms of equal employment opportunity. Therefore, if "exempt" employees previously have not had opportunity for employment in union jobs, (or vice-versa) such opportunities should be created, publicized, and employees enabled to compete for such jobs on the basis of their company seniority, regardless of any contrary provisions in the bargaining agreement.

>   *   *   *   *   *

> If any . . . steps conflict with existing contract provisions, get together with your union and make needed revisions to comply with the law.

>   *   *   *   *   *

> Both employer and unions are responsible for non-discrimination under Title VII. An employer may not blame his failure to take

affirmative action on barriers in the union contract or threat of a suit if such action is taken. Courts have held that this is not a justifiable "business necessity."

Union and employer must assure that the contract provides equal opportunity.

If your self-audit of employment practices finds discriminatory barriers in the collective bargaining agreement, you should notify the union of sections which must be changed. Some unions have already requested changes to advance their minority and female members; others may be resistant. Legally, the union is obligated to revise any provisions which have a discriminatory effect regardless of membership preference. If the union is unwilling to negotiate such changes, you should make them unilaterally. Such unilateral action to comply with Title VII does not violate the "good faith bargaining" provisions of the National Labor Relations Act.[65]

As long-time students and teachers of labor relations and labor law, the present authors could not pretend to assess the full import of the above statements from the EEOC manual. All we can properly do is suggest that our readers and their legal counsel make their own interpretations based in part on reviewing the relevant cases cited in Chapters 3 and 7 of this book, as well as in this chapter. We urge those needing up-to-date information with latest developments in litigation to subscribe to at least one of the authoritative labor law services reporting current developments.

Disciplinary Penalties for Alleged Crimes

Criminal statutes in and of themselves impose no restrictions on management's rights to discipline its own employees, including the right to discharge and to prosecute, or rather to seek prosecution. That is to say, a person whose employer considers him to be a thief may be discharged without let or hindrance from the law. But the discharge may not stick if a grievance is filed on behalf of the employee and is ultimately upheld in arbitration. We do not mean to imply that arbitrators condone thievery or other crimes. They do consider, however, the job relationship, if any, between the offense for which an employee may be charged and/or found guilty in determining what penalty to impose on the employee whose discipline has been presented for their review.

Much has been said in grievance arbitration hearings about the plight of employees who assertedly are subject to double jeopardy by being disciplined or perhaps discharged for illegal con-

---

[65]Equal Opportunity Employment Commission, AFFIRMATIVE ACTION AND EQUAL EMPLOYMENT, Vol. 1 (Washington: U.S. Government Printing Office, 1974), pp. 15, 22, 47-49, 57.

duct that might have resulted in a fine or imprisonment. But an employer may find himself in double jeopardy too, at least in a financial sense, by his handling of a disciplinary case where a crime is alleged and not proven.

To illustrate, assume an employer had substantial reason to believe that an employee has stolen several hundred dollars' worth of the company's small tools. The employee is fired forthwith. The employer presses criminal charges but the employee is acquitted. The employee then seeks reinstatement through arbitration and simultaneously files a suit against the employer for personal damages caused by false arrest. It is possible although not inevitable in such a situation that an arbitrator might order the reinstatement of the employee and that the employee might collect a considerable sum in court proceedings against the employer.

Arbitrators, it must be emphasized, are not bound by rules of evidence as practiced by civil and criminal courts. They may find an employee guilty of theft after a judge or jury has held him innocent, or vice versa. If a union and an employer vest in an arbitrator the authority to decide a dispute over the propriety of the discharge of a possible criminal, this usually means he is empowered to determine whether or not there was a justifiable basis for discharge and not necessarily if the employee was a criminal under the standards set by the courts of the state.

When arbitration of discharges for alleged criminal acts is under consideration, the question may arise as to which proceeding should proceed first, i.e., the trial in court or the arbitration hearing. In one unpublished but still significant case the union and management agreed to avoid the long delay involved in awaiting trial by court and to go immediately to arbitration. Management thought it had what it termed "an open and shut case." It had caught the culprit red-handed. And the culprit was no less a personage than the president of the local union and a *guard* to boot. (Anyone thoroughly familiar with Taft-Hartley may wonder why a guard was an official of a union representing production and maintenance employees as here was the case. Actually, the law does not prevent guards from being represented by the same union that represents other plant employees. It does, however, enable management to insist that guards, if organized at all, be in an entirely separate union. But in this instance the management had agreed to perpetuate beyond the effective date of Taft-Hartley a combined unit of production and protection employees.)

As for the facts in this case, minor shortages in raw materials used in the plant production process and having ready resale value had been detected by management. The missing materials seemingly had been pilfered on more than one occasion on weekends when the plant was not in operation. So the plant protection chief decided to maintain a lookout one Sunday. He stationed himself in his car with a set of binoculars, a block away from the plant. From this distance he saw the guard, who was also the union official, throwing materials over the fence and in close proximity to the latter's own car. He at once confronted the guard and fired him on the spot.

When the grievance of the guard protesting his discharge was heard in arbitration it was not such an "open and shut" matter as the management assumed. First there was the issue of credibility, the guard's denial of pilferage against the protection chief's eyewitness account. Then the union presented a second defense. It argued that even assuming the guard had thrown some material of inconsequential value over the plant fence, it was common knowledge that minor management employees had openly walked out of the plant with quantities of the same material without challenge or disciplinary action. The arbitrator sustained the discharge without giving an opinion in support of his reasons. The management then decided to quit while it was ahead. It withdrew the charges it had previously filed with the police, accusing its guard of thievery. So he was never tried in court.

Another case that went to arbitration after the management had discharged a production worker for alleged theft of semiprecious metals had seriocomic overtones. The management was convinced the employee had tried to steal the material because he was seen toting it through the plant yard and some hundred pounds of it were found lying next to the workman's pickup truck, parked on a public street. Near the end of the shift, the police were notified. They parked their clearly identifed patrol car behind the truck. What's more, the shift superintendent tailed the employee as he left the plant until he got into his truck, leaving the company material on the curb. As the workman drove off the superintendent shouted to the police to arrest him. Simultaneously the superintendent fired the man. He was then carted off to jail. The next morning he was quickly sprung by his attorney, and the charges of theft were withdrawn by the company.

The matter did not end here. The plant management insisted on sustaining the discharge, which the union promptly took to arbitration. Meanwhile the employee had caused a suit for false arrest to be instituted. To settle this out of court, the company had to pay a substantial sum. Curiously, it might seem, the arbitrator sustained the discharge when the company during the hearing of the case before him changed its reasons to attempted theft and to lying in front of the arbitrator while under oath. (There can be no citation of this case, for none of the parties, including the arbitrator, who was then a law professor and later president of the National Academy of Arbitrators, had any inclination to air developments in what on hindsight seemed to be mostly ludicrous.)

Arbitration Case Law on Discipline for Dishonesty, etc.

"Case law" is no doubt a misnomer when applied to arbitrators' decisions in matters relating to alleged dishonesty of employees and the disciplinary penalties imposed therefor. Arbitrators are not bound by the decisions of other arbitrators in such matters even when construing identical contract provisions. Neither are they necessarily bound by court or jury verdicts regarding employees who have been tried on charges of dishonesty.

Professor Lawrence Stessin gave a terrific jolt to the thinking of many management people when he wrote in 1960:

> To an employer, discharge for stealing or dishonesty seems so in keeping with accepted mores of society that he is surprised and sometimes shocked when his action is questioned by a union and reversed by an arbitrator. And yet *mitigation and reversal are exactly what happen in a high majority of cases which come to arbitration involving employee dishonesty or deceit.* [Italics supplied] About two-thirds of the arbitrations covering this triumvirate (theft, dishonesty and disloyalty) end up in upsetting the management's original decision of discharge. The reason for the large percentage of employer reversals in theft arbitrations is based not only on arbitrator doubt as to the employee's guilt; the leniency can be traced to the future consequences of an allowed discharge.[66]

To put it in another way, many arbitrators have accepted the concept that discharge for dishonesty blackens an individual's record for life and eliminates or decimates his chances of ever reentering the respectable labor market. This concept, we submit, is not completely valid. If it were, thousands of ordinary workmen who have rehabilitated themselves and hundreds of important businessmen who have regained a decent place in society might be languishing on the government's permanent relief rolls. Even worse, they might be permanently relegated to illicit occupations in the nation's underworld.

There is, however, logic behind the views of arbitrators who insist on stringent standards of proof "beyond a reasonable doubt" in

---

[66]Stessin, p. 103.

adjudicating cases of discipline for dishonesty. The case for this viewpoint was well stated by Arbitrator Harold M. Somers when he said:

> Discharge for stealing involves an unfavorable reflection on the *moral* character of the employee which is almost impossible to erase and which will seriously hamper if not altogether prevent his getting a job elsewhere in his line of work and will even hurt innocent members of his family. He and they are branded for life. The company therefore has a very heavy obligation in such a case. It carries the burden of proving beyond a reasonable doubt — in its own conscience as well as before the arbitrator — that the employee committed the offense of stealing.[67]

Discharge Sustained After Acquittal for Theft

The lack of anything like unanimity in arbitrators' decisions on cases involving discharge for alleged dishonesty was strikingly demonstrated in a landmark case in which a seasoned arbitrator, Burton B. Turkus, upheld the discharge of an employee who had been acquitted in a state criminal court at a trial where he faced a charge of theft of valuable company property. In this particular case the arbitration proceeding was not instituted until after the court verdict of the employee's innocence. As Arbitrator Turkus, a former prosecuting attorney himself, explained the rationale of this almost unprecedented decision, the contract that he was called upon to construe and apply defined the term "proven theft" to mean proven to the satisfaction of the arbitrator hearing the case and *not* to the satisfaction of a criminal court. Highlight passages of this Turkus decision are quoted below:

> A mere "nodding" acquaintance with the trial of a criminal case would indicate the wisdom and providence of avoiding an arbitration hearing with its far less stingent evidentiary procedures and the subjection of the defendant (grievant) to an intensive and binding cross-examination in advance of the determination of the criminal case.
>
> *   *   *   *   *
>
> The acquittal of the criminal charge is not conclusive or "res judicata" of a subject matter which was in dispute between the same parties and has been finally and authoritatively determined by the decision of a court of competent jurisdiction. The parties to the two proceedings are not the same. The parties to the criminal case were the People of the State as plaintiff and M— — as defendant. The parties to the arbitration are the Company and the Union. The Company was not a party to the criminal case either directly or indirectly.

---

[67]Marlin Rockwell Corp., Harold M. Somers, Arbitrator, 24 LA 728.

It had no standing in the criminal case nor any control thereof which at all times was vested exclusively in the public prosecutor.

The collective bargaining agreement of the parties, moreover, in enumerating "proven theft" as a ground for discharge expressly provides that when the just cause thereof is challenged or tested in arbitration through access to the grievance procedures of the agreement, that a "proven theft" is one which is proven to the satisfaction of the arbitrator duly designated to determine the issue — not to the satisfaction of a criminal court in which a criminal charge for the same offense may be pending.

*   *   *   *   *

Accordingly, the test or criteria which has been here applied to determine whether or not M— — was discharged for just cause is, as follows: Has the Company sustained the burden of establishing the grievant's guilt (proven theft) in this proceeding by reliable, accurate and credible proof beyond a reasonable doubt, giving due consideration to the persuasive force of his acquittal for the same offense in a criminal court of competent jurisdiction?

The Company has successfully met that test. [Italics supplied][68]

Relevance of Employee's Past Record

There are vast differences among and between arbitrators and the courts in their holdings as to what types of evidence are admissible when allegations of past misconduct are made. In discharge cases, employers frequently want to put into the record of arbitration proceedings previous offenses of the employee that they think add justification for their disciplinary action. They have abundant reason for such attempts. After all, a common argument of union spokesmen in disciplinary cases is that an employee's past exemplary record warrants leniency in meting out the penalty for current dereliction. If the past record that is *good* should be considered by an arbitrator, why not a past record that is *bad?*

On this knotty issue, R. W. Fleming in an analytical study, *The Labor Arbitration Process,* had this to say:

Does it make any difference, for instance, whether the company is using the past record to: (1) prove that the penalty which has been imposed is appropriate; (2) suggest the likelihood that the employee committed the present offense; or (3) undermine the credibility of the employee as a witness? The courts in criminal cases, have certainly thought there was a difference. Former convictions are certainly relevant in connection with the degree of penalty, but if the evidence of past misconduct is offered for the purpose of proving the likelihood that the present offense has been committed, there is what

---

[68]Service Trucking Company, Inc. and International Brotherhood of Teamsters, Chauffeurs, Warehousemen and Helpers, Local 560, Barton B. Turkus, Arbitrator, 41 LA 377 (1963).

appears at first glance to be a flat rule against admission. Thus, "the doing of one act is in itself no evidence that the same or a like act was done again by the same person," and "where the doing of an act is the proposition to be proved, there can never be a direct inference from an act of former conduct to the act charged." There are, however, numerous exceptions to this rule. And it would be unrealistic to distinguish between "proving likelihood" and "degree of penalty" when discussing the admissibility of past misconduct in arbitration proceedings because of two fundamental differences between the arbitrator and the judge. The first is that the arbitrator sits in review of a penalty which has already been imposed by the company, while the judge has the duty of setting the penalty. Second, the judge normally assesses the penalty *after* the jury has decided the question of guilt or innocence, whereas the arbitrator is both judge and jury. It is impractical for the arbitrator to hear the evidence, decide whether an employee deserves to be penalized, and then return to hear evidence of past misconduct which might bear on the degree of penalty. In this connection it may be worth noting that state statutes which permit the jury to fix a criminal sentence and allow the fact of prior convictions to be considered by jurors before verdict have been severely criticized, although not held unconstitutional.[69]

Special Expertise of Arbitrators

From the foregoing passage indicating great diversity as to the views of practicing arbitrators on major issues it should not be inferred that grievance arbitration is not a good substitute for court action in settling disputes arising under labor agreements. One of the staunch defenders of the arbitration process has been the Chief Justice of the United States, Warren E. Burger. Addressing the American Arbitration Association in 1968, while still on the federal circuit court bench, he said:

> One thing an appellate judge learns very quickly is that a large part of all the litigation in the courts is an exercise in futility and frustration. The anomaly is that there are better ways of resolving private disputes, and we must in the public interest move toward taking a large volume of private conflicts out of the courts and into the channels of arbitration. . . .
>
> We must learn from the experience of labor and management that courts are not the best places to resolve these special kinds of claims. My own experience for over twenty years, for three years as Assistant Attorney General, and now a dozen years as a judge, satisfies me that in terms of cost, time, human wear and tear, arbitration is vastly better than conventional litigation.[70]

---

[69]R. W. Fleming, THE ARBITRATION PROCESS (Urbana, Ill: University of Illinois Press, 1967). p. 166

[70]Warren F. Burger, Address at American Arbitration Association meeting, N.Y., 1968; quoted in ARBITRATION NEWS (New York: American Arbitration Association) June 1969, No. 2, p. 6.

As indicated earlier in this chapter, the U.S. Supreme Court in one of its Trilogy cases *(Enterprise)* emphatically declared that "so far as the arbitrator's decision concerns construction of the contract, the courts have no business overruling him because their interpretation of the contract is different from his." It is true, arbitrators' decisions can be set aside by the courts for improper practices that are proscribed by some state laws.

There is, however a dearth of reported cases where arbitrators' awards have been set aside by the courts. If all the pertinent facts became generally known, a 1974 federal court decision upsetting an arbitrator's award in a discharge case could no doubt be regarded as of much less importance than some commentators have attached to it. This was *Holodnak* v. *Avco Corp.*[71]

The American Bar Association committee that annually reviews developments in labor management arbitration had only the briefest of references to the case. In its 1975 report the committee said:

> [In *Holodnak*] it was found that a union attorney (1) failed to adequately investigate and prepare for discharge arbitration, (2) failed to object at the arbitration hearing to the arbitrator and opposing counsels' interrogation of plaintiff concerning his political views, and (3) was harsh in his characterization of plantiff's political knowledge and views in the union's post-hearing brief. The court held that such conduct violated the union's duty. The court also vacated the arbitrator's award for evident partiality and bias.[72]

The arbitrator in this case has refrained from public comment. When he rendered his decision, he became *functus officio*. Liberally translated, this means the assignment was completed. There was a lot more to the *Holodnak* case than has been aired in the press and in critical articles in professional publications. The American Arbitration Association sought to present the other side of the case, i.e., why the arbitrator might have had ample grounds for deciding as he did. The AAA's editor of publications, Morris Stone, has suggested that those who may be inclined to cite the *Holodnak* case as the proverbial "horrible example" would do well to conduct independent research. Stone's comments reinforced our own observations to the effect that the full significance of court decisions is often graspable only by diligent reading of the footnotes of leading cases and sometimes the footnotes to the footnotes. Stone has given a few clues as to where to look and what to look for to those in

---

[71]87 LRRM 2237 (1974).

[72]American Bar Association, *Report of the Committee on Labor Arbitration and the Law of Collective Bargaining*, p. 158.

management or labor who would want to use the *Holodnak* decision in support of or in opposition to a position in an arbitrational proceeding or court appeal therefrom. To be fully cognizable, the following quotes from Stone would have to be weighed in the light of the entire record.

> During the arbitration hearing, Holodnak admitted he was advocating wildcat strikes, and admitted also that he knew that course of action was expressly contrary to the union contract and an arbitrator's cease-and-desist order. . . .
>
> A few lines taken from the transcript seem to show [the arbitrator] questioning Holodnak vigorously, in a manner intended to extract admission that his accusations were objectionable. But when the same exchange of questions and answers is read in the context of surrounding material, it appears that the arbitrator was trying to get the grievant to express his views in a manner that could justify mitigation of the penalty. Moreover, the arbitrator specifically excluded from consideration Holodnak's radical views.
>
> A reading of the entire transcript of the arbitration hearing and the trial reveals that: Holodnak was aware of the wildcat strike situation and of two cease-and-desist orders by arbitrators; he admitted he had no information at the time he wrote the article of union-busting activities by the employer; he was unable to give any instances of Avco buying off unionists with the offer of foremanships, as alleged; he could not cite any example of arbitral bias; he would not have written the article had he known at the time what he knew by the time the hearing took place; and he agreed that the hearing was fair and that he was fairly represented.[73]

One of the most obvious reasons for the paucity of cases of reversible errors by arbitrators is that practicing arbitrators usually work in a figurative goldfish bowl. They have their own professional association, the National Academy of Arbitrators, that has helped to formulate and police a rigid code of ethics and procedural standards. As for the figurative goldfish bowl, it is common knowledge that many employer groups constantly exchange information on their own experiences with arbitrators; so do many labor organizations. The two chief national organizations that recommend or designate arbitrators, the American Arbitration Association and the Federal Mediation and Conciliation Service, maintain elaborate dossiers on the arbitrators they propose to the respective parties. Moreover, the commercial reporting services such as BNA and CCH compile and publish voluminous data on arbitral awards. If one of the parties to an arbitration proceeding has any basis for assuming that the arbitrator whose award he disapproves of has been guilty of unethical conduct or has used bad judgment,

---

[73]STUDY TIME, American Arbitration Association, Jan. 1976, pp. 2-3.

that party often has only himself to blame for agreeing to utilize the services of that arbitrator.

The high standards for professional conduct, self-imposed on arbitrators who have been admitted to membership in the National Academy of Arbitrators, can best be illustrated, perhaps, by citing some of the tenets prescribed in their code. To wit:

> The arbitrator should be conscientious, considerate and patient in the discharge of his functions. There should be no doubt as to his complete impartiality. He should be fearless of public clamor and indifferent to private, political or partisan influences.
>
> The arbitrator should not undertake or incur obligations to either party which may interfere with the impartial determination of the issue submitted to him.
>
> *　　　　*　　　　*　　　　*　　　　*
>
> Unless the parties approve the arbitrator should not, in the absence of or without notice to one party, hold interviews with, or consider arguments or communications from the other party. If such communications be received, their contents should be disclosed to all parties and an opportunity afforded to comment thereon.[74]

CONCLUDING OBSERVATIONS

Arbitrators are neither omniscient nor omnipotent, even though Mr. Justice Douglas suggested in his *Warrior* opinion that the courts think they should be both. Arbitrators expect the parties in labor arbitration cases to know the basics of the law and to be filled in on recent rulings of the courts. As Professor Sam Kagel has said:

> Law is a volatile field. The law on a subject may be changed by the act of a legislature or by a court decision. This is happening every minute. The law on a particular subject must be checked for the latest laws and decisions on that subject.[75]

It has been the present authors' hope in preparing this book that it will help personnel administrators become sufficiently familiar with the law so that they will know when to consult labor relations counsel, *before* making vital decisions. By so doing they can well prove how wrong Carl Sandburg was when he said: "Why does a hearse horse snicker/Hauling a lawyer away?" We imply no disrespect for the legal profession, whether members of the bar or the

---

[74]American Arbitration Association and National Academy of Arbitrators, *Code of Ethics and Practical Standard for Labor Management Arbitration* (New York: Bernheimer Foundation 1962).

[75]Kagel, pp. 139-140.

bench. Nor can any disrespect be imputed by quoting the sage remarks made in 1967 by Judge Mathew O. Tobriner of the California Supreme Court when, in speaking before the National Academy of Arbitrators, he said:

> . . . I am particularly interested in the impact upon the arbitration process of judicial due process. But, lest you take my observations too seriously, let me tell you the story told recently by retired Supreme Court Justice Charles E. Whittaker. It seems that in the course of argument of a case before the United States Supreme Court, a lawyer repeatedly cited as precedent the judgments of Mr. Justice Peffley. Finally the Chief Justice leaned over and said, "Counsel, the Court does not readily identify Mr. Justice Peffley. Would you please tell us who he is?"
>
> "Why," replied the attorney, "Mr. Justice Peffley is the Justice of the Peace of the Fifth District of Kaw Township of Jackson County, Missouri."
>
> Thereupon the Chief Justice said, "Well, now, Counsel, the Court does not care to hear any more references to Mr. Justice Peffley. He is not considered to be persuasive authority here."
>
> Whereupon the lawyer retorted: "That is a coincidence. Only last week I heard Mr. Justice Peffley make an identical statement about the judgment of this court."[76]

---

[76]Mathew O. Tobriner, *An Appellate Judge's View of the Labor Arbitration,* in THE ARBITRATOR, THE NLRB, AND THE COURTS; PROCEEDINGS OF THE TWENTIETH ANNUAL MEETING, NATIONAL ACADEMY OF ARBITRATORS, ed. Dallas L. Jones (Washington: The Bureau of National Affairs, Inc., 1967), p. 37.

Topical Index